The POEMS of
JONATHAN SWIFT

The History of Vanbrug's House. 1706.

When Mother Clud had rose from Play,
And call'd to take the Cards away,
Van saw, but seem'd not to regard,
How Miss pickt ev'ry painted Card,
And busy both with Hand and Eye
Soon rear'd a House two Storyes high;
Van's Genius without Thought or Lecture
Is hugely turn'd to Architecture,
He saw the Edifice and smil'd,
Vow'd it was pretty for a Child;
It was so perfect in its kind,
He kept the Model in his Mind
But when he found the Boys at play,
And saw them dabling in their Clay,
He stood behind a Stall to lurk,
And mark the Progress of their Work,
With true Delight observ'd them all
Raking up mud to build a Wall,
The Plan he much admir'd, and took
The Model in his Table book;
Thought himself now exactly Skill'd,
And so resolv'd a House to build;

Δ

See p. 86

THE
POEMS
OF
JONATHAN
SWIFT

Edited by HAROLD WILLIAMS

VOLUME I

SECOND EDITION

OXFORD
AT THE CLARENDON PRESS

Oxford University Press, Ely House, London W. 1

GLASGOW NEW YORK TORONTO MELBOURNE WELLINGTON
CAPE TOWN SALISBURY IBADAN NAIROBI LUSAKA ADDIS ABABA
BOMBAY CALCUTTA MADRAS KARACHI LAHORE DACCA
KUALA LUMPUR HONG KONG

PR
3721
W.5

FIRST EDITION 1937
SECOND EDITION 1958, 1966

53605

REPRINTED LITHOGRAPHICALLY IN GREAT BRITAIN
AT THE UNIVERSITY PRESS, OXFORD
BY VIVIAN RIDLER
PRINTER TO THE UNIVERSITY

PREFACE
TO THE SECOND EDITION

IN 1937 the earlier edition of this work, which, with some intermissions, had been in my hands for seven years, was published. It was the first attempt to edit Swift's poems by a textual standard which they demanded and with an exegetical commentary linking them with the events of his life. The long-drawn labour's courteous reception was unexpectedly gratifying. The work, still selling, is virtually out of print. Without the need for major correction these volumes have stood the test of time; but the discovery of two important manuscripts in Swift's hand, previously untraced; the appearance of several notable contemporary transcripts; and minor additions to biographical and bibliographical information now present the opportunity for a measure of revision. The reader will find major additions or modifications at pp. 125–7, 159–60, 259–69, 444, 531, 576–9, 673, 680, 683, 799, 863–73, and 1154.

The interest and helpfulness of friends, owners of manuscripts, scholars, librarians, and booksellers, whose names appeared in my earlier preface recall kindly memories. Some are no longer here, some have changed title, situation, or description, some have rendered me further service. I ask those who remember the first appearance of this work to accept again the acknowledgements I offered twenty years ago. Among those unnamed in the Preface of 1937 I here record the help I have received from the late Norman Ault and the late E. St. John Brooks. Among new-comers whose advice and help have been of service to me are L. W. Hanson, David Woolley, Irvin Ehrenpreis, James M. Osborn, George Mayhew, and Robert Halsband. Others there may be whom here I have not named. They will find due acknowledgements embodied in my commentary and notes. I add my thanks to Mrs. Cartwright of Aynho for permission to make use of contemporary transcripts of poems.

Once more, as earlier, I am indebted to the Delegates of the Clarendon Press and their staff for patient guidance and assistance.

H. W.

LONDON,
July 1957.

PREFACE

SWIFT, as the Introduction to these volumes shows, was at little pains to ensure the publication of an authoritative collection of his writings, whether in prose or in verse. Two miscellany gatherings, 1711 and 1727–32, and six volumes of a Dublin edition of his *Works* received some measure of editorial attention from him. But at his death a large proportion of his verse lay scattered in manuscripts, in broadsides, and in pamphlets. These stray leaves were gradually brought together by successive editors, combined with many conjectural attributions which have little or no claim to be regarded as Swift's. Scarcely any effort at an arrangement of the poems was made by early editors, Faulkner, Deane Swift, Sheridan, and John Nichols. Sir Walter Scott, in his editions of Swift's *Works*, 1814 and 1824, attempted a partial grouping by subject-matter; but the poems were distributed through several volumes, the arrangement was imperfectly executed, the text was little considered, and many questionable pieces, together with poems by other hands, were indiscriminately included. Little has since been done; and the need for a new edition of Swift's poems requires no emphasis or argument.

In this edition I have attempted to determine, as nearly as may be, the exact date of composition of each poem. In each section, grouped by subject-matter, the poems are arranged in chronological sequence, following the date of composition, not that of first publication. Poems written by others, which it was necessary to print for an understanding of Swift's reply, appear in smaller type. In two sections, 'Riddles' and 'Trifles', in which Swift's share could not be clearly determined, this differentiation by type has not been observed.[1]

---

[1] Nor has a type differentiation been observed at pp. 184–8, 665–72.

A large part of the time spent in the preparation of this edition has been devoted to bibliographical scrutiny and textual collation. Nearly every poem has its separate bibliography, and a list of editions collated, together with autographs and early transcripts, whenever these are preserved, is given at the head of each poem. I have printed the text from manuscript, from a first edition, or from an authoritative early text. In only one instance, 'Verses on the Death of Dr. Swift' (see p. 551), have I printed a recension.

The introductory notes to each poem, or group of poems, discuss the date, the occasion, the bibliography, and the text. They have, in effect, together with the footnotes, a biographical design and purpose.

I have many acknowledgements to make for the helpful interest of older friends, and I recognize gratefully the kindness of the new friends my work has brought me.

The courtesy of Dr. F. Elrington Ball is a happy memory. He was ever ready to answer questions. His death, in 1928, deprived me of his unrivalled knowledge of Anglo-Ireland. But my chief debt for encouragement, advice, and active help, is due to Professor D. Nichol Smith, whom I have consulted throughout the progress of this work. He has, furthermore, read the proofs, contributed valuable suggestions, and saved me from oversights and mistakes. It would be difficult to assess the sum of my obligation to him.

I have received many courtesies from owners of manuscripts, rare books, and annotated volumes, who have afforded me access to their collections and the use of manuscripts in their possession. I am gratefully indebted to the Duke of Bedford, the Duke of Portland, the Marquis of Bath, Lord Mount Temple, Major-General Sir W. J. Maxwell-Scott, Major Evelyn Shirley of Lough Fea, co. Monaghan, Mrs. Baker, Malahow, Naul, co. Dublin, Mrs. W. G. Panter, the Rev. John Longe, the Rev. J. J. Antrobus, Mr. T. J. Wise, Mr. Cecil Harmsworth, and Mr. Seumas O'Sullivan. Mr. Victor (now Lord) Rothschild has always been ready to place his fine collection of manuscripts and printed pieces fully at my disposal. Mr., now Sir Shane Leslie, Bt., has been generous with his help, and obtained entries for me to private libraries. Among those who have drawn my attention to manuscripts, or furnished me with rotographs, are Professor G. C. Moore Smith, Professor Herbert Davis, Professor George Sherburn, Dr. A. S. W. Rosenbach, Mr. Arthur Pforzheimer, Dr. Francis S. Bourke, and Mr. Francis Needham. I cannot sufficiently thank Dr. Robin Flower for the assistance he has often given me in the examination of manuscripts and rotographs, and for the helpfulness of his opinion on questions of handwriting. I am particularly under an obligation to Mr. M. B. Gold for examining the Orrery Papers in the library of Harvard College, and for sending me rotographs.

My thanks are due to the Very Rev. D. F. R. Wilson, Dean of St. Patrick's, the Very Rev. W. J. Askins, Dean of Kilmore, the Rev. H. C. Armour, Professor Edward Bensly, Mrs. Arundell Esdaile, Mr. I. A. Williams, and Mr. Séamus Ó Casaide for answers readily given to questions addressed to them. For help, none the less valuable because difficult to define, I am most grateful to Mr. John Hayward and to Dr. T. Percy Kirkpatrick.

Messrs. Bernard Quaritch, Ltd., Messrs. P. J. and A. E. Dobell (and especially I thank Mr. Percy Dobell), Messrs. Pickering and Chatto, and Mr. M. J. Mac-Manus have kindly allowed me to examine volumes which have passed through their hands, and given me information about other books.

I have been received with unfailing courtesy and helpfulness in many libraries. In Dublin Mr. J. Hanna, Assistant Librarian at Trinity College, Dr. Best of the National Library of Ireland, Mr. Newport B. White of Archbishop Marsh's Library, the staff of the Royal Irish Academy, and Mr. Fennelly, custodian of the Gilbert Collection, belonging to the City of Dublin, have been generous of their time and knowledge. I thank, in general, the staff of the British Museum, the Bodleian Library, the University Library, Cambridge, the National Library of Scotland, the Public Record Office, the Victoria and Albert Museum, the Goldsmiths' Library, and the John Rylands Library, Manchester.

I acknowledge the generosity of the trustees of the Pierpont Morgan Library, New York, in supplying me with photographs of manuscripts in that library, and for kind permission accorded me to make full use of them in this work. Captain Haselden and Mr. H. C. Schulz, Curator and Assistant Curator of manuscripts in the Henry E. Huntington Library, San Marino, California, have been at much pains to supply me with information and rotographs; and I have the permission of Dr. Max Farrand, Director of Research, to make use of the information thus obtained. The authorities of Harvard College have generously allowed me the use of rotographs from the Orrery Papers.

I am obliged to the publishers, Messrs. G. Bell & Sons, for allowing me to quote extensively from Dr. Elrington Ball's edition of Swift's *Correspondence*.

I am indebted to the Delegates of the Clarendon Press and their staff for their careful attention to a work which has not been without problems and difficulties while it was passing through the press.

H. W.

ASPENDEN,
HERTFORDSHIRE,
February 1937.

C O N T E N T S

VOLUME I

LIST OF PLATES

Grateful acknowledgements are made to his Grace the Duke of Bedford, to Lord Rothschild, and to the Trustees of the Pierpont Morgan Library, for kind permission to reproduce manuscripts in their possession.

INTRODUCTION

(i)

AS a prose-writer Swift won the immediate recognition of his contemporaries. Even the pedantic Orrery praised the 'masterly conciseness', which he regarded as unequalled by any writer; and Delany, for once, echoed his lordship's words.[1] A few have cavilled at what they considered the bareness of Swift's prose, its want of decorative epithets or graceful turns of phrase; but the passage of time has served to establish his fame securely. The judgement of Dr. Johnson stands: 'He studied purity . . . and whoever depends on his authority may generally conclude himself safe.'[2]

The ideal Swift consciously pursued in the writing of prose he followed in his verse. The very conciseness, clarity, and directness which lend to his prose a deceptive simplicity, seemingly so easy to imitate and so impossible to attain in practice, led him into the paths of satire and tended too frequently to narrow his range. The sceptism of enthusiasms, pretentions, and cant which underlies his counsel in the 'Directions for a Birth-Day Song', and in his rhapsody 'On Poetry' confined a natural genius within self-imposed barriers. His poetic vesture was too small for him. In Swift's verse, as in his life, we are conscious of a frustration. In prose he was free. Although there are poems 'which are as dreadful and as easy as though one of the major prophets had written *vers de société*',[3] he had something to give to English poetry that he never wholly gave.

---

[1] Orrery, *Remarks*, 1752, p. 63; Delany, *Observations*, 1754, p. 272.
[2] *Lives of the English Poets*, ed. G. Birkbeck Hill, iii. 51–2.

[3] *Miscellaneous Poems by Jonathan Swift*, ed. R. Ellis Roberts, 1928, p. viii.

The unhappiness of Swift's life was in no small part chargeable against himself. But even when toiling under unnatural conditions there is an occasional illumination which bids us remember what manner of man he was.

> But what does our proud Ign'rance Learning call,
>   We odly *Plato*'s Paradox make good,
> Our Knowledge is but mere Remembrance all,
>   Remembrance is our Treasure and our Food;
> Nature's fair Table-book our tender Souls
> We scrawl all o'er with old and empty Rules,
>   Stale Memorandums of the Schools;
>   For Learning's mighty Treasures look
>   In that deep Grave a Book.[1]

If this be Cowley, it is Cowley with a sombre power. But when Swift recognized the futility of unnatural pindarics, and turned, after a pause in which he seems hardly to have written verse at all, to a style more natural, he allowed the pendulum to swing too far, and fell into an opposite error. In a poem half-earnest, half-satire, he represents Apollo as appointing him vicegerent in Ireland, and bidding other poets to follow his example in rejecting similes and picturesque figures of speech.

> No Simile shall be begun,
> With *rising* or with *setting* Sun:
>   And let the *secret Head of Nile*
>   Be ever banish'd from your Isle.
> When wretched Lovers live on Air,
> I beg you'll the *Camelion* spare.
>   And when you'd make a Heroe grander,
>   Forget he's like a *Salamander*.
>
>   .   .   .   .
> When you describe a lovely Girl,
> No Lips of *Coral* Teeth of *Pearl*.[2]

[1] *Ode to the Honble Sir William Temple*, ll. 28–36; see p. 27. I am indebted to Mr. W. B. Yeats for calling my particular attention to these lines.
[2] *Apollo's Edict*; see pp. 270–72.

These and the like phrases litter the '*beaten* Paths' of
poetry the old stock-in-trade of those who make a business
of it, for it is they only who deserve the name of poet. And
Swift scarcely claimed himself a poet by profession. Nevertheless he was constantly turning verses as a common part
of his everyday life, so much so that no part of his writing
is as complete an autobiography, and no part of his writing
so calls for annotation. No part of his writing, furthermore,
has been so neglected and mishandled by editors. Two
hundred years ago Deane Swift described the arrangement
of the Dean's poetical writings as a 'heap of confusion';[1]
and little has since been done to improve matters. Sir
Walter Scott loosely sorted the growing heap into smaller
heaps; but Dr. Elrington Ball's essay on *Swift's Verse* was
the first informed attempt to bring order where none had
been.

The poems of Jonathan Swift have been undeservedly
overshadowed. The perfection of his prose, the satirical and
imaginative genius of *A Tale of a Tub*, *Gulliver's Travels*,
and *Polite Conversation*, the incisive mastery of his political
pamphlets have screened off his pages of verse. Nevertheless
it must be recognized that his standing was within the
circle of the Augustan poets; and in prose his range was
far beyond their compass. In verse Pope was his superior.

> In POPE, I cannot read a Line,
> But with a Sigh, I wish it mine.[2]

Gay and Prior had a more lyrical gift. Swift's genius lay
in the succession of Samuel Butler. *Hudibras* he knew
by heart. But Butler's stream ran in a narrow channel
through a monotonous country. His antipathies and sympathies were limited by a confined experience and limited
responsiveness. Swift's powers of mind were far greater

---

[1] *Essay*, 1755, p. 232.
[2] *Verses on the Death of Dr. Swift*, ll. 47-8; see p. 555.

than Butler's; his experience of life was more complex; he knew more intimately the extremes of joy and pain, love and hate. The content of his verse shows a diversity Butler's lacks; his variations of theme and metre are frequent. *Cadenus and Vanessa* may want the porcelain elegance of *The Rape of the Lock*, but it is a definite achievement of sustained artifice and fancy. The metrical accomplishment and vigour of *On Poetry: A Rapsody*, which moved the admiration of contemporaries, are not less apparent to-day. No verse satire in English, or in any language, pierces, wounds, and scarifies like that of Swift. There was no warding off the thrust, whether the attack was personal, directed at Nottingham, Richard Tighe, Lord Allen, or Bettesworth, or general, against the ministry and parliamentary measures. And here there is all the wide range from a squib or lampoon of a few lines to lengthy and polished pieces like the *Libel on Dr. Delany*, or *Epistle to Mr. Gay*, or the typical social satire of *The Journal of a Modern Lady*, or, finally, the uncontrolled outburst of *The Legion Club*. Again, there is the everyday friendliness of his familiar verse, the addresses to Stella, to the Rochforts, Achesons, Sheridan, Delany, and other Irish friends, and the great *Verses on the Death of Dr. Swift*, which are also of this order, if with a difference. And, yet again, is not *Mrs. Harris's Petition* one of the best of all colloquial pieces? Add to these the nonsense poems and frolics in rhyme, and we have not exhausted a variety which rarely falters or fails.

Swift's verse has been shabbily treated by his editors. Perhaps readers and critics may plead this neglect in excuse for theirs. Much of his verse is not readily, or completely, intelligible until ordered chronologically and annotated. If this be an admission that the chief interest of Swift's verse lies elsewhere than in poetic content, it is unnecessary to plead the contrary. Poetry is there, and the instinct to poetry, though trammelled and impeded. Further, the events of Swift's life, his character, his standing with his fellows, and his place in history can only be adequately interpreted if his verse is closely read and understood. Swift, like Marlborough, is not easily explicable. Each was an enigma to his contemporaries; and each has left to succeeding generations unsolved problems of life and character. If a better text and clearer arrangement of Swift's poems can serve to bring us a fuller knowledge of the author, the editor of these volumes will have been repaid for his long task. Lacunae there may be, and unavoidably; mistakes there must be; but, at the least, the attempt has been made to edit Swift's poetical writings by a standard they merited.

(ii)

The editor of Swift's verse is, from beginning to end, beset by the constant problem of determining the canon. The apocrypha spring like weeds choking the good seed. Omitting riddles and epigrams from separate enumeration, not less than one hundred and fifty attributions and supposititious pieces may be counted, over against two hundred and fifty genuine poems. During Swift's life, and after, any witty, grotesque, or indecent piece, of Irish origin and uncertain parentage, was ascribed to the great Dean of St. Patrick's, as if by a standing affiliation order. It is to the credit of Swift's earliest editors, Faulkner in Dublin, Hawkesworth, Deane Swift, and Sheridan in England, that they admitted comparatively few of the doubtful poems. Unfortunately, before Faulkner published his edition of the *Works* in 1735, the Swift and Pope *Miscellanies* of 1727-32, for which Pope was responsible as editor, included, without indication of authorship, pieces both in prose and verse written by others, as indeed their joint preface particularly informs the reader. These *Miscellanies*, reprinted from time to time, and extended, became the façade of all the London editions of the *Works*, until Sheridan, in 1784, removed to his seventeenth volume those pieces for which Swift was not directly or wholly responsible.

In Bathurst's small octavo edition of the *Miscellanies*, 1742, an attempt was made to assign to Arbuthnot and Gay their parts. In the fourth volume, which contains the verse, fifty-four pieces out of a total of one hundred are marked with an asterisk, explained in a note—'Whatever are not mark'd with a Star, are Dr. SWIFT's.' This may, presumably, be taken also to mean that no piece marked with a star is Swift's. Many of those so marked are attributable to Pope.

This arrangement of the *Miscellanies* led to confusion and misunderstanding. Charles Ford admonished Swift that a careful edition of his *Works* was 'become absolutely necessary, since that jumble with Pope, etc., in three volumes', which put him 'in a rage' whenever he met with them.[1] The first move in this direction came from Dublin with the publication of Faulkner's edition of the *Works* in four volumes, dated 1735. Although this edition aroused protests from Motte, the London bookseller, and adverse criticism from successive London editors, Hawkesworth, Sheridan, and even Nichols, the Dublin volumes, rather than Hawkesworth's 1755 volumes, merit the description of the 'earliest regular edition'.[2]

Only two collections of Swift's writings issued before 1735 were authoritative, or recognized by him, the *Miscellanies in Prose and Verse* printed for John Morphew in 1711, and the *Miscellanies* in four volumes, 1727–32. The remaining pieces, scattered in pamphlet and broadsheet form, had been partially 'scraped up' by Curll and other publishers, together with 'trash' which Swift disowned.[3] These unauthorized publications, together with the haphazard 1727–32 *Miscellanies*, became a source of confusion from which editors failed to escape.

[1] 6 Nov. 1733; *Correspondence of Jonathan Swift*, ed. F. Elrington Ball, v. 37, subsequently cited as *Corresp.*; *Letters of Swift to Ford*, ed. Nichol Smith, p. 156.

[2] *Works*, ed. John Nichols, 1801, ii, Preface, p. v.

[3] *Journal to Stella*, 14 May, 1711. For these unauthorized collections see the Bibliographical Summary.

(iii)

As early as 1708 Swift began to draw up a list of occasional pieces suitable for publication in a miscellany volume. This was during a residence in London extending from 1707 to 1709. The list, written on the back of a letter directed to him in October, 1708,[1] contained, in addition to prose, nine verse pieces. The projected miscellany is referred to in Swift's correspondence, and in the *Journal to Stella*.[2] From these references it appears that originally there was some thought of a preface by Steele; and that, although the volume finally appeared with Morphew's imprint, Benjamin Tooke was earlier busied with it. The book was published at the end of February, 1711.[3] It contained the nine verse pieces proposed by Swift in 1708, and four others, or five if we count the verse portion of 'Merlin's Prophecy'. They are (1) 'Verses Wrote in a Lady's Ivory Table Book'; (2) 'Mrs. Harris's Petition'; (3) the ballad 'To the Tune of the Cutpurse'; (4) 'Vanbrug's House'; (5) 'The Description of a Salamander'; (6) 'Baucis and Philemon'; (7) 'To Mrs. Biddy Floyd'; (8) 'The History of Vanbrug's House'; (9) 'Elegy on Patrige'; (10) 'Apollo Outwitted'; (11) 'A Description of the Morning'; (12) 'A Description of a City Shower'; (13) 'Sid Hamet'. Five of these, (1), (3), (4), (5), and, apparently, (10),[4] were here printed for the first time. A second edition of these *Miscellanies*, dated 1713, was published by Morphew early in 1714.[5]

---

[1] See Biographical Anecdotes prefixed to Nichols's *Supplement*, 1779, and Forster, *Life*, p. 257 n.

[2] *Corresp.* i. 167, 185–6; *Journal to Stella*, 17 October, 1710.

[3] *The Post-Boy*, 24–7 February, 1711; *The Daily Courant*, 28 February, 1711; and frequently thereafter in various newspapers.

[4] An undated broadsheet edition of 'Apollo Outwitted' appears in the catalogue of the Gilbert Collection, Dublin; but this cannot now be found, and may have been of later date.

[5] *The London Gazette*, 23–7 February, 1714. There were two different printings of the second edition.

(iv)

Fifteen years passed before Swift was again moved to collect his scattered writings. His brief span of power and fame during the last four years of Queen Anne was over, and he had endured twelve years of separation from his English friends. In the summer of 1726 he visited England again; and during that visit he and Pope concerted a joint miscellany. After his return to Dublin we find him writing to Pope: 'I am mustering, as I told you, all the little things in verse that I think may be safely printed, but I give you despotic power to tear as many as you please.'[1] In February of the following year Pope was able to report, but it would seem prematurely, 'Our Miscellany is now quite printed';[2] for the first two volumes did not appear till the latter part of June,[3] and his accompanying remarks give a completely erroneous description of the set as it was finally published. He speaks of 'this joint volume, in which methinks we look like friends side by side'. In the first volume, consisting wholly of prose, the only piece by Pope is the preface, jointly signed by Swift and himself. In the second volume, also prose, one piece only can be wholly assigned to Pope, with some further share in a series of pieces in which Arbuthnot, Gay, and Fortescue, as well as Swift, were represented.[4] And, further, Pope's statement that 'The third volume consists of verses' is evidence only of his intention at the time, for this volume, called 'The Last', did not appear till March, 1728,[5] and contained, as well as verse, Pope's *Art of Sinking in Poetry* occupying over ninety pages. The truth is that Pope was not, as his letters might suggest, an equal partner in the venture. His contribution to the three volumes was far less than Swift's; he enjoyed any advantages to be derived from publication; and he reserved material for future use.

[1] 15 October, 1726; *Corresp.* iii. 349.
[2] *Ib.* 380.
[3] *The Evening Post,* 15–22 June, 1727; *The Craftsman,* 24 June, 1727.
[4] See *Alexander Pope: A Bibliography,* Griffith, Nos. 184, 185.
[5] Griffith, *op. cit.,* No. 196.

The delay in the publication of the third (so-called 'Last') volume may also be attributed to Pope. Courthope suggests that, 'though ready', it was kept back 'in anticipation of the appearance of the "Dunciad"'.[1] But the volume was certainly not ready, and, although delayed till March of the following year, it then appeared more than two months before the *Dunciad*.[2] Pope evidently found himself with insufficient copy to fill out a third volume, unless, and for this he seems to have been unprepared, he drew upon his own resources. He fell back on Swift, who was during 1727 again in England, and for a visit extending from April to September, over six months. In July Swift, then at Twickenham, wrote to Sheridan for a copy of the verses addressed to Stella on her collecting his poems, as these, although he did not propose to print them entire, were wanted to enlarge the miscellany.[3] Pope, however, succeeded in obtaining much more additional copy. The particular poem was printed in full, and six other Stella pieces also appeared, including even the verses written for her birthday 1726–7. 'It might excite surprise at any time', writes Dr. Ball, 'that Swift could have borne the publication of these verses, but especially so when he believed her to be dying and was writing to Sheridan in an agony of affliction. The only explanation seems to be that Swift had delivered himself in his infatuation for Pope completely into his hands. Pope is recorded to have said that he wished the verses to Stella had never been written, but none the less he had the power to prevent their inclusion in the Miscellanies and did not use it.'[4] It may be questioned, however, whether Pope is accurately reported; and Dr. Ball's suggestion that Swift was a puppet in his hands cannot be entertained. We, at least, have good reason to be thankful that the Stella verses were included in the *Miscellanies*.

1 *Works of Alexander Pope*, Elwin and Courthope, v. 213.
2 Griffith, *op. cit.*, No. 198.
3 *Corresp.* iii 403–4.
4 *Swift's Verse*, pp. 212–13. It is

Delany, *Observations*, 1754, p. 103, who states that Pope expressed a wish that the poems to Stella had never been written.

The volume, as finally published, contained as Swift's contribution the thirteen verse pieces included in the *Miscellanies* of 1711, 'Cadenus and Vanessa', the Stella poems, the imitation of Horace addressed to Oxford in 1713, the imitation of *Hoc erat*, 'The South-Sea', 'Newgate's Garland' (if by Swift), 'Prometheus', 'Corinna', 'The Quidnuncki's' (if by Swift), 'Phyllis: Or the Progress of Love', 'The Progress of Poetry', 'The Progress of Beauty', 'Pethox the Great', 'Epilogue to a Play for the Benefit of the Weavers', the 'Epitaph on a Miser' (Demar), and 'On Dreams'. Swift was evidently prepared to make even further contributions;[1] but apparently these came too late to the printer's hand. In the result the 'Last' volume bears all the marks of editorial and printing indecision. It falls into three sections, each with a separate register and pagination: (1) 'The Art of Sinking in Poetry'; (2) 'Cadenus and Vanessa'; (3) miscellaneous verses by Swift, Pope, and others.

(v)

Miscellanies. The Last Volume was published a few weeks after Stella's death on the 28th of January, 1727-8. New-formed friendships with the Achesons and Leslies, and long summer visits to Market Hill, 1728-29-30, served to fill Swift's time and occupy his mind in the first years of bereavement. From the autumn of 1730 to the fateful decay of his mental powers he became more and more of a recluse, immured in the large and bare deanery house. But these six years, 1731-6, saw the composition of several of his greatest poems. If the number declined, and more rapidly towards the end, in wit, in power of invective, and in versification, there was, in the major pieces, gain rather than loss, until the terrible 'Legion Club' (1736) finished the tale of his greater poems.

In these latter years his Irish friends, including even Sheridan and Delany, became less to him; and several of

---

[1] *Corresp.* iv. 7.

his English friends were removed. Congreve died on
19 January, 1729; Gay died on 4 December, 1732; and
the news of Arbuthnot's death, 27 February, 1735,
struck him to the heart.[1] As he withdrew himself from
social life his poems began to owe less to the passing
occasion, and to become more general in character.
Furthermore, in these years three important groups of
collected poems saw the light. The story of their
publication, severally associated with the names of Pope,
Pilkington, and Faulkner, is, in each instance, complicated by some uncertainty and mystery. The three
groups are:

(1) A further volume of the *Miscellanies*, called 'The
Third', edited by Pope, and published in 1732 with
the joint imprint of Benjamin Motte and Lawton
Gilliver.

(2) *On Poetry: A Rapsody*, 1733; *An Epistle to a Lady*,
... *Also a Poem, Occasion'd by Reading Dr. Young's
Satires*, 1734; *A Beautiful Young Nymph*. ... *To
which are added, Strephon and Chloe. And Cassinus
and Peter*, 1734. These six poems, appearing in
three separate publications, were, in August, 1733,
conveyed by Mrs. Barber to Matthew Pilkington,
then in London. He was responsible for negotiating
their publication; and was also concerned in the
publication by Roberts, through Motte, of *The Life
and Genuine Character of Dr. Swift*, 1733.

(3) The second volume of Faulkner's 1735 four-
volume edition of Swift's *Works*. In the publication of this important collection Faulkner received
assistance not only from the Dean's friends, but from
Swift himself.

The story of Pilkington's connexion with the pieces
named under (2) can best be followed in the introductory
notes to each poem; but (1) and (3) call for fuller discus-
sion.

[1] See *Corresp.* iv. 58, 365–6; v. 140.

(vi)

Three volumes of the Swift and Pope *Miscellanies*, distinguished as 'First', 'Second', and 'Last', had been published in 1727–8. During the summer of 1732 Pope projected a further volume and applied to Swift for copy. On 12 June Swift wrote in reply to a letter of Pope's which has been lost, naming those issues of *The Intelligencer*[1] written by him, and giving a list of pieces in prose and verse composed 'since I left you'.[2] The verse pieces enumerated by him are 'a Libel on Dr. Delany and Lord Carteret, a Letter to Dr. Delany on the Libels writ against him, the Barrack (a stolen copy), the Lady's Journal, the Lady's Dressing-room (a stolen copy), [and] the [Place] of the Damned (a stolen copy). . . . Besides these there are five or six, perhaps more, papers of verses writ in the North, but perfect family things, two or three of which may be tolerable, the rest but indifferent, and the humour only local, and some that would give offence to the times'. It is evident that several letters relating to the publication of this volume have been lost; but Pope, it is clear, was too much concerned with the commercial side of the transaction, and paid too little regard to Swift's feelings in the matter. He intended originally to issue the volume through Lawton Gilliver, his new publisher, but deferred so far to Motte, on account of his previous association with Swift, that the two names were joined on the imprint. The volume was published at the beginning of October, 1732.[3] A month later, on 4 November, Swift wrote to tell Motte that 'two copies of the last Miscellany' had just reached him. He was annoyed to find that Pope had taken his own course in selecting the verse, with the result that 'almost six-sevenths of the whole verse part in the book' was his, and chosen with insufficient regard for the list he

[1] For *The Intelligencer* see p. 772.
[2] *Corresp.* iv. 307–9.
[3] *The Daily Post*, 2 October; *Grub-Street Journal*, 4 October, 1732; Griffith, *op. cit.*, No. 276. Concerning the two publishers see *Elwin and Courthope, op. cit.* ix. 524–9, and Plomer's *Dictionary of Booksellers and Printers*.

had sent Pope in June.[1] He was particularly aggrieved that the 'Libel on Delany', which he considered the best thing he had written, was omitted. Much the greater part of the volume consisted of prose, followed by one hundred pages of verse, paged separately, containing the following pieces by Swift: (1) 'The Journal of a Modern Lady'; (2) 'The Country Life'; (3) 'On Cutting down the Old Thorn at Market-Hill'; (4) 'A Pastoral Dialogue'; (5) 'Mary the Cook-Maid's Letter to Dr. Sheridan'; (6) 'A Dialogue between Mad Mullinix and Timothy'; (7) 'Epigram On seeing a worthy Prelate go out of Church'; (8) 'Dr. Sw— to Mr. P—e, While he was writing the Dunciad'; (9) 'A Soldier and a Scholar'; (10) 'To Doctor D—l—y on the Libels Writ against him'. There were, in addition, three short poems and a few epigrams not by Swift.

Furthermore, in the prose section of the volume Pope had printed several pieces disowned by Swift; and it is hardly to be wondered at that Swift found difficulty in reconciling himself to such negligent and inconsiderate editorial practices. On 9 December he wrote again to Motte to express his dissatisfaction, complaining, though hardly with justification, that his part in the verses was 'very uncorrect'. He went on to say he had reason to believe certain Dublin 'printers will collect all they think to be mine, and print them by subscription, which I will neither encourage nor oppose'.[2] This was the first hint of Faulkner's edition of the *Works*, a project which soon began to take more definite shape.

(vii)

Meanwhile, as Pope's volume was in course of preparation, Matthew Pilkington, a young Irish clergyman, was, with Swift's recognition, negotiating the publication of a rival volume. This transaction was distinct from the publication through Pilkington, in 1733–4, of the pieces

[1] *Corresp.* iv. 359–61.   [2] *Ib.* 367.

conveyed to him by Mrs. Barber. Once again, for want of all the papers and correspondence, the affair is not wholly clear.

As noted above, on 12 June, 1732, Swift sent to Pope a list of pieces suitable for the miscellany volume in preparation. A month later[1] he wrote to Motte, in answer to a letter which has not been preserved, but which evidently related to Pope's desire to relegate Motte to a secondary position. In this letter Swift affirms categorically that (*a*) he wished Motte alone to issue anything published with his consent when alive, or with the consent of his executors after his death; (*b*) he intended to entrust any posthumous pieces to Pope with a recommendation that Motte alone should be employed in their publication; (*c*) he hoped also that anything he acknowledged and approved during his life should be published by Motte 'by themselves', provided it turned to his advantage; (*d*) Motte was authorized to emphasize these points to Pope.

Within a week of this letter, however, on 22 July, Swift executed a surprising document assigning 'all manner of right' in his 'scattered papers, in prose and verse, for three or four years last past' to Matthew Pilkington.[2] Following upon this assignment Pilkington wrote to Bowyer on 17 August to say that the Dean was reading over 'two or three of those papers' to see if any revision was necessary. He inquired whether Bowyer possessed copies of '*The Journal of a Dublin Lady*, *The Ballad on the English Dean*, and *Rochford's Journal*, because you shall have the copies sent to you and the property effectually secured'. He added: 'The Dean says

[1] *Corresp.* iv. 317–18.

[2] This assignment, together with Pilkington's correspondence with William Bowyer, was printed by Nichols in his *Supplement*, 1779. A manuscript copy from the original in Nichols's possession will be found in the British Museum (Add. MS. 38730. f. 185), showing one or two unimportant verbal differences from the printed version. There is also a similar document in the Harvard University Library. The correspondence, with other relative letters, is also printed by Ball, *Corresp.* iv. 480–7, Appendix X. William Bowyer, the younger, printed the London edition of Pilkington's poems in 1730. *Cf.* also Nichols, *Lit. Anec.* ii. 10–11.

he thinks the assignment as full as it is possible for him to write; but that he will comply with any alterations we think proper.' This was sufficiently comprehensive and definite. On the 28th of the same month he informed Bowyer that the parcel of pamphlets with the Dean's corrections had been dispatched, and promised shortly to forward 'another pamphlet at least, and a new assignment from the Dean'. He also reported that Swift had 'received a letter from Mr. Pope and Mr. Motte; but neither have been of the least disadvantage to my request'. He added: 'I desire that you will insist upon your right by the assignment I formerly sent; and let Mr. Motte shew you anything under the Dean's hand which will invalidate it!' He appended to this letter a list of 'some of' the pieces in prose and verse which Bowyer was entitled to print. The verse pieces were: (1) 'The Barrack'; (2) 'An Ode to Ireland from Horace'; (3) 'A Libel on Dr. Delany and Ld. Carteret'; (4) 'To Dr. Delany on the Libels against him'; (5) 'O'Rourk'; (6) 'The Dressing-room'; (7) 'The Journal at Rochford's'; (8) 'The Thorn'; (9) 'Poem on the English Dean'; (10) 'Journal of a Dublin Lady'; and any pieces from *The Intelligencer* which were by Swift. It will be seen that this list misses only one piece, 'The Place of the Damn'd', of those Swift named to Pope in his letter of 12 June, 1732. On the other hand, (2), (3), (5), (6), and (9) were not included in the volume edited by Pope.

By this time Pope had become aware of what was going on. He adopted a characteristic method of conveying a reproach. On 28 August, 1732, the Duchess of Queensberry and Gay wrote a joint letter to Swift, in the course of which Gay quoted a paragraph from a letter of Pope's containing the complaint that 'Motte and another idle fellow, I find, have been writing to the Dean to get him to give them some copyright, which surely he will not be so indiscreet as to do, when he knows my design, and has done these two months and more'.[1] He suggested,

---

[1] *Corresp.* iv. 342.

further, that the Dean was acting unadvisedly in committing his affairs to 'mercenaries'. Gay also added a line of caution. To this letter Swift made no response till 3 October; and, unfortunately, that part of his reply in which he promised 'two or three full answers' to Pope's complaint has not been preserved.[1] It seems evident, however, that he was in no mood of conciliation. Two days later Pilkington conveyed his right, under Swift's assignment of 22 July, to William Bowyer, thus empowering him to make what use he would of the Dean's scattered writings. It was then, however, too late to proceed. *Miscellanies. The Third Volume* had just been published by Motte and Gilliver.

All the facts are not before us, and the correspondence between Swift and Pope, relating to the publication of the 1732 volume of *Miscellanies*, has been, for the most part, destroyed; but so far as these tortuous transactions can be followed, they reflect no credit on either Pope or Swift. Pope's chief interest seems to have been a display of editorial activity at little personal sacrifice. He cut down to narrow limits his own contribution to the forthcoming volume, at the same time playing off Gilliver against Motte to draw the best fee he could from the publisher, or publishers. Motte, aggrieved at the attempt to pass him over, must have written to Swift insinuating, probably, that Pope was negotiating with little regard to the Dean's interest. Swift's letter of 15 July[2] was a reply to Motte's complaint; and thereupon, also, to forestall Pope's volume, he commissioned Pilkington to treat with Bowyer. By this secret transaction he hoped, no doubt, to checkmate Pope, pleading ignorance if necessary, bestow a kindness on his protégé the young Irish clergyman, and regain control over the publication of his writings. As it proved, nothing came of the scheme. Pilkington's and Bowyer's methods were too dilatory; whereas they should have made the utmost speed to publish their volume first.

[1] *Corresp.* iv. 354.   [2] *Ib.* 317.

(viii)

To George Faulkner,[1] the Dublin bookseller and printer, belongs the credit of first realizing that the time had come for a standard edition of the Dean's works. The plan took shape in his mind towards the end of 1732, or the beginning of 1733. In a letter dated 16 February, 1732–3, commending Faulkner to Lord Oxford, Swift referred to the Dublin printer's project as 'a work that very much discontents me', although he admitted that he would rather have it fall into his hands 'than any other's on this side'.[2] The hint of a Dublin edition reached Pope, and possibly aroused a fear that he would be deprived of writings which might be used in a further volume of *Miscellanies*. On 1 May, 1733, Swift wrote to say that a printer in Dublin intended to publish 'my works, as he called them, in four volumes by subscription', despite his own expressed disfavour and preference for a London edition. 'Much of this discourse passed,' he continues, 'and he goes on with the matter, wherein I determined not to intermeddle.'[3] Swift may have regarded Faulkner's proceedings with qualified approval; he would probably have preferred a London edition; but he certainly exaggerated the degree of his indifference.

Faulkner went forward but slowly. In August, 1734, Oxford inquired why publication had been so long delayed.[4] Swift artlessly explained that he was not interested, that, indeed the whole affair was a 'great vexation' to him, that Faulkner was dependent upon others for copy, and that delays had arisen through his ordering 'certain things to be struck out after they were printed'.[5] More than six months later Lord Carteret had not received the copies for which he had subscribed.[6] The four volumes were, however, issued about this time. During 1733 and 1734 Faulkner made a practice of appending to his various

[1] For a good account of Faulkner see Gilbert's *History of the City of Dublin*, ii. 30–53.
[2] *Corresp.* iv. 390. See also Faulkner's advertisement in the *Dublin Journal*, 10 Feby. 1732–3.
[3] *Corresp.* iv. 431.
[4] *Ib.* v. 81.
[5] *Ib.* 85.
[6] *Ib.* 142.

publications a lengthy advertisement[1] of his intention to publish in four volumes 'all the Works that are generally allowed to have been written' by Swift. Subscriptions were invited and delivery promised upon dates which proved to be continuously movable, as were also the dates given for the closing of the subscription lists. In January, 1735, however, the complete set was at last published,[2] and attracted an unexpected notoriety, for in the *Dublin Gazette* of 15–19 April Faulkner advertised a reward for the detection of persons who had stolen copies from his warehouse to hawk them in the streets.

After publication Swift continued to pretend a displeasure with Faulkner. Writing to William Pulteney, 12 May, 1735, he repeated his earlier observations upon 'some volumes of what are called my Works', protesting that the printer 'consulted some friends, who were readier to direct him than I desired they should'.[3] He affirmed categorically to Motte that, 'Mr. Faulkner in printing those volumes did what I much disliked, and yet what was not in my power to hinder, and all my friends pressed him to print them, and gave him what manuscript copies they had occasionally gotten from me'.[4] Nevertheless when Motte, who considered himself to have a prior claim to the Dean's writings, filed a bill in Chancery to stop the sale of Faulkner's edition in England, Swift wrote sternly to his English bookseller asserting that Irish printers were morally, if not legally, justified in trying to sell their publications in England.[5]

These and other references by Swift to Faulkner's edition of his writings are, at the least, equivocal. He protests overmuch. Faulkner consulted him in the first

[1] Some of Faulkner's advertisements are printed by Ball, *Corresp.* v. 449–52, Appendix V.

[2] Faulkner's *Dublin Journal*, 7 January, 1734–5. Three volumes were, apparently, issued earlier. See *Dublin Journal*, 23 November, and *Dublin Evening Post*, 26 November, 1734. But the fourth volume, completing the set, was held over.

[3] *Corresp.* v. 179–80.

[4] 1 Nov. 1735; *Corresp.* v. 257. This letter, given only in part by Ball, is printed in full in *Historical MSS. Commission, MSS. of the Earl of Bathurst*, p. 10.

[5] 25 May, 1736; *Corresp.* v. 338–40.

instance; he knew that friends were furnishing Faulkner with copy; yet he pretends an inability to stay either him or them. It was but a part of his ingrained habit of dissociating himself from the open publication of his own writings.

There is, on the other hand, evidence, internal and external, which leaves no doubt that Swift was trying to conceal the real measure of his co-operation with Faulkner. The evidence, so far as it relates to the third volume of the *Works*, containing *Gulliver's Travels*, shows that Swift wrote to his friends for a manuscript list of errata and a corrected copy of Motte's edition, with the intention of allowing Faulkner to make use of them. There are further corrections in the text of Faulkner's third volume which could have come, directly or indirectly, only from the author. Swift's co-operation with the printer of the third volume is beyond a doubt.[1] It is hardly likely that where assistance went far with one volume it was withheld from the other three; and an examination of their text supports this inference. In the second volume, which contains the poems, corrections are embodied which Swift made with his own hand in a copy of the *Miscellanies*, 1727–32.[2] Furthermore a set of Faulkner's edition, in six volumes, appears in the sale catalogue of Swift's library, lot number 486, marked as annotated by the Dean himself. This set is, possibly, that now in the Shirley library, Lough Fea, co. Monaghan, Ireland. The second volume has a number of corrections in Swift's hand. These are quite unimportant, relating chiefly to printer's errors and the like, and suggest that he approved both of Faulkner's selection and text.

In a letter written to Pope, 8 July, 1733, Swift drops into an important admission: 'As to the printing of my

[1] See Hubbard's *Contributions towards a Bibliography of Gulliver's Travels*, 1922, pp. 44–62, and Harold Williams's edition of *Gulliver's Travels*, 1926, pp. xxxviii–l.
[2] This copy, formerly in Lord Powerscourt's library, passed into the possession of Mr. W. G. Panter, The Bawn, Foxrock, co. Dublin. It is now in the possession of Lord Rothschild, Merton Hall, Cambridge.

things going on here, it is an evil I cannot prevent. I shall not be a penny the richer. Some friends correct the errors, and now and then I look on them for a minute or two.'[1] This can be read only as a confession that he sometimes examined the proof-sheets. Orrery, who knew Swift well in his later years, has a more circumstantial story: 'FAULKNER's edition, at least the four first volumes of it (for there are now eight) were published, by the permission and connivance, if not by the particular appointment of the Dean himself.'[2] And later he grows more explicit: 'The four first volumes were published by subscription, and every sheet of them was brought to the Dean for his revisal and correction. The two next were published in the same manner. . . . In the publication of the six first volumes, the situation and arrangement of each particular piece, in verse and prose, was left entirely to the editor. In that point, the Dean either could not, or would not give him the least assistance. The dates were often guessed at.'[3] The last remark is interesting, for it aptly fits the second volume containing the verses. Some of the dates are clearly wrong, and the result of pure guess-work. If we allow something for exaggeration, Orrery's evidence cannot be wholly set aside; and some years later it was emphatically corroborated by Deane Swift, who states that the first four volumes 'were actually revised and corrected by *Swift* himself, as indeed were afterwards the two subsequent volumes, printed by Faulkner in the year 1738: and, what is very surprising, these six volumes, as far as they run, are still by many degrees, notwithstanding they want at present many illustrations, the best edition of the Dr.'s Works now extant. If any one doubt this, let him compare *Cadenus* and *Vanessa*, or the poem on the *South-Sea Project*, as printed by Faulkner, with the English edition; especially the latter'.[4] The statement is clear; the examples cited are to the point. Nevertheless Faulkner's edition has

[1] *Corresp.* v. 1.
[2] *Remarks*, 1752, p. 79.
[3] *Ib.*, pp. 81–2.

[4] *Letters, Written by the Late Jonathan Swift, D.D.*, ed. Deane Swift, 1768, footnote to Letter LII.

been depreciated, its textual value overlooked for nearly two centuries, owing to the jealousy with which it was regarded by the English booksellers, furthered by a bitter but ignorant and misguided attack made upon it by Hawkesworth, in 1755, in the Preface to his edition of the Dean's *Works* issued in London by Bathurst and others.[1]

Swift's admissions, the testimony of Orrery and Deane Swift, and the nature of the textual revisions, combine to give to Faulkner's first six volumes a semi-authoritative character. And Faulkner's prefaces are a further testimony in his favour. These are skilfully phrased, discreetly reserved, and may, very probably, have been written by Swift himself.[2] 'The Publisher's Preface' to the set, appearing in the first volume, repeats in similar words Swift's remarks upon the edition in his letters. The *'supposed Author'*, we are told, was almost indifferent to the fate of any *'Copies of Verses'* he ever wrote, which had, for the most part, found their way into print from transcripts made by friends. The *'supposed Author'* could not be prevailed on by argument to lend assistance in the preparation of the new edition, although it was represented to him that disagreements between different booksellers on the question of partnership rights would prevent the publication of a full edition in London, that literary property was not recognized in Ireland, and that, failing Faulkner, a less desirable printer would seize upon his works. He would not, however, do more than permit some friends to revise proofs, and occasionally offer an opinion himself. In the 'Advertisement' prefixed to the volume of poems we are told that *'Our Intentions were to print the Poems according to the Time they were writ in;' but*

---

[1] See further A. E. Case, *Four Essays on Gulliver's Travels*, 1945, pp. 1–49; and Harold Williams, *The Text of Gulliver's Travels*, 1952.

[2] In a letter addressed to William Bowyer by Faulkner (1 Oct. 1745; *Corresp.* vi. 223–4) the latter says: 'As you are famous for writing pre-

faces, pray help me to one for Advice to Servants.' John Forster, noting this statement, gave it as his conviction that the prefaces to Faulkner's volumes were written by Swift. Nichols, *Lit. Anec.* ii. 177, states that Bowyer wrote the preface for the Irish edition of *Directions to Servants*.

we could not do it so exactly as we desired, because we could never get the least Satisfaction in that or many other Circumstances from the supposed Author.' The style of these prefaces strongly resembles Swift's; and several of the phrases ring familiarly like those in his letters in which he had affected indifference to the whole project.

It seems plain that Faulkner was precluded from professing any direct communication with the author. And for years he loyally accepted a pose which cannot have been to his liking. A charge of piratical practices, however, stung him, and in 1744 he published a notice in his *Dublin Journal* declaring that his edition of the Dean's *Works* was published at the request of Swift's friends, that 'the Author was pleased to consent, and was so kind as to correct the whole work, ready for printing, and, in order to have them appear in the most accurate manner, the Author was pleased to revise every Proof Sheet'.[1] Years later, after Hawkesworth's attack, he repeated this statement, affirming that it was his practice to attend the Dean and read aloud from the proof-sheets, not only to the author but to two men servants, 'Which, if they did not comprehend, he would alter and amend, until they understood it perfectly well, and then would say, *This will do; for I write to the Vulgar, more than to the Learned*. Not satisfied with this Preparation for the Press, he corrected every Sheet of the first seven Volumes that were published in his Life Time, desiring the Editor to write Notes, being much younger than the Dean, acquainted with most of the Transactions of his Life.'[2]

If Faulkner's later preface, which is directed against Hawkesworth and the London booksellers, be suspected of overstating the measure of Swift's co-operation, the earlier prefaces, probably written by Swift himself, as definitely understate it. Faulkner's edition of the *Works*,

[1] I am indebted to Dr. T. Percy Kirkpatrick for drawing my attention to this notice in the *Dublin Journal* for 29 September–2 October, 1744. See further *Times Literary Supplement*, 12 April, 1934, p. 262.

[2] *Works*, 1762, vol. i, 'To the Reader'. The whole of this lengthy preface by Faulkner is instructive.

so far as the first six[1] volumes are concerned, was secretly recognized by the author, and at least partially revised by him. In the third volume, *Gulliver's Travels*, revision was extensive; in the second volume, with which we are here concerned, it was more casual and desultory, nevertheless definitely apparent, as a study of the textual apparatus will show.[2]

(ix)

Faulkner's second volume, containing the *Poetical Works*, more than doubled the quantity of Swift's verse gathered in the miscellany volumes of 1711 and 1727–32. Among pieces of importance here first collected were 'The Fable of Midas', 'To the Earl of Peterborough', 'The Description of an Irish Feast', 'Stella at Wood-Park', 'A Receipt to restore Stella's Youth', 'A Pastoral Dialogue between Richmond-Lodge and Marble-Hill', four of the Market Hill poems, poems relating to Wood's coinage and Irish politics, the epistle 'To Mr. Gay', 'On Mr. Pulteney being put out of the Council', 'The Place of the Damn'd', and the poems published in London, 1733–4, through the agency of Pilkington. Here also appeared 'A Libel on Dr. Delany and Lord Carteret', omitted from the *Miscellanies* by Pope, although Moore included it in his slender volume of Swift *Miscellanies*, 1734. Faulkner's claim, in the 'Advertisement' to his second volume, that he had rejected what was not by Swift in the *Miscellanies* and added '*above a*

---

[1] Deane Swift says 'seven'; and he also stated (Nichols, *Lit. Illustrations*, v. 379) that he was the only person who could give a true account of how Faulkner's seventh volume came to be published. But this volume, containing correspondence, was not printed till 1741, and was based on Pope's *Works of Mr. Alexander Pope, in Prose. Vol. II.* It may be doubted whether Swift would have assisted Faulkner with this volume. On the publication of this correspondence see further Dilke, *Papers of a Critic*, i. 312–28; Elwin and Courthope, *Works of Alexander Pope*, i. pp. lxxxiii–cxix; *Corresp.* vi. 197–202, Appendix I; Griffith, *Pope: A Bibliography*, Nos. 529–34; Pope's *Correspondence*, ed. Sherburn, i, pp. xi–xviii.

[2] See *The Journal, Journal of a Modern Lady, To Dr. Delany on the Libels*.

third Part, which was never collected before', was fully justified.

Indications of editorial work, which proceeded while the volume was in the press, carry a suggestion of the author's rather than the publisher's hand. O8 is cancelled by *O, pp. 207–8. Further signs of cancellation appear at *Z, pp. 343–4, *Aa, pp. 357–8, *Bb2, pp. 371–2, *Bb, pp. 379–80. In each of these instances the recto or verso of the starred leaf has a prefatory note to the poem, or poems, following. It seems most probable that these notes were written by Swift, and that the original leaves were cancelled to admit the insertion or recasting of the notes. T5–T8, pp. 281–8, representing the earlier part of 'A Panegyrick on the Dean', appears also to have been replaced by a cancel half-sheet signed *T.

Faulkner published his edition of Swift's *Works* concurrently in octavo and duodecimo formats. 'Prometheus' was inadvertently omitted from the second volume of the octavo edition, and inserted at the close of the fourth volume. It appears in the proper volume in the duodecimo edition. There was, apparently, a greater demand for the octavo edition of the *Poetical Works* than for the other three volumes, for it was published separately in a new edition in 1737, with the addition of 'Prometheus' and a reshuffling of the order in which the pieces were printed. This 1737 volume was followed as a model throughout subsequent Faulkner editions. In 1746 (vol. viii) more poems were added; and more again in 1762–3.[1]

(x)

The successive *Miscellanies* issued by Samuel Fairbrother are the only other Dublin editions of Swift's verse which call for notice. In 1728 he published two piratical volumes of *Miscellanies in Prose and Verse*, called 'The Second Edition', taken, with some changes and slight

---

[1] Volume numbers differ according to format.

additions, from the three volumes edited by Pope in 1727. 'The Third Edition' of these two volumes was published in 1732, followed, in 1733, by 'The Second Edition' of a third volume, reproducing, with some additions, Pope's 1732 volume of *Miscellanies*. Faulkner's edition of the *Works* in 1735 gave Fairbrother a further opportunity to pilfer, which he seized upon by publishing *Vol. IV. of the Miscellanies . . . To which are added Several other Poems by the same Author, many of which are Printed from Original Manuscripts, not in any former Edition. . . . 1735.* This volume contained an unblushing preface in which Fairbrother announced that he had extracted from the 'Author's Works, in Four Volumes 8vo' pieces not in his own edition for 'the Accommodation of all those Gentlemen' who were supplied with his first three volumes. And he repeated the claim made on his title-page that several poems 'never before Printed' had been added 'from the D—ns own Original Manuscripts'. A first instinct is to dismiss this for the usual puff of a piratical bookseller; but there is substance in Fairbrother's claim.

The first poem printed in the verse section of Fairbrother's fourth volume is a pindaric 'Ode to the King on his *Irish* Expedition'. Swift is known to have written a poem on this subject. Deane Swift tells us he had seen it, and that it was written in a 'Pindarique way'. The 'Ode to King William' which has found its way into Swift's *Works*, on the authority of Nichols, is not a pindaric, and it seems most probable that the poem printed by Fairbrother is authentic.[1] Fairbrother's volume also printed for the first time a number of trifles in verse passing between Swift and his Irish friends, two of which are presented in an arrangement which differs from that of the accepted versions. In addition there are four trifling pieces hitherto not printed elsewhere.[2] It seems most likely that Fairbrother had access to the manuscript collection now in the library of Trinity College, Dublin,

---

[1] See further pp. 4–13.
[2] See pp. 994, 996, 998 n., 1003 n., 1006, 1007.

known as *The Whimsical Medley*, and to other manuscripts of an authoritative character. His exceedingly
rare fourth volume, which has not previously been noted
by any editor, is both curious and important.

(xi)

The London booksellers had long been aware of
Faulkner's project. Motte, as has been noted, complained
of it to Swift; but neither he nor Lawton Gilliver, with
whom he was joined in the publication of the 1732
volume of *Miscellanies*, appears to have taken sufficiently
active steps to protect their common commercial interests, unless Motte thought he had gone far enough by
filing a bill in Chancery.[1] Or they may have delegated
the work to Charles Davis, who, as early as the end of
January, or beginning of February, 1735,[2] published a
fifth and supplementary volume of *Miscellanies, in Prose
and Verse*, in which full use was made of Faulkner's four
volumes. It is clear that he was working from advance
sheets, whether with, or without, Faulkner's knowledge.

If we confine our attention to the verse only we find
that Davis omitted several poems contained in Faulkner's
second volume. These he printed in a supplement, as
*A Collection of Poems, &c. Omitted in the Fifth Volume of
Miscellanies in Prose and Verse*, with pagination in sequence,
and intended to be bound up with 'Volume the Fifth'.
In the 'Advertisement' to his supplement Davis frankly
admitted that the 'Copy of the *Dublin* Edition' transmitted
to him 'from the Press' was not as complete as 'the Editor
afterwards thought fit to make it'. Davis's omissions
cannot be satisfactorily explained by the lack of specific
sheets as they were gathered in Faulkner's second volume;
but we know that this volume underwent revision in the
press, and it is possible that alterations, now indistinguisable
by us, may be reflected in Davis's publication.

---

[1] See p. xxx.
[2] *The Grub-Street Journal*, 30 Jany.,

6, 13 Feby., 27 March, 3 April, 1735;
London Magazine, Jany. 1735, iv. 51.

On the other side it is noteworthy that Davis included three pieces which did not appear in Faulkner's edition, namely the two parts of 'Traulus' and an 'Epigram on Fasting'.[1]

(xii)

The four volumes published in 1735 presented a more complete body of verse than prose, for although, during the next thirty years, Faulkner extended the *Works* to twenty volumes, the additions in verse, though numerous, occupied a comparatively inconsiderable space. These additions immediately found their way into the London trade editions. To trace the extension of the verse canon, step by step, in this introduction would serve little purpose and occupy needless space. The Bibliographical Summary provides a working check-list of collected editions. Furthermore the textual and bibliographical notes accompanying each poem, or group of poems, as arranged in this edition, show how and when additions were made.

Both in London and Dublin Swift's *Works* commanded a sale; and the trade on one side, Faulkner on the other, continued to reprint and extend. The *Miscellanies* begun by Pope, supplemented by Davis's borrowings from Faulkner in 1735, were continued volume by volume by the London booksellers. *Miscellanies. The Tenth Volume*, published by Dodsley in 1745, added the 'Ode to the Athenian Society', the 'Ode to Temple', and some lesser pieces. *Miscellanies. . . . The Eleventh Volume*, 1746, carrying the imprint of four members of the trade, drew upon Faulkner's eighth volume published earlier in the same year. These *Miscellanies* were variously reprinted until the booksellers commissioned Dr. Hawkesworth to edit a definitive set of the Dean's *Works* in opposition to that of Faulkner. The result was the handsome but indifferently edited volumes of 1755, which were published as six in

[1] See pp. 794–801, 948.

quarto, or twelve in octavo.[1] The first continuation of this set came in 1762–4 (vol. vii, 4to; xiii and xiv, 8vo), when William Bowyer reprinted pieces in prose and verse which had been collected and published by Faulkner in 1762.

So far the London booksellers had, in the main, been dependent upon appropriations from Faulkner; but in 1765 Deane Swift carried the English edition further with vol. viii, 4to, vols. xv and xvi, 8vo, in which several important poems appeared for the first time. Thus matters stood when John Nichols, that great printer, chronicler, and literary commentator, began, among his many labours, his long task of making additions to Swift's *Works*. Between twenty and thirty verse pieces were added by him in the volume of 1775. In his *Supplement*, 1776 and 1779, he gathered together many poems by Swift and 'his Friends', a medley which has encouraged unfortunate conjectural attributions. Nichols, an untiring worker, was by no means a careful editor, but he brought genuine enthusiasm to his self-appointed task of presenting a complete collection of Swift's writings.

The result of these disconnected printing and editorial labours, extending over twenty-four years, was an irregular and disordered edition, running to twenty-five octavo volumes, in which shares were held by five different sets of proprietors. After some opposition an arrangement was reached with the shareholders for an amalgamation; and Thomas Sheridan, the son of Swift's friend, was commissioned to write a life of the Dean and compile a regular edition of his *Works*. He was to receive £300 for the *Life*, and £300 more as an editor. The whole, embodying the contents of the previous trade editions and the accumulations of Nichols, sorted into a better semblance of order, appeared in seventeen volumes, 1784.[2]

---

[1] Deane Swift described this edition as 'the vilest that ever yet was published'. He added: 'I could, if I had a mind to it, point you out one part, which is so intolerably wretched, that you would suppose the compositor had been drunk while he was setting the press.' Nichols's *Lit. Illustr.* v. 376.

[2] *Lit. Illustr.* v. 394–5.

Within a few years the indefatigable Nichols produced
a supplement to Sheridan's edition, *Miscellaneous Pieces,
In Prose and Verse. . . . Not inserted in Mr. Sheridan's
Edition of the Dean's Works*, published by Charles Dilley
in 1789. Most of the verse additions in this volume were
minor Swiftiana; but the 'Ode to King William on his
Successes in Ireland', previously printed, as Swift's, by
Nichols in his *Select Collection of Poems*, was here included
with the works, and three early odes, 'To Sancroft', 'To
Congreve', and that 'Occasioned by Sir William Temple's
Late Illness', here first appeared in print, with a note
stating that they were taken 'from an authentic Manuscript fairly and correctly written out as if intended for
the Press'. No trace of this manuscript survives; nor is
it affirmed to have been in Swift's hand, although the
poems are certainly his. The 'Ode to King William', as
noted above,[1] is probably a mistaken ascription.

In 1801 the London booksellers invited Nichols to
prepare a new edition incorporating his further collections
and notes. This appeared in the same year, in nineteen
volumes, embodying Sheridan's *Life* and following the
general outline of the 1784 edition. Nichols's additions
are, for the most part, to be found in vols. xviii and
xix. This edition was republished in twenty-four volumes,
1804, and in nineteen volumes, 1808. The 1808 edition
was indebted to suggestions from Malone and to the
researches of Barrett's *Essay on the Earlier Part of the Life
of Swift*.[2]

To John Nichols's immense industry and energy all
students of eighteenth-century literature, biography, and
printing owe a large debt. In addition to many other
activities he busied himself with Swift over a period of
nearly fifty years; and there is an irony, which he felt
himself, in the fact that his last edition·was so quickly
supplanted by that of Sir Walter Scott, who, as he remarks
caustically, 'having made a solid breakfast on John
Dryden, conceived the idea of a pleasant dinner and

---

[1] See p. xxxvii.   [2] *Lit. Illustr.* v. 396.

supper on Jonathan Swift; which, from the entertainment I had prepared, he found a task of no great difficulty'. And it was a bitter reflection that Scott, who, in a 'brief compliment', could not even spell Nichols's name correctly, received for his one edition thirty times the remuneration the latter 'had received, or expected' for three.[1]

(xiii)

The anecdotal and other additions of Wilson's *Swiftiana*, 1804, were not of special importance; but both Nichols, in 1808, and Scott, in 1814, regarded the contributions of John Barrett, eccentric Greek scholar and Vice-Provost of Trinity College, Dublin, with unnecessary respect. The *Essay on the Earlier Part of the Life of Swift* was published in 1808 with a prefatory 'Advertisement' by Nichols. Barrett's *Essay* supplies interesting details from the registers of Trinity College, Dublin, relative to Swift's residence there. It proceeds to ascribe to Swift, upon strained evidence which Scott himself questioned, the composition of a Tripos[2] pronounced in the college in July, 1688. The text of the Tripos Barrett extracted from the manuscript collection in the library of Trinity College known as *The Whimsical Medley*;[3] and, incited by this discovery, rummaging further, he selected a number of pieces included in that collection, which he ascribed to Swift on the slenderest grounds of internal evidence. They may, nearly all, be characterized as more than doubtful, and do little credit to Barrett's critical faculty. The only exceptions to a singularly unfortunate choice were 'The Intended Speech of a Famous Orator', which was already known as Swift's, although Barrett was unaware of it, and a few *jeux d'esprit* passing between the Dean and his friends, which were now printed for the first time. Barrett's eccentricities of temper and character hardly fitted him to weigh evidence or to judge of style. His great merit was his examination of the college registers and his use of

---

[1] *Lit. Illustr.* v. 396-7.　　　[2] See pp. 1055-7.　　　[3] See p. xlviii.

the neglected, but extremely valuable, collections of Lord Newtown-Butler known as *The Whimsical Medley*.

(xiv)

The aggrieved Nichols characterized Scott's edition of Swift as 'somewhat similar' to his, and 'consisting of the same number of volumes' compiled by 'a neat shuffling of the cards'. The description is only just in so far as it is fair to admit that so extensive was the work done for Swift by Nichols that all editors must, from time to time, turn to him. Scott's acknowledgement might have been more generous. But the fact remains that his edition, carried through with the extraordinary pace he commanded, is even now, in some respects, the most useful working set of the Dean's complete writings. The letters have been superseded by Dr. Elrington Ball's great edition of the *Correspondence*; the prose-writings have been re-edited by Temple Scott and Herbert Davis; single works have been documented with a research to which Scott made no pretence; but, taken as a whole, his editions of 1814 and 1824 have not yet been displaced. The verse, especially, may be better consulted there than in the more recent edition of W. E. Browning, which, if it adds something to our knowledge, makes no attempt at a revision of the canon, is unreliable textually, is less complete than Scott, and is sometimes misleading.

Scott claimed, in the 'Advertisement' to his edition of 1814, to have included over one hundred letters, essays, and poems not previously printed as a part of Swift's *Works*. These were drawn from manuscript communications and collections received from Theophilus Swift, son of Deane Swift, Major Tickell, a grandson of Tickell the poet, Leonard Macnally, the discreditable Irish barrister and playwright, the Rev. Edward Berwick, who furnished the correspondence between Swift and Vanessa,[1]

---

[1] See further *Corresp.* iii. 466–7. These letters have since been re-edited by A. Martin Freeman in *Vanessa and her Correspondence with Jonathan Swift*.

Thomas Steele, a nephew of the Rev. John Lyon who had charge of Swift's person during the last years, W. M. Hartstonge, and others. The verse, with some attempt at arrangement by subject-matter, appears in vols. x, xiii, xiv, and xv. Poems additional to those printed in previous editions appear chiefly in the tenth volume. Verse ascriptions also appear in the Appendix to vol. i, including suggestions by Barrett from *The Whimsical Medley*, and other poems from the same source.

In his second edition Scott made some rearrangement of the contents and inserted additions from papers of Theophilus Swift,[1] which were saved by James Smith. These papers, bound in two folio volumes, are now in the Huntington Library, San Marino, California. But the passages deleted from 'On Poetry: A Rapsody',[2] which are added in footnotes to Scott's second edition, do not appear to have been among these papers, and, unfortunately, he gives no indication of the source from which he derived them.

Scott's edition was hurried, and no endeavour was made to present a faithful text. Careful collation was not, in his day, regarded as part of an editor's duty. But, despite all shortcomings, his editions of Swift, together with those of Nichols, are of permanent value to the critic and scholar as well as good library sets for the general reader. Roscoe's slighting observations upon Scott are not without justification if we adopt an exacting standard, but his own popular edition of Swift in two ungainly volumes, 1841, can scarcely be accepted as an improvement; nor is there much evidence of the research and collation which he professed.

The text, the canon, and the arrangement of Swift's verse, as these were left by Scott, were appropriated in the handy Aldine Edition of the *Poetical Works*, 1833–4, and its reprints, and persist, with some modifications and additions, in the *Poems* as edited by W. E. Browning in two volumes, 1910, which were published to accompany Temple Scott's edition of the *Prose Works*.

[1] Theophilus Swift died in 1815.   [2] See pp. 639, 658–9.

(xv)

The extent and character of supplementary researches since the time of Scott, which throw light upon the canon and text of Swift's verse, are set out fully in their appropriate contexts, and here need only be summarized.

In 1849 Sir W. R. Wilde published his *Closing Years of Dean Swift's Life*. He was the first to make use of an interleaved copy of Harward's *Almanack*[1] and of a folio volume[2] of manuscripts and broadsides now in the Huntington Library. He was, however, mistaken in supposing the writing in either volume to be in Swift's autograph, he was not an accurate transcriber, he was too ready in his attributions, and his work cannot be accepted as it stands.

In 1875 John Forster published the first, and only, volume of his *Life of Swift* in which he gave some account of discoveries he had made among the Fountaine papers at Narford.[3] His statement was by no means complete. These manuscripts are now in the Pierpont Morgan Library, New York.

In the *Gentleman's Magazine* for June, 1882, cclii. 731–43, Churton Collins printed the 'Holyhead Journal' from the manuscript in the Forster Collection, South Kensington. In the same year this piece appeared as Appendix IX to Craik's *Life of Swift*.[4]

Swift's Verse: An Essay, written by that true scholar, Dr. F. Elrington Ball, was the first genuine attempt to arrange the poems in their chronological order and to link them with the story of Swift's life. For this Dr. Ball was peculiarly fitted by his wide knowledge of Anglo-Irish history. It may be, as he declares in his preface, and as he confessed to the present writer, that 'circumstances rather than inclination' connected him with Swift; but, embarked on the task which fell to him, he carried it

[1] See p. l.
[2] See p. l.
[3] See p. xlix.
[4] The 'Journal' and the verses which form part of it were also reprinted in Temple Scott's edition of the *Prose Works*, xi. 391–403.

through in his great edition of the *Correspondence* and in his essay on the verse as no one else could have done.

In 1935 Professor D. Nichol Smith, in his edition of the *Letters of Jonathan Swift to Charles Ford*, printed from the Ford papers two poems, 'The Bubble' and 'To Charles Ford Esqr. on his Birth-day', surviving in Swift's autograph, and four poems by Swift transcribed by Ford.[1] The Ford transcripts reveal a singularly interesting secret. No one had suspected, although the patchwork now becomes apparent, that the poem printed by Faulkner as 'Stella at Wood-Park' was a combination of two separate pieces.

We are closer to Swift in his verse, and in his letters, than in his prose-writings. In Dr. Ball's words: 'Without knowledge of his verse a true picture of Swift cannot be drawn. In his verse he sets forth his life as in a panorama, he shows more clearly than in his prose his peculiar turn of thought, and he reveals his character in all its phases. ... Before the testimony of his verse the work of many of his biographers cannot stand.'[2]

If the editor of these volumes has made easier the approach to Swift he will be happy in the consciousness of having continued the work of Dr. Ball. And if he is compelled on occasion to dissent from him, it is with fitting respect and regard. He must, however, place it on record that he cannot accept a number of the conjectural attributions proffered in *Swift's Verse*. Dr. Ball believed that, outside the acknowledged metrical pieces, and others tentatively assigned to Swift, a large number 'owed their origin to his inspiration if not to his pen'. There exist certainly poems written by others at Swift's suggestion; but these, shining with a reflected light, are no part of the central system. If anything the canon, as it has been expanded by previous editors, calls for curtailment. Nichols, Scott, and Barrett have been responsible for questionable accretions. And, beyond these, is an untidy heap of meaningless, fanciful attribu-

---

[1] See p. li. [2] *Swift's Verse*, p. viii.

tions. An attempt has here been made to consider or note all these ascriptions so far as any purpose is served thereby. But it will be found that this edition has narrowed the boundary of the canon, a service to Swift which was long overdue. Nevertheless, doubtful poems are printed in full if they have a reasonable claim to recognition, or if they are elsewhere scarcely available. Conjectural attributions, supported by little or no evidence, are noted with a varying degree of consideration.

A
BIBLIOGRAPHICAL
SUMMARY

THE following lists make no pretence to furnish a complete bibliography of Swift's verse writings. List A presents a conspectus of the manuscript collections, and single manuscripts, which have been used to correct and establish the text of his poems as printed in these volumes; list B miscellanies, collected works, and other publications, containing the text of poems, or contributions to textual, chronological, and bibliographical problems; list C some general sources of reference. In list B titles are set in roman type, abbreviated imprints in italic. Unauthorized collections have been ranged in their chronological order; but doubtful single works, fully discussed in their place, have been excluded.

A list of separate publications, in broadsheet or pamphlet form, would involve needless repetition of fuller details given with each poem; and this has not, therefore, been provided.

A
MANUSCRIPT SOURCES
INCLUDING PRINTED VOLUMES WITH ANNOTATIONS

I.   *LIBRARIES*

TRINITY COLLEGE, DUBLIN. MS. 879 [I. 5. 1–3]: *The Whimsical Medley*: Three quarto volumes, containing transcripts of contemporary verse, latter part of the seventeenth and early part of the eighteenth century, made for Theophilus, first Lord Newtown-Butler. MS. 1050 [I. 4. 7]: Contemporary transcript of 'The Legion Club' on seven octavo leaves. Two volumes (Press 3, and Press A. 7. 6³⁸) containing manuscript miscellanies.

ROYAL IRISH ACADEMY, DUBLIN. MS. 24. C. 31: A small quarto volume, bound in vellum, containing transcripts of verses in an unidentified hand. In the same volume are a letter (7 Oct. 1737, to Lord Mayor Walker), and accounts relating to 1734–5, both in Swift's hand.

FORSTER COLLECTION, VICTORIA AND ALBERT MUSEUM, SOUTH KENSINGTON. The valuable collection made by John Forster in preparation for his *Life of Swift*. Contains many MSS. in Swift's hand; papers by Percy, Malone, and others; transcripts, collations, and notes by Forster. Also a copy of Hawkesworth's *Life of Swift*, 1755, with marginal annotations by Dr. Lyon.

BRITISH MUSEUM, LONDON. Add. MSS. 4804–6: *Journal to Stella* and correspondence. Add. MS. 39839: Swift and Vanessa correspondence. Also a few further MSS., Add., Lansdowne, Harley, and Stowe; including the Marmaduke Coghill and Edward Southwell correspondence, which throws some light on the history of verse pieces.

GOLDSMITHS' LIBRARY, IMPERIAL INSTITUTE, SOUTH KENSINGTON. A copy of the *Hibernian Patriot*, 1730, with a couplet added in the hand of Lady Acheson (?).

BODLEIAN LIBRARY, OXFORD. MS. Malone 37. On ff. 68–98 contains matter which appeared in Barrett's *Essay on the earlier Part of the Life of Swift*, 1808.

UNIVERSITY LIBRARY, CAMBRIDGE. Contemporary transcripts in the Bradshaw Collection. See pp. 769, 801.

JOHN RYLANDS LIBRARY, MANCHESTER. English MS. 659. See pp. 662–4, 680.

SIR WALTER SCOTT'S LIBRARY, ABBOTSFORD. Principal Library, Press N. Shelf 7: A 12mo volume containing transcripts of poems by Swift in an unidentified hand. The volume was presented to Scott by a Mr. Bembridge, as being in Swift's hand. The copies are certainly neither by Swift, nor by Stella, as Scott conjectures. A collection made about the middle of the eighteenth century. The volume has no textual value.

PIERPONT MORGAN LIBRARY, NEW YORK. Contains the valuable Fountaine MSS., for nearly two hundred years preserved at Narford, in Norfolk. Five poems in this collection are in Swift's hand. See further pp. 61, 78, 85, 88, 122. Manuscripts from the Ford papers are also in the library. See p. 744.

HARVARD COLLEGE LIBRARY, CAMBRIDGE, MASSACHUSETTS. MS. Eng. 218. 2: Orrery Papers. MS. Eng. 218. 14: A copy of

Orrery's *Remarks*, 1752, annotated by the author. Also MS. Eng. 629 F: A verse miscellany.

HENRY E. HUNTINGTON LIBRARY, SAN MARINO, CALIFORNIA. Two miscellaneous volumes of Swiftiana salvaged by James Smith, after the death of Theophilus Swift. See the 'Advertisement', p. ix, to Scott's second edition of Swift's *Works*, 1824. The papers were at one time in the possession of Frederick Locker, who bound them. Later they were in the library of William Bixby of St. Louis, from whom Mr. Huntington bought them. Also a volume of annotated broadsheets and manuscripts (113198–259) first used by W. R. Wilde in his *Closing Years of Dean Swift's Life*, and mistakenly supposed by him to be in Swift's hand.

II. PRIVATE COLLECTIONS

MRS. BAKER, MALAHOW, NAUL, CO. DUBLIN. A copy of Harward's *Almanack*, 1666, with transcripts of poems erroneously supposed to be in Swift's hand. For a description of this volume and its contents see pp. 1058–63. This book was formerly in the possession of the Christie family, at Newtown House, Swords, co. Dublin.

SHIRLEY LIBRARY, LOUGH FEA, CO. MONAGHAN, IRELAND. A set of Faulkner's edition of Swift's *Works*, six volumes, 1737–8, with textual annotations in Swift's hand. It is doubtful whether any of the notes or markings are by Swift, save those in vol. ii, which contains the verses, and even these are of little textual importance. The set is of value, however, in showing that Swift substantially approved of Faulkner's edition.

SIR SHANE LESLIE, BT., GLASLOUGH, CO. MONAGHAN, IRELAND. A commonplace book belonging to Florence O'Crowley, an Irish priest, and evidently in use by him from about 1736 onward. See further *The Irish Book Lover*, vol. xxi, no. 3, July–August, 1933. Contains transcripts of Swift's 'Advice to a Parson' and epigram on Hort (pp. 807–9). Also ascribes to him three doubtful pieces. See pp. 1115, 1137, 1138.

DUKE OF BEDFORD, WOBURN ABBEY, BEDFORDSHIRE. A volume containing transcripts of Swift's poems carefully written by Stella. This book has eighty-five leaves, not counting binder's fly leaves, two in number. The format is small quarto, the leaves measuring 19·8 × 15·5 cm.; and the binding is eighteenth century calf with gilt back.

The volume contains a note by the fourth Duke of Bedford: 'This Manuscript was given me, by Sr Archibald Acheson at Bath 9^{ber} 2^d 1768. It was given to his Father, by the Dean of St Patrick, and is of the hand writing of Stella, Mrs Johnson. B.'

Only forty leaves have been used for the transcripts. The book contains nineteen pieces, of which eighteen are copies by Stella. The last piece, 'On the five Lady's at Sots-hole and the Doctor at their head', is in a different and unidentified handwriting.

DUKE OF PORTLAND, WELBECK ABBEY, NOTTINGHAMSHIRE. Several contemporary transcripts of poems by Swift among the Harley Papers. Now deposited in the British Museum and Nottingham University Library.

MARQUIS OF BATH, LONGLEAT, WILTSHIRE. Portland Papers, vols. xi, xiii, xvii, xviii, xix, xx. Verses in Swift's autograph, and contemporary transcripts.

LORD ROTHSCHILD, MERTON HALL, CAMBRIDGE. Letters and papers belonging to Charles Ford, Swift's friend, passed, on Ford's death, into the possession of Sir John Hynde Cotton, his executor, and were long preserved at Madingley Hall, Cambridge. They came, through the Cotton family, to Mrs. Rowley Smith of Shortgrove. See *Letters of Jonathan Swift to Charles Ford*, ed. D. Nichol Smith, 1935, p. vii. Among these papers are six of Swift's poems, two, 'The Bubble' and 'To Charles Ford Esqr. on his Birth-day', in Swift's hand, and four in the handwriting of Charles Ford. See pp. 78, 248, 309, 459, 744. Swift autographs of 'Atlas', p. 159; and 'The Grand Question Debated', p. 863.

A copy of the Pope and Swift *Miscellanies*, 4 vols. 1727–32, with many corrections in Swift's hand. Previously in the libraries of Viscount Powerscourt, and of Mr. W. G. Panter, The Bawn, Foxrock, co. Dublin.

YELVERTON RECTORY, NORFOLK. Among papers formerly at Yelverton, which had come down from the family of Sir William Temple, were 'A description of Mother Ludwell's cave' (see p. 1068), and a contemporary copy of 'The Journal'. See p. 276.

BROADLANDS, ROMSEY, HANTS. Among Lord Mount Temple's MSS. were copies of 'Apollo to the Dean', and two sets of verses written on the windows of St. Patrick's Deanery. See pp. 259, 262.

SIR HAROLD WILLIAMS, 43 ALBERT COURT, KENSINGTON GORE, LONDON, S.W. 7. Two contemporary manuscripts of 'The Legion Club'; and two copies of Faulkner's editions of 'Verses on the

Death of Dr. Swift' with the blanks, in text and notes, completed
in contemporary hands. Also a copy of the first edition of 'On
Poetry: A Rapsody' with the rejected lines added in the hand of
Lord Orrery. See pp. 551, 827.

Mrs. Cartwright, Aynho. Contemporary transcripts of several
poems. See pp. 63, 161, 343, 374, 683.

Miscellaneous. A few other manuscripts have been used—the
holograph of Swift's lines 'From Catullus' (see p. 679); lines
written in a copy of Le Sage's *Devil upon Two Sticks* (see p. 1139);
and lines in a copy of Pope's *Iliad* (see p. 1136).

B

MISCELLANIES, COLLECTED WORKS, BIOGRAPHIES, CRITICISM, &c.

1692 The Supplement to the Fifth Volume of the Athenian
Gazette; . . . *London, Printed for John Dunton* . . . [1692].
The Gentleman's Journal: Or the Monthly Miscellany [Feby.,
June, and July, 1692]. Ed. P. A. Motteux.

1707 The Muses Mercury: Or The Monthly Miscellany.... *London, Printed by J. H. for Andrew Bell*, . . . *1707.* [April–
June, 1707.]

1709 Baucis and Philemon; A Poem On the ever lamented Loss
Of the two Yew-Trees, In the Parish of Chilthorne, . . .
Together with Mrs. Harris's Earnest Petition. . . . *London:
Printed and Sold by H. Hills . . . 1709.* [Another edn. 1710.]
The Works of the Right Honourable The Earls of Rochester,
And Roscommon. . . . The Third Edition. To which is
added, A Collection of Miscellany Poems. . . . *London: . . .
E. Curll*, . . . *1709*
Poetical Miscellanies: The Sixth Part. . . . *London, Printed for
Jacob Tonson*, . . . *1709.*
The Tatler. . . . *Sold by John Morphew* . . . [No. 9, 30 April,
1709; No. 238, 17 October, 1710; and No. 301, 13 March,
1710–11].

1710 A Meditation upon a Broom-Stick, And Somewhat Beside;
Of the Same Author's. . . . *London: Printed for E. Curll*, . . .
1710. [The B.M. Copy of this pamphlet (C. 28. b. 11⁵) has
on the title a note in Curll's handwriting: 'Given me by John
Cliffe Esq.; who had them of the Bp. of Killala, in Ireland,
whose Daughter he married & was my Lodger.—E Curll'.]

1711 Miscellanies in Prose and Verse. *London: Printed for John Morphew*, . . . *MDCCXI*. [The first authorized collection of Swift's prose and verse. 2nd edn. 1713.]

Miscellanies by Dr. Jonathan Swift . . . *London, Printed for E. Curll*, . . . *1711*.

1714 A Collection of Original Poems, Translations, and Imitations, by Mr. Prior, Mr. Rowe, Dr. Swift, And other Eminent Hands. . . . *London: Printed for E. Curll*, . . . *1714*.

1718 Letters, Poems, and Tales, Amorous, Satirical; and Gallant. . . . *London: Printed for E. Curll . . . 1718*.

1719 Ars Punica, sive Flos Linguarum: The Art of Punning; Or the Flower of Languages; . . . *Dublin: Printed by and for James Carson*, . . . *1719*. [Also London edns., *Roberts*, in the same year.]

1720 A Defence of English Commodities. . . . To which is Annexed, An Elegy upon the much lamented Death of Mr. Demar, . . . *Printed at Dublin: And Reprinted at London, by J. Roberts . . . MDCCXX*.

The Swearer's-Bank: . . . (With The Best in Christendom. A Tale.) Written by Dean Swift. . . . *Reprinted at London by J. Roberts*. . . .

Miscellaneous Works, Comical & Diverting: By T. R. D. J. S. D. O. P. I. I. In Two Parts. I. The Tale of a Tub; . . . II. Miscellanies in Prose & Verse, . . . *London, Printed by Order of the Society de propagando, &c. M.DCC.XX*.

1721 Miscellanies in Prose and Verse. The Fourth Edition, . . . *Dublin: Printed by S. Fairbrother*, . . . *2721* [*sic*].

A Miscellaneous Collection of Poems, Songs and Epigrams. By several Hands. Publish'd by T. M. Gent . . . *Dublin: Printed by A. Rhames, 1721*. 2 vols.

1722 Miscellanies, Written By Jonathan Swift, D.D. . . . The Fourth Edition. *London: Printed in the Year M.DCC.XXII*.

1724 Miscellaneous Poems, Original and Translated, By Several Hands. . . . Published by Mr. Concanen. . . . *London: Printed for J. Peele*, . . . *MDCCXXIV*.

1725 Fraud Detected. Or, The Hibernian Patriot. . . . *Dublin: Re-printed and Sold by George Faulkner . . . 1725*.

A New Collection Of Poems On Several Occasions, By Mr. Prior, and Others. . . *London: Printed for Tho. Osborne*, . . . *MDCCXXV*.

1726 Miscellanea. In Two Volumes. Never before Published.
. . . *London: Printed in the Year, 1727.* [Published July,
1726.]

Whartoniana: Or Miscellanies, In Verse and Prose. By the
Wharton Family, . . . *Printed in the Year, 1727.* 2 vols.
[Published September, 1726. Re-issued as The Poetical
Works of Philip Late Duke of Wharton.]

1727–8. Miscellanies In Prose and Verse. The First Volume.
London: Printed for Benjamin Motte, . . . *M.DCC.XXVII.*

Miscellanies. The Second Volume. *London: Printed for Benjamin Motte . . . M DCC XXVII.*

Miscellanies. The Last Volume. . . . *London: Printed for B.
Motte,* . . . *1727.* [The 'First' and 'Second' volumes were
published in June, 1727; the 'Last' volume in March, 1728.
The first three volumes of the famous Pope and Swift *Miscellanies,* and edited by the former. They were variously
reprinted; and continued with 'The Third Volume', 1732,
and 'Volume the Fifth', 1735.]

1728 Miscellanies In Prose and Verse. In Two Volumes. . . .
*London Printed, and Re-printed in Dublin, By and for Sam.
Fairbrother,* . . . *1728.* [Reprinted 1732; a third volume added
in 1733, and a fourth in 1735.]

Gulliveriana: Or, A Fourth Volume of Miscellanies. . . .
London: Printed for J. Roberts, . . . *M.DCC.XXVIII.*

The Intelligencer. Numb. I Saturday. May, 11, To be Continued Weekly, *Dublin: Printed by S. Harding,* . . . *172[8].*
[Continued for twenty numbers inclusive. London collected
editions, *A. Moor,* 1729, *Francis Cogan,* 1730.]

1729 Miscellaneous Poems, By Several Hands: . . . Publish'd by
Mr. Ralph. *London: Printed by C. Ackers,* . . . *MDCCXXIX.*

1730 The Metamorphosis Of The Town: . . . To which is added,
The Journal of a Modern Lady. . . . By Dr. Swift. . . .
London: Printed for J. Wilford, . . . *MDCCXXX.* [Later edns.
1731, 1743.]

An Epistle To His Excellency John Lord Carteret . . . To which
is added, an Epistle upon an Epistle; . . . *Dublin: Printed, in
the Year 1730.*

A Satire On Dr. D—ny. . . . To which is added, the Poem which
occasion'd it. *Printed at Dublin: And Re-printed at London,
for A. Moore,* . . . *M DCC XXX.*

A Libel On Dr. D—ny, . . . The Second Edition. *Printed at*

Dublin: And Re-printed at London, for A. Moore. M DCC XXX.
[Another edn., 1730, *Reprinted for Capt. Gulliver.*]

A Vindication of the Libel On Dr. Delany, . . . Together with a Panegyric On Dean Sw—t; . . . *Dublin: Printed, London: Re-printed for J. Wilford* . . . *M.DCC.XXX.*

Select Poems from Ireland: Part I. [Part II.] . . . *Printed at Dublin: London, Reprinted and Sold by T. Warner* . . . *M.DCC.XXX.*

The Hibernian Patriot: . . . To which are added, Poems and Songs . . . *Printed at Dublin. London: Reprinted and Sold by A. Moor* . . . *MDCCXXX.* [Reprinted from Fraud Detected, 1725, with alterations and additions.]

Poems On Several Occasions. . . . By Jonathan Smedley, Dean of Clogher. . . . *London: Printed in the Year M.DCC.XXX.*

1731 A Proposal Humbly offer'd to the P—t, . . . To which is added, The Humble Petition of the Weavers. . . . As also two Poems, viz. Helter Skelter, . . . and The Place of the Damn'd. *Dublin Printed. London, Re-printed for J. Roberts* . . . *MDCCXXXI.* [2nd edn. 1732.]

The Flower-Piece: A Collection Of Miscellany Poems. By Several Hands. . . . *London: Printed for J. Walthoe* . . . *and H. Walthoe,* . . . *M.DCC.XXXI.* [Republished 1733.]

1732 The Grand Question debated: Whether Hamilton's Bawn Should be turn'd into a Barrack, or a Malt-house. . . . *London Printed for A. Moore. And, Dublin Re-printed by George Faulkner* . . . *M,DCC,XXXII.*

The Lady's Dressing Room. To which is added, A Poem on Cutting down the Old Thorn at Market Hill. . . . *London, Printed for J. Roberts* . . . *MDCCXXXII.* [2nd edn. in the same year.]

An Elegy On Dicky and Dolly, . . . To which is Added The Narrative of D. S. when he was in the North of Ireland. *Dublin: Printed by James Hoey,* . . . *MDCCXXXII.*

Miscellanies. The Third Volume. *London: Printed for Benj. Motte,* . . . *and Lawton Gilliver* . . . *1732.* [Variously reprinted. See under 1727–8.]

1733 The Drapier's Miscellany. . . . *Dublin: Printed by and for James Hoey,* . . . *1733.* [At least three editions.]

The Presbyterians Plea of Merit; . . . To which is added, An Ode to Humphry French, Esq; . . . *London: Reprinted from the Dublin Edition, for G. F. and Sold by A. Dodd,* . . .

1734 Miscellanies. Consisting chiefly of Original Pieces in Prose
and Verse. . . . *Dublin Printed. London: Reprinted for A.
Moore . . . 1734.* [Two edns.]

An Epistle to a Lady, . . . Also A Poem, Occasion'd by Reading
Dr. Young's Satires, . . . *Dublin, Printed: And Reprinted at
London for J. Wilford,* . . . *M.DCC.XXXIV.*

A New Miscellany For the Year 1734. Part I.

An Account Of A Strange and Wonderful Apparition Lately
Seen in Trinity-College, Dublin. . . . *Printed in the Year
MDCCXXXIV.*

Mezentius on the Rack . . . *Printed in the Year MDCCXXXIV.*

A Beautiful Young Nymph Going to Bed. . . . To which are
added, Strephon and Chloe. And Cassinus and Peter. *Dublin
printed: London reprinted for J. Roberts . . . MDCCXXXIV.*

1734 (?) The History of John Bull. And Poems on several
Occasions, . . . *Sold by D. Midwinter and A. Tonson in the
Strand.*

1734–5 The Works of J. S, D. D, D. S. P. D. in Four Volumes.
Containing, I. The Author's Miscellanies in Prose. II. His
Poetical Writings. III. The Travels of Captain Lemuel
Gulliver. IV. His Papers relating to Ireland, . . . *Dublin:
Printed by and for George Faulkner,* . . . *M DCC XXXV.*
[Issued Nov. 1734–Jany. 1735. Another edn. of vol. ii in
1737. The set increased to six volumes in 1738, with some
additional verse pieces in vol. vi. Gradually extended to
twenty volumes, 1772. Vol. viii, 1746, contained more
verse. The chief verse addition thereafter was in 1762;
reprinted in the London edition of the *Works* in the same
year.]

1735 Miscellanies, In Prose and Verse. Volume the Fifth. . . .
London: Printed for Charles Davis, . . . *MDCCXXXV.* [See
under 1727–8. This volume is based on Faulkner.]

A Collection of Poems, &c. Omitted in the Fifth Volume of
Miscellanies in Prose and Verse. *London: Printed for
Charles Davis,* . . . *MDCCXXXV.*

Miscellaneous Poems on Several Occasions. By Mr. Dawson,
. . . And a Copy of Verses Spoke Extempore by Dean Swift
upon his Curate's Complaint of hard Duty. . . . *1735.*

1736 The Poetical Works, Of J. S. D. D. D. S. P. D. . . . Reprinted from the Second Dublin Edition, with Notes and
Additions. . . . *Printed in the Year. MDCCXXXVI.*

S—t contra Omnes. An Irish Miscellany. . . . *London . . .
Mrs. Dod . . .*

Miscellanies. . . . *London: Printed for Benjamin Motte, and
Charles Bathurst,* . . . MDCCXXXVI. [6 vols., 12mo, 1736, a
trade venture, with other printers' names in later volumes.
Vols. vii, viii, and ix added, *T. Cooper,* 1742. The first extension of the Pope and Swift Miscellanies, 1727–8–32–35,
into sets which developed into Swift's works.]

1739 A Supplement to Dr. Swift's And Mr. Pope's Works. . . .
*Dublin: Printed by S. Powell, For Edward Exshaw . . .
MDCCXXXIX.*

1740 Poems on Various Subjects, . . . By Laurence Whyte. . . .
Dublin: Printed by S. Powell, And Sold by L. Dowling, . . .
M DCC XL.

1742 Miscellanies. In Four Volumes. . . . The Fourth Edition
Corrected: . . . Vol. I. By Dr. Swift. *London: Printed for
Charles Bathurst,* . . . MDCCXLII. [A further trade develop-
ment of the Miscellanies. Other printers' names in subsequent volumes. Extended to eleven volumes, 1742–6; and
followed by reprints of varying dates, 1747, 1749, 1750,
1751, 1753.]

A New Miscellany In Prose and Verse. Containing, Several
Pieces never before made public. By the Reverend Dr.
Swift, . . . And other Eminent Hands. *London: Printed for
T. Read,* . . . MDCCXLII.

1744 The Muse in Good Humour. Or, a Collection of Comic
Tales, &c. . . . *London: Printed for J. Noble,* . . . *1744.*
[Other edns. 1745, 1751, 1766; a second volume, 1757.]

1746 The Story Of The Injured Lady. . . . With Letters and
Poems. . . . *Printed for M. Cooper,* . . . MDCCXLVI.

1749 Poems on Several Occasions, from Genuine Manuscripts of
Dean Swift, . . . *London: Printed for J. Bromage,* . . .
1749.

1750 (?) The Poetical Works of Dr. Jonathan Swift, . . . In Two
Volumes. . . . *London: Sold by A. Manson, R. Dilton, J.
Thomson, H. Gray, T. Nelson, and P. Bland.* [A trade edi-
tion, not earlier than 1745.]

1750 A Supplement To The Works of The Most celebrated
Minor Poets. . . . To which are added, Pieces omitted in the
Works of . . . Dean Swift. *London: Printed for F. Cogan,* . . .
MDCCL.

1751 The Works of Dr. Jonathan Swift, . . . Vol. I. . . . *London: Printed for C. Bathurst,* . . . *MDCCLI.* [Fourteen volumes, 12mo. The first four vols. and vols. vi, and viii, carry the name of Bathurst only; other names added, or differing names, in subsequent volumes.]

1752 A Supplement to the Works of Dr. Swift. *London: Printed for F. Cogan,* . . . *1752.*

Remarks on the Life and Writings of Dr. Jonathan Swift, . . . In a Series of Letters from John Earl of Orrery To his Son, the Honourable Hamilton Boyle. . . . *London, Printed for A. Millar,* . . . *MDCCLII.* [Several further London edns. in the same year, and Dublin edns., *Printed by George Faulkner.*]

Brett's Miscellany. Vol. II., *Dublin.*

1754 The Dreamer. . . . *London: Printed for W. Owen,* . . . *MDCCLIV.* [By Dr. William King. Contains the first printing of 'Paulus' and 'The Answer'.]

Observations Upon Lord Orrery's Remarks . . . To which are added, Two Original Pieces of the same author . . . *London, Printed: And Sold by W. Reeve* . . . *MDCCLIV.* [By Delany.]

Poems on Various Subjects: Viz. The Legion Club, by D—n S—t. . . . *Glasgow: Printed by Sawney McPherson. M.DCC.LIV.* [Another edn. 1756.]

1754-5. The Works of Jonathan Swift, D.D. . . . Accurately revised In Six Volumes, . . . *London, Printed for C. Bathurst,* . . . *MDCCLV.* [Edited by Hawkesworth, for the London trade, in opposition to Faulkner's Dublin edn. of the *Works.* The six volumes 4to also appeared as twelve volumes large and small 8vo. Gradually extended, 1755–79, to fourteen, twenty-five, and twenty-seven volumes respectively. Additions to the verse were made in 1762–4 by Bowyer, from Faulkner, 1762; by Deane Swift in 1765; and by Nichols in his *Supplement,* 1776 and 1779. This trade edn. was the basis of Sheridan's edn. of the *Works,* 1784, and Nichols, 1801. It was also used by Edinburgh, Glasgow, and Dublin publishers, whose edns. have no independent value, and are not here noted.]

1755 An Essay upon the Life, Writings, and Character, Of Dr. Jonathan Swift. . . . By Deane Swift, Esq; . . . *London, Printed for Charles Bathurst,* . . . *MDCCLV.*

1767 An Appendix To Dr. Swift's Works . . . *London, Printed for W. B. and sold by S. Bladon,* . . . *MDCCLXVII.*

1770 (?) The Trader's Garland, Composed of Five Excellent

New Songs. . . . *Licensed and entered according tn* [*sic*] *order.*

1776 Additions to the Works of Alexander Pope, Esq. Together with Many Original Poems and Letters, Of Cotemporary Writers, Never Before Published. In Two Volumes. . . . *London: Printed for H. Baldwin,* . . . *1776.*

1779 The Works of the English Poets. With Prefaces, . . . by Samuel Johnson. . . . [Vols. 39 and 40 contain Swift's Poems; but this trade edition has no textual or editorial value.]

1780–2. A Select Collection of Poems: With Notes Biographical and Historical. . . . *London: Printed By and For J. Nichols,* . . . [Eight volumes.]

1784 The Works of the Rev. Dr. Jonathan Swift, . . . Arranged, Revised, and Corrected, with Notes, By Thomas Sheridan, A.M. A New Edition, in Seventeen Volumes. *London: Printed for C. Bathurst,* . . . M DCC LXXXIV. [See under 1754–5.]

1789 Miscellaneous Pieces, In Prose and Verse. By the Rev. Dr. Jonathan Swift, . . . Not Inserted in Mr. Sheridan's Edition Of the Dean's Works. *London: Printed for C. Dilly,* . . . *MDCCLXXXIX.*

Literary Relics: Containing Original Letters from . . . Swift, To which is prefixed, An Inquiry into the Life of Dean Swift. By George-Monck Berkeley, Esq.; . . . *London: Printed for C. Elliot* . . . *M,DCC,LXXXIX.* [2nd edn. 1792.]

1801 The Works of the Rev. Jonathan Swift, D.D., Dean of St. Patrick's, Dublin. Arranged by Thomas Sheridan, . . . A New Edition, In Nineteen Volumes; Corrected and Revised By John Nichols, . . . *London: Printed for J. Johnson, J. Nichols,* . . . *1801.* [See under 1784. Further edns., 1803, 24 vols., 1808, 19 vols.]

1804 Swiftiana. Vol. I. [Vol. II.] . . . *Printed for Richard Phillips, 71, St. Pauls Church Yard. 1804.*

1806–7 The Poetical Works of Jonathan Swift; . . . by Thomas Park, Esq. F.S.A. In Four Volumes. . . . *London: Printed at the Stanhope Press, by Charles Whittingham,* . . . *1806–7.* [No independent value.]

1808 An Essay On The Earlier Part of the Life of Swift. By the Rev. John Barrett, D.D. . . . To Which are Subjoined Several Pieces Ascribed to Swift; . . . *London: Printed for J. Johnson; J. Nichols and Son;* . . . *1808.*

1814 The Works of Jonathan Swift, D.D. Dean of St. Patrick's, Dublin; Containing Additional Letters, Tracts, and Poems, Not Hitherto Published; With Notes and A Life of the Author, By Walter Scott, Esq. . . . *Edinburgh: Printed for Archibald Constable and Co. . . . 1814.* [In nineteen volumes. A 2nd edn. in nineteen volumes, 1824, containing further additions. Reprinted in nineteen volumes, 1883.]

1822 [The British Poets. Vols. 37–9.] The Poems of Jonathan Swift. . . . *Chiswick: From the Press of C. Whittingham, College House.* [No independent value.]

1833–4. The Poetical Works of Jonathan Swift. [Aldine Edition.] . . . *London William Pickering.* [In three volumes, based on Scott's 2nd edn., 1824. Further edns. 1853, 1866.]

1841 The Works of Jonathan Swift, . . . Containing Interesting and Valuable Papers, Not Hitherto Published. In Two Volumes. With Memoirs of the Author, by Thomas Roscoe; . . . *London: Henry Washbourne, . . . 1841.* [A number of later edns.]

1849 The Closing Years of Dean Swift's Life; . . . By W. R. Wilde, . . . *Dublin: Hodges and Smith . . . 1849.* [2nd edn. in the same year.]

1875 The Life of Jonathan Swift. By John Forster. Volume the First. 1667–1711. *London: John Murray, Albemarle Street. 1875.*

1882 The Life of Jonathan Swift . . . By Henry Craik, M.A. . . . *London: John Murray, Albemarle Street, 1882.* [2nd edn. 1894, 2 vols.]

1897–1908. The Prose Works of Jonathan Swift, D.D. Edited by Temple Scott . . . *London George Bell and Sons.* [Twelve volumes.]

1910 The Poems of Jonathan Swift, D.D. Edited by William Ernst Browning . . . *London G. Bell and Sons, Ltd. 1910.* [Two volumes.]

1910–14. The Correspondence of Jonathan Swift, D.D. Edited by F. Elrington Ball . . . *London G. Bell and Sons, Ltd.* [Six volumes.]

1921 Vanessa And Her Correspondence with Jonathan Swift . . . With an Introduction by A. Martin Freeman . . . *London Selwyn & Blount, Ltd.*

1929 Swift's Verse An Essay By F. Elrington Ball, Litt. D. . . . *London John Murray, Albemarle Street, W.*

1931 Studies in English . . . *The University of Toronto Press 1931.* [Contains an essay on 'Swift's View of Poetry' by Herbert Davis.]

1934 Swift Gulliver's Travels and Selected Writings in Prose & Verse. Ed. John Hayward. *Nonesuch Press, Bloomsbury, 1934.*

1935 The Letters of Jonathan Swift to Charles Ford. Ed. D. Nichol Smith . . . *Oxford At the Clarendon Press MCMXXXV.* [Prints six of Swift's poems from the Ford papers,—two from Swift's autograph.]

1935 The Drapier's Letters to the People of Ireland . . . Ed. Herbert Davis. *Oxford At the Clarendon Press MCMXXXV.* [Contains notes and bibliographical detail relative to verses connected with the Drapier.]

C

MISCELLANEOUS BIBLIOGRAPHICAL AND TEXTUAL AIDS

In addition to eighteenth-century periodicals specifically mentioned in the preceding list useful information has been derived from Abel Boyer's *Political State of Great Britain,* the *Gentleman's Magazine, London Magazine,* and *European Magazine.* At a later date valuable communications have appeared in *Notes and Queries, The Antiquarian Magazine and Bibliographer, The Times Literary Supplement,* the *Review of English Studies,* the *Book-Collector's Quarterly,* and other publications.

The published correspondence and memoirs of Swift's contemporaries, the various reports of the *Historical Manuscripts' Commission,* Nichols's *Literary Anecdotes* and *Literary Illustrations* throw light upon dates, ascriptions, and other matters.

Sale catalogues of libraries dispersed during the last two centuries have been laid under contribution.

The *Catalogue of the Bradshaw Collection of Irish Books in the University Library Cambridge* and the *Catalogue of the Books & Manuscripts Comprising the Library of the late Sir John T. Gilbert,* a collection now in the keeping of the City of Dublin, are valuable reference works for all students of Dublin printed books, pamphlets, and broadsheets; and Sir J. T. Gilbert's scholarly *History of the City of Dublin* contains occasional notices of printers and their publications. To these should be added Plomer's *Dictionary of Booksellers and Printers*, which contains, in the 1726–75 volume, a section devoted to Irish printers, booksellers, and stationers, compiled by Mr. E. R. M^cC. Dix.

THE
EARLY ODES

THE
EARLY ODES

For the periods of Swift's residences under the roof of Sir William Temple at Moor Park consult Forster's *Life*,* pp. 53–103, Craik's *Life*, 2nd edn., i. 26–94, and Lecky's 'Biographical Introduction' to Temple Scott's edition of the *Prose Works*, i, pp. xv–xxii.

It is at this time, when Swift was between twenty-two and twenty-three years old, that we meet with the earliest essays in the art of verse which are, beyond doubt, authentically his. Cowley's attempts to transplant the pindaric ode set a fashion, and, in common with others, Swift was beguiled into imitation. The first of his pindarics to appear in print was his 'Ode to the Athenian Society', published in *The Supplement to the Fifth Volume of the Athenian Gazette*, 1692; the second, if it be Swift's, was the 'Ode to the King on his Irish Expedition', printed in vol. iv of Fairbrother's *Miscellanies*, 1735; the third was the 'Ode to Sir William Temple', printed in vol. x of the *Miscellanies*, 1745; the fourth was the 'Ode to Dr. William Sancroft', included by Nichols in *Miscellaneous Pieces*, 1789.

In a group with these are two odes, or addresses, in heroic couplets, also first printed in 1789, the ode 'To Mr. Congreve', and that 'Occasioned by Sir William Temple's late Illness and Recovery'.

An 'Ode to King William on his Successes in Ireland', composed in quatrains, was rescued by Nichols from *The Gentleman's Journal* for July, 1692, and attributed to Swift; but there is good reason to suppose that the ode written in honour of King William was in pindaric form, and that the authentic ode is that printed by Fairbrother in 1735.

The odes are here arranged in their order of composition, not that of publication.

Apparently also, in these early days, Swift began another ode called 'The Poet', from which he quotes in the ode 'To Mr. Congreve' (see p. 49 n.). In a letter of 3 May, 1692, he speaks of a translation of Virgil which he was then attempting, and refers to a poem called 'the Ramble' (*Corresp.* i. 365–6). These three pieces have not been traced.

---

* Forster calls for some correction. See Craik, i. 35 n.[1], and *Corresp.* i. 3 n.[3].

ODE to the KING.

On his *Irish* Expedition.

AND

The Success of his Arms in general.

Written in the Year 1691.

The troubles following upon the revolution led to an exodus of refugees from Ireland; and with them came Swift early in 1689. After a visit to his mother at Leicester he entered the household of Sir William Temple at Moor Park before the close of the same year. In May, 1690, he returned to Ireland armed with a letter (*Corresp.* i. 1) of recommendation from Temple to Sir Robert Southwell, Secretary of State. He was back in England about August, 1691; and, after visits to Leicester and Oxford, he reached Moor Park in December.

On 1 July (o.s.), 1690, while Swift was in Ireland, was fought the battle of the Boyne. He is known to have written an ode celebrating William's Irish successes, composed presumably 1690–1. In his 'Ode to the Athenian Society' he refers to 'an *Humble Chaplet for the King*', and explains the allusion with a marginal note,—'*The Ode I writ to the King in* Ireland'. Furthermore, Deane Swift, writing 7 June, 1778, says that 'five or six and forty years ago' Mrs. Whiteway showed him the Dean's 'Ode to King William', apparently in printed form, but that, owing to its 'Pindarique way' he was unable to drudge through more than fifty or sixty lines of it (Nichols's *Literary Illustrations*, v. 382). He had previously in his *Essay on the Life of Swift*, 1755, p. 118, counted the 'Ode to King William' with the pindarics, although he was mistaken in supposing that it had appeared in the *Athenian Oracle*. But when as an editor, in 1765, he added a number of verse pieces hitherto omitted from the *Works* he made no attempt to recover the ode addressed to King William, perhaps because he regarded it as unreadable.

In 1780, however, the industrious John Nichols, in his *Select Collection of Poems*, printed an 'Ode to King William, On his Successes in Ireland', with the following footnote: 'With much pleasure I here present to the publick an Ode which had long been sought after without success. That it is Swift's, I have not the least doubt; . . . He refers to it in the second stanza of his "Ode to the Athenian Society", . . . See the "English Poets", vol. xxxix, p. 10; and "The Gentleman's Journal", July, 1692, p. 13.' At the reference given by Nichols to Johnson's *English Poets* a footnote merely states that the ode to the king 'cannot now be recovered'; in *The Gentleman's Journal, loc. cit.*, appears the poem which Nichols claimed for Swift. It is entitled 'TO THE KING', and a prefatory note informs the reader that 'I have here some Verses upon the KING's Success in *Ireland:* You will find that tho they were written long ago, they carry their Recommendation by their Value, and it had been Pity to have conceal'd them, as their Author does himself'. Following upon the text of the poem, which runs to twelve four-line stanzas, some clue is offered to the author: 'I need not tell you that the Gentleman that wrote these Verses, hath merited highly the name of *Vates* in every respect. The intire Reduction of *Ireland,* and our late Victory over the *French* at Sea, make it obvious enough'. This does not carry us very far; but, if anything, suggests reference to an older and better-known person than was Swift at the time. Nor does the poem in the least resemble the ode which Deane Swift avers that he and Mrs. Whiteway understood to be Swift's. It is not pindaric in form; and it does not run to the fifty or sixty lines after which Deane Swift desisted from reading. Furthermore, we know that at this time Swift was immersed in ambitious imitations of Cowley. An ode to the king would almost certainly have been thrown into pindaric form, as he understood it. And, if it were, we should get the most probable grouping of his six early odes. Four in pindarics would then be followed by two in heroic couplets,* suggesting that he had learned to abandon a form unnatural to him. There is indeed no evidence to support Nichols's confident attribution to Swift of the poem he unearthed from *The Gentleman's Journal.* He included it, however, as Swift's, in the volume of *Miscellaneous Pieces,* 1789, which was published as a supplement to Sheridan's edition of the Dean's *Works,* 1784, whence it has been adopted by subsequent editors.

Between 1728 and 1735 Samuel Fairbrother, the Dublin printer, published four volumes of *Miscellanies,* the earlier volumes drawn from the Swift and Pope miscellany volumes published in London, the fourth extracted from the edition of Swift's *Works* in four volumes published in Dublin, by Faulkner, in 1735. Fairbrother claimed, over and above his borrowings from Faulkner, to have added in his fourth volume several poems 'taken from the D—ns own Original Manuscripts'. An examination of the verse section of his 1735 volume leaves no doubt that he had access to manuscripts unused by Faulkner.† The first poem printed by him is a pindaric 'Ode to the King on his Irish Expedition'. Its turgid style reads uncommonly like Swift's other attempts in the same form; and

---

* (1) 'To King William', 'To the Athenian Society', 'To Sir William Temple', 'To Dr. William Sancroft'; (2) 'To Mr. Congreve', 'Occasioned by Sir William Temple's late Illness and Recovery'.

† See Introduction, pp. xxxvii–xxxviii.

it is reasonable to believe that this is the lost ode for which Nichols and others sought in vain. It has the merit also of answering to Deane Swift's description.

This may be Swift's lost ode, and Nichols was probably wrong; but convincing evidence is lacking. Both pieces are, therefore, here printed, the pindaric ode first, as it appeared in *Vol. IV. of the Miscellanies Begun by Jonathan Swift, D.D. and Alexander Pope, Esq. . . . Dublin, Printed by and for Samuel Fairbrother, . . . 1735*, Verse section, pp. 1–6.

I.

SURE there's some Wondrous Joy in *Doing Good*;
Immortal Joy, that suffers no Allay from Fears,
　　Nor dreads the Tyranny of Years,
By none but its Possessors to be understood:
　　Else where's the Gain in being *Great?*
　　Kings would indeed be Victims of the State;
　　What can the Poet's humble Praise?
　　What can the Poet's humble Bays?
　　(We Poets oft our Bays allow,
　　Transplanted to the Hero's Brow)　　　　　　10
　　Add to the Victor's Happiness?
　　What do the Scepter, Crown and Ball,
Rattles for Infant Royalty to play withal,
　　But serve t' adorn the Baby-dress
　　Of one poor Coronation-day,
　　　　To make the Pageant gay:
　　A three Hours Scene of empty Pride,
　　And then the Toys are thrown aside.

II.

But the Delight of *Doing Good*
Is fix't like Fate among the Stars,
　　And Deifi'd in Verse;　　　　　　　　　　20
'Tis the best Gemm in Royalty,

The Great Distinguisher of Blood,
Parent of Valour and of Fame,
Which makes a Godhead of a Name,
And is Contemporary to Eternity.
This made the Ancient Romans to afford
To *Valour* and to *Virtue* the *same Word:*
To shew the Paths of both must be together trod,
Before the *Hero* can commence *a God*.   30

III.

These are the Ways
By which our happy Prince carves out his Bays;
Thus he has fix'd His Name
First, in the mighty List of Fame,
And thus He did the Airy Goddess Court,
He sought Her out in Fight,
And like a Bold Romantick Knight
Rescu'd Her from the Giant's Fort:
The Tyrant Death lay crouching down,
Waiting for Orders at his Feet,   40
Spoil'd of his Leaden Crown;
He trampled on this Haughty *Bajazet*,
Made him his Footstool in the War,
And a Grim Slave to wait on his Triumphal Car.

IV.

And now I in the Spirit see
(The Spirit of Exalted Poetry)
I see the *Fatal Fight* begin;
And, lo! where a Destroying Angel stands,
(By all but Heaven and Me unseen,)
With Lightning in his Eyes, and Thunder in his Hands;
In vain, said He, *does* *Utmost Thule *boast*   51
No poys'nous Beast will in Her breed,
Or no Infectious Weed,

* *Ireland.*

When she sends forth such a malignant Birth,
When Man himself's the Vermin *of Her Earth;*
When Treason *there in* Person *seems to stand,*
And Rebel *is the* growth *and* manufacture *of the Land.*
 He spake, and a dark Cloud flung o're his light,
  And hid him from Poetick sight,
  And (I believe) began himself the Fight,   60
   For strait I saw the Field maintain'd,
 And what I us'd to laugh at in *Romance,*
 And thought too great ev'n for effects of Chance,
The Battel almost by *Great William's* single Valour gain'd;
 The *Angel* (doubtless) kept th' Eternal Gate,
  And stood 'twixt Him and every Fate;
And all those flying Deaths that aim'd him from the Field,
  (Th' impartial Deaths which come
  Like Love, wrapt up in Fire;
 And like that too, make every breast their home)   70
  Broke on his everlasting Shield.

V.

 The *Giddy Brittish Populace,*
  That *Tyrant-Guard* on *Peace,*
  Who watch Her like a Prey,
  And keep Her for a Sacrifice,
 And must be sung, like *Argus,* into *ease*
Before this *Milk-white Heifer* can be stole away,
 Our *Prince* has charm'd its many hundred Eyes;
  Has lull'd the Monster in a Deep
  And (I hope) an Eternal Sleep,   80
 And has at last redeem'd the *Mighty Prize*
The *Scots* themselves, that Discontented Brood,
Who always loudest for *Religion* bawl,
 (*As those still do wh' have none at all*)
Who claim so many Titles to be *Jews,*
(But, surely such whom God did never for *his People*
  chuse)

Still murmuring in *their Wilderness* for *Food*,
Who pine us like a *Chronical Disease*;
And one would think 'twere past Omnipotence to
     please;
Your Presence all their *Native Stubborness* controuls, 90
And for a while unbends their contradicting Souls:
     As in old Fabulous Hell,
When some *Patrician* God wou'd visit the Immortal Jayl,
     The very Brightness of His Face
Suspended every Horror of the Place,
The Gyants under *Ætna* ceas'd to groan,
And *Sisiphus* lay sleeping on his Stone.
Thus has our Prince compleated every Victory,
     And glad *Iërne* now may see
Her Sister Isles are *Conquered* too as well as She.   100

VI.

How vainly (Sir) did Your fond *Enemy* try
Upon *a rubbish Heap of broken Laws*
     To climb at Victory
     Without the Footing of a *Cause*;
His Lawrel now must only be a Cypress Wreath,
     And His best Victory a Noble Death;
His scrap of Life is but a Heap of Miseries,
     The Remnant of a falling Snuff,
     Which hardly wants another puff,
And needs must *stink* when e're it dies;   110
Whilst at Your Victorious Light
     All lesser ones expire,
Consume, and perish from our sight,
Just as the Sun puts out a Fire;
And every foolish *Flye* that dares to aim
     To buzz about the mighty Flame;
The wretched Insects singe their Wings, and fall,
     And humbly at the bottom crawl.

VII.

That *Restless Tyrant*, who of late
Is grown so impudently Great,   120
   That Tennis-Ball of Fate;
This Gilded Meteor which flyes
As if it meant to touch the Skies;
   For all its boasted height,
For all its Plagiary Light,
   Took its first Growth and Birth
From the worst *Excrements of Earth;
Stay but a little while and down again 'twill come,
And end as it began, in Vapour, Stink, and Scum.
   Or has he like some fearful Star appear'd?   130
Long dreaded for his *Bloody Tail* and *Fiery Beard*,
   Transcending Nature's ordinary Laws,
   Sent by just Heaven to threaten Earth
   With War, and Pestilence, and Dearth,
Of which it is at once the Prophet and the Cause.
   Howe're it be, the Pride of *France*
   Has finish'd its short Race of Chance,
And all Her boasted Influences are
Rapt in the *Vortex* of the *Brittish* Star;
Her *Tyrant* too an unexpected Wound shall feel   140
   In the last wretched Remnant of his Days;
Our Prince has hit Him, like *Achilles*, in the *Heel*,
   The poys'nous Darts has made him reel,
   Giddy he grows, and down is hurl'd,
And as a Mortal to his †*Vile Disease*,
Falls sick in the *Posteriors* of the World.

---

* *The* French *King suppos'd a Bastard.*
† *Fistula in Ano.*

ODE to KING WILLIAM,

ON HIS SUCCESSES IN IRELAND

The Gentleman's Journal: Or the Monthly Miscellany, July, 1692, p. 13.
The Whimsical Medley, ii. 391. [Ref. *W.M.*]
*A Select Collection of Poems: . . . London: Printed by and for J. Nichols,
Red Lion Passage, Fleet-Street. MDCCLXXX.* iv. 303.
*Miscellaneous Pieces, in Prose and Verse. By the Rev. Dr. Jonathan Swift,
. . . Not inserted in Mr. Sheridan's Edition of the Dean's Works. London:
Printed for C. Dilly, in the Poultry. MDCCLXXXIX.* p. 239.

The text of this ode, attributed to Swift by Nichols, and since included
in editions of the Dean's *Works*, is reprinted from *The Gentleman's Journal*,
1692. The poem found a place in the manuscript miscellany, *The Whimsical Medley*, preserved in the library of Trinity College, Dublin. The poem
is there headed,

> 'On King William's Success in Ireland.
> To the King.'

Two variants in the manuscript are noted.

I.

TO *purchase Kingdoms, and to buy Renown,*
    Are Arts *peculiar to dissembling* France:
You, Mighty Monarch, Nobler Actions Crown,
And solid Virtue does Your Name advance.

II.

Your matchless Courage with Your Prudence joins
The glorious Structure of Your Fame to raise;
With its own Light Your dazling Glory shines,
And into Adoration turns our Praise.

III.

Had You by dull Succession gain'd Your Crown,
(Cowards are Monarchs by that Title made)   10
Part of Your Merit Chance wou'd call her own,
And half Your Virtues had been lost in Shade.

8 *our*] your *W.M.*

IV.

But now Your Worth its just Reward shall have;
What Trophies and what Triumphs are Your Due!
Who cou'd so well a dying Nation save,
At once deserve a Crown, and gain it too.

V.

You saw how near we were to Ruin brought,
You saw th' impetuous Torrent rolling on;
And timely on the coming Danger thought,
Which we cou'd neither obviate, nor shun.   20

VI.

Britannia *stript from her sole* Guard *the* Laws,
Ready to fall Rome's *bloody Sacrifice;*
You strait stept in, and from the Monster's Jaws
Did bravely snatch the lovely helpless Prize.

VII.

Nor is this all: As glorious is the Care
To preserve Conquests, as at first to gain:
In this Your Virtue claims a double share,
Which, what it bravely Won, do's well Maintain.

VIII.

Your Arm has now Your Rightful Title show'd;
An Arm on which all Europe's *Hopes depend,*   30
To which they look as to some Guardian God
That must their doubtful Liberty *defend.*

IX.

Amaz'd Thy Action at the BOYNE *we see!*
When Schonberg *started at the* Vast *Design:*
The boundless Glory all Redounds to Thee,
Th'Impulse, the Fight, *th'Event, were wholly Thine.*

14 *Due!*] due; 1780   due! 1789   16 *too.*] too! 1780, 1789   33 *Action*]
Actions *W.M.*   34 Schonberg] 1780 Schomberg 1789

34. *Schonberg.* The Duke of Schom-   in Ireland, was killed at the battle of
berg, William's commander-in-chief   the Boyne, and buried in St. Patrick's

X.

The brave Attempt do's all our Foes disarm,
You need but now give Orders and Command;
Your Name shall the remaining Work perform,
And spare the Labour of Your Conquering Hand.   40

XI.

France *do's in vain her feeble* Arts *apply*
To interrupt the Fortune of Your *Course:*
Your Influence do's the vain Attacks defy
Of secret Malice, or of open Force.

XII.

Boldly we hence the brave Commencement Date
Of glorious Deeds, that must all Tongues Employ:
WILLIAM'*s the* Pledge *and* Earnest *given by Fate*
Of England'*s Glory, and her lasting* Joy.

O D E

TO THE

Athenian Society.

The Supplement to the Fifth Volume of the Athenian Gazette; . . . London,
Printed for John Dunton at the Raven in the Poultry, . . . [1691–2], *p.* 1.
A Supplement to the Athenian Oracle: . . . London, Printed for Andrew
Bell, . . . 1710. *p.* 111.
Sphinx: A Poem, Ascrib'd to Certain Anonymous Authors. By the Rev'd.
Dean S—T. . . . Dublin: Printed in the Year 1724–5.

Cathedral. In 1729 Swift wrote to Schomberg's grand-daughter, the Countess of Holderness, suggesting that she should assign a sum of money for the erection of a monument to his memory. No reply was received, whereupon a monument was placed in the cathedral at the charges of the dean and chapter. Swift wrote an epitaph reflecting upon the ingratitude of Schomberg's heirs and descendants. The inscription has been reprinted in editions of Swift's *Works*. See more particularly *Corresp.* iv. 85, 144, 218 n., 230 n.[3]

The Athenian Oracle: . . . Vol. IV. The Third Edition. . . . London, . . . MDCCXXVIII. p. 111.
Miscellanies. The Tenth Volume. By Dr. Swift. London: Printed for R. Dodsley in Pall-mall. M.DCC.XLV. p. 178 (1750, p. 178).
Miscellanies, 1751, xiii. 175.
The Works of Jonathan Swift, D.D., ed. Hawkesworth, 1755, 4to, iv (1), 229.

With this ode (if we ignore doubtful attributions) Swift saw himself in print for the first time. The poem was 'rough drawn in a week, and finished in two days after' (*Corresp.* i. 363). It was published by John Dunton, in the supplement to the Fifth Volume of the *Athenian Gazette*, early in 1692, prefaced with a letter from Swift, dated from Moor Park. The *Athenian Gazette*, renamed the *Athenian Mercury*, was a periodical published weekly from 17 March, 1691, to 14 June, 1697, resolving all queries addressed to it by correspondents. In 1710, and again in 1728, the ode was reprinted in a fourth, and supplementary, volume of selections from the *Athenian Gazette*, of which three volumes first appeared in 1703 under the title of *The Athenian Oracle*. The poem also appeared in a curious little eight-leaf Dublin pamphlet, entitled *Sphinx*. It was included with Swift's works in the *Miscellanies* volume of 1745. The prefatory letter was not included in *Sphinx*, or in the successive editions of Swift's works.

Swift's interest in Dunton's venture may have been due to the fact that Sir William Temple was a contributor (Dunton's *Life and Errors*, 1705, p. 261). In the same work (p. 260) Dunton refers to Swift as 'a Country Gentleman' who sent 'an ingenious Poem', which 'was prefixt to the *Fifth Supplement* of the *Athenian Mercury*'. According to Johnson, in his life of Swift, this was the poem which led Dryden to observe, 'Cousin Swift, you will never be a poet', words which were 'the motive of Swift's perpetual malevolence to Dryden'.

The text is here given as it appeared in the supplement to the *Athenian Gazette*.

TO THE

Athenian Society.

Moor-park, Feb. 14. 1691.

GENTLEMEN,

S*INCE* every Body *pretends to trouble you with their* Follies, *I thought I might claim the Priviledge of an* English-man, *and put in my share among the rest. Being* *last year in* Ireland, (*from whence I returned about half a year ago*) *I heard only a* loose talk of your Society, *and believed the design to be only some new* Folly *just suitable to the Age, which* God *knows, I little expected ever to produce any thing* extraordinary. *Since my being in* England, *having still continued in the Countrey, and much out of Company; I had but little advantage of knowing any more, till about two Months ago* passing through *Oxford,* a very learned Gentleman *there, first shew'd me two or three of your* Volumes, *and gave me his Account and Opinion of you; a while after, I came to this place, upon a Visit to* —— *where I have been ever since, and have seen all the* four Volumes with their Supplements, *which answering my Expectation. The perusal has produced, what you find inclosed.*

As I have been somewhat inclined to this Folly, *so I have seldom wanted some-body to flatter me in it. And for the* Ode *inclosed, I have sent it to a Person of very great* Learning and Honour, *and since to some others, the best of my Acquaintance,* (to which I thought very proper to inure it for a greater light) *and they have all been pleased to tell me, that they are sure it will not be unwelcome, and that I should* beg the Honour *of You to let it be Printed before Your* next Volume (*which I think, is soon to be published,*) *it being so usual before most Books of any great value among Poets, and before it's seeing the World, I submit it wholly to the* Correction of your Pens.

I intreat therefore one of You would descend *so far, as to write two or three lines to me of your Pleasure upon it. Which as I cannot but expect from Gentlemen, who have so well shewn upon so many occasions, that* greatest Character *of Scholars, in being favourable to the* Ignorant, *So I am sure nothing at present, can more highly oblige me, or make me happier.*

I am,

(Gentlemen)
Your ever most Humble,
and most
admiring Servant.

Jonathan Swift.

I.

AS when the *Deluge* first began to fall,
  That *mighty Ebb* never to flow again,
    (When this huge Bodies Moisture was so great
It quite o'recame the vital Heat,)
That Mountain which was highest first of all
Appear'd, above the Universal Main,
To bless the *Primitive Sailer*'s weary sight,
And 'twas perhaps *Parnassus*, if in height
  It be as great as 'tis in Fame,
  And nigh to Heaven as is its Name.   10
So after th' Inundation of a War
When *Learnings little Houshold* did embark
With her World's fruitful System in her sacred Ark,
  At the first Ebb of Noise and Fears,
  Philosophy's exalted head appears;
And the *Dove-muse*, will now no longer stay
But plumes her Silver Wings and flies away,
  And now a Laurel wreath she brings from far,
  To Crown the happy Conquerour,
  To shew the Flood begins to cease,   20
And brings the dear Reward of *Victory and Peace*.

II.

The eager *Muse* took wing upon the Waves decline,
  When War her cloudy aspect just withdrew,
  When the *Bright Sun* of Peace began to shine,
And for a while in heav'nly Contemplation sate
  On the high Top of peaceful *Ararat*;
And pluckt a *Laurel* branch (for Laurel was the first
        that grew,
The first of Plants after the Thunder, Storm, and Rain)
  And thence with joyful, nimble Wing
The Ode I writ to the King in Ireland. Flew dutifully back again,   30
  And made an *Humble* Chaplet for the King.*

    31. *Humble Chaplet.* The marginal note is Swift's. See p. 4.

And the *Dove-muse* is fled once more,
(Glad of the Victory, yet frighted at the War)
And now discovers *from afar*
A Peaceful and a Flourishing Shore:
No sooner does she land
On the delightful *Strand*,
When strait she sees the *Countrey all around*,
Where fatal *Neptune* rul'd e'rewhile,
Scatter'd with *flowry Vales*, with fruitful Gardens crown'd,
And many a pleasant Wood,
As if the Universal *Nile*
Had rather water'd it, than drown'd:
It seems some floating piece of *Paradice*,
Preserv'd by wonder from the Flood,
Long *wandring thrô the Deep*, as we are told
Fam'd *Delos* did of old,
And the transported Muse imagin'd it
To be a fitter *Birth-place for the God of Wit;*
Or the much-talkt Oracular Grove
When with amazing Joy she hears,
An *unknown Musick* all around,
Charming her greedy Ears
With many a heavenly Song
Of Nature and of Art, of deep *Philosophy and Love,*
Whilst Angels tune the Voice, and God inspires the Tongue.
In vain she catches at the empty Sound,
In vain pursues the Musick with her longing Eye,
And *Courts* the wanton Echoes as they fly.

III.

Pardon **Ye great Unknown**, and far-exalted Men,
The wild excursions of a youthful pen;

36 does] 1710, 1725, 1728, 1745 did 1750, 1751, 1755 38 When] 1710, 1725, 1728 Then 1745 Than 1750, 1751, 1755 61 excursions of a youthful] Attempts of an unskilful 1725

47. *Fam'd Delos* . . . The floating isle, raised from the sea by Neptune, and later secured to the bottom by Zeus that Latona might there bring forth Apollo and Diana. Ovid, *Metam.*, vi. 191, 333.

Forgive a young and (almost) *Virgin-muse*,
Whom blind and eager Curiosity
　　(Yet Curiosity they say,
　Is in her Sex a Crime needs no excuse)
　　Has forc't to grope her uncouth way
After a *mighty Light* that leads her wandring Eye;
No wonder then she quits the *narrow Path of Sense*
　　For a dear Ramble thro' Impertinence,
　　Impertinence, the *Scurvy* of Mankind,　　　　70
And all we Fools, who are the greater part of it,
　　Tho' we be of two different Factions still,
　　　Both the Good-natur'd and the Ill,
　　Yet wheresoe're you look you'll always find
We join like Flyes, and Wasps, in buzzing about Wit.
　　In me, who am of the first Sect of these,
　　All Merit that transcends the humble Rules
　　　Of my own dazled, scanty Sense
　　Begets a kinder Folly and Impertinence
　　　Of Admiration and of Praise:　　　　80
　　And our good Brethren of the *Surly Sect*
　　Must e'en all herd with us their *Kindred Fools*,
　For tho' possess'd of present Vogue they've made
Railing a Rule of Wit, and Obloquy a Trade,
Yet the same want of Brains produces each effect;
　And you whom *Pluto*'s Helm does wisely shroud
　　From us the Blind and thoughtless Croud,
　Like the fam'd Hero in his Mother's Cloud,
Who both our Follies and Impertinencies see,
Do laugh perhaps at theirs, and pity mine and me.　　90

　　　　　　　IV.

　　But Censure's to be understood
　　Th'*Authentick mark* of the Elect,
The publick Stamp Heav'n sets on all that's Great and
　　　　Good,
　Our shallow Search and Judgment to direct.

The War methinks has made
Our Wit and Learning, narrow as our Trade;
Instead of boldly sailing far to buy
A Stock of Wisdom and Philosophy,
We fondly stay at home in fear
Of ev'ry censuring Privateer,   100
Forcing a wretched Trade by beating down the sale,
And selling *basely* by Retail,
The Wits, I mean the Atheists of the Age,
Who fain would rule the Pulpit, as they do the Stage,
Wondrous *Refiners* of Philosophy,
Of Morals and Divinity,
By the new *Modish System* of reducing all to sense,
Against all Logick and concluding Laws,
Do own th'Effects of Providence,
And yet deny the Cause.   110

V.

This *hopeful Sect,* now it begins to see
How little, very little do prevail
Their *first and chiefest force*
To censure, to cry down, and rail,
Not knowing What, or Where, or Who, You be,
Will quickly take another course
And by their never-failing ways
Of Solving all Appearances they please,
We soon shall see them to their ancient Methods fall,
And straight deny you to be *Men, or any thing at all;*   120
I laugh at the grave Answer they will make,
Which they have always ready, general and Cheap;
'Tis but to say, that what we daily meet,
And by a fond mistake

100 *censuring*] pilfering 1725

95–100. *The War . . .* Swift's
reference is to the war on the Continent, not that in Ireland. In 1689
William formed an alliance with Austria, Spain, and the Dutch against
France. The campaign of 1691 had
been indecisive.

Perhaps imagine to be *wondrous Wit*
And think, alas, to be by mortals writ,
Is but a *Crowd of Atoms* justling in a heap,
      Which from Eternal Seeds begun,
      Justling some thousand years till ripen'd by
        the Sun,
They're now, just now, as naturally born,   130
As from the *Womb of Earth* a field of Corn.

VI.

    But as for poor contented Me,
Who must my Weakness and my Ignorance confess,
That I believe in much, I ne're can hope to see;
    Methinks I'm satisfied to guess
That this New, Noble, and Delightful Scene
Is wonderfully mov'd by some exalted Men,
    Who have well studied in the *Worlds Disease*,
(That Epidemick Error and Depravity
      Or in our Judgment or our Eye)   140
That what *surprises us* can only please:
We often search contentedly the whole World round,
    To make some *great Discovery*,
      And scorn it when 'tis found.
Just so the Mighty *Nile* has suffer'd in it's Fame,
    Because 'tis said, (and perhaps only said)
We've found a little inconsiderable Head
      That feeds the huge unequal stream.
Consider *Humane Folly*, and you'll quickly own,
    That all the Praises it can give,   150
By which some fondly boast they shall for ever live,
    Won't pay th'*Impertinence* of being known;
      Else why should the fam'd *Lydian* King,
Whom all the *Charms* of an Usurped Wife and State,

153. *Lydian King.* Plato, *Rep.* II, 359 C; Cicero, *De Off.*, iii. 9.

With all that Power unfelt, courts Mankind to be Great,
    Did with new, unexperienc't Glories wait,
Still wear, still doat on his *Invisible Ring*.

VII.

  Were I to form a regular *Thought of Fame*,
  Which is perhaps as hard t'imagine right
    As to paint Eccho to the Sight: 160
I would not draw th'*Idea* from an empty Name;
    Because, alas, when we all dye
    Careless and Ignorant Posterity,
    Although they praise the Learning and the Wit,
      And tho' the Title seems to show
    The Name and Man, by whom the Book was writ,
      Yet how shall they be brought to know
Whether that very Name was *He, or You, or I?*
Less should I dawb it o're with transitory Praise,
    And *water-colours* of these Days,   170
These Days! where ev'n th'Extravagance of Poetry
    Is at a loss for Figures to express
    Men's Folly, Whimsyes, and Inconstancy,
    And by a faint Description make them less.
Then tell us what is Fame? where shall we search for it?
Look where exalted Vertue and Religion sit
    Enthron'd with Heav'nly Wit,
    Look where you see
    The greatest scorn of *Learned Vanity*,
    (And then how much a nothing is Mankind!   180
    Whose Reason is weigh'd down by Popular air,
Who by that, vainly talks of bafling Death,
And hopes to lengthen Life by a *Transfusion of Breath*,
    Which yet whoe're examines right will find
To be an Art as vain, as *Bottling up of Wind:*)
And when you find out these, believe true Fame is there.
Far above all Reward, yet to which all is due,
And this 𝔜𝔢 𝔤𝔯𝔢𝔞𝔱 𝔘𝔫𝔨𝔫𝔬𝔴𝔫, is only known in You.

157 *Ring*.] Ring? 1710, 1725, 1728, 1745, 1750, 1751   ring? 1755   174
make] 1751   makes 1710, 1725, 1728, 1745, 1750, 1755

VIII.

The *Jugling Sea-god* when by chance trepann'd
By some instructed *Querist* sleeping on the Sand,   190
  Impatient of all *Answers*, straight became
  A *Stealing Brook*, and strove to creep away
     Into his Native Sea,
  Vext at their Follies, murmur'd in his Stream;
  But disappointed of his fond Desire
  Would vanish in a *Pyramid of Fire*.
This Surly, *Slipp'ry God*, when He design'd
    To furnish his Escapes,
  Ne'er borrow'd more *variety of Shapes*
Than *You* to please and satisfie Mankind,   200
And seem (almost) transform'd to *Water, Flame, and Air*,
  So well *You* answer all *Phænomenaes there*;
Tho' Madmen and the Wits, Philosophers and Fools,
With all that Factious or Enthusiastick Dotards dream,
And all the incohærent Jargon of the Schools,
  Tho' all the Fumes of Fear, Hope, Love, and Shame,
Contrive to shock your Minds, with many a sensless doubt,
Doubts, where the *Delphick God* would grope in Ignorance
  and Night,
    The God of Learning and of Light   *θεὸς ἀπὸ
*Would want a * God Himself to help him out.*   μηχανῆς.

IX.

Philosophy, as it before us lyes,   211
  Seems to have borrow'd some ungrateful tast
Of *Doubts*, Impertinence, and Niceties,
    From ev'ry Age through which it pass't,
But always with a stronger relish of the Last.
    This beauteous Queen by Heaven design'd
      To be the great Original
For Man to *dress and polish* his Uncourtly Mind,
In what *Mock-habits* have they put her, since the Fall!

189 *Jugling Sea-god.* Proteus, Ovid, *Metam.*, viii. 731 ff.

More oft in Fools and Mad-mens hands than Sages 220
 She seems a Medly of all Ages,
With a huge Fardingal to swell her Fustian Stuff,
 A new Commode, a *Top-knot,* and a Ruff,
 Her Face patch't o'er with *Modern Pedantry,*
  With a long sweeping Train
Of Comments and Disputes, ridiculous and vain,
 All of old Cut with a new Dye,
 How soon have You restor'd her Charms!
And rid her of her *Lumber and Her Books,*
 Drest her again Genteel and Neat,   230
  And rather Tite than Great,
How fond we are to court Her to our Arms!
How much of Heav'n is in her naked looks.

X.

Thus the *deluding Muse* oft blinds me to her Ways,
 And ev'n my very Thoughts transfers
 And changes all to Beauty, and the Praise
  Of that proud Tyrant Sex of Hers.
  The *Rebel Muse,* alas, takes part
  But with my own Rebellious Heart,
And You with *fatal and Immortal Wit* conspire   240
  To fann th'unhappy Fire:
𝕮𝖗𝖚𝖊𝖑 𝖀𝖓𝖐𝖓𝖔𝖜𝖓! what is it You intend!
Ah, could You! could you hope *a Poet for your Friend!*
 Rather forgive what my first Transport said,
May all the Blood, which shall by *Womans scorn* be shed
 Lye on you, and on your Childrens Head,
For You (ah, did I think I e'er should live to see
  The fatal Time when that cou'd be)
 Have ev'n encreas't their *Pride and Cruelty.*

233 *looks.*] Looks! 1710, 1725, 1728, 1750, 1751   looks! 1745, 1755   242
intend!] intend ? *remainder*   246 Lye on] Lie upon *remainder*

 222–3. *Fardingal . . . Commode, . . .*   consisting of a wire frame-work
Top-knot. A farthingale was a hooped   covered with lace or silk; a top-knot,
petticoat; a commode, a tall head-dress,   a bow of ribbon worn on the top of the
fashionable at the time with women,   head by women.

Woman seems now above all Vanity grown,   250
  Still boasting of Her Great Unknown;
Platonick Champions, gain'd without one Female Wile,
  Or the vast 𝕮𝖍𝖆𝖗𝖌𝖊𝖘 𝖔𝖋 𝖆 𝕾𝖒𝖎𝖑𝖊;
Which 'tis a shame to see how much of late
You've taught the *Cov'tous* Wretches to o're-rate,
And which they've now the Conscience to way
  In the same Ballance with our Tears,
  And with such *Scanty* Wages pay
  The Bondage and the Slavery of Years.
Let the *vain sex* dream on, their Empire comes from Us, 260
  And had they *common* Generosity
    They would not use Us thus.
  Well—tho' you've rais'd Her to this high Degree,
    Our selves are rais'd as well as she,
  And 'spight of all that They or You can do,
  'Tis Pride and Happiness enough to Me
Still to be of the same exalted Sex with You.

XI.

  Alas, how fleeting, and how vain,
Is even the *nobler Man*, our Learning and our Wit,
    I sigh when e're I think of it   270
  As at the closing an unhappy Scene
    Of some *great King* and Conqu'rors Death,
    When the sad, melancholy Muse
    Stays but to catch his *utmost breath*,
I grieve, this Noble Work so happily begun,
So quickly, and so wonderfully carried on,
Must fall at last to Interest, Folly, and Abuse.
    There is a *Noon-tide* in our Lives
    Which still the sooner it arrives,

254 to see] *Om.* 1750, 1751, 1755   259 the Slavery] 1710, 1725, 1728, 1745
Slavery 1750, 1751, 1755   271 closing] 1710, 1725, 1728 1745   closing
of 1750, 1751, 1755   273 sad,] said 1728   275 Noble Work so]
noble Work so 1710, 1725, 1728, 1745   nobler Work most 1750   noble Work
most 1751   nobler work most 1755   277 Must] May *remainder*

Altho' we boast our *Winter-Sun looks bright*,   280
And foolishly are glad to see it at it's height
Yet so much sooner comes the long and gloomy Night.
        No Conquest ever yet begun
And by one mighty Hero carried to it's height
E'er flourish't under a Successor or a Son;
It lost some mighty Pieces thro' all hands it past
And vanisht to an *empty Title in the Last.*
    For when the animating Mind is fled,
        (Which Nature never can retain,
            Nor e'er call back again)   290
The Body, tho' Gigantick, lyes all *Cold and Dead.*

XII.

    And thus undoubtedly 'twill fare,
        With what unhappy Men shall dare,
    To be Successors to these Great Unknown,
        On Learning's high-establish't Throne.
        Censure, and Pedantry, and Pride,
    Numberless Nations, stretching far and wide,
Shall (I foresee it) soon with *Gothick* Swarms come forth
        From Ignorance's Universal North,
And with blind Rage break all this peaceful Government;
Yet shall these *Traces of your Wit* remain   301
    Like a *just Map* to tell the vast Extent
    Of Conquest in your short and Happy Reign;
        And to all future Mankind shew
        How strange a *Paradox* is true,
That Men, who liv'd and dy'd without a Name,
Are the chief Heroes in the sacred List of Fame.

Jonathan Swift.

Jonathan Swift. The signature does not appear in the *Miscellanies* or collected *Works.*

O D E

To the Honble Sir WILLIAM TEMPLE.

Miscellanies. The Tenth Volume. By Dr. Swift. London: Printed for R. Dodsley in Pall-mall. M.DCC.XLV. p. 194 (1750, p. 194).
Miscellanies, 1751, xiii. 190.   [(1), 239.
The Works of Jonathan Swift, D.D., ed. Hawkesworth, 1755, 4to, iv

In the *Miscellanies* of 1745, where this ode was first printed, it is said to have been 'Written at *Moorpark, June* 1689'. This, however, is an extremely unlikely date. At that time Swift had barely entered Temple's service. Further, although Professor Homer E. Woodbridge, *Sir William Temple*, 1940, p. 219, inclines to accept 1689 as a probable date, he forgot that during the revolutionary disturbance of 1688 Temple, with his wife and sister, retired to Sheen and there remained till the end of 1689. See below, pp. 33–4, introductory notes to the 'Ode to Sancroft'. It is not improbable that, like that ode, the 'Ode to Temple' was antedated; and, if begun in 1689, not completed till a year or two later. Hawkesworth's footnote (1755) says that 'When the author's posthumous pieces were reprinted in *Ireland*', this poem and the 'Ode to the Athenian Society' were omitted. The note is intended as a stricture upon Faulkner's editions.

The text of the poem is here reprinted from the *Miscellanies* of 1745.

VIRTUE, the greatest of all Monarchies,
   Till its first Emperor rebellious Man
     Depos'd from off his Seat
  It fell, and broke with its own Weight
Into small States and Principalities,
   By many a petty Lord possess'd,
But ne'er since seated in one single Breast.
     'Tis you who must this Land subdue,
     The mighty Conquest's left for you,
     The Conquest and Discovery too: 10
    Search out this *Utopian* Ground,
    Virtue's *Terra Incognita*,
     Where none ever led the Way,
Nor ever since but in Descriptions found,
   Like the Philosopher's Stone,
With Rules to search it, yet obtain'd by none.

II.

We have too long been led astray,
Too long have our misguided Souls been taught
  With Rules from musty Morals brought,
  'Tis you must put us in the Way;   20
  Let us (for shame) no more be fed
  With antique Reliques of the Dead,
  The Gleanings of Philosophy,
  Philosophy! the Lumber of the Schools,
  The Roguery of Alchymy,
    And we the bubbled Fools
Spend all our present Stock in hopes of golden Rules.

III.

But what does our proud Ign'rance Learning call,
  We odly *Plato*'s Paradox make good,
Our Knowledge is but mere Remembrance all,   30
  Remembrance is our Treasure and our Food;
Nature's fair Table-book our tender Souls
We scrawl all o'er with old and empty Rules,
  Stale Memorandums of the Schools;
  For Learning's mighty Treasures look
    In that deep Grave a Book,
  Think she there does all her Treasures hide,
And that her troubled Ghost still haunts there since she
    dy'd;
  Confine her Walks to Colleges and Schools,
  Her Priests, her Train and Followers show   40
  As if they all were Spectres too,
  They purchase Knowledge at the Expence
  Of common Breeding, common Sense,
  And at once grow Scholars and Fools;
  Affect ill-manner'd Pedantry,
Rudeness, Ill-nature, Incivility,
  And sick with Dregs of Knowledge grown,
  Which greedily they swallow down,
Still cast it up and nauseate Company.

IV.

Curst be the Wretch, nay doubly curst,   50
   (If it may lawful be
To curse our greatest Enemy)
Who learnt himself that Heresy first
   (Which since has seiz'd on all the rest)
That Knowledge forfeits all Humanity;
Taught us, like *Spaniards*, to be proud and poor,
   And fling our Scraps before our Door.
Thrice happy you have 'scap't this gen'ral Pest;
Those mighty Epithets, Learn'd, Good, and Great,
Which we ne'er join'd before, but in Romances meet,   60
   We find in you at last united grown.
     You cannot be compar'd to one,
   I must, like him that painted *Venus'* Face,
   Borrow from every one a Grace;
Virgil and *Epicurus* will not do,
   Their courting a Retreat like you,
Unless I put in *Caesar*'s Learning too,
     Your happy Frame at once controuls
     This great triumvirate of Souls.

V.

Let not old *Rome* boast *Fabius*'s Fate,   70
   He sav'd his Country by Delays,
     But you by Peace,
   You bought it at a cheaper Rate;
Nor has it left the usual bloody Scar,
   To shew it cost its Price in War,
War! that mad Game, the World so loves to play,
   And for it does so dearly pay;

63. *like him that painted Venus' Face.* Apelles, painter of the celebrated Venus Anadyomene. Pliny, *Hist. Nat.*, xxxv. 87, 91.

72. *But you by Peace.* Temple, whose diplomacy was constantly directed towards peace, effected the Triple Alliance in 1668, the Treaty of Westminster in 1674, and played a part in the congress which led to the Treaty of Nimeguen (1679), of which, however, he disapproved.

For though with Loss or Victory awhile
  Fortune the Gamesters does beguile,
Yet at the last the Box sweeps all away.   80

VI.

Only the Laurel got by Peace
    No Thunder e'er can blast,
    Th' Artillery of the Skies
    Shoots to the Earth and dies;
Forever green and flourishing 'twill last,
Nor dipt in Blood, nor Widow's Tears, nor Orphan's
      Cries:
  About the Head crown'd with these Bays,
  Like Lambent Fire the Lightning plays;
Nor its triumphal Cavalcade to grace
  Make up its solemn Train with Death;   90
It melts the Sword of War, yet keeps it in the Sheath.

VII.

The wily Shafts of State, those Juggler's Tricks
Which we call deep Design and Politicks
(As in a Theatre the Ignorant Fry,
  Because the Cords escape their Eye
  Wonder to see the Motions fly)
  Methinks, when you expose the Scene,
  Down the ill-organ'd Engines fall;
Off fly the Vizards and discover all,
  How plain I see thro' the Deceit!   100
  How shallow! and how gross the Cheat!
  Look where the Pully 's ty'd above!
  Great God! (said I) what have I seen!
    On what poor Engines move

85 Forever] For ever 1751 Nor ever 1750, 1755

85. *Forever.* By a printer's error this became, in successive editions of the works, 'Nor ever'. Sheridan in his edition (1784, vii. 6) conjecturally emended to 'And ever', and this mistake has since been followed by editors.

The Thoughts of Monarchs, and Designs of States,
   What petty Motives rule their Fates!
How the Mouse makes the mighty Mountain shake!
The mighty Mountain labours with its birth,
   Away the frighted Peasants fly,
    Scar'd at th' unheard-of Prodigy,   110
Expect some great gigantick Son of Earth;
      Lo, it appears!
   See, how they tremble! how they quake!
Out starts the little Beast, and mocks their idle Fears.

VIII.

    Then tell (dear fav'rite Muse)
  What Serpent's that which still resorts,
  Still lurks in Palaces and Courts,
    Take thy unwonted Flight,
    And on the Terras light.
     See where she lies!   120
    See how she rears her Head,
  And rolls about her dreadful Eyes,
To drive all Virtue out, or look it dead!
'Twas sure this Basilisk sent *Temple* thence,
And tho' as some ('tis said) for their Defence
  Have worn a Casement o'er their Skin,
    So he wore his within,
Made up of Virtue and transparent Innocence:
   And tho' he oft renew'd the Fight,
And almost got priority of Sight,   130
   He ne'er could overcome her quite,
(In pieces cut, the Viper still did reunite)
  Till at last tir'd with loss of Time and Ease,
Resolv'd to give himself, as well as Country Peace.

IX.

Sing (belov'd Muse) the Pleasures of Retreat,
  And in some untouch'd Virgin Strain

135 *Pleasures of Retreat.* Retiring   lived at Sheen, and, from 1686, at
from public life, in 1680, Temple first   Moor Park, near Farnham.

Shew the Delights thy Sister Nature yields,
Sing of thy Vales, sing of thy Woods, sing of thy Fields;
    Go publish o'er the Plain
    How mighty a Proselyte you gain!   140
How noble a Reprisal on the Great!
        How is the Muse luxuriant grown,
            Whene'er she takes this Flight
            She soars clear out of sight,
These are the Paradises of her own;
        (The Pegasus, like an unruly Horse
            Tho' ne'er so gently led
To the lov'd Pasture where he us'd to feed,
Runs violently o'er his usual Course.)
        Wake from thy wanton Dreams,   150
        Come from thy dear-lov'd Streams,
    The crooked Paths of wandering *Thames*.
        Fain the fair Nymph would stay,
        Oft she looks back in vain,
    Oft 'gainst her Fountain does complain,
And softly steals in many Windings down,
As loth to see the hated Court and Town,
        And murmurs as she glides away.

                            X.

        In this new happy Scene
    Are nobler Subjects for your learned Pen;   160
        Here we expect from you
More than your Predecessor, *Adam*, knew;
Whatever moves our Wonder or our Sport,
Whatever serves for innocent Emblems of the Court;
    (How that which we a Kernel see,
Whose well-compacted Forms escape the Light,
    Unpierc'd by the blunt Rays of Sight)
    Shall e'er long grow into a Tree,
Whence takes it its Increase, and whence its Birth,
Or from the Sun, or from the Air, or from the Earth, 170

Where all the fruitful Atoms lye,
How some go downward to the Root,
Some more ambitiously upwards fly,
And form the Leaves, the Branches, and the Fruit.
You strove to cultivate a barren Court in vain,
Your Garden's better worth your noble Pain,
Hence Mankind fell, and here must rise again.

XI.

Shall I believe a Spirit so divine
Was cast in the same Mold with mine?
Why then does Nature so unjustly share   180
Among her Elder Sons the whole Estate?
And all her Jewels and her Plate,
Poor we *Cadets* of Heav'n, not worth her Care,
Take up at best with Lumber and the Leavings of a Fate:
Some she binds 'Prentice to the Spade,
Some to the Drudgery of a Trade,
Some she does to *Egyptian* Bondage draw,
Bids us make Bricks, yet sends us to look out for Straw;
Some she condemns for Life to try
To dig the leaden Mines of deep Philosophy: 190
Me she has to the Muse's Gallies ty'd,
In vain I strive to cross this spacious Main,
In vain I tug and pull the Oar,
And when I almost reach the Shore
Strait the Muse turns the Helm, and I launch out again;
And yet to feed my Pride,
Whene'er I mourn, stops my complaining Breath,
With promise of a mad Reversion after Death.

XII.

Then (Sir,) accept this worthless Verse,
The Tribute of an humble Muse,   200
'Tis all the Portion of my niggard Stars;
Nature the hidden Spark did at my Birth infuse,

And kindled first with Indolence and Ease,
  And since too oft debauch'd by Praise,
'Tis now grown an incurable Disease:
In vain to quench this foolish Fire I try
  In Wisdom and Philosophy;
  In vain all wholsome Herbs I sow,
    Where nought but Weeds will grow.
Whate'er I plant (like Corn on barren Earth)   210
    By an equivocal Birth
  Seeds and runs up to Poetry.

O D E

To Dr. WILLIAM SANCROFT,

Late Lord Archbishop of CANTERBURY.

Miscellaneous Pieces, in Prose and Verse. By The Rev. Dr. Jonathan Swift,
Dean of St. Patrick's, Dublin. Not inserted in Mr. Sheridan's Edition of
The Dean's Works. London: Printed for C. Dilly, in the Poultry.
MDCCLXXXIX. p. 215.
Works, ed. Nichols, 1801, xviii. 395.
Works, ed. Scott, 1814, xiv. 3.

    This poem was first printed by John Nichols in 1789, together with the
'Ode to Congreve' and the verses occasioned by Temple's illness. The three
were prefaced with a note: 'Now first published from an authentic Manuscript, fairly and correctly written out as if intended for the Press.' Below,
in square brackets, was added: 'From the dates, it is supposed that these
were among the first, if not the very first, productions of his muse.' No
trace of this manuscript remains; and it is not stated whether the hand was
Swift's, unless the word 'authentic' is to be read in that sense; but that the
poems are by Swift cannot fairly be doubted. The 'Ode to Sancroft' is
expressly mentioned by Swift in a letter to his cousin, Thomas Swift, dated
3 May, 1692 : 'I have had an ode in hand these five months inscribed to
my late Lord of Canterbury, Dr. Sancroft' (*Corresp.* i. 363). Nine stanzas,
he says, are finished, but he finds difficulty in completing a poem which he
had undertaken upon 'half a promise' to the Bishop of Ely. As it stands,
with twelve stanzas, the poem is still unfinished.

The date of Swift's letter is of interest and importance. Nichols, presumably copying from the manuscript, heads the poem: 'Written May 1689, at the Desire of the late Lord Bishop of E—.' But three years later it was still in hand, denying every effort. Furthermore, stanza iii refers to Sancroft's 'divin'ty of retreat', and xi to his 'exaltation of retreat'. Although Sancroft was suspended 1 August, 1689, and deprived 1 February, 1690, for refusing the oath of allegiance to William and Mary, he did not leave Lambeth until his ejectment, 23 June, 1691. We may surmise that the poem was begun in 1689, at the request of Francis Turner, Bishop of Ely, also a non-juror, and abandoned incomplete in 1692.

This poem is one of Swift's four attempts to emulate a contemporary fashion, wholly unnatural to him, the so-called Pindaric ode. In the letter to his cousin Thomas, above referred to, he confesses that he is continually altering, and can 'seldom write above two stanzas in a week'. But 'when I write what pleases me I am Cowley to myself and can read it a hundred times over'. In his *Letter concerning the Sacramental Test*, 1708, he quotes 'Mr. *Cowley*'s Love Verses', which, even at fifteen, he 'thought extraordinary' (*Prose Works*, ed. Temple Scott, iv. 10). For the greater part of his life a copy of Cowley's works was in his library. But the modern reader will agree with Deane Swift, that this 'was not a style of poetry that he excelled in' (Nichols's *Literary Illustrations*, v. 382). Sheridan (*Life*, 1784, p. 15) has said all that need be said: 'The sentiments were strained and crowded; and the numbers irregular and harsh.' Nevertheless, these early poems deserve study for the personal characteristics they reflect.

The text is here reprinted from *Miscellaneous Pieces*, 1789.

I.

TRUTH is eternal, and the Son of Heav'n,
　　Bright effluence of th' immortal ray,
Chief cherub, and chief lamp of that high sacred Seven,
Which guard the throne by night, and are its light by
　　　　day:
　　First of God's darling attributes,
　　　　Thou daily seest Him face to face,
Nor does thy essence fix'd depend on giddy circumstance
　　　　Of time or place,
Two foolish guides in ev'ry sublunary dance:
　　How shall we find Thee then in dark disputes?　　10
　　How shall we search Thee in a battle gain'd,
　　Or a weak argument by force maintain'd?

In dagger-contests, and th' artillery of words,
(For swords are madmen's tongues, and tongues are mad-
        men's swords)
        Contriv'd to tire all patience out,
        And not to satisfy the doubt:

II.

    But where is ev'n thy Image on our earth?
        For of the person much I fear,
Since Heaven will claim its residence as well as birth,
And God himself has said, He shall not find it here.   20
For this inferior world is but Heaven's dusky shade,
By dark reverted rays from its reflection made;
    Whence the weak shapes wild and imperfect pass,
Like sun-beams shot at too far distance from a glass;
        Which all the mimic forms express,
Tho' in strange uncouth postures, and uncomely dress;
        So when Cartesian artists try
        To solve appearances of sight
        In its reception to the eye,
And catch the living landscape thro' a scanty light,   30
        The figures all inverted shew,
        And colours of a faded hue;
Here a pale shape with upward footstep treads,
        And men seem walking on their heads;
        There whole herds suspended lie
    Ready to tumble down into the sky;
    Such are the ways ill-guided mortals go
    To judge of things above by things below.
Disjointing shapes as in the fairy-land of dreams,
    Or images that sink in streams;   40
    No wonder, then, we talk amiss
    Of truth, and what, or where it is:

        16 doubt:] doubt? 1801, 1814

30. *And catch* . . . 'The experiment   light to be by reception of the object
of the dark chamber, to demonstrate   and not by emission.'—1789.

Say Muse, for thou, if any, know'st
Since the bright essence fled, where haunts the reverend
　　ghost?

III.

If all that our weak knowledge titles virtue, be
(High Truth) the best resemblance of exalted Thee,
　　If a mind fix'd to combat fate
With those two pow'rful swords, Submission and Humility,
　　Sounds truly good, or truly great;
Ill may I live, if the good SANCROFT in his holy rest,　　50
　　In the divin'ty of retreat,
　　Be not the brightest pattern Earth can shew
　　　Of heav'n-born Truth below:
　　But foolish Man still judges what is best
　　　In his own balance, false and light,
　　　Foll'wing Opinion, dark, and blind, .
　　　That vagrant leader of the mind,
Till Honesty and Conscience are clear out of sight.

IV.

And some, to be large cyphers in a state,
Pleas'd with an empty swelling to be counted great;　　60
Make their minds travel o'er infinity of space,
　　　Rapp'd through the wide expanse of thought,
　　And oft in contradiction's vortex caught,
To keep that worthless clod, the body, in one place:
Errors like this did old Astronomers misguide,
Led blindly on by gross philosophy and pride,
　　　Who, like hard masters, taught the Sun
　　　Thro' many a needless sphere to run,
Many an eccentric and unthrifty motion make,
　　And thousand incoherent journies take,　　　　70
　　　Whilst all th' advantage by it got,
　　Was but to light Earth's inconsiderable spot.

The herd beneath, who see the weathercock of state
   Hung loosely on the Church's pinnacle,
Believe it firm, because perhaps the day is mild and still;
But when they find it turn with the first blast of fate,
     By gazing upwards giddy grow,
     And think the Church itself does so;
     Thus fools, for being strong and num'rous known,
     Suppose the truth, like all the world, their own; 80
And holy Sancroft's motion quite irregular appears,
     Because 'tis opposite to theirs.

V.

In vain then would the Muse the multitude advise,
   Whose peevish knowledge thus perversely lies
     In gath'ring follies from the wise;
   Rather put on thy anger and thy spight,
     And some kind pow'r for once dispense
Thro' the dark mass, the dawn of so much sense,
To make them understand, and feel me when I write;
   The muse and I no more revenge desire, 90
Each line shall stab, shall blast, like daggers and like fire;
   Ah, Britain, land of angels! which of all thy sins,
     (Say hapless Isle, altho'
     It is a bloody list we know)
   Has given thee up a dwelling-place to fiends?
     Sin and the plague ever abound
In governments too easy, and too fruitful ground;
     Evils which a too gentle king,
     Too flourishing a spring,
     And too warm summers bring: 100
     Our British soil is over-rank, and breeds
Among the noblest flow'rs a thousand pois'nous weeds,
     And ev'ry stinking weed so lofty grows,
     As if 'twould overshade the Royal Rose,
     The Royal Rose the glory of our morn,
     But, ah, too much without a thorn.

77 upwards] upward 1801, 1814

VI.

Forgive (Original Mildness) this ill-govern'd zeal,
   'Tis all the angry slighted Muse can do
     In the pollution of these days;
   No province now is left her but to rail,   110
   And Poetry has lost the art to praise,
     Alas, the occasions are so few:
     None e'er but you,
     And your Almighty Master, knew
     With heavenly peace of mind to bear
(Free from our tyrant-passions, anger, scorn, or fear)
     The giddy turns of pop'lar rage,
And all the contradictions of a poison'd age;
   The Son of God pronounc'd by the same breath
   Which strait pronounc'd his death;   120
   And tho' I should but ill be understood
   In wholly equalling our sin and theirs,
   And measuring by the scanty thread of wit
   What we call holy, and great, and just, and good,
(Methods in talk whereof our pride and ignorance make
     use)
   And which our wild ambition foolishly compares
     With endless and with infinite;
   Yet pardon, native ALBION, when I say
Among thy stubborn sons there haunts that spirit of Jews,
   That those forsaken wretches who to-day   130
     Revile His great ambassador,
   Seem to discover what they would have done
   (Were his humanity on earth once more)
To his undoubted Master, Heaven's Almighty Son.

VII.

But zeal is weak and ignorant, tho' wond'rous proud,
   Though very turbulent and very loud;
     The crazy composition shews,
Like that fantastic medley in the idol's toes,

Made up of iron mixt with clay,
This, crumbles into dust,   140
That, moulders into rust,
Or melts by the first show'r away.
Nothing is fix'd that mortals see or know,
Unless, perhaps, some stars above be so;
    And those, alas, do show
Like all transcendent excellence below;
    In both, false mediums cheat our sight,
And far exalted objects lessen by their height:
    Thus, primitive SANCROFT moves too high
    To be observ'd by vulgar eye,   150
    And rolls the silent year
    On his own secret regular sphere,
And sheds, tho' all unseen, his sacred influence here.

VIII.

Kind Star, still may'st thou shed thy sacred influence here,
    Or from thy private peaceful orb appear;
    For, sure, we want some guide from Heav'n to show
    The way which ev'ry wand'ring fool below
        Pretends so perfectly to know;
    And which for ought I see, and much I fear,
        The world has wholly miss'd;   160
    I mean, the way which leads to Christ:
Mistaken Ideots! see how giddily they run,
    Led blindly on by avarice and pride,
        What mighty numbers follow them;
        Each fond of erring with his guide:
Some whom ambition drives, seek Heaven's high Son
    In Caesar's court, or in Jerusalem;
        Others, ignorantly wise,
Among proud Doctors and disputing Pharisees:
What could the Sages gain but unbelieving scorn;   170
    Their faith was so uncourtly when they said
That Heaven's high Son was in a village born;

That the world's Saviour had been
In a vile manger laid,
And foster'd in a wretched inn.

IX.

Necessity, thou tyrant conscience of the great,
Say, why the Church is still led blindfold by the State?
  Why should the first be ruin'd and laid waste,
  To mend dilapidations in the last?
And yet the world, whose eyes are on our mighty Prince,
    Thinks Heav'n has cancel'd all our sins,   181
And that his subjects share his happy influence;
Follow the model close, for so I'm sure they should,
But wicked kings draw more examples than the good;
  And divine SANCROFT, weary with the weight
Of a declining Church, by Faction her worse foe opprest,
    Finding the Mitre almost grown
    A load as heavy as the Crown,
Wisely retreated to his heavenly rest.

X.

  Ah, may no unkind earthquake of the State,   190
    Nor hurricano from the Crown,
Disturb the present Mitre, as that fearful storm of late,
  Which in its dusky march along the plain,
    Swept up whole churches as it list,
    Wrapp'd in a whirlwind and a mist;
Like that prophetic tempest in the virgin reign,
  And swallow'd them at last, or flung them down.
  Such were the storms good SANCROFT long has borne;
  The Mitre, which his sacred head has worn,
  Was, like his Master's Crown, inwreath'd with thorn.
Death's sting is swallow'd up in victory at last,   201
    The bitter cup is from him past:
    Fortune in both extremes,

175 inn.] inn? 1801, 1814   177 State?] state; 1801, 1814

Tho' blasts from contrariety of winds,
    Yet to firm heavenly minds,
  Is but one thing under two different names;
And even the sharpest eye that has the prospect seen,
    Confesses ignorance to judge between;
And must, to human reasoning opposite, conclude
To point out which is moderation, which is fortitude. 210

XI.

Thus SANCROFT, in the exaltation of retreat,
    Shews lustre that was shaded in his seat;
    Short glimm'rings of the prelate glorify'd;
Which the disguise of greatness only served to hide;
    Why should the Sun, alas, be proud
    To lodge behind a golden cloud;
Tho' fring'd with ev'ning gold the cloud appears so
        gay,
'Tis but a low-born vapor kindled by a ray;
    At length 'tis over-blown and past,
    Puff'd by the people's spightful blast,   220
The daz'ling glory dimms their prostituted sight,
    No deflower'd eye can face the naked light:
    Yet does this high perfection well proceed
        From strength of its own native seed,
This wilderness the world, like that poetic wood of old,
    Bears one, and but one branch of gold,
    Where the bless'd spirit lodges like the dove,
And which (to heavenly soil transplanted) will im-
        prove,
To be, as 'twas below, the brightest plant above;
    For, whate'er theologic lev'llers dream,   230
        There are degrees above I know
        As well as here below,
(The goddess Muse herself has told me so)
Where high patrician souls dress'd heavenly gay,
Sit clad in lawn of purer woven day,

There some high spiritual throne to SANCROFT shall be
    given,
    In the metropolis of heaven;
Chief of the mitred saints, and from arch-prelate here,
    Translated to arch-angel there.

XII.

Since, happy Saint, since it has been of late   240
    Either our blindness or our fate,
    To lose the providence of thy cares,
Pity a miserable Church's tears,
That begs the pow'rful blessing of thy pray'rs.
Some angel say, what were the nation's crimes,
That sent these wild reformers to our times;
    Say what their senseless malice meant,
    To tear Religion's lovely face;
Strip her of ev'ry ornament and grace,
In striving to wash off th'imaginary paint: 250
    Religion now does on her death-bed lie,
Heart-sick of a high fever and consuming atrophy;
How the physicians swarm to shew their mortal skill,
And by their college-arts methodically kill:
Reformers and physicians differ but in name,
    One end in both, and the design the same;
    Cordials are in their talk, whilst all they mean
      Is but the patient's death, and gain—
      Check in thy satire, angry muse,
      Or a more worthy subject chuse: 260
    Let not the outcasts of this outcast age
    Provoke the honour of my Muse's rage,
      Nor be thy mighty spirit rais'd,
      Since Heaven and Cato both are pleas'd—

[The rest of the poem is lost.]

236 high spiritual] high-spirited 1801, 1814   250 paint:] 1801 paint?
1814

To Mr. CONGREVE.

Written November 1693.

Miscellaneous Pieces, in Prose and Verse....MDCCLXXXIX. p. 225.
Works, ed. Nichols, 1801, xviii. 407.
Works, ed. Scott, 1814, xiv. 36.

When only six years old Swift was sent by his uncle, Godwin Swift, to the grammar school of Kilkenny, where he remained 1674–82. Two years later he was joined by his cousin Thomas. In 1681, or 1682, William Congreve, who was two years Swift's junior, was sent to the same school. There is no evidence that they formed any acquaintance at this time. But later they were together at Trinity College, Dublin, which Swift entered 24 April, 1682, and Congreve 5 April, 1685, where, also, they had the same tutor, St. George Ashe.

In 1693 Swift was still in the household service of Sir William Temple, and obscure, while Congreve had risen to fame with the brilliant success of his first play, *The Old Batchelor*, which appeared in January of that year. His second play, *The Double-Dealer*, was performed at Drury Lane in October, 1693, and published on the 4th of December. Following the appearance of *The Double-Dealer*, Swift composed the following poem, to which he makes detailed reference in a letter addressed to his cousin, Thomas, 6 December, 1693, evidently from Moor Park: 'I desire you would inform yourself what you mean by bidding me keep my Verses for Will Congreve's next Play, for I tell you they were calculated for any of his, and if it were but acted when you say, it is as early as ever I intended, since I only design they should be printed before it, so I desire you will send me word immediately how it succeeded, whether well, ill or indifferently, because my sending them to Mr. Congreve depends upon knowing the Issue. They are almost 250 lines not Pindarick.' (*Corresp.* i. 368.)

There is no record that Congreve ever received a copy of the poem. It was first printed by Nichols in 1789. The text is here reprinted as given by him.

THRICE, with a prophet's voice and prophet's pow'r,
   The Muse was call'd in a poetic hour,
And insolently thrice, the slighted Maid
Dar'd to suspend her unregarded aid;
Then with that grief we form in spirits divine,
Pleads for her own neglect, and thus reproaches mine:

Once highly honour'd! False is the pretence
You make to truth, retreat, and innocence;
Who, to pollute my shades, bring'st with thee down
The most ungen'rous vices of the town;   10
Ne'er sprang a youth from out this isle before
I once esteem'd, and lov'd, and favour'd more,
Nor ever maid endur'd such court-like scorn,
So much in mode, so very city-born;
'Tis with a foul design the muse you send,
Like a cast mistress to your wicked friend;
But find some new address, some fresh deceit,
Nor practise such an antiquated cheat;
These are the beaten methods of the stews,
Stale forms of course, all mean deceivers use,   20
Who barbarously think to 'scape reproach,
By prostituting her they first debauch.
    Thus did the Muse severe unkindly blame
This off'ring long design'd to CONGREVE's fame;
First chid the zeal as unpoetic fire,
Which soon his merit forc'd her to inspire;
Then call this verse, that speaks her largest aid,
The greatest compliment she ever made,
And wisely judge, no pow'r beneath divine
Could leap the bounds which part your world and mine; 30
For, youth, believe, to you unseen, is fix'd
A mighty gulph unpassable betwixt.
    Nor tax the goddess of a mean design
To praise your parts by publishing of mine;
That be my thought when some large bulky writ
Shews in the front the ambition of my wit;
There to surmount what bears me up, and sing
Like the victorious wren perch'd on the eagle's wing;
This could I do, and proudly o'er him tow'r,
Were my desires but heighten'd to my pow'r.   40
    Godlike the force of my young CONGREVE's bays,
Soft'ning the muse's thunder into praise;
Sent to assist an old unvanquish'd pride
That looks with scorn on half mankind beside;

A pride that well suspends poor mortals fate,
Gets between them and my resentment's weight,
Stands in the gap 'twixt me and wretched men,
T'avert th'impending judgments of my pen.
　　Thus I look down with mercy on the age,
By hopes my CONGREVE will reform the stage;   50
For never did poetic mine before
Produce a richer vein or cleaner ore;
The bullion stampt in your refining mind
Serves by retail to furnish half mankind.
With indignation I behold your wit
Forc'd on me, crack'd, and clipp'd, and counterfeit,
By vile pretenders, who a stock maintain
From broken scraps and filings of your brain.
Through native dross your share is hardly known,
And by short views mistook for all their own;   60
So small the gain those from your wit do reap,
Who blend it into folly's larger heap,
Like the sun's scatter'd beams which loosely pass,
When some rough hand breaks the assembling-glass.
　　Yet want your critics no just cause to rail,
Since knaves are ne'er oblig'd for what they steal.
These pad on wit's high road, and suits maintain
With those they rob, by what their trade does gain.
Thus censure seems that fiery froth which breeds
O'er the sun's face, and from his heat proceeds,   70
Crusts o'er the day, shadowing its parent beam
As antient nature's modern masters dream;
This bids some curious praters here below
Call Titan sick, because their sight is so;
And well, methinks, does this allusion fit
To scribblers, and the god of light and wit;
Those who by wild delusions entertain
A lust of rhiming for a poet's vein,
Raise envy's clouds to leave themselves in night,
But can no more obscure my CONGREVE's light   80

45-8] *Rom.* 1801, 1814

Than swarms of gnats, that wanton in a ray
Which gave them birth, can rob the world of day.
   What northern hive pour'd out these foes to wit?
Whence came these Goths to overrun the pit?
How would you blush the shameful birth to hear
Of those you so ignobly stoop to fear;
For, ill to them, long have I travell'd since
Round all the circles of impertinence,
Search'd in the nest where every worm did lie
Before it grew a city butterfly;   90
I'm sure I found them other kind of things
Than those with backs of silk and golden wings;
A search, no doubt, as curious and as wise
As virtuosoes' in dissecting flies;
For, could you think? the fiercest foes you dread,
And court in prologues, all are country-bred;
Bred in my scene, and for the poet's sins
Adjourn'd from tops and grammar to the inns;
Those beds of dung, where schoolboys sprout up beaus
Far sooner than the nobler mushroom grows: 100
These are the lords of the poetic schools,
Who preach the saucy pedantry of rules;
Those pow'rs the criticks, who may boast the odds
O'er Nile, with all its wilderness of gods;
Nor could the nations kneel to viler shapes,
Which worship'd cats, and sacrific'd to apes;
And can you think the wise forbear to laugh
At the warm zeal that breeds this golden calf?
   Haply you judge these lines severely writ
Against the proud usurpers of the pit;   110
Stay while I tell my story, short, and true;
To draw conclusions shall be left to you;
Nor need I ramble far to force a rule,
But lay the scene just here at Farnham school.
   Last year, a lad hence by his parents sent
With other cattle to the city went;
Where having cast his coat, and well pursu'd
The methods most in fashion to be lewd,

Return'd a finish'd spark this summer down,
Stock'd with the freshest gibberish of the town; 120
A jargon form'd from the lost language, wit,
Confounded in that Babel of the pit;
Form'd by diseas'd conceptions, weak, and wild,
Sick lust of souls, and an abortive child;
Born between whores and fops, by lewd compacts,
Before the play, or else between the acts:
Nor wonder, if from such polluted minds
Should spring such short and transitory kinds,
Or crazy rules to make us wits by rote
Last just as long as ev'ry cuckow's note: 130
What bungling, rusty tools, are us'd by fate!
'Twas in an evil hour to urge my hate,
My hate, whose lash just heaven has long decreed
Shall on a day make sin and folly bleed;
When man's ill genius to my presence sent
This wretch, to rouse my wrath, for ruin meant;
Who in his idiom vile, with Gray's-inn grace,
Squander'd his noisy talents to my face;
Nam'd ev'ry player on his fingers ends,
Swore all the wits were his peculiar friends; 140
Talk'd with that saucy and familiar ease
Of Wycherly, and you, and Mr. Bays;
Said, how a late report your friends had vex'd,
Who heard you meant to write heroics next;
For, tragedy, he knew, would lose you quite,
And told you so at Will's but t'other night.
  Thus are the lives of fools a sort of dreams,
Rend'ring shades, things, and substances of names;

133–4] *Rom.* 1801, 1814

133–4. *My hate, . . .* 'Thus early in life did Swift feel the efforts of his genius struggling for birth, and prognosticate its vigorous exertions against vice and folly, when arrived at maturity.'—1789.

142. *Mr. Bays.* Dryden is satirized under the name in Buckingham's *Rehearsal. Cf.* note to l. 23 of 'The Discovery', p. 63.

143–6. *Said, how a late report . . .* If suggestive of a premonitory rumour, it can hardly be supposed that, at this time, Congreve had thought of *The Mourning Bride,* 1697.

Such high companions may delusion keep,
Lords are a footboy's cronies in his sleep.   150
As a fresh miss, by fancy, face, and gown,
Render'd the topping beauty of the town,
Draws ev'ry rhyming, prating, dressing sot,
To boast of favours that he never got;
Of which, whoe'er lacks confidence to prate,
Brings his good parts and breeding in debate;
And not the meanest coxcomb you can find,
But thanks his stars, that Phyllis has been kind;
Thus prostitute my CONGREVE's name is grown
To ev'ry lew'd pretender of the town.   160
'Troth I could pity you; but this is it,
You find, to be the fashionable wit;
These are the slaves whom reputation chains,
Whose maintenance requires no help from brains.
For, should the vilest scribbler to the pit,
Whom sin and want e'er furnish'd out a wit;
Whose name must not within my lines be shewn,
Lest here it live, when perish'd with his own;
Should such a wretch usurp my CONGREVE's place,
And chuse out wits who ne'er have seen his face;   170
I'll be my life but the dull cheat would pass,
Nor need the lion's skin conceal the ass;
Yes, that beau's look, that voice, those critic ears,
Must needs be right, so well resembling theirs.
    Perish the Muse's hour, thus vainly spent
In satire, to my CONGREVE's praises meant;
In how ill season her resentments rule,
What's that to her if mankind be a fool?

                    167–8] *Rom.* 1801, 1814

167–8. *Whose name* . . . 'To this resolution Swift ever after adhered; for of the infinite multitude of libellers who personally attacked him, there is not the name mentioned of any one of them throughout his works; and thus, together with their writings, have they been consigned to eternal oblivion. How much more noble was this conduct than that of Pope's; whose low vindictive spirit prompted him to collect together in his Dunciad all the names of all the scribblers who in any shape had incurred his displeasure.'— 1789.

Happy beyond a private muse's fate,
In pleasing *all that's good among the great*,   180
Where tho' her elder sisters crowding throng,
She still is welcome with her inn'cent song;
Whom were my CONGREVE blest to see and know,
What poor regards would merit all below!
How proudly would he haste the joy to meet,
And drop his laurel at *Apollo*'s feet.
    Here by a mountain's side, a reverend cave
Gives murmuring passage to a lasting wave;
'Tis the world's wat'ry hour-glass streaming fast,
Time is no more when th'utmost drop is past;   190
Here, on a better day, some druid dwelt,
And the young Muse's early favour felt;
Druid, a name she does with pride repeat,
Confessing Albion once her darling seat;
Far in this primitive cell might we pursue
Our predecessors foot-steps, still in view;
Here would we sing—But, ah! you think I dream,
And the bad world may well believe the same;
Yes; you are all malicious standers-by,
While two fond lovers prate, the Muse and I.   200
    Since thus I wander from my first intent,
Nor am that grave adviser which I meant;
Take this short lesson from the god of bayes,
And let my friend apply it as he please:

Beat not the dirty paths where vulgar feet have trod,
    But give the vigorous fancy room.
For when like stupid alchymists you try
    To fix this nimble god,
    This volatile mercury,
The subtil spirit all flies up in fume;   210

---

180 *all that's good among the great,*] Rom. 1801, 1814   205–6] Rom. 1801, 1814

    180. *In pleasing all that's good* . . .   205–12. *Beat not* . . . *left behind.*
'This alludes to Sir W. Temple, to   'Out of an Ode I writ, inscribed The
whom he gives the name of Apollo in   Poet. The rest is lost.'—1789.
a few lines after.'—1789.

Nor shall the bubbl'd virtuoso find
More than a fade insipid mixture left behind.

Whilst thus I write, vast shoals of critics come,
And on my verse pronounce their saucy doom;
The Muse, like some bright country virgin, shows,
Fall'n by mishap amongst a knot of beaux;
They, in their lewd and fashionable prate,
Rally her dress, her language, and her gait;
Spend their base coin before the bashful maid,
Current like copper, and as often paid: 220
She, who on shady banks has joy'd to sleep
Near better animals, her father's sheep;
Sham'd and amaz'd, beholds the chatt'ring throng,
To think what cattle she has got among;
But with the odious smell and sight annoy'd,
In haste she does th'offensive herd avoid.
'Tis time to bid my friend a long farewell,
The muse retreats far in yon chrystal cell;
Faint inspiration sickens as she flies,
Like distant echo spent, the spirit dies.   230
In this descending sheet you'll haply find
Some short refreshment for your weary mind,
Nought it contains is common or unclean,
And once drawn up, is ne'er let down again.

213 Whilst] While 1801, 1814   216 amongst] among 1801, 1814   223–6]
Rom. 1801, 1814

223–6. *Sham'd and amaz'd, . . .*
avoid. 'Would not one imagine that
Swift had at this time first conceived
his idea of the Yahoos?'—1789.

231–4. *In this descending sheet . . .*
A reference to the vision of St. Peter,
Acts, x. 9–16.

OCCASIONED BY SIR W— T—'s
LATE ILLNESS AND RECOVERY.

Written December 1693

Miscellaneous Pieces, in Prose and Verse. . . . *MDCCLXXXIX.* p. 233.
Works, ed. Nichols, 1801, xviii. 415.
Works, ed. Scott, 1814, xiv. 45.

Sir William Temple was a constant sufferer from the gout and other
complaints. In 1693 he was for some time seriously ill. See Courtenay's
Memoirs of Sir William Temple, 1836, ii. 135.
The text follows that of *Miscellaneous Pieces,* 1789.

STRANGE to conceive, how the same objects strike
  At distant hours the mind with forms so like!
Whether in time, deduction's broken chain
Meets, and salutes her sister link again;
Or hunted fancy, by a circling flight,
Comes back with joy to its own seat at night;
Or whether dead imagination's ghost
Oft hovers where alive it haunted most;
Or if thought's rolling globe her circle run,
Turns up old objects to the soul her sun;   10
Or loves the muse to walk with conscious pride
O'er the glad scene whence first she rose a bride:
  Be what it will; late near yon whisp'ring stream,
Where her own TEMPLE was her darling theme;
There first the visionary sound was heard,
When to poetic view the Muse appear'd.
Such seem'd her eyes, as when an evening ray
Gives glad farewell to a tempestuous day;
Weak is the beam to dry up nature's tears,
Still ev'ry tree the pendent sorrow wears;   20
Such are the smiles where drops of chrystal show,
Approaching joy at strife with parting woe.

21, 22] Rom. 1801, 1814

As when to scare th'ungrateful or the proud
Tempests long frown, and thunder threatens loud,
Till the blest sun to give kind dawn of grace
Darts weeping beams across heaven's wat'ry face;
When soon the peaceful bow unstring'd is shown,
A sign God's dart is shot, and wrath o'erblown;
Such to unhallowed sight the Muse divine
Might seem, when first she rais'd her eyes to mine.   30
     What mortal change does in thy face appear,
Lost youth, she cry'd, since first I met thee here!
With how undecent clouds are overcast
Thy looks, when every cause of grief is past!
Unworthy the glad tidings which I bring,
Listen while the muse thus teaches thee to sing:
     As parent earth, burst by imprison'd winds,
Scatters strange agues o'er men's sickly minds,
And shakes the atheist's knees; such ghastly fear
Late I beheld on every face appear;   40
Mild Dorothea, peaceful, wise and great,
Trembling beheld the doubtful hand of fate;
Mild Dorothea, whom we both have long
Not dar'd to injure with our lowly song;
Sprung from a better world, and chosen then
The best companion for the best of men:
As some fair pile, yet spar'd by zeal and rage,
Lives pious witness of a better age;
So men may see what once was womankind,
In the fair shrine of Dorothea's mind.   50
     You that would grief describe, come here and trace
It's watery footsteps in Dorinda's face;

41. *Mild Dorothea* . . . Lady Temple, *née* Dorothy Osborne. She married Sir William Temple in 1655. See her *Letters*, ed. E. A. Parry, 1888, 1903; ed. G. C. Moore Smith, 1928. Nichols and Scott mistakenly take this to refer to Lady Giffard, for whom, even before his quarrel, Swift had no regard.

52. *Dorinda's face*. Martha, Lady Giffard, Temple's sister. The tragedy of her life was the death of her husband, Sir Thomas Giffard, in 1662, within thirteen days of their marriage. In 1709 she caused an advertisement to be inserted in *The Postman* accusing Swift of having published the third part of Temple's *Memoirs* from an unfaithful copy. Swift easily vindicated himself, and thereafter declined all further intercourse with her. See

Grief from Dorinda's face does ne'er depart
Further than its own palace in her heart:
Ah, since our fears are fled, this insolent expel,
At least confine the tyrant to his cell.
And if so black the cloud, that heaven's bright queen
Shrouds her still beams; how should the stars be seen?
Thus, when Dorinda wept, joy ev'ry face forsook,
And grief flung sables on each menial look;   60
The humble tribe mourn'd for the quick'ning soul,
That furnish'd spirit and motion through the whole;
So would earth's face turn pale, and life decay,
Should heaven suspend to act but for a day;
So nature's craz'd convulsions make us dread
That time is sick, or the world's mind is dead.—
Take, youth, these thoughts, large matter to employ
The fancy furnish'd by returning joy;
And to mistaken man these truths rehearse,
Who dare revile the integrity of verse: 70
Ah fav'rite youth, how happy is thy lot!—
But I'm deceiv'd, or thou regard'st me not;
Speak, for I wait thy answer, and expect
Thy just submission for this bold neglect.
    Unknown the forms we the high-priesthood use
At the divine appearance of the Muse,
Which to divulge might shake profane belief,
And tell the irreligion of my grief;
Grief that excus'd the tribute of my knees,
And shap'd my passion in such words as these.   80
    Malignant goddess! bane to my repose,
Thou universal cause of all my woes;
Say, whence it comes that thou art grown of late
A poor amusement for my scorn and hate;
The malice thou inspir'st I never fail
On thee to wreak the tribute when I rail;
Fools common-place thou art, their weak ensconcing fort,
Th'appeal of dullness in the last resort:

Corresp. i. 150 n.4, 170–4; iii. 297   i. 212; *Journal to Stella, passim.* Lady
n.4; *Prose Works,* ed. Temple Scott,   Giffard died in 1722.

Heaven with a parent's eye regarding earth,
Deals out to man the planet of his birth;   90
But sees thy meteor blaze about me shine,
And passing o'er, mistakes thee still for mine:
Ah, should I tell a secret yet unknown,
That thou ne'er hadst a being of thy own,
But a wild form dependent on the brain,
Scatt'ring loose features o'er the optic vein;
Troubling the chrystal fountain of the sight,
Which darts on poets eyes a trembling light;
Kindled while reason sleeps, but quickly flies,
Like antic shapes in dreams, from waking eyes: 100
In sum, a glitt'ring voice, a painted name,
A walking vapor, like thy sister fame.
But if thou be'st what thy mad vot'ries prate,
A female pow'r, loose-govern'd thoughts create;
Why near the dregs of youth perversely wilt thou stay,
So highly courted by the brisk and gay?
Wert thou right woman, thou shouldst scorn to look
On an abandon'd wretch by hopes forsook;
Forsook by hopes, ill fortune's last relief,
Assign'd for life to unremitting grief;   110
For, let heaven's wrath enlarge these weary days,
If hope e'er dawns the smallest of its rays.
Time o'er the happy takes so swift a flight,
And treads so soft, so easy, and so light,
That we the wretched, creeping far behind,
Can scarce th'impression of his foot-steps find;
Smooth as that airy nymph so subtly borne
With inoffensive feet o'er standing corn;
Which bow'd by evening-breeze with bending stalks,

112. *If hope e'er dawns* . . . 'What a miserable state of mind must Swift have been in when he wrote this! which was owing to the state of dependence in which he had always lived from his birth to that time, with but little prospect of his being relieved from it. How grating must this have been to such a proud and generous spirit!'—1789.

117–18. *Smooth as that airy nymph* . . . Virg. *Aen.* vii. 808–9. And compare Pope (who follows Dryden), *Essay on Criticism*, ll. 372–3.
'Not so, when swift Camilla scours the plain,
Flies o'er th'unbending corn, and skims along the main.'

Salutes the weary trav'ller as he walks;   120
But o'er th'afflicted with a heavy pace
Sweeps the broad scythe, and tramples on his face.
Down falls the summer's pride, and sadly shews
Nature's bare visage furrowed as he mows:
See Muse, what havock in these looks appear
These are the tyrant's trophies of a year;
Since hope his last and greatest foe is fled,
Despair and he lodge ever in its stead;
March o'er the ruin'd plain with motion slow,
Still scatt'ring desolation where they go.   130
To thee I owe that fatal bent of mind,
Still to unhappy restless thoughts inclin'd;
To thee, what oft I vainly strive to hide,
That scorn of fools, by fools mistook for pride;
From thee whatever virtue takes its rise,
Grows a misfortune, or becomes a vice;
Such were thy rules to be poetically great,
"Stoop not to int'rest, flattery, or deceit;
"Nor with hir'd thoughts be thy devotion paid;
"Learn to disdain their mercenary aid;   140
"Be this thy sure defence, thy brazen wall,
"Know no base action, at no guilt turn pale;
"And since unhappy distance thus denies
"T'expose thy soul, clad in this poor disguise;
"Since thy few ill-presented graces seem
"To breed contempt where thou hast hop'd esteem."—
    Madness like this no fancy ever seiz'd,
Still to be cheated, never to be pleas'd;
Since one false beam of joy in sickly minds
Is all the poor content delusion finds.—   150
There thy enchantment broke, and from this hour
I here renounce thy visionary pow'r;
And since thy essence on my breath depends,
Thus with a puff the whole delusion ends.

123 Down] Downs 1798

OCCASIONAL
POEMS
1698—1710

Occasional Poems

1 6 9 8 — 1 7 1 0

In this section are arranged, in chronological order, poems written after the death of Sir William Temple and before the period, 1710–14, in which Swift became a notable figure in the political world. He was between thirty and forty-three years of age. Abandoning imitative exercises he found a natural style. His movements during these years may be briefly indicated:

27 January, 1699: Sir William Temple died.
Summer of 1699 to the beginning of April, 1701: In Ireland with Lord Berkeley.
April to September, 1701: In England.
To April, 1702: In Ireland.
April to October, 1702: In England.
October, 1702, to November, 1703: In Ireland.
To May, 1704: In England.
June, 1704, to November, 1707: In Ireland.
November, 1707, to end of June, 1709: In England.
July, 1709, to end of August, 1710: In Ireland.
7 September, 1710: Arrived in London.

V E R S E S

wrote in a

Lady's *Ivory Table-Book.*

Anno. 1698.

Miscellanies in Prose and Verse, 1711, p. 351 (2nd edn., 1713, p. 349). *Miscellanies. The Last Volume,* 1727, p. 54 (1731, p. 166; 1733, p. 166). Faulkner, 1735, ii. 11 (1737, ii. 9). [Ref. F.]

The exact date of composition cannot be fixed. In the *Miscellanies* of 1711 it was assigned to 1698. No date is stated in the *Miscellanies,* 1727. Faulkner gives 1706. Deane Swift, *Essay,* 1755, p. 127, places it between 1703 and 1706. It may have been written early and revised about 1706. The text is reprinted from the *Miscellanies,* 1711.

PERUSE my Leaves thro' ev'ry Part,
　And think thou seest my owners Heart,
Scrawl'd o'er with Trifles thus, and quite
As hard, as sensless, and as light:
Expos'd to every Coxcomb's Eyes,
But hid with Caution from the Wise.
Here you may read (*Dear Charming Saint*)
Beneath (*A new Receit for Paint*)
Here in Beau-spelling (*tru tel deth*)
There in her own (*far an el breth*)　　　　10
Here (*lovely Nymph pronounce my doom*)
There (*A safe way to use Perfume*)
Here, a Page fill'd with Billet Doux;
On t'other side (*laid out for Shoes*)
(*Madam, I dye without your Grace*)
(Item, *for half a Yard of Lace.*)
Who that had Wit would place it here,
For every peeping Fop to Jear.

Title: in] on 1727, F.　　3 thus,] 1727　thus; F.　　8 *Receit*] *Receipt* 1727, F.
18 Jear.] jeer? 1727, F.

To think that your Brains Issue is
Expos'd to th' Excrement of his,   20
In power of Spittle and a Clout
When e're he please to blot it out;
And then to heighten the Disgrace
Clap his own Nonsence in the place.
Whoe're expects to hold his part
In such a Book and such a Heart,
If he be Wealthy and a Fool
Is in all Points the fittest Tool,
Of whom it may be justly said,
He's a Gold Pencil tipt with Lead.   30

The Discovery.

An. 1699.

Swift's autograph in the Pierpont Morgan Library, New York, formerly in
the Fountaine Collection.
Orrery Papers, Harvard College Library, MS. Eng. 218. 14, vol. iii,
pp. 112–14. [Ref. H.C.L.]
Miscellanies, 1746, xi. 261 (1749, xi. 261; 1751, xiv. 231).
The Works of Jonathan Swift, D.D., ed. Hawkesworth, 1755, 4to, iv (1),
298.
Essay, Deane Swift, 1755, p. 110. [Ref. D.S.]

Swift arrived in Dublin with Lord Berkeley in the summer of 1699,
having, on the voyage, acted both as secretary and chaplain. According to
his own statement it was intended that he should continue to hold both
offices. It seems doubtful whether this could have been Lord Berkeley's
intention. After the arrival of the party in Dublin Swift was superseded
as secretary by Arthur Bushe, who had not travelled over with Berkeley
(B.M., Add. MS. 28,884. f. 167; *Corresp.* i. 31 n.[1]). Later Swift was
further incensed by Bushe, to whom he believed Dr. John Bolton (see
p. 72 n.) was indebted for the Deanery of Derry, a preferment he desired for
himself. 'The Discovery' was written towards the end of 1699; or at least
before February, 1700, when Bolton was presented to the Deanery of

19, 20] *Om.* 1727, F.   30 Gold] Golden 1727   *Gold* F.   30 Lead.]
1727 *Lead.* F.
The 1731 and 1733 12mo. editions follow the 1727 readings.

Derry, for the satire is not markedly bitter. Swift's manuscript gives the date as 'An. 1699.'; and this is the date stated by Deane Swift in his *Essay*.

On the whole incident see further Forster, *Life*, pp. 110–11; Craik, *Life*, 2nd edn., i. 98–100; *Corresp.* i. 33 n.[1]. The account of the transaction given by Sheridan, *Life*, pp. 33–4, is based on hearsay, and its details are open to doubt.

The text is printed from the Fountaine MS., which is Swift's hand with an attempt, not unnatural, at disguise. Swift was copying from an earlier draft. Line 2, blotted out, originally stood as in the printed version; and the first line of the tenth stanza was copied four lines out of place, and then scratched out. The H.C.L. MS., in a clerical hand, has only one verbal variant. Both manuscripts divide the stanzas. There are no stanza divisions in the printed versions. Variants from Swift's spelling and punctuation are ignored in the apparatus, save in two instances.

When wise L^d B— first came here,
We Irish Folks expected wonders,
Nor thought to find so great a Peer
E'er a week pas't committing Blunders:

Till on a Day cut out by Fate,
When Folks came thick to make their Court
Out slipp't a Mystery of State
To give the Town and Country Sport.

Now Enter *Bush with new State-Airs,   *my L^{ds} wise
                                        Secretary
His Lordship's premier Ministre,   10
And who in all profound Affairs   *always taken
Is held as needfull as His Glyster   before my L^d
                                          went to Council

2 We Irish Folks] We Irish Fools H.C.L. Statesmen and Mob *printed versions*
9 Enter] enter H.C.L. enters *printed versions*   12 Is] H.C.L., 1749, 1751, 1755, D.S. It's 1746

1. L^d B—. Hawkesworth and Deane Swift, in 1755, were the first to print the name of Berkeley in full. Charles, second Earl of Berkeley, came to Ireland as Lord Justice in 1699. He returned to England in April 1701, and virtually retired from public life. He died at Berkeley Castle, in Gloucestershire, 24 Sept., 1710. A Latin epitaph to his memory was composed by Swift (see p. 1132). In a copy of Macky's *Characters* Swift characterized his former patron as 'Intolerably lazy and indolent, and somewhat covetous' (*Prose Works*, ed. Temple Scott, x. 279). Swift, however, was several times at Cranford, as the guest of Berkeley, who does not seem to have divined the opinion in which he was held. His daughter, Elizabeth, who became Lady Betty Germain, was Swift's lifelong friend and correspondent (see p. 76).

9, 12. The marginal notes by Swift

With Head reclining on his Shoulder,
He deals, and Hears mysterious Chat;
While every ignorant Beholder
Asks of his Neighbor; Who is that?

With this He putt up to My L——d
The Courtiers kept their Distance due,
He twitcht his sleeve, and stole a word,
Then to a Corner both withdrew.   20

Imagine now My L——d and Bu——sh
Whisp'ring in Junto most profound,
Like good King Phys: and good King Ush:
While all the rest stood gaping round

At length, a spark not too well bred
Of forward Face, and Ear acute,
Advanc't on tiptoe, lean'd his Head
To overheare the grand Dispute.

To learn what Northern Kings design,
Or from Whitehall some new Express,   30
Papists disarm'd, or Fall of Coin,
For sure (thought He) it can't be less.

My L^d, s^d Bush, a Friend and I
Disguis'd in two old thredbare Coats
Ere Mornings dawn stole out to spy
How Markets went for Hey and Oats.

With that he draws two Handfulls out,
The one was Oats, the other Hay,
Putts This to's Excellency's Snout,
And begs, He would the other weigh.   40

22 Junto] H.C.L., D.S. Junta *remainder*

appear also in the H.C.L. MS., and
in the printed versions. It may be
noted, further, that the H.C.L. MS.
follows the Fountaine MS. save for one
word, 'Fools' for 'Folks', l. 2; and

even to the spelling 'Branford', l. 48.
23. *Phys . . . Ush.* The two usurping
Kings of Buckingham's satire, *The
Rehearsal,* 1672.

My Lord seems pleas'd, but still directs
By all means to bring down the Rates,
Then with a Congee circumflex
Bush smiling round on all, retreats

Our Listner stood a while confus'd,
But gath'ring spirits, wisely ran for't,
Enrag'd to see the World abus'd
By two such whisp'ring Kings of Branford.

The P R O B L E M.

Orrery Papers, Harvard College Library, MS. Eng. 218. 14, vol. iii, pp. 110–12.
Miscellanies, 1746, xi. 263 (1749, xi. 263; 1751, xiv. 233).
The Works of Jonathan Swift, D.D., ed. Hawkesworth, 1755, 4to, iv (1), 299.

A sub-title to this poem, as first printed, runs, '*That my Lord B—ly stinks, when he's in Love—*', and the satire has been interpreted as an attack upon Berkeley in consequence of Swift's anger at the preferment of Bolton to the Deanery of Derry. But Swift never broke off relationship with Berkeley, despite no great love for him; and it is a little difficult to believe that the satire of 'The Problem' was directed against a man with whom he was on sufficiently friendly terms (see n. p. 62, l. 1). The satire of 'The Discovery' is comparatively harmless. Moreover, immediately before coming to Ireland, as chaplain to Berkeley, Swift conceived himself to have been injured by a man of very different character, Henry Sidney, Earl of Romney, who had promised to prefer to the King his petition for a prebend of Canterbury or Westminster, and gone no further in the matter (*Essay,* Deane Swift, 1755, Appendix, p. 50; Forster, *Life,* pp. 15–16). See also Sheridan, *Life,* 1784, pp. 32–3. He never lost his dislike of Romney, describing him in the Fragment of Autobiography as 'an old, vicious, illiterate rake, without any sense of truth or honour'; and in a note to Macky's *Characters* (*Prose Works,* ed. Temple Scott, x. 274) denied him any honesty or capacity. It is therefore of the utmost significance that a manuscript copy of this poem, among the Orrery Papers at Harvard

48 Branford.] H.C.L. *Brentford. printed versions*

48. *whisp'ring Kings. The Rehearsal,*   are always whispering to each other.
i. 2, and ii. 1. The usurping Kings

carries the sub-title: 'That Sidney E. of R—mn—y st—ks, when he is
in Love'. In addition, the satire is more directly applicable to Romney
than to Berkeley.

Henry Sidney, fourth and youngest son of Robert, second Earl of
Leicester, was born at Paris in 1641. While envoy at The Hague, 1679–
81, he gained the confidence of William of Orange. He carried over the
secret invitation to William, and accompanied him to England. In 1692
he was Lord Lieutenant of Ireland, where he acquitted himself in-
competently, and was recalled. Nevertheless he was created Earl of Romney in 1694. He died in 1704. The handsomest man of his time, he was a
notorious profligate, and the terror of husbands. He was the cause of an
estrangement between the Duke and Duchess of York; and maintained a
long intrigue with the wife of his nephew Sunderland. See *Diary* and
letters, edited in two volumes, 1843, by R. W. Blencowe.

In 'The Problem' the object of the satire is described as 'So sweet a
Passion', and 'an universal Lover'. Three women are named as his loves.
All this applies much more aptly to the libertine bachelor, Romney, than to
Berkeley. On the other hand l. 35, 'Ambitious of a Regent's Heart', may
be thought more appropriate to Berkeley, who was one of the Lords
Justices with the Duke of Bolton and Lord Galway; but Romney had served
in the same capacity, and as Lord Lieutenant. On the face of it, therefore,
it is more than probable that Orrery is right in his attribution of the satire.
The poem was not printed till after Swift's death, and there is no evidence
for the suggestion that it was directed against Berkeley.

The Harvard MS. is more careful than the first printed text, and is here
used.

> Did ever Problem thus perplex,
> Or more employ the Female Sex?
> So sweet a Passion who cou'd think,
> Jove ever form'd to make a S—k?
> The Ladys vow, and swear they'll try,
> Whether it be a Truth, or Lye.
> Love's Fire, it seems, like inward Heat,
> Works in my Lord by St—l and Sweat,
> Which brings a St—k from ev'ry Pore,
> And from behind, and from before;   10
> Yet, what is wonderful to tell it,
> None but the Fav'rite Nymph can smell it.
> But now, to solve the Nat'ral Cause
> By sober, Philosophick Laws,

4 S—k?] Stink? 1746, 1749, 1751   7] *N.P.* 1746, 1749, 1751   8 St—l]
Stool 1746, 1749, 1751   9 St—k] Stink 1746, 1749, 1751   13] *No
break* 1746, 1749, 1751

Whether all Passions, when in Ferment,
Work out, as Anger does in Vermin?
So, when a Weasel you torment,
You find his Passion by his Scent.
We read of Kings, who in a Fright,
Tho' on a Throne, wou'd fall to sh—.   20
Beside all this, deep Scholars know,
That the main String of Cupid's Bow,
Once on a Time, was an A— Gut,
Now to a nobler Office put,
By Favour, or Desert preferr'd
From giving Passage to a T—.
But still, tho' fixt among the Stars,
Does sympathize with Human A—.
Thus when you feel an hard-bound B—
Conclude Love's Bow-String at full Stretch;   30
Till the kind L—seness comes, and then
Conclude the Bow relax'd again.
     And now the Ladys all are bent,
To try the great Experiment;
Ambitious of a Regent's Heart
Spread all their Charms to catch a F—;
Watching the first unsav'ry Wind,   ·
Some ply before, and some behind.
My Lord, on Fire amidst the Dames,
F—s like a Laurel in the Flames.   40
The Fair approach the speaking Part,
To try the Back-way to his Heart;
For, as when we a Gun discharge,
Altho' the Bore be ne'er so large,
Before the Flame from Muzzle burst,
Just at the Breech it flashes first:
So from my Lord his Passion broke,
He f—ted first, and then he spoke.
     The Ladys vanish, in the Smother,
To confer Notes with one another;   50

16 Vermin?] Vermin; 1746   29 B—] Breech, 1746, 1749, 1751   31
L—seness] Looseness 1746, 1749, 1751

And now they all agree, to name
Whom each one thought the happy Dame:
Quoth Neal, whate'er the rest may think,
I'm sure, 'twas I that smelt the S—k.
You smell the S—k? by — you lye,
Quoth Ross, for, I'll be sworn, 'twas I.
Ladys, quoth Levens, pray forbear,
Let's not fall out; We all had Share.
And, by the most we can discover,
My Lord's an universal Lover.   60

54 S—k.] Stink. 1746, 1749, 1751   55 S—k? by —] Stink, by G— 1746,
1749, 1751   59 we] I 1746 *and remainder*

53. *Neal.* Mary, daughter of Charles, Duke of Bolton, who married Colonel Charles O'Neill, a descendant of the O'Neills who were Kings of Ulster.

56. *Ross.* Sir Richard Parsons, grandson of the Sir William Parsons who was a Lord Justice of Ireland, was created Baron of Oxmantown and Viscount Rosse in 1681. His third wife, whom he married in 1685, was Elizabeth, eldest daughter of Sir George Hamilton and niece of Sarah, Duchess of Marlborough.

57. *Levens.* Richard Levinge, born in Staffordshire, was called to the bar at the Inner Temple in 1678. He went over to Ireland, and had a distinguished career. He was successively M.P. for Blessington, Longford, and Kilkenny city. From 1690 to 1695 he was Solicitor-General of Ireland; and for a second time 1704–9. Speaker of the Irish House of Commons 1692–5; Attorney-General 1711–14; Lord Chief Justice of the Common Pleas 1720 to his death in 1724. He was knighted in 1692, and created a baronet in 1704. The 'Levens' referred to would be his first wife, Mary, daughter of Gawen Corbyn of London. G.E.C., *Complete Baronetage,* iv. 234–5; *D.N.B.* xxxiii. 158; Ball, *Judges in Ireland,* ii. 195-6.

TO THEIR

EXCELLENCIES

THE

Lords Justices of IRELAND.

The Humble Petition of Frances Harris,

Who must Starve, and Die a Maid if it miscarries.

Anno. 1700.

Baucis and Philemon; . . . Together with Mrs. Harris's Earnest Petition. . . .
    London: . . . H. Hills, . . . 1709 (and 1710), p. 9. [Ref. H.]
Works of . . . Rochester and Roscommon. . . . To which is added, a Collection
    of Miscellany Poems. . . . London: . . . Curll, . . . 1709. p. 175.
A Meditation upon a Broom-Stick, and Somewhat Beside; . . . London: . . .
    Curll, . . . 1710. p. 19. [Ref. C.]
The Whimsical Medley, ii. 368. (Copied from a printed edition.)
Miscellanies, 1711, p. 353 (2nd edn., 1713, p. 351).
A Collection of Original Poems, . . . London: . . . Curll, . . . 1714.
The Bee. A Collection of Choice Poems. Part I. . . . London. . . . T. Ilive:
    . . . MDCCXV. p. 20.
Miscellanies. The Last Volume, 1727, p. 56. (One manuscript correction in
    Swift's own copy of this volume.)
Faulkner, 1735, ii. 1 (1737, ii. 1). [Ref. F.]

    Deane Swift, *Essay,* 1755, p. 119 n., is certainly wrong in placing this
poem as early as 1699. The *Miscellanies,* 1711, gives the date as 1700, and
Faulkner as 1701. It was composed early in 1701 during the latter part of
Berkeley's residence in Ireland. The arrival of the 'Earl of Drogheda, who
was one of the lords justices designated to succeed Berkeley and his col-
league, . . . is mentioned in the Petition as imminent' (Ball, *Swift's Verse,*
p. 46). After some delay Berkeley left Ireland early in April, 1701.
    Swift's poem on Mrs. Harris, one of Lady Berkeley's gentlewomen,
passed in manuscript for nine years, and was then published by the pirate
printers, Hills and Curll. *A Meditation upon a Broom-Stick* was published
in April, 1710.
    The text here printed is that of the *Miscellanies,* 1711. The unauthorized

publications of Hills and Curll generally agree against 1711, 1727, and Faulkner. The poem, as it appeared in *The Bee*, was printed from a Hills edition.

Humbly Sheweth.

THAT I went to warm my self in Lady *Betty*'s Chamber, because I was cold,
And I had in a Purse, seven Pound, four Shillings and six Pence, besides Farthings, in Money, and Gold;
So because I had been buying things for my *Lady* last Night,
I was resolved to tell my Money, to see if it was right:
Now you must know, because my Trunk has a very bad Lock,
Therefore all the Money, I have, which, *God* knows, is a very small Stock,
I keep in a Pocket ty'd about my Middle, next my Smock.
So when I went to put up my Purse, as *God* would have it, my Smock was unript,
And, instead of putting it into my Pocket, down it slipt:
Then the Bell rung, and I went down to put my *Lady* to Bed,   10
And, *God* knows, I thought my Money was as safe as my Maidenhead.
So when I came up again, I found my Pocket feel very light,
But when I search'd, and miss'd my Purse, *Lord!* I thought I should have sunk outright:

Title: THE *Lords Justices of* IRELAND.] &c. H., C.   2 seven Pound, four Shillings] 7*l.* and 4*s.* H.   seven Pound, and four Shillings, C.   2 and six Pence,] *om.* H.   7 a Pocket] H., C.   my Pocket 1713, 1727, F.   10 down] 1727, F. down stairs H.   down Stairs C.   11 And,] 1727, F.   When, H., C.   12 feel] 1727, F. *om.* H., C.

Title: Lords Justices . . . The Earl of Berkeley and the Earl of Galway. For the latter see *D.N.B.* xxxvii. 17. He became commander of the English forces in Portugal, and a rival in popular favour of Peterborough, Swift's friend. He was again for a brief period, 1715–16, a Lord Justice in Ireland.

Lord! Madam, says *Mary*, how d'ye do? Indeed, says I,
    never worse;
But pray, *Mary*, can you tell what I have done with my
    Purse!
Lord help me, said *Mary*, I never stirr'd out of this Place!
Nay, said I, I had it in Lady *Betty*'s Chamber, that's a plain
    Case.
So *Mary* got me to Bed, and cover'd me up warm,
However, she stole away my Garters, that I might do
    my self no Harm:
So I tumbl'd and toss'd all Night, as you may very well
    think,   20
But hardly ever set my Eyes together, or slept a Wink.
So I was a-dream'd, methought, that we went and search'd
    the Folks round,
And in a Corner of Mrs. *Dukes*'s Box, ty'd in a Rag, the
    Money was found.
So next Morning we told *Whittle*, and he fell a Swearing;
Then my Dame *Wadgar* came, and she, you know, is
    thick of Hearing;
Dame, said I, as loud as I could bawl, do you know what
    a Loss I have had?
Nay, said she, my Lord *Collway*'s Folks are all very sad,
For my Lord *Dromedary* comes a *Tuesday* without fail;
Pugh! said I, but that's not the Business that I ail.
Says *Cary*, says he, I have been a Servant this Five and
    Twenty Years, come Spring,   30
And in all the Places I liv'd, I never heard of such a
    Thing.

14 says I,] said I, F.   22 a-dream'd,] 1727, F. dream'd, H., C.   25 Then
my Dame *Wadgar*] 1727, F.   Then Mrs. *Wadgar* H., C.   25 of Hearing;]
1727, F. o'hearing; H. o'Hearing; C.   29 that] 1727, F. *om*. H., C.

17. *Lady Betty's Chamber*] Writing
to Swift, 19 Sept., 1730, Lady Elizabeth Germain, twenty-nine years
later, recalls this line. See *Corresp*. iv.
165.

23. *Mrs. Dukes's* . . . Wife to one of
the footmen.

24. *Whittle*. Valet to the Earl of
Berkeley.

25. *Dame Wadgar*. The old deaf
housekeeper.

27. *Collway's* . . . Galway's.

28. *Dromedary*. Drogheda, one of
the Lords Justices appointed in place
of Berkeley and Galway.

30. *Cary*. Clerk of the Kitchen.

Yes, says the *Steward*, I remember when I was at my
    Lady *Shrewsbury's*,
Such a thing as this happen'd, just about the time of
    Goosberries.
So I went to the Party suspected, and I found her full of
    Grief;
(Now you must know, of all Things in the World, I hate
    a Thief.)
However, I was resolv'd to bring the Discourse slily
    about,
Mrs. *Dukes*, said I, here's an ugly Accident has happen'd
    out;
'Tis not that I value the Money three Skips of a Louse;
But the Thing I stand upon, is the Credit of the
    House;
'Tis true, seven Pound, four Shillings, and six Pence,
    makes a great Hole in my Wages,   40
Besides, as they say, Service is no Inheritance in these
    Ages.
Now, Mrs. *Dukes*, you know, and every Body under-
    stands,
That tho' 'tis hard to judge, yet Money can't go without
    Hands.
The *Devil* take me, said she, (blessing her self,) if I ever
    saw't!
So she roar'd like a *Bedlam*, as tho' I had call'd her all
    to naught;
So you know, what could I say to her any more,
I e'en left her, and came away as wise as I was before.

---

32 I remember] 1727, F. *om.* H., C.   34 I found] 1727, F. found H., C.
35 you must know,] 1727, F.   you know, H., C., *and also omit brackets*
40 seven Pound, four Shillings,] 7*l.* and 4*s.* H. seven Pound, and four Shillings,
C.   43 judge, yet Money] 1727, F. judge—Mony H. judge—Money C.
44 I ever] ever I H., C., 1727, F.   45 tho'] H., C., 1727, thof F.   45 all]
Om. H., C.

    32. *Steward*. His name was Ferris.
Referred to as a 'scoundrel dog' by
Swift, *Journal to Stella*, 21 Dec., 1710.
    38. *three Skips of a Louse*. According
to a note in Faulkner's edition, 1735,
this was a common saying of Mrs.
Harris's.

Well: But then they would have had me gone to the
   Cunning Man;
No, said I, 'tis the same Thing, the *Chaplain* will be here
   anon.
So the *Chaplain* came in; now the Servants say, he is my
   Sweet-heart,   50
Because he's always in my Chamber, and I always take
   his Part;
So, as the *Devil* would have it, before I was aware, out I
   blunder'd,
Parson, said I, can you cast a *Nativity*, when a Body's
   plunder'd?
(Now you must know, he hates to be call'd *Parson*, like
   the *Devil*.)
Truly, says he, Mrs. *Nab*, it might become you to be
   more civil:
If your Money be gone, as a Learned *Divine* says, d'ye see,
You are no *Text* for my Handling, so take that from me:
I was never taken for a *Conjurer* before, I'd have you to
   know.
Lord, said I, don't be angry, I'm sure I never thought
   you so;
You know, I honour the Cloth, I design to be a *Parson*'s
   Wife,   60
I never took one in *Your Coat* for a *Conjurer* in all my
   Life.
With that, he twisted his Girdle at me like a Rope, as
   who should say,
Now you may go hang your self for me, and so went away.

50 in; now] H., C.   in: Now 1727   in. Now F.   54] H., C. *omit brackets*
55 says] C. 1727, F.   said H., Curll *Miscellany Poems*, 1709   57 so take]
1727, F.   take H., C.   59 I'm] H., C.   I am 1713, 1727, F.   62
at me] *Om.* H., C.

48. *Cunning Man.* A fortune-teller;
one who professes the power of dis-
covering stolen goods.
49. *the Chaplain.* Swift himself.
56. *Learned Divine.* Said to be a
reference to Dr. John Bolton, who,
through the instrumentality of Bushe

(see p. 61), was preferred to the
Deanery of Derry, which Swift re-
garded as his due. Bolton died as
Dean of Derry in 1724; and was suc-
ceeded by Swift's friend, George
Berkeley, the philosopher, afterwards
Bishop of Cloyne.

Well; I thought I should have swoon'd; *Lord*, said I,
    what shall I do?
I have lost my *Money*, and shall lose my *True-Love* too.
Then my *Lord* call'd me; *Harry*, said my *Lord*, don't cry,
I'll give something towards thy Loss; and says my *Lady*,
    so will I.
Oh but, said I, what if after all my Chaplain won't
    come to?
For that, he said, (an't please your *Excellencies*) I must
    Petition You.

The Premises tenderly consider'd, I desire your *Excel-*
    lencies Protection,   70
And that I may have a Share in next *Sunday*'s Collection:
And over and above, that I may have your *Excellencies*
    Letter,
With an Order for the *Chaplain* aforesaid; or instead of
    Him, a Better:
And then your poor *Petitioner*, both Night and Day,
Or the *Chaplain*, (for 'tis his *Trade*) as in Duty bound,
    shall ever *Pray*.

64 swoon'd;] H., C., 1727 swoon'd: F.   65 shall] H., C., 1727   I shall
F.   66 Then my] So, my F.   66 *Harry*,] 1727, F.   *Harris*, H., C.
68 my] the F.   68 *come to?*] 1727, F.   come to? H., C.   75 shall ever
Pray.] 1727   shall ever *pray*. F.   shall *Pray* H., C.   H., C., *also omit brackets*
    Swift, in his own copy of the *Miscellanies. Last Vol.*, 1727, makes one correction
in this poem, altering 'my', in line 68, to 'the'; and this correction appears in
Faulkner's edition.
    In the miscellaneous poems added to the *Works of the Earls of Rochester and
Roscommon*, 1709, and in the *Collection of Original Poems*, 1714, Curll follows the
text printed in *A Meditation upon a Broom-Stick*.

A
B A L L A D
on the Game of TRAFFICK.

Volume VIII. of the Author's Works, . . . *Dublin:* . . . *Faulkner*,
M,DCC,XLVI. p. 312. [Ref. F.]
Miscellanies, 1746, xi. 240 (1749, xi. 240; 1751, xiv. 215). [Refs. 1746,
1751.]
The Works of Jonathan Swift, D.D., ed. Hawkesworth, 1755, 4to, iv (1),
282.

This poem, which is closely connected with that which follows, was not
printed till 1746, in the year after Swift's death, although its sequel appeared in 1711, under the author's supervision. Faulkner, misled by the
references to Berkeley's household, assigned a wrong date to the poem,
adding, under the title, '*Written at the Castle of* Dublin, *in the Time of the
Earl of* Berkeley's *Government*'. Its immediate sequel, the 'Ballad to the
Tune of the Cutpurse', is dated '*August, 1702.*' in the *Miscellanies* of 1711;
and the mention of Jack Howe in the 'Ballad on the Game of Traffick'
shows that this poem was probably written after the election of July, 1702.
The family scene depicted took place in Berkeley Castle, not Dublin
Castle, and in 1702. It is known that Swift visited Lord Berkeley, after
he had ceased to be his chaplain (see p. 62 n.); and he was in England
between April and October, 1702.

Faulkner's text is printed.

MY Lord to find out who must deal
  Delivers Cards about,
But the first Knave does seldom fail
  To find the *Doctor* out.

But then his *Honour* cry'd, Godzooks!
  And seem'd to knit his Brow;
For on a Knave he never looks
  But H' thinks upon *Jack How*.

8. *Jack How*. John Grubham Howe, 1657–1722. *D.N.B.* xxviii. 89. A notorious politician of his day. At first a strong Whig, he became a violent Tory from 1692 onward. He was returned for Gloucestershire in 1698, and again in January, 1701; but at the election of December, 1701, the Whigs succeeded in ejecting him. In July, 1702, he was returned for four constituencies.

My *Lady* tho' she is no Player
  Some bungling Partner takes,   10
And wedg'd in Corner of a Chair
  Takes Snuff, and holds the Stakes.

Dame *Floyd* looks out in grave Suspence
  For Pair-royals and Sequents;
But wisely cautious of her Pence,
  The Castle seldom frequents.

Quoth *Herries*, fairly putting Cases,
  I'd won it on my Word,
If I had but a Pair of Aces,
  And could pick up a Third.   20

But *Weston* has a new-cast Gown
  On *Sundays* to be fine in,
And if she can but win a *Crown*,
  'Twill just new dye the Lining.

"With these is Parson *Swift*,
  "Not knowing how to spend his Time,
"Does make a wretched Shift,
  "To deafen 'em with Puns and Rhime.

9 My *Lady* tho'] My *Lady,* tho' 1746, 1751 My *lady,* though 1755   19 but]
1755, *and later editions*   put F., 1746, 1751   23 And if] 1746   And, if
1751, 1755   28 'em] them 1746, 1751, 1755

13. *Dame Floyd.* Dr. Elrington Ball (*Swift's Verse*, p. 52) suggests that this lady was probably the mother of Mrs. Biddy Floyd, companion to Lady Betty Germain. See the verses addressed 'To Mrs. Biddy Floyd', p. 117.

17. *Herries.* The Mrs. Frances Harris of the preceding poem.

21. *Weston.* Apparently another gentlewoman attached to Berkeley's household.

25–8. Faulkner, 1746, has the following note: '*Lady* Betty Berkeley *finding this Ballad in the Author's Room unfinished, she underwrit the last Stanza, and left the Paper where she had found it; which occasioned the following Song, that the Author wrote in a counterfeit Hand, as if a third Person had done it.*'

Lady B——— B——— *finding in
the Authors* R**o**om *some Verses
Unfinished, underwrit a* Stanza
*of her own, with Railery upon
him, which gave Occasion to this
Ballade.*

August, 1702.

To the Tune of the Cutpurse.

The Whimsical Medley, i. Appendix, p. 51 (no significant variants).
Miscellanies, 1711, p. 361 (2nd edn., 1713, p. 359).
Miscellanies. The Last Volume, 1727, p. 65 (1731, p. 174; 1733, p. 174).
Faulkner, 1735, ii. 9 (1737, ii. 7). [Ref. F.]
Miscellanies, 1742, iv. 73.

Lady Betty Berkeley occasioned these verses by adding a stanza to the
last poem. Born in 1680, she was the second daughter of the Earl of
Berkeley. At the age of twenty-six she married Sir John Germain, a rake
and soldier of fortune, reputed to be the son of William II, Prince of
Orange. She remained one of Swift's firmest friends, and a constant correspondent. See especially *Corresp.*, vols. iv and v *passim*; also *D.N.B.* xxi.
230. She lived a widow for over fifty years, dying in 1769. *Cf.* p. 1069.

Swift's verses are modelled upon the song of Nightingale, the ballad-
singer, in Ben Jonson's *Bartholomew Fair,* iii. i.

The text printed is that of the *Miscellanies,* 1711. Swift's reasons for
omitting from that collection the poem which prompted it are obvious.
Swift made one correction in his copy of the *Miscellanies,* 1727.

I.

ONCE on a time, as old Stories reherse,
A Fryer would needs show his Talent in *Latin;*
But was sorely put to't in the midst of a Verse,
 Because he could find no Word to come pat in.
  Then all in the Place
  He left a void Space,

5 all in the Place] F. at the Place 1727, 1742 (*corrected back to* 'all in the Place'
by Swift, *in his copy of Miscellanies, Last Vol.* 1727)

And so went to Bed in a desperate Case.
When, Behold the next Morning, a wonderful Riddle,
He found it was strangely fill'd in the Middle.

Cho. *Let Censuring Criticks then think what they list on't,* 10
    Who would not Write Verses with such an assistant.

II.

This put me the Fryar into an Amazement,
   For he wisely consider'd it must be a Sprite,
That came through the Key-Hole, or in at the Casement,
   And it needs must be one that could both Read and
          Write:
        Yet he did not know
        If it were Friend or Foe,
   Or whether it came from Above or Below.
Howe'er it was civil in Angel or Elf,
For he ne're could have fill'd it so well of himself.   20

Cho. *Let Censuring,* &c.

III.

Even so Master Doctor had Puzzled his Brains
   In making a Ballad, but was at a Stand,
He had mixt little Wit with a great deal of Pains,
   When he found a new Help from Invisible Hand.
      Then Good Dr. *S——*
      Pay Thanks for the Gift,
   For you freely must own you were at a Dead lift;
And tho' some Malicious Young Spirit did do't,
You may know by the Hand, it had no Cloven Foot.   30

Cho. *Let Censuring Criticks then think what they list on't,*
    Who would not Write Verses with such an assistant.

8 When, Behold] When, behold 1713 When behold 1727, F. when behold 1742
9 fill'd] fill'd up 1727, F., 1742
The *Miscellanies* 1731, 1733, follow the 1727 readings.

Vanbrug's House.

An. 1703.

Built from the burnt Ruins of Whitehall.

In 1703 Whitehall was partially burnt down, and John Vanbrugh set out to build himself a house on the site. Swift, who had been meeting Vanbrugh at the coffee-houses, composed a poem jeering at his gifts as an architect, reflecting, at the same time, upon the dramatic verse of the period.

The version of the poem published by Swift in the *Miscellanies*, 1711, was a revision, probably made in 1708. John Forster discovered an earlier version, in manuscript, at Narford, the paternal home of the Fountaine family, and quoted it in part (*Life of Swift*, pp. 163–4). This manuscript, with others in Swift's hand, is now in the Pierpont Morgan Library (see p. xlix). A transcript of the earlier version, in the hand of Charles Ford, is preserved among the Ford papers, and has been printed by Professor D. Nichol Smith (*Letters of Jonathan Swift to Charles Ford*, 1935, pp. 179–82). Ford's transcript omits the date from the title.

The earlier version of the poem is here printed for the first time, completely and exactly, from Swift's manuscript. The variants of Ford's transcript are indicated by 'Ford'. The printed version appears below, p. 105.

Sir Andrew Fountaine, 1676–1753, probably made Swift's acquaintance in early days, when an official at the viceregal court in Dublin during the lieutenancy of Lord Pembroke, and their friendship continued till the death of Queen Anne, after which no communication passed between them for many years. He is frequently mentioned in the *Journal to Stella*. Fountaine was given favoured positions in the Hanoverian court, which would not commend him to his old friend; and in 1727 he was appointed Warden of the Mint in succession to Sir Isaac Newton. He formed a noble collection of coins, pictures, and objects of art. An authority on early English coins, his remarkable 'Numismata Anglo-Saxonica et Anglo-Danica breviter illustrata' was included in Hickes's great *Thesaurus*, 1705. The identification of Fountaine with 'Annius' of the *Dunciad* (iv. 347 ff.) is questionable.

Scott, *Works*, 1814, i. 46–9, on doubtful evidence, attributes a poem, 'On the Burning of Whitehall, in 1697', to Swift (see p. 1069). The old palace was burnt to the ground on the 4th of January, 1698.

In addition to a revised version of 'Vanbrug's House', Swift again attacked Vanbrugh in 'The History of Vanbrug's House' (see p. 85).

[p. 1] In times of old, when Time was young,
And Poets their own Verses sung,
A Song could draw a Stone or Beam,
That now would overload a Team,
Lead them a Dance of many a Mile,
Then rear 'em to a goodly Pile,
Each Number had it's diff'rent Power;
Heroick Strains could build a Tower;
Sonnets and Elegyes to Chloris
Would raise a House about two Storyes;   10
A Lyrick Ode would Slate; a Catch
Would Tile; an Epigram would Thatch.
    Now Poets find this Art is lost,
Both to their own and Landlord's Cost;
Not one of all the tunefull Throng
Can hire a Lodging for a Song;
For Jove consider'd well the Case,
That Poets were a numerous Race,
And if they all had Power to build,
The Earth would very soon be filld: 20
[p. 2] Materials would be quickly spent,
And Houses would not give a Rent.
The God of Wealth was therefore made
Sole Patron of the building Trade,
Leaving to Wits the spatious Air,
With License to build Castles there;
And 'tis conceiv'd, their old Pretence
To lodge in Garrats comes from thence.
    There is a Worm by Phœbus bred,
By Leaves of Mulberry is fed;   30
Which unprovided where to dwell,
Consumes it self to weave a Cell.
Then curious Hands this Texture take,
And for themselves fine Garments make.

---

6 rear 'em] raise them Ford   13] Ford *does not mark a new paragraph*
27 And 'tis conceiv'd,] Swift *first wrote, and blotted out,* 'In right whereof,'
28 comes] came Ford   30 By] On Ford

Mean time a Pair of awkward Things
Grew to his Back instead of Wings;
He flutters when he Thinks he flyes,
Then sheds about his Spaun, and dyes.
    Just such an Insect of the Age
Is he that scribbles for the Stage;   40
His Birth he does from Phœbus raise,
And feeds upon imagin'd Bays:

[p. 3] Throws all his Witt and Hours away
In twisting up an ill-spun Play:
This gives him Lodging, and provides
A Stock of tawdry Stuff besides,
With the unravelld Shreds of which
The Under-wits adorn their Speech.
And now he spreads his little Fans,
(For all the Muses Geese are Swans)   50
And borne on fancy's Pinions, thinks,
He soars sublimest when he Sinks:
But scatt'ring round his Fly-blows, dyes;
Whence Broods of insect Poets rise.
    Premising thus in Modern way
The greater half I had to say,
Sing Muse the House of Poet Van
In higher Strain than we began.
    Van, (for 'tis fit the Reader know it)
Is both a Herald and a Poet;   60
No wonder then, if nicely skill'd
In each Capacity to Build:
As Herald, he can in a Day
Repair a House gone to decay;

[p. 4] Or by Atchievments, Arms, Device
Erect a new one in a Trice;

35 Mean time] Mean while Ford   39] Ford *does not mark a new paragraph*
45 gives] *Written above the line in place of* 'pays' *struck out*   47 Shreds]
Written above the line in place of 'Scraps' *struck out*   49–50] *Line 49 first ran*
'Apollo's Bird now spreads his Fans,' *the reading followed in Ford's transcript.*
Swift *has drawn a perpendicular stroke in the right-hand margin against ll. 49/50,
and written* 'Thats not right'. *The first three words of l. 49 are struck out, and above*
Swift *has written* 'And now he ... little'.   59] Ford *does not mark a new paragraph*

And Poets if they had their Due,
By antient Right are Builders too.
This made him to Apollo pray
For Leave to build the Poet's Way.   70
His Pray'r was granted, for the God
Consented with the usuall Nod.
After hard Throws of many a Day
Van was deliver'd of a Play,
Which in due time brought forth a House;
Just as the Mountain did the Mouse;
One Story high, one postern Door,
And one small Chamber on a Floor.
Born like a Phœnix from the Flame,
But neither Bulk nor Shape the same: 80
As Animals of largest Size
Corrupt to Maggots Worms and Flyes.
A Type of Modern Witt and Style,
The Rubbish of an antient Pile.
So Chymists boast they have a Power
From the dead Ashes of a Flow'r
[p. 5] Some faint Resemblance to produce,
But not the Virtue Tast nor Juyce.
So, Modern Rhymers strive to blast
The Poetry of Ages past,   90
Which having wisely overthrown,
They from it's Ruins build their own.

70 Poet's] modern Ford   80 Bulk nor Shape] shape, nor bulk Ford
88 nor] or Ford   89 Rhymers strive to] *Written above the line over* 'Rhymers
wisely', *which* ẛ *struck out.* 'Wisely' *occurs in l. 91. In the revised version of the
poem the reading is* 'Rhymers wisely'.

  89–90. As Craik, *Life*, i. 174 n.,   ing memory of the controversy which
observes, there is evidently here a pass-   prompted *The Battle of the Books*.

THE

DESCRIPTION

OF A

Salamander.

Out of Pliny *Nat. Hist.* L. 10. C. 67 *and* L. 29 C. 4.

Anno. 1705.

The Whimsical Medley, i, Appendix, p. 42. [Ref. *W.M.*]
Miscellanies, 1711, p. 372 (2nd edn., 1713, p. 370).
Miscellanies. The Last Volume, 1727, p. 89 (1731, p. 189; 1733, p. 189).
Faulkner, 1735, ii. 13 (1737, ii. 10). [Ref. F.]

The date, 1705, assigned to this piece in the *Miscellanies* of 1711, is, almost undoubtedly, correct. From June, 1704, to November, 1707, Swift was in Ireland. In 1705 Lord Cutts was appointed commander-in-chief in that country. Faulkner, in 1735, gives the date as 1706, which is possible. See also Deane Swift, *Essay*, 1755, p. 127.

John Cutts, 1661–1707, created Baron Cutts of Gowran in 1690, was one of the most distinguished soldiers of his day. He fought at the Boyne; and at the siege of Namur in 1695 he won the name of 'Salamander' for his intrepidity under withering fire. He took part in negotiating the Treaty of Ryswick; and fought at Blenheim. See further, *D.N.B.* xiii. 367.

Swift's scurrilous invective against a brave man is inexcusable, and excited indignation (*Journal to Stella*, 24 October, 1711). His dislike of Cutts endured; for, nearly thirty years later, he described him in a copy of Macky's *Characters* as 'The vainest old fool alive'. That he was inordinately vain is the testimony of contemporaries; and he may have personally offended Swift.

There is a manuscript copy in *The Whimsical Medley*. The text is here printed from the *Miscellanies*, 1711.

AS Mastive Dogs in Modern Phrase are
Call'd *Pompey*, *Scipio* and *Cæsar*;
As *Pies* and *Daws* are often stil'd
With Christian Nick-names like a Child;

Title: *Anno.* 1705.] *Om.* 1727, 1731 Written in the YEAR 1706. F.

As we say, *Monsieur*, to an *Ape*
Without offence to Human Shape:
So men have got from Bird and Brute
Names that would best their Natures suit:
The *Lyon*, *Eagle*, *Fox* and *Bear*
Were Hero's Titles heretofore,   10
Bestow'd as Hi'roglyphicks fit
T'express their Valor, Strength or Wit.
For, what is understood by *Fame*
Beside the getting of a Name?
But e're since Men invented Guns,
A different way their Fancy runs;
To paint a Hero, we enquire
For something that will conquer Fire,
Would you describe *Turenne* or *Trump*
Think of a Bucket or a Pump.   20
Are these too low?—then find out grander,
Call my Lord *C*— a *Salamander*.
'Tis well.—But since we live among
Detractors with an evil Tongue,
Who may object against the Term,
Pliny shall prove what we affirm:
Pliny shall prove, and we'll apply,
And I'll be judg'd by standers-by.

FIRST then, our Author has defin'd
This Reptil, of the Serpent kind,   30
With gawdy Coat, and shining Train,
But loathsom Spots his Body stain:

9 *Bear*] *Boar* 1727, 1731, F. The Lion, Eagle, and the Bear *W.M.*   12 T'express]
W.M., 1727, 1731 To shew F. *and most later editions*   14 Beside] Besides 1727,
1731, F.   18 Fire,] *Fire.* 1727, 1731, F.   22 *C*—] 1727, 1731 *Cutts*, F.

19. *Turenne or Trump*. Marshal Turenne, 1611–75, one of France's greatest soldiers; and Martin Harpertzoon Tromp, 1597–1653, the famous Dutch admiral and opponent of Blake.
29–36. The Spotted or Fire Salamander is common in Europe. Its colouring is striking, bright yellow patches on a black surface. These lines follow Pliny's account, *Hist. Nat.* x. 67, 'Animal lacertae figura, stellatum, numquam nisi magnis imbribus proveniens et serenitate desinens'.

Out from some Hole obscure he flies
When Rains descend, and Tempests rise,
Till the Sun clears the Air; and then
Crawls back neglected to his Den.

SO when the War has rais'd a Storm
I've seen a *Snake* in human Form,
All stain'd with Infamy and Vice,
Leap from the Dunghill in a trice,   40
Burnish and make a gaudy show,
Become a General, Peer and Beau,
Till Peace hath made the Sky serene,
Then shrink into it's Hole again.

All this we grant—why, then look yonder
Sure that must be a Salamander!

FARTHER, we are by *Pliny* told
This *Serpent* is extreamly cold,
So cold, that put it in the Fire,
'Twill make the very Flames expire,   50
Beside, it Spues a filthy Froth,
(Whether thro' Rage or Love, or both)
Of Matter purulent and white
Which happ'ning on the Skin to light,
And there corrupting to a Wound
Spreads Leprosy and Baldness round.

SO have I seen a batter'd Beau
By Age and Claps grown cold as Snow,

54 happ'ning] happen'd 1713, 1727, 1731   happening F. *and most later
editions*

47-56. *Hist. Nat.* x. 67. 'Huic tantus rigor, ut ignem tactu restinguat non alio modo quam glacies. Ejusdem sanie, quae lactea ore vomitur, quacumque parte corporis humani contacta toti defluunt pili, idque quod contactum est colorem in vitiliginem mutat.' And xxix. 4 (23): 'Inter omnia venenata salamandrae scelus maximum est. . . . nam si arbori inrepsit omnia poma inficit veneno, et eos qui ederint necat frigida vi nihil aconito distans.' Pliny, however, admits that, on the one occasion on which he tried the experiment of placing a salamander in fire, the creature was soon reduced to a powder. Despite its evil reputation the salamander is quite harmless.

Whose Breath or Touch, where e'er he came,
Blew out Love's Torch or chill'd the Flame: 60
And should some Nymph who ne'er was cruel,
Like *Carleton* cheap, or fam'd *Duruel,*
Receive the Filth which he ejects,
She soon would find, the same Effects,
Her tainted Carcase to pursue,
As from the *Salamander's* Spue;
A dismal shedding of her Locks
And, if no Leprosy, a Pox.

> Then *I'll appeal to each By-stander,*
> *Whether this ben't a* Salamander.   70

The History of Vanbrug's House.
1706.

Swift's autograph: Pierpont Morgan Library, New York.
The Whimsical Medley, i, Appendix, p. 61.
Two transcripts among the Harley Papers, in the possession of the Duke of
  Portland, Welbeck Abbey. [Refs. W.¹, W.².]
A Meditation upon a Broom-Stick, and Somewhat Beside; . . . London: . . .
  Curll, . . . 1710. p. 27. [Ref. C.]
Miscellanies, 1711, p. 389 (2nd edn., 1713, p. 387).
A Collection of Original Poems, . . . London: . . . Curll, . . . 1714.
Miscellanies. The Last Volume, 1727, p. 77 (1731, p. 182; 1733, p. 182).
Faulkner, 1735, ii. 36 (1737, ii. 29). [Ref. F.]

In the *Miscellanies,* 1711, this poem is assigned to 1708; and the date is
accepted by Faulkner and Deane Swift (*Essay,* 1755, p. 137). There are
two transcripts of the poem among the Harley Papers at Welbeck Abbey.

62 *Duruel,*] Du-Ruel, 1727, 1731, F. *and later editions*   64 find, the same Effects,]
find the same Effects 1713, 1727, 1731, F.   find the same Effects, 1733   70
Whether this be'nt a Salamander.] . . . Salamander ? *W.M.,* 1713 *Is not this same*
a Salamander ? 1727, 1731 *If this be not a* Salamander ? F. *and most later editions*
Miscellanies 1733 follows 1727 save for one noted variant in punctuation

62. *Carleton cheap.* Mary Carleton, German princess'. See *D.N.B.* ix. 95.
1642 ?–1673, the adventuress and Duruel has not been identified.
criminal, popularly known as 'the

One, with the title 'The History of Vanbrugh's House', is written on the first two pages of a folded folio sheet; the other, entitled 'The Architect', is written on the first and third pages of a folio half-sheet folded to quarto size. The latter transcript is endorsed by Edward Harley 'The Architect. 1709', and 'Dr Swift'. But Swift's autograph copy, formerly in the Fountaine collection, gives '1706'. Swift was then in Ireland; but this would be a natural date for his second lampoon on Vanbrugh, who was called to be 'Architect at Blenheim' in 1705.

The first appearance of the poem in print was in *A Meditation on a Broom-Stick*, which was published in April, 1710 (*Daily Courant*, 6, 7 April). Swift records that Vanbrugh, though 'a good-natured fellow', was incensed (*Journal to Stella*, 7, 11 Nov. 1710; and see *Prose Works*, ed. Temple Scott, xii. 79 n.) especially as 'Lady Marlborough used to tease him' with the verses.

The text is here printed from Swift's manuscript. In title and text Vanbrugh's name, or 'Van', was not printed in full prior to Faulkner, except by Curll.

[p. 1]   When Mother Clud had rise[n] from Play,
       And call'd to take the Cards away,
       Van saw, but seemd not to regard,
       How Miss pickt ev'ry painted Card,
       And busy both with Hand and Eye
       Soon reard a House two Storyes high;
       Van's Genius without Thought or Lecture
       Is hugely turnd to Architecture,
       He saw the Edifice and smil'd,
       Vow'd it was pretty for a Child;   10
       It was so perfect in its kind,
       He kept the Model in his Mind.
       But when he found the Boys at play,
       And saw them dabling in their Clay,
       He stood behind a Stall to lurk,
       And mark the Progress of their Work,

1 rise[n]] rose W., C., 1711, 1727, 1731, F.   6 Storyes] Story W.², C., 1711 Stories 1727, 1731, F.   8 Is] This C.   8 Is hugely] This highly W.¹ This quickly W.²   9 Saw] view'd C., 1711 *and later editions*   13] *N.P. printed editions*   14 them] 'em C.   16 their] yᵉ W.²

1. *Mother Clud*. See 'The Reverse', pp. 118, 1082.   8. Swift first wrote 'His', but the 'H' is partly rubbed out.

With true Delight observed them all
Raking up Mud to build a Wall;
The Plan he much admir'd, and took
The Model in his Table-book;   20
Thought himself now exactly skill'd,
And so resolv'd a House to build;
[p. 2] A reall House with Rooms and Stairs,
Five times at least as big as theirs,
Taller than Misse's by two yards,
Not a sham Thing of Clay or Cards.
And so he did; for in a while
He built up such a monstrous Pile,
That no two Chairmen could be found
Able to lift it from the Ground;   30
Still at Whitehall it stands in view,
Just in the Place where first it grew,
There all the little School-boys run
Envying to see themselves outdone.
        From such deep Rudiments as these
Van is become by due Degrees
For Building fam'd, and justly reckond
At Court, Vitruvius the second,
No wonder, since wise Authors shew,
That best Foundations must be low.   40
And now the Duke has wisely ta'ne him
To be his Architect at Blenheim.
[p. 3]   But Raillery, for once, apart,
If this Rule holds in ev'ry Art,

17 them] W.² 'em W.¹, C., 1711, 1727, 1731, F.   18 up Mud] of dirt W.²
23 with] C., 1711, F. and 1713, 1727, 1731   24 Five] six W.²   40 That]
The W.²   40 must] should W.¹   42 at] of W.²   43] *No break early printed*
editions   44 holds] hold W.²

31. *Still at Whitehall* . . . See
p. 78.
38. *Vitruvius the second.* M. Vitruvius Pollio, a military and civil engineer employed by Augustus Caesar.
His *De Architectura* is the one work of
its kind which has come down to us

from classical times. The point of
Swift's reference lies in the fact that
Vanbrugh had been appointed Comp-
troller of the Board of Works.
40. *be low.* First written by Swift as
one word and blotted out.

Or if his Grace were no more skilld in
The Art of battring Walls, than building,
We might expect to find next Year
A Mousetrap-man chief Engineer.

The Story of Baucis & Philemon.
Ov. Met. l. 8.

Swift's autograph: Pierpont Morgan Library, New York.

There are, as in the case of 'Vanbrugh's House', two versions of this poem. It has always been known that the printed version represented a revision advised by Addison. According to Delany, *Observations*, 1754, p. 19, Swift 'was often wont to mention: that in a poem of not two hundred lines (*Baucis* and *Philemon*) Mr. *Addison* made him blot out fourscore, add fourscore, and alter fourscore'.

John Forster discovered the manuscript of the earlier version, in Swift's hand, among the Fountaine papers at Narford, and printed the variant passages in his *Life of Jonathan Swift*, pp. 164–74. I am indebted to the trustees of the Pierpont Morgan Library, New York, where the Fountaine manuscripts are now preserved, for the opportunity of printing the text as Swift wrote it.

The differences between the original and revised version, if not exactly as Swift described them, are, as the comparison afforded in this volume (see p. 110) will show, almost equally substantial. The changes prompted by Addison are no improvement; much of the homeliness and vigour of the original has been lost.

I have been unable to reconcile Forster's description of the manuscript at Narford, or the text printed by W. E. Browning (*Poems of Jonathan Swift*, i. 62–8), with the Pierpont Morgan manuscript. Among the Forster papers in the Victoria and Albert Museum, South Kensington, are two collations made by Forster against the Narford manuscript, and they differ. In one collation the metamorphosis of the 'wooden Jack' follows the passages describing the chair, the mortar, the porringers, and the ballads; in the other it precedes these passages, as Forster gives it in the *Life* and as Browning prints the poem. Forster in one of his collations deletes the six lines beginning 'At christ'nings well could act his part'; in the *Life* he

---

45 were] is W.[2]   46 battring Walls, than building,] battering than of building; W.[2]   47 find] C., W. see 1711, 1727, 1731, F.

In *A Collection of Original Poems*, 1714, Curll prints the text of *A Meditation on a Broom-Stick*.

includes them, and Browning follows. But Forster never professed to have seen two manuscripts. Furthermore Forster's retention of the two lines,

> 'His waistcoat to a cassock grew,
> And both assum'd a sable hue;'

which belong to the printed version, seems to be a careless oversight. Browning rejects these two lines, and has six verbal differences from Forster. In any event Browning, who never saw the original manuscript, concocted his version from the material left behind by Forster, which is clearly irreconcilable and untrustworthy.

The Pierpont Morgan MS. extends to 180 lines, followed by '&c', which seems to indicate that it was not proposed to revise the last part of the poem. Forster (*op. cit.*, p. 165) says: 'The poem as printed contains one hundred and seventy-eight lines; the poem as I found it at Narford has two hundred and thirty.' If the six lines beginning 'At christ'nings well could act his part', and the forty-four final lines of the version as printed, be added to the 180 lines of the Pierpont Morgan text we have a poem 230 lines long. This may be the explanation of Forster's statement; but there are further difficulties. The long dash 'marked in Swift's manuscript', according to Forster (*op.cit.*, p. 170), does not appear in the Pierpont Morgan MS.; and there are several verbal differences in the version of the original given by Forster in the *Life*. These have been indicated in the apparatus. The 180 lines are here printed as they appear in the Pierpont Morgan MS.

When Swift included the poem in his *Miscellanies*, 1711, he, or the printer, stated that it was 'Written, 1706', and this may be accepted. It belongs to the same period as the earlier version of 'Vanbrug's House', during a time of comparative leisure in Ireland, 1704–7. And it is interesting to reflect that this racy sketch of typical English country-folk was written in alien surroundings. Faulkner and Deane Swift, *Essay*, 1755, p. 137, assign the poem to 1708, the date of the Addisonian revision. For the printed version see p. 110.

Swift's acquaintance with Addison appears to have begun during the early part of that visit to England which lasted from November, 1707, to June, 1709. The first letter passing between them, an invitation to dinner from Addison, dated 29 February, 1707/8, suggests that they had not long been known to each other (*Corresp.* i. 79–80, and note). The friendship soon ripened, and was accompanied by a respect which continued despite political differences. Delany (*Observations*, 1754, p. 32) reports Swift as having said of Addison, 'that often as they spent their evenings together, they neither of them ever wished for a third person, to support or enliven their conversation'. And entries in Swift's account-books, preserved in the Forster Library, South Kensington, point to many evenings on which the two dined or drank wine together to the exclusion of further company. It is probable that Philip Frowde, a poetaster and one time pupil of Addison, brought the two together; but Dr. Ball (*Swift's Verse*, p. 66) suggests that

Sir Andrew Fountaine (see p. 78) may have been partly instrumental in procuring the introduction. For several years Swift was upon the most intimate and friendly terms with both Fountaine and Addison, and it is of peculiar interest, therefore, that the original drafts of the two poems, 'Vanbrug's House' and 'Baucis and Philemon', so largely altered upon Addison's suggestions, should have been found at Fountaine's house at Narford.

For the story of Baucis and Philemon see Ovid, *Met.* viii. 611–724.

[p. 1] In antient Time, as Story tells
The Saints would often leave their Cells
And strole about, but hide their Quality,
To try the People's Hospitality.
    It happen'd on a Winter's night,
As Authors of the Legend write
Two Brother-Hermits, Saints by Trade
Taking their Tour in Masquerade
Came to a Village hard by Rixham
Ragged, and not a Groat betwixt 'em.   10
It rain'd as hard as it could pour,
Yet they were forc't to walk an Hour
From House to House, wett to the Skin
Before one Soul would let 'em in.
They call'd at ev'ry Dore; Good People,
My Comrade's Blind, and I'm a Creeple
Here we ly starving in the Street
'Twould grieve a Body's Heart to see't:
No Christian would turn out a Beast
In such a dreadfull Night at least;   20
Give us but Straw, and let us Ly
In yonder Barn to keep us dry.
Thus in the Strolers usuall Cant
They beg'd Relief which none would grant;
[p. 2] No Creature valu'd what they se'd:
One Family was gone to bed;
The Master Bawl'd out half asleep
You Fellows, what a Noise you keep!
So many Beggers pass this way,
We can't be quiet Night nor day;   30

We can not serve You every One,
Pray take your Answer and be gone.
One swore he'd send 'em to the Stocks,
A third could not forbear his Mocks,
But bawl'd as loud as he could roar,
You're on the wrong side of the Door.
One surly Clown lookt out, and said,
I'll fling the P— pot on your head;
You sha'n't come here nor get a Sous
You look like Rogues would rob a House   40
Can't you go work, or serve the King?
You blind and lame! tis no such Thing
That's but a counterfeit sore Leg:
For shame! two sturdy Rascalls beg;
If I come down, I'll spoil your Trick
And cure You both with a good Stick.

[p. 3]   Our wand'ring Saints in wofull State,
Treated at this ungodly Rate
Having thro all the Village pass't,
To a small Cottage came at last   50
Where dwelt a poor old honest Yeman
Call'd thereabouts Goodman Philemon;
Who kindlly did the Saints invite
In his poor House to pass the Night;
And then the hospitable Sire
Bade Goody Baucis mend the Fire
Whilst he from out the Chimny took
A Flitch of Bacon off the Hook,
And freely from the fattest Side
Cutt off large Slices to be fry'd;   60
Which tosst up in a Pan with Batter,
And serv'd up in an earthen Platter;
Quoth Baucis, this is wholsom Fare,
Eat, Honest Friends, and never spare,

38 the P— pot] a brick-bat Forster   51 poor] good Forster   52 thereabouts] thereabout Forster   54 House to] 'Hutt to' *first written and blotted out.*
This is the reading of the revised version   60 off] out Forster

And if we find our Vittels fail
We can but make it out in Ale.
    To a small Kilderkin of Beer
Brew'd for the good time of the Year
Philemon by his Wife's consent
Step't with a Jug, and made a Vent;   70
[p. 4] And having fill'd it to the Brink,
Invited both the Saints to Drink.
When they had took a second Draught,
Behold, a Miracle was wrought
For, Baucis with Amazement found
Although the Jug had twice gone round
It still was full up to the Top
As if they ne're had drunk a drop.
You may be sure, so strange a Sight
Put the old People in a Fright;   80
Philemon whisper'd to his Wife,
These Men are Saints I'll lay my Life
The Strangers overheard, and said,
You're in the right, but be'n't afraid
No hurt shall come to You or Yours;
But for that Pack of churlish Boors
Not fitt to live on Christian Ground,
They and their Village shall be droun'd,
Whilst You shall see your Cottage rise,
And grow a Church before your Eyes.   90
    Scarce had they spoke when fair and soft
The Roof began to mount aloft
[p. 5] Aloft rose ev'ry Beam and Rafter,
The heavy Wall went clamb'ring after.
The Chimny widen'd and grew high'r,
Became a Steeple with a Spire:
The Kettle to the Top was hoist
And there stood fastned to a Joyst,
But with the upside doun to shew
It's Inclination for below;   100

78 As] 'Has' *first, and blotted out*

In vain; for a superior Force
Apply'd at Bottom stops it's Course;
Doomd ever in suspense to dwell,
Tis now no Kettle but a Bell.
The groaning Chair began to crawll
Like a huge Insect up the Wall,
There stuck, and to a Pulpitt grew,
But kept it's Matter and it's Hue,
And mindfull of it's antient State,
Still Groans while tatling Gossips prate.   110
  The Mortar onely chang'd it's Name,
In it's old shape a Font became
  The Porrengers that in a Row
Hung high and made a glitt'ring Show
[p. 6] To a less noble Substance chang'd
Were now but leathern Buckets rang'd.
  The Ballads pasted round the Wall,
Of Chivy-chase, and English Mall,
Fair Rosamond, and Robin Hood,
The little Children in the Wood,   120
Enlarg'd in Picture, Size and Letter
And painted, lookt abundance better
And now the Heraldry describe
Of a Churchwarden or a Tribe.
  The wooden Jack which had almost
Lost by Disuse the Art to roast
A sudden Alteration feels,
Encreas't by new intestin Wheels
But what adds to the Wonder more,
The Number made the Motion slower   130
The Fly'r, altho't had leaden Feet,
Would turn so quick you scarce could see't
But now stopt by some hidden Pow'rs
Moves round but twice in twice twelve Hours

117 round] on Forster 131 altho'] 'which tho' ' *first written;* 'which' *struck out,* 'al-' *above line* 133 But] It Forster 133 But now stopt] *Above the line in place of* 'Now slackned' *which is struck out.* 'But slacken'd' *in the revised version* 134 But twice] *First at the beginning of the line and struck out.* 'Now hardly moves an Inch an Hour' *in the revised version*

While in the Station of a Jack
'Twas never known to turn its back
A Friend in Turns and Windings try'd
Nor ever left the Chimny side.

[p. 7] The Chimny to a Steeple grown,   140
The Jack would not be left alone
But up against the Steeple rear'd,
Became a Clock, and still adher'd,
And still it's Love to Houshold Cares
By a shrill Voice at noon declares,
Warning the Cook-maid not to burn
That Roast-meat which it cannot turn.

A Bed-sted in the antique mode
Compos'd of Timber many a Load;
Such as our Grandfathers did use,
Was Metamorphos't into Pews;   150
Which yet their former Virtue keep,
By lodging Folks dispos'd to sleep.

     The Cottage with such Feats as these
Grown to a Church by just Degrees,
The holy Men desir'd their Host
To ask for what he fancy'd most.
Philemon having paus'd a while
Reply'd in complementall Style:
Your Goodness more than my Desert
Makes you take all things in good Part: 160
[p. 8] You've rais'd a Church here in a Minute,
And I would fain continue in it;
I'm good for little at my days;
Make me the Parson if you please.
He spoke. and presently he feels
His Grazier's Coat reach down his Heels,
The Sleeves new border'd with a List
Widn'd and gatherd at his Wrist;
But being old continued just
As threadbare, and as full of Dust.   170

136 turn] show Forster   138 Chimny] chimney's Forster   146 That]
The Forster

A shambling awkward Gate he took,
With a demure dejected Look.
Talkt of his Off'rings, Tyths, and Dues,
Could Smoak, and Drink, and read the News;
Or sell a Goose at the next Toun
Decently hid beneath his Goun.
Contrivd to preach his Sermon next
Chang'd in the Preface and the Text:
Carry'd it to his Equalls high'r,
But most obsequious to the Squire.   180

&c

V E R S E S

said to be written on the

U N I O N.

Faulkner, 1746, viii. 314.
Miscellanies, 1746, xi. 242 (1749, xi. 242). [Ref. 1746.]
Miscellanies, 1751, xiv. 216.
The Works of Jonathan Swift, D.D., ed. Hawkesworth, 1755, 4to, iv (1),
283.

The poem is one of those added to the canon of Swift by Faulkner in
1746. The poems printed in vol. viii of the *Works* in that year are for the
most part undoubtedly genuine. These verses are in the manner of Swift,
and, with hardly a doubt, may be accepted as his. They are, further, of a
piece with his inveterate dislike for Scotland.

If by Swift, these lines must have been written while he was in Ireland;
for the Act of Union was formally ratified by the Parliament of Scotland on
the 16th of January, 1707, and came into operation on the 1st of May in
that year.

The text is given as first printed by Faulkner.

177 his Sermon] old Sermons Forster *and revised version*

T HE Queen has lately lost a Part
    Of her entirely-*English* Heart,
For want of which by way of Botch,
She piec'd it up again with *Scotch*.
Blest Revolution, which creates
Divided Hearts, united States.
See how the double Nation lies;
Like a rich Coat with Skirts of Frize:
As if a Man in making Posies
Should bundle Thistles up with Roses.   10
Whoever yet a Union saw
Of Kingdoms, without Faith or Law.
Henceforward let no Statesman dare,
A Kingdom to a Ship compare;
Lest he should call our Commonweal,
A Vessel with a double Keel:
Which just like ours, new rigg'd and man'd,
And got about a League from Land,
By Change of Wind to Leeward Side
The Pilot knew not how to guide.   20
So tossing Faction will o'erwhelm
Our crazy double-bottom'd Realm.

2 entirely-*English*] 1746, 1751   *entirely-english* 1755   6 united States.] 1746,
1751   united states! 1755   11 Whoever] 1746, 1755   Who ever 1751   12
Law.] 1746 Law? 1751 law. 1755

1–4. Dr. Ball (*Swift's Verse*, p. 92) sees in these lines 'a suggestion that Queen Anne's support of the measure was given to obtain compensation for her loss of revenue by the grant of the tenths and first-fruits to the church'.

17. *ours.* The reference is to Ireland and the new order which followed the victory of William III.

An ELEGY on
Mr. *PATRIGE*, the Almanack-maker,
who Died on the 29th of this Instant *March*, 1708.

An Elegy on Mr. Patrige, . . . *London: Printed in the Year 1708.* Broadside.
An Elegy On Mr. Patrige, . . . *Edinburgh Re-printed in the Year 1708.* Broadside. [Ref. E.]
The Whimsical Medley, i, Appendix, p. 47. [Ref. *W.M.*]
Miscellanies, 1711, p. 392 (2nd edn., 1713, p. 390).
Miscellanies. The Last Volume, 1727, p. 97 (1731, p. 195; 1733, p. 195).
Faulkner, 1735, ii. 114 (1737, ii. 91). [Ref. F.]

John Partridge, 1644–1715, a shoemaker, turned to the publication of astrological booklets. In 1680 his almanac, *Merlinus Liberatus,* first appeared; and he became one of the best-known of the 'philomaths' as these quacks styled themselves. Swift seized upon the idea of demolishing him with his own weapons. In March, 1708, he published *Predictions for the Year 1708,* in which he foretold the death of Partridge 'upon the 29th of *March* next, about Eleven at night, of a raging Feaver'. On the 30th of March appeared *The Accomplishment of the first of Mr. Bickerstaff's Predictions,* in which a detailed account is given of Partridge's death. Swift also ridiculed the wretched almanac-maker in *An Elegy on Mr. Patrige.* Many thought him really dead; and the Stationers' Hall struck his name from its rolls. Others joined in the joke at Partridge's expense. In his almanac for 1709 he protested that he was still alive; but he was too late. Swift conclusively proved his death in *A Vindication of Isaac Bickerstaff Esq.* See further Forster, pp. 221–5; Craik, i. 219–24; *Prose Works,* i. 298 ff.; Aitken, *Life of Steele,* i. 211–14.

In his *History of the City of Dublin,* i. 192–3, Gilbert states that several lines of Swift's elegy were distributed in Dublin as an epitaph on John Whalley, an astrologer of the city, who died 17 Jany. 1724. In actual fact the whole, with the exception of ll. 95–102, was adapted and reprinted as a broadside.

The text is here reprinted from the first broadside edition. In the *Miscellanies,* 1711, the title becomes 'A Grubstreet Elegy on the supposed Death of Patrige the Almanack-Maker'. In 1727, and later, 'Grubstreet' is omitted. From 1713, in title and text, 'Patrige' becomes 'Partrige'. The change in spelling of the proper name takes place in the second printing of the second edition of the *Miscellanies,* 1713.

Title: this Instant *March,*] *March* last, E.

WELL, 'tis as *Bickerstaff* has guest,
    Tho' we all took it for a Jest:
Patrige is Dead, nay more, he dy'd
E'er he could prove the good *Squire* ly'd.
Strange, an Astrologer should Die,
Without one Wonder in the Sky;
Not one of all his *Crony* Stars,
To pay their Duty at his Hearse!
No Meteor, no Eclipse appear'd!
No Comet with a Flaming Beard!   10
The Sun has rose, and gone to Bed,
Just as if *Patrige* were not Dead;
Nor hid himself behind the Moon,
To make a dreadful Night at Noon:
He at fit Periods walks through *Aries*,
Howe'er our Earthly Motion varies,
And 'twice a Year he'll cut th' *Æquator*,
As if there had been no such Matter.
    Some Wits have wondred what Analogy
There is 'twixt *Cobling and *Astrology*;   20
How *Patrige* made his *Opticks* rise,
From a *Shoe Sole* to reach the Skies;
A *List* the Coblers Temples ties,
To keep the Hair out of their Eyes;
From whence 'tis plain the *Diadem*
That Princes wear derives from them;
And therefore *Crowns* are now-a-days
Adorn'd with *Golden Stars* and *Rays*,
which plainly shews the near Alliance
'Twixt *Cobling* and the *Planet Science*.   30
    Besides, that slow-pac'd Sign *Bo-otes*
As 'tis miscall'd, we know not who 'tis;

* *Patrige was a Cobler.*

8, 9, 10] *followed by interrogation marks* 1727, 1731, 1733, F.   10 Flaming]
fiery *W.M.*   23] *N.P.* 1711, 1713, 1727, *and later editions*   26 wear] wear,
E.   30 *Planet*] *Planets* 1711, 1713, 1727, 1731, 1733, F.   planets' Scott,
planet's Browning

But *Patrige* ended all Disputes,
He knew his Trade, and call'd it †*Boots*.
The *Horned Moon* which heretofore
Upon their Shoes the *Romans* wore,
Whose Wideness kept their Toes from Corns,
And whence we claim our *shoeing horns*,
Shews how the Art of *Cobling* bears
A near Resemblance to the *Spheres*.   40
    A Scrap of *Parchment* hung by *Geometry*,
A great Refinement in *Barometry*,
Can like the Stars foretel the Weather;
And what is *Parchment* else but *Leather?*
Which an Astrologer might use,
Either for *Almanacks* or *Shoes*.
    Thus *Patrige*, by his Wit and Parts,
At once did Practice both these Arts:
And as the Boding Owl, or rather
The Bat, because her Wings are *Leather*,   50
Steals from her Private Cell by Night,
And flies about the Candle-Light;
So Learned *Patrige* could as well
Creep in the Dark from *Leathern* Cell,
And in his Fancy fly as far,
To peep upon a twinkling Star.
    Besides, he could confound the *Spheres*,
And set the *Planets* by the Ears:
To shew his Skill, he *Mars* would join
To *Venus* in *Aspect Mali'n*,   60
Then call in *Mercury* for Aid,
And Cure the Wounds that *Venus* made.
    Great Scholars have in *Lucian* Read,
When *Philip* King of *Greece* was Dead,
His *Soul* and *Spirit* did divide,
. And each Part took a diff'rent Side;

† *See his Almanack.*
35] *N.P.* 1711 *and later editions*

36. *Upon their Shoes the Romans wore.*   clasp on the shoes of patricians.
An allusion to the crescent-shaped   63. *Luciani Opera,* xi. 17.

One rose a Star, the *other fell*
Beneath, and mended Shoes in Hell.
  Thus *Patrige* still shines in each Art,
The *Cobling* and *Star-gazing* Part,   70
And is *Install'd* as good a Star,
As any of the *Cæsars* are.
  Thou, high-exalted in thy Sphere,
May'st follow still thy Calling there.
To thee the *Bull* will lend his *Hide*,
By *Phœbus* newly Tann'd and Dry'd.
For thee they *Argo's* Hulk will Tax,
And scrape her Pitchy Sides for *Wax*.
Then *Ariadne* kindly Lends
Her Braided Hair to make thee *Ends;*   80
The Point of *Sagittarius* Dart,
Turns to an *Awl* by Heav'nly Art;
And *Vulcan* wheedled by his Wife,
Will Forge for thee a *Paring-Knife*,
For want of Room by *Virgo's* Side,
She'll strain a Point, and sit *astride,
To take thee kindly in *between*,
And then the *Signs* will be *Thirteen*.
  Triumphant Star! Some Pity show
On *Coblers Militant* below,   90
Whom Roguish Boys in Stormy Nights
Torment, by pissing out their Lights;
Or thro' a Chink convey their Smoke,
Inclos'd *Artificers* to Choke.
  †But do not shed thy Influence down
Upon St. *James's* End o' th' Town;
Consider where the *Moon* and *Stars*
Have their devoutest Worshippers,

---

  * Tibi brachia contrahet Ingens Scorpius, &c.   † Sed nec in Arctoo
sedem tibi legeris Orbe, &c.   89–94] *Inserted after l.* 72 1711, 1713, 1727
and later editions   95–102] *Om.* 1711, 1713, 1727 *and later editions*

  86, 95, 102. The footnotes are those   i. 34–5, and Lucan, *De bello civili*, i.
of the broadside. See Virgil, *Georg.*   53–5.

Astrologers and *Lunaticks*
Have in *More Fields* their Stations fix,   100
Hither thy gentle Aspect bend,
*Nor look Asquint on an old Friend.

The EPITAPH.

HERE *Five Foot deep lyes on his Back*
A Cobler, Starmonger, *and* Quack,
Who to the Stars in pure Good-will,
Does to his best look upward still.
Weep all you Customers that use
His Pills, *his* Almanacks, *or* Shoes.
And you that did your Fortunes seek,
Step to this Grave but once a Week,   110
This Earth which bears his Body's Print,
You'll find has so much Virtue in't,
That I durst Pawn my Ears, 'twill tell
Whate'er concerns you full as well,
In Physick, Stolen Goods, *or* Love,
As he himself could, when above.

A Famous Prediction of *MERLIN*, the *British* Wizard; written above a Thousand Years ago, and re-lating to this present Year.

With Explanatory Notes. By *T. N.* Philomath.

A Famous Prediction of Merlin, ... London: *Printed and Sold by A. Baldwin,*
... *MDCCIX.* Half-sheet.
A Famous Prediction of Merlin, ... Edinburgh Re-printed by *James Watson*
1709. Half-sheet.
A Famous Prediction of Merlin, ... London: *Printed and Sold by H. Hills, in*
Black-fryars, near the Water-side, 1708. Half-sheet.

* Neve tuam videas obliquo sidere Romam.
100 Have] Do E.

Miscellanies, 1711, p. 305 (2nd edn., 1713, p. 303).
Miscellanies, 1727, ii. 253.

This was Swift's last contribution to the Partridge practical joke; and it took a political character. Although more properly a prose piece it contains twenty lines of verse prophecy, and is here reprinted for the sake of completeness. Swift mentions the piece in the *Journal to Stella*, 24 December, 1711. Deane Swift, *Essay*, 1755, p. 139, suggests, and doubtless rightly, that Swift had no serious intention; but so far as the *Prediction* had any purpose it was an appeal to Queen Anne to marry again.

Dr. Johnson was deceived into believing it a genuine piece of ancient verse, and, before him, Ames included it in his *Typographical Antiquities*, 1749, a mistake in which he was followed by Philip Luckombe in his *Concise History of Printing*, 1770, p. 60.

There was a severe frost during the winter of 1708–9. The *Prediction* appeared in the early part of the latter year.

LAST Year was publish'd a Paper of Predictions pretended to be written by one *Isaac Bickerstaff*, Esq; but the true Design of it was to Ridicule the Art of Astrology, and Expose its Professors as ignorant, or Impostors. Against this Imputation, Dr. *Partridge* hath vindicated himself in his Almanack for the present Year.

For a further Vindication of this famous Art, I have thought fit to present the World with the following Prophecy. The Original is said to be of the famous *Merlin*, who lived about a Thousand Years ago: And the following Translation is Two Hundred Years old; for it seems to be written near the End of *Henry* the Seventh's Reign. I found it in an Old Edition of *Merlin*'s Prophecies; imprinted at *London* by *Johan Haukyns*, in the Year 1530, *Pag*. 39. I set it down Word for Word in the Old Orthography, and shall take Leave to subjoin a few Explanatory Notes.

Seven and Ten addyd to nyne,
Of Fraunce hir woe thys is the sygne,
Tamys rivere twys y-frozen,
Walke sans wetynge Shoes ne hosen.
Then compth foorthe, Ich understonde,
From Toune of Stoffe to fattyn Londe

An herdie Chiftan, woe the morne
To Fraunce, that evere he was borne.
Than shall the Fyshe beweyle his Bosse;
Nor shall grin Berris make up the Losse.
Yonge Symnele shall agayne miscarrye:
And Norways pryd agayne shall marreye.
And from the Tree where Blosums fele,
Ripe fruit shall come, and all is wele.
Reaums shall daunce honde in honde,
And it shall be merye in olde Inglonde.
Then olde Inglonde shall be noe more,
And no Man shall be sorie therefore.
Geryon shall have three Hedes agayne
Till Hapsburge makyth them but twayne.

Explanatory Notes.

Seven and Ten. This Line describes the Year when
these Events shall happen. Seven and Ten makes Seventeen, which I Explain Seventeen Hundred, and this Number added to Nine, makes the Year we are now in; for it
must be understood of the Natural Year, which begins the
First of *January*.

Tamys River twice, &c. The River *Thames* frozen
twice in one Year, so as Men to walk on it, is a very signal
Accident; which perhaps hath not fallen out for several
Hundred Years before, and is the Reason why some Astrologers have thought that this Prophecy could never be
fulfilled, because they imagined such a Thing would never
happen in our Climate.

From Town of Stuff, &c. This is a plain designa-
tion of the Duke of *Marlborough*; One kind of Stuff used
to fatten Land is called *Marle*, and every body knows that
Borough is a Name for a Town; and this way of Expression is
after the usual dark manner of Old Astrological Predictions.

Then shall the Fish, &c. By the *Fish* is understood the *Dolphin* of *France*, as their Kings Eldest Sons are
called: 'Tis here said, He shall lament the Loss of the

Duke of *Burgundy*, called the *Bosse*, which is an Old
English Word from *Hump-Shoulder*, or *Crook-Back*, as that
Duke is known to be; and the Prophecy seems to mean,
that he shall be overcome or slain. By the *Green Berrys*
in the next Line is meant the Young Duke of *Berry*, the
Dauphin's Third Son, who shall not have Valour or
Fortune enough to supply the Loss of his Eldest Brother.

Young Symnele, &c. By *Symnel* is meant the Pretended Prince of *Wales*, who if he offers to attempt any
thing against *England*, shall miscarry as he did before.
Lambert Symnel is the Name of a Young Man noted in
our Histories for Personating the Son (as I remember) of
Edward the Fourth.

And Norways Pride, &c. I cannot guess who is meant
by *Norway*'s *Pride*, perhaps the Reader may, as well as the
Sense of the Two following Lines.

Reaums shall, &c. *Reaums*, or, as the Word is now,
Realms, is the old Name for *Kingdoms*: And this is a very
plain Prediction of our Happy *Union*, with the Felicities
that shall attend it. It is added, That *Old England* shall be
no more, and yet no Man shall be sorry for it. And indeed,
properly speaking, *England* is now no more; for the whole
Island is one Kingdom, under the Name of *Britain*.

Geryon shall, &c. This Prediction, though somewhat obscure, is wonderfully adapt. *Geryon* is said to have
been a King of *Spain*, whom *Hercules* slew. It was a Fiction
of the Poets, that he had Three Heads, which the Author
says he shall have again. That is, *Spain* shall have Three
Kings; which is now wonderfully verify'd: For besides
the King of *Portugal*, which properly is Part of *Spain*, there
are now Two Rivals for *Spain*; *Charles* and *Philip*. But
Charles being descended from the Count of *Hapsburgh*,
Founder of the *Austrian* Family, shall soon make those
Heads but Two; by Overcoming *Philip*, and Driving him
out of *Spain*.

Some of these Predictions are already fulfilled; and it
is highly probable the rest may be in due time: And, I

think, I have not forced the Words by my Explication, into any other Sense than what they will naturally bear. If this be granted, I am sure it may be also allow'd, that the Author, whoever he were, was a Person of extraordinary Sagacity; And that Astrology brought to such a Perfection as this, is by no means an Art to be despis'd; whatever Mr. *Bickerstaff*, or other Merry Gentlemen are pleased to think. As to the Tradition, of these Lines having been writ in their Original by *Merlin*; I confess, I lay not much Weight upon it: But it is enough to justify their Authority, that the Book from whence I have transcrib'd them, was printed 170 Years ago, as appears by the Title-Page. For the Satisfaction of any Gentleman, who may be either Doubtful of the Truth, or Curious to be inform'd; I shall give Order to have the very Book sent to the Printer of this Paper, with Directions to let any Body see it that pleases; because, I believe, it is pretty scarce.

V——'s H O U S E
Built from the Ruins of White-Hall *that was Burnt.*

Miscellanies, 1711, p. 364 (2nd edn., 1713, p. 362).
Miscellanies. The Last Volume, 1727, p. 68 (1731, p. 176; 1733, p. 176).
Faulkner, 1735, ii. 30 (1737, ii. 24). [Ref. F.]

For an account of the occasion of this poem, and Swift's earlier version, see above, p. 78. The *Miscellanies* of 1711 gives the date of composition as 1703, when Whitehall was burnt. Faulkner assigns the poem to 1708, the date of the revised version, as printed.

The earlier version runs to 92, the printed version to 134 lines. Apart from minor differences, ll. 29–54 are peculiar to the earlier version, ll 53–120 to the printed version.

The text printed is that of the *Miscellanies*, 1711. Swift made one correction, l. 105, in his copy of the *Miscellanies*, 1727.

Title: *V*—'s] *VANBRUG*'s F.

IN Times of *Old*, when Time was *Young*,
And Poets their own Verses Sung,
A Verse could draw a Stone or Beam
That now would overload a Team;
Lead 'em a Dance of many a Mile,
Then rear 'em to a goodly Pile.
Each Number had it's diff'rent Pow'r;
Heroick Strains could build a Tow'r;
Sonnets, or Elogies to *Chloris*
Might raise a House about two Stories;   10
A Lyrick Ode would Slate; a Catch
Would Tile; an Epigram would Thatch.

BUT, to their own, or Landlord's Cost,
Now Poets feel this Art is lost:
Not one of all our tuneful Throng
Can raise a Lodging *for a Song*.
For, *Jove* consider'd well the Case,
Observ'd, they grew a num'rous Race.
And should they *Build* as fast as *Write*,
'Twould ruin Undertakers quite.   20
This Evil, therefore to prevent,
He wisely chang'd their Element:
On Earth, the God of Wealth was made
Sole Patron of the Building Trade,
Leaving the Wits the Spacious Air
With Licence to *build Castles* there:
And 'tis conceiv'd, their old Pretence
To lodge in Garrats, comes from thence.

PREMISING thus in Modern way
The better Half we had to say;   30
Sing Muse the House of Poet *V*—
In higher Strains than we began.

2 own] one 1711   8 build] will 1731, 1733   30 had] 1713 have 1727,
1731, 1733, F.   31 *V*—] 1713, 1727, 1731, 1733 *Van* F.

8. The reading 'will' for 'build' was   returned to 'build'; and Hawkesworth,
followed in the *Miscellanies*, 1736,   1755, reads 'build'.
1742, 1749. The 12mo edn. of 1751

V— (for 'tis fit the Reader know it)
Is both a Herald and a Poet,
No wonder then, if nicely skill'd
In both Capacities, to Build.
As Herald, he can in a Day
Repair a *House* gone to Decay,
Or by *Atchivement, Arms, Device,*
Erect a new one in a trice.   40
And as a Poet, he has Skill
To build in Speculation still.
Great *Jove,* he cry'd, the Art restore
To build by Verse as heretofore,
And make my Muse the Architect;
What Palaces shall we erect!
No longer shall forsaken *Thames*
Lament his old *Whitehall* in Flames,
A Pile shall from its Ashes rise
Fit to Invade or prop the Skies.   50

    JOVE Smil'd, and like a gentle God,
Consenting with the usual Nod,
Told *V—* he knew his Talent best,
And left the Choice to his own Breast.
So *V—* resolv'd to write a Farce,
But well perceiving Wit was scarce,
With Cunning that Defect supplies,
Takes a *French* Play as lawful Prize,
Steals thence his Plot, and ev'ry Joke,
Not once suspecting, *Jove* would *Smoak,*   60
And, (like a Wag) sat down to Write,
Would whisper to himself; *A Bite,*

33 *V—*] *VAN,* F.   43 *Jove,*] 1713   *Jove!* 1727, 1731, 1733, F.   52 the]
1713, 1727, 1731, 1733   his F.   53 *V—*] *Van* F.   55 *V—*] *Van* F.

34. *Is both a Herald and a Poet.* Vanbrugh held the office of Clarenceux King-of-Arms, 1704–26.

39. *Atchivement.* A variant spelling of achievement, the older form of hatchment, an escutcheon.

58. *Takes a French Play* . . . Although Vanbrugh's two best plays, *The Relapse* and *The Provok'd Wife,* were original, he borrowed largely and adapted from Boursault, Le Sage, Molière, and Dancourt.

Then, from the motly mingled Style
Proceeded to erect his Pile:
So, Men of old, to gain Renown, did
Build *Babel* with their Tongues confounded.
Jove saw the Cheat, but thought it best
To turn the Matter to a Jest;
Down from *Olympus* Top he Slides,
Laughing as if he'd burst his Sides:
Ay, thought the God, are these your Tricks?   70
Why then, *old Plays* deserve *old Bricks*,
And since you're sparing of your Stuff,
Your Building shall be small enough.
He spake, and grudging, lent his Ayd;
Th' experienc't Bricks that knew their Trade,
(As being Bricks at Second Hand,)
Now move, and now in Order Stand.

THE Building, as the Poet Writ,
Rose in proportion to his Wit: 80
And first the Prologue built a Wall
So wide as to encompass all.
The Scene, a Wood, produc'd no more
Than a few Scrubby Trees before.
The Plot as yet lay deep, and so
A Cellar next was dug below:
But this a Work so hard was found,
Two Acts it cost him under Ground.
Two other Acts we may presume
Were spent in Building each a Room;   90
Thus far advanc't, he made a shift
To raise a Roof with Act the Fift.
The Epilogue behind, did frame
A Place not decent here to name.

NOW Poets from all Quarters ran
To see the House of Brother *V—*:

63 the] 1713, 1727, 1731, 1733   this F.   79–94] *Rom.* 1727, 1731, 1733, F.
96 *V—*:] *Van:* F.

Lookt high and low, walkt often round,
But no such House was to be found;
One asks the Watermen hard by,
Where may the Poets Palace ly?   100
Another, of the *Thames* enquires,
If he has seen its gilded Spires.
At length they in the Rubbish spy
A Thing resembling a Goose Py,
Farther in haste the Poets throng,
And gaze in silent Wonder long,
Till one in Raptures thus began
To praise the Pile, and Builder *V—*.

THRICE happy Poet, who may trail
Thy House about thee like a Snail;   110
Or Harness'd to a Nag, at ease
Take Journies in it like a Chaise;
Or in a Boat when e're thou wilt
Canst make it serve thee for a Tilt.
Capacious House! 'tis own'd by all
Thou'rt well contriv'd, tho' thou art small;
For ev'ry Wit in *Britain*'s Isle
May lodge within thy Spacious Pile.
Like *Bacchus* Thou, as Poets feign,
Thy Mother burnt, art Born again;   120
Born like a *Phœnix* from the Flame,
But neither *Bulk*, nor *Shape* the same:
As Animals of largest Size
Corrupt to Maggots, Worms and Flyes.
A Type of *Modern* Wit and Style,
The Rubbish of an Antient Pile.
So *Chymists* boast they have a Pow'r
From the dead Ashes of a Flow'r
Some faint Resemblance to produce,
But not the Virtue, Tast or Juice.   130

102 Spires.] 1713   Spires? 1727, 1731, 1733, F.   105 Farther] 1713, 1727,
1731, 1733   Thither Swift *in his copy of Miscellanies, 1727; and followed by* F.
108 *V—*.] *Van.* F.

So *Modern* Rimers wisely *Blast*
The Poetry of Ages past,
Which after they have overthrown,
They from its Ruins build their own.

B A U C I S

AND

P H I L E M O N.

Imitated, From the Eighth Book of OVID.

Baucis and Philemon, Imitated from Ovid.... Printed An. Dom. MDCCIX,
  Price Two-Pence. (4 leaves.) [Ref. 1709.] Another issue omits price.
Poetical Miscellanies: The Sixth Part.... London,... Tonson,... 1709.
  p. 237.
Baucis and Philemon;... Together with Mrs. Harris's Earnest Petition....
  London:... Hills,... 1709 (and 1710), p. 3. [Ref. H.]
Works of... Rochester, and Roscommon.... The Third Edition. To which is
  added, A Collection of Miscellany Poems.... London,... Curll,...
  1709. p. 129.
A Meditation upon a Broom-Stick,... London:... Curll,... 1710. p. 9.
  [Ref. C.]
Miscellanies, 1711, p. 377 (2nd edn., 1713, p. 375).
A Collection of Original Poems,... London:... Curll,... 1714.
Miscellanies. The Last Volume, 1727, p. 1 (1731, p. 132; 1733, p. 132).
Faulkner, 1735, ii. 21 (1737, ii. 17). [Ref. F.]

For an account of the occasion of this poem, and Swift's earlier version,
see above, p. 88. The *Miscellanies* of 1711 gives the date 1706, which is
probably approximately right for the earlier form. Faulkner assigns it to
1708, the date of the revised and printed version.

It is possible that its first appearance in print was in Tonson's *Miscellanies,*
1709. It was immediately pirated. The title in the Hills piracy is, 'The
Metamorphosis of Baucis *and* Philemon, *Burlesqu'd; from the* 8th *Book of*
Ovid'; and there are no paragraph divisions.

Variations in the detail of the title heading, which would serve no purpose, are not given below.

Swift made one correction, l. 19, in his copy of the *Miscellanies*, 1727,
and one, l. 38, in his copy of Faulkner, vol. ii, 1737.

The text is printed from the *Miscellanies* of 1711.

IN antient Times, as Story tells,
The Saints would often leave their Cells,
And strole about, but hide their Quality,
To try good People's Hospitality.

IT happen'd on a Winter Night,
As Authors of the Legend write;
Two Brother Hermits, Saints by Trade,
Taking their *Tour* in Masquerade;
Disguis'd in tatter'd Habits, went
To a small Village down in *Kent*;   10
Where, in the Strolers Canting Strain,
They beg'd from Door to Door in vain;
Try'd ev'ry Tone might Pity win,
But not a Soul would let them in.

OUR wand'ring Saints in woful State,
Treated at this ungodly Rate,
Having thro' all the Village pass'd,
To a small Cottage came at last;
Where dwelt a good old honest Yeoman,
Call'd, in the Neighbourhood, *Philemon*.   20
Who kindly did the Saints invite
In his Poor Hut to pass the Night;
And then the Hospitable Sire
Bid *Goody Baucis* mend the Fire;

5 Winter] Winter's 1709   6] F. *places in round brackets*   19 good old
honest] C., F. good old godly 1709   good honest old 1727, 1731, 1733 (*corrected
back by* Swift *to* 'good old honest' *in his copy of the Miscellanies, 1727*) good
honest H.   21 the] 1709 H., C., 1713, F. these 1727, 1731, 1733   24
mend] light 1709

10. *To a small Village down in Kent.*   thorne, near the County Town of
Swift's MS. reads 'a Village hard by   *Somerset*'.
Rixham'; and the title-page of Hills's   24. *Goody.* A contracted form of
pirated edition 'the Parish of *Chil*-   'goodwife'.

While He from out of Chimney took
A Flitch of Bacon off the Hook;
And freely from the fattest Side
Cut out large Slices to be fry'd:
Then stept aside to fetch 'em Drink,
Fill'd a large Jug up to the Brink;   30
And saw it fairly twice go round;
Yet (what is wonderful) they found,
'Twas still replenished to the Top,
As if they ne'er had toucht a Drop.
The good old Couple was amaz'd,
And often on each other gaz'd;
For both were frighted to the Heart,
And just began to cry; —What ar't!
Then softly turn'd aside to view,
Whether the Lights were burning blue.   40
The gentle *Pilgrims* soon aware on't,
Told 'em their Calling, and their Errant:
Good Folks, you need not be afraid,
We are but *Saints*, the Hermits said;
No Hurt shall come to You, or Yours;
But, for that Pack of churlish Boors,
Not fit to live on Christian Ground,
They and their Houses shall be drown'd:
Whilst you shall see your Cottage rise,
And grow a Church before your Eyes.   50

THEY scarce had Spoke; when, fair and soft,
The Roof began to mount aloft;
Aloft rose ev'ry Beam and Rafter,
The heavy Wall climb'd slowly after.

25 While He from out of] C., 1713   Whilst he from out the H.   While he from
out the 1709, 1727, 1731, 1733, F.   32 is] was 1709, F.   is *remainder*   34
toucht] drunk 1709   35 Couple] People 1709   35 was] C., 1713, 1727,
1731, 1733, F.   were 1709, H.   38 What ar't!] What art? 1709   What art!
remainder   41 *Pilgrims*] 1713 *and others*   Saints 1709, H., Curll *Miscellany
Poems 1709*

38. In Swift's copy of Faulkner, vol.   margin in pencil against this line.
ii, 1737, 'Wha art' is written in the

THE Chimney widen'd, and grew higher,
Became a Steeple with a Spire.

THE Kettle to the Top was hoist,
And there stood fast'ned to a Joist:
But with the Upside down, to shew
Its Inclinations for below;   60
In vain; for a Superior Force
Apply'd at Bottom, stops its Course,
Doom'd ever in Suspence to dwell,
'Tis now no Kettle, but a Bell.

A wooden Jack, which had almost
Lost, by Disuse, the Art to Roast,
A sudden Alteration feels,
Increas'd by new Intestine Wheels:
And, what exalts the Wonder more,
The Number made the Motion slow'r: 70
The Flyer, tho't had Leaden Feet,
Turn'd round so quick, you scarce cou'd see't;
But slacken'd by some secret Power,
Now hardly moves an Inch an Hour.
The Jack and Chimney near ally'd,
Had never left each other's Side;
The Chimney to a Steeple grown,
The Jack wou'd not be left alone,
But up against the Steeple rear'd,
Became a Clock, and still adher'd: 80
And still its Love to Houshold Cares
By a shrill Voice at Noon declares,
Warning the Cook-maid, not to burn
That Roast-meat which it cannot turn.

THE Groaning Chair began to crawl
Like an huge Snail along the Wall;

60 Its] His 1709   62 stops] stop'd 1709   69 And,] C., 1713   But H.
And 1709, 1727, 1731, 1733, F.   71 Flyer, tho't] 1709, C., 1713, 1727,
1731, 1733 Flyer, though't H.   Flyer which, tho't F.   73 But] Now F.
74 Now hardly moves] Can hardly move F.   84 it cannot turn] it now
can't turn 1709   85 began] was seen F.   86 along] half up F.

There stuck aloft, in Publick View,
And with small Change, a Pulpit grew.

THE Porringers, that in a Row
Hung high, and made a glitt'ring Show,   90
To a less Noble Substance chang'd,
Were now but Leathern Buckets rang'd.

THE Ballads pasted on the Wall,
Of *Joan* of *France*, and *English Moll*,
Fair *Rosamond*, and *Robin Hood*,
The *Little Children in the Wood*:
Now seem'd to look abundance better,
Improv'd in Picture, Size, and Letter;
And high in Order plac'd, describe
The Heraldry of ev'ry Tribe.   100

A Bedstead of the Antique Mode,
Compact of Timber many a Load,
Such as our Ancestors did use,
Was Metamorphos'd into Pews;
Which still their antient Nature keep;
By lodging Folks dispos'd to Sleep.

THE Cottage by such Feats as these,
Grown to a Church by just Degrees,

87 stuck] stretcht 1709   90 glitt'ring] mighty 1709   102 Timber
many a Load,] 1709, C., 1713 *and others*   Timber, (many a Load) H.   103
Ancestors did] Grandsires wont to F.

89. *Porringers.* Small basins. From *potager*, as porridge from *pottage*.

94. *Of Joan of France, and English Moll.* Quoted from *Hudibras*, Part I, c. 2, 367–8, where Trulla is described as—

'A bold virago, stout and tall
As Joan of France, or English Mall.'

Swift knew his *Hudibras* by heart. 'English Moll' was Mary Ambree, reputed to have fought at the siege of Ghent, 1584. See Percy's *Reliques*, Ser. II, Bk. ii. 19. Ben Jonson refers to her several times, and she is mentioned in Fletcher's *Scornful Lady*, Act v.

95. *Fair Rosamond.* Daughter of Walter, Lord Clifford, and mistress of Henry II. See Percy's *Reliques*, Ser. II, Bk. ii. 7.

100 *The Heraldry of ev'ry Tribe.* Hawkesworth observes, in a note, that, in country churches, the twelve tribes of Israel 'are sometimes distinguished by the ensigns appropriated to them by *Jacob* on his death-bed'.

The Hermits then desir'd their Host
To ask for what he fancy'd most:　　110
Philemon, having paus'd a while,
Return'd 'em Thanks in homely Stile;
Then said; my House is grown so Fine,
Methinks, I still wou'd call it mine:
I'm Old, and fain wou'd live at Ease,
Make me the *Parson*, if you please.

HE spoke, and presently he feels,
His Grazier's Coat fall down his Heels;
He sees, yet hardly can believe,
About each Arm a Pudding-sleeve;　　120
His Wastcoat to a Cassock grew,
And both assum'd a Sable Hue;
But being Old, continu'd just
As Thread-bare, and as full of Dust.
His Talk was now of *Tythes* and *Dues*,
Cou'd smoak his Pipe, and read the News;
Knew how to preach old Sermons next,
Vampt in the Preface and the Text;
At Christnings well could act his Part,
And had the Service all by Heart;　　130
Wish'd Women might have Children fast,
And thought whose *Sow* had *farrow'd* last:
Against *Dissenters* wou'd repine,
And stood up firm for *Right Divine:*
Found his Head fill'd with many a System,
But Classick Authors—he ne'er miss'd 'em.

THUS having furbish'd up a Parson,
Dame *Baucis* next, they play'd their Farce on:
Instead of Home-spun Coifs were seen,
Good Pinners edg'd with Colberteen:　　140

109 desir'd] desire F.　　117 spoke,] 1709, C., 1713 *and others*　spake, H.
126 Cou'd smoak] C.　Could smoak H., 1713　He smok'd 1727, 1731, 1733
Could smoke 1709, F.　　129 act] 1709, C., 1713 *and others*　get H.　　137 Thus]
1709, C., 1713 *and others* They H.　138 their] 1709, C., 1713 *and others*　the H.

140. *Colberteen*. A lace named after　Baptiste Colbert, 1619–83.
the celebrated French minister, Jean

Her Petticoat transform'd apace,
Became Black Sattin, Flounc'd with Lace.
Plain *Goody* would no longer down,
'Twas *Madam*, in her Grogram Gown.
Philemon was in great Surprize,
And hardly could believe his Eyes,
Amaz'd to see Her look so Prim,
And she admir'd as much at Him.

THUS, happy in their Change of Life,
Were several Years this Man and Wife,   150
When on a Day, which prov'd their last,
Discoursing on old Stories past,
They went by chance, amidst their Talk,
To the Church-yard, to take a walk;
When *Baucis* hastily cry'd out;
My Dear, I see your Forehead sprout:
Sprout, quoth the Man, What's this you tell us?
I hope you don't believe me Jealous:
But yet, methinks, I feel it true;
And re'ly, Yours is budding too—   160
Nay,—now I cannot stir my Foot:
It feels as if 'twere taking Root.

DESCRIPTION would but tire my Muse:
In short, they both were turn'd to *Yews*.
Old Good-man *Dobson* of the Green
Remembers he the Trees has seen;
He'll talk of them from Noon till Night,
And goes with Folks to shew the Sight:
On *Sundays*, after Ev'ning Prayer.
He gathers all the Parish there;   170
Points out the Place of either *Yew*;
Here *Baucis*, there *Philemon* grew.

141 Petticoat] C., 1713 *and others* Petticoats H. Petti-Coats 1709   150
this] the 1709, F.   152 on] H., C. 1713 o'er 1709, 1727, 1731, 1733, F.
154 take] fetch F.   157 this] that 1709   160 re'ly,] trûly 1709, H.
truly, C. re'lly, 1713 really, 1727, 1731, 1733, F.   162 feels] seems 1709
165] *N.P.* 1709, 1727, 1731, 1733, F.   167 till] H., C., 1733 to 1709, 1713,
1727, 1731, F.

Till once, a Parson of our Town,
To mend his Barn, cut *Baucis* down;
At which, 'tis hard to be believ'd,
How much the other Tree was griev'd,
Grew Scrubby, dy'd a-top, was stunted:
So, the next Parson stub'd and burnt it.

177 Scrubby,] C., 1713 *and others* scrubb'd, 1709 Surly, H.

The poem as printed in the *Works of Rochester and Roscommon, &c.*, 1709, follows Hills's text. Tonson follows the readings of Curll and Hills, without peculiar variants. In *Original Poems*, 1714, the text is that printed in *A Meditation on a Broom-Stick*. In the unpriced issue of 1709 line 19 reads 'good old honest', and in line 117 there is no comma after 'spoke'.

T O
Mrs. BIDDY FLOYD.

Anno. 1708.

Poetical Miscellanies: The Sixth Part. . . . *London,* . . . *Tonson,* . . . *1709.*
p. 249. [Ref. T.]
Works of . . . *Rochester, and Roscommon.* . . . *The Third Edition. To which is
added, A Collection of Miscellany Poems,* . : . *London,* . . . *Curll,* . . . *1709.*
p. 187.
The Whimsical Medley, i. 102; iii. 288.
Two transcripts among the Harley Papers, in the possession of the Duke of
Portland, Welbeck Abbey. [Ref. W.]
A Meditation upon a Broom-Stick, . . . *London:* . . . *Curll,* . . . *1710.* p. 26.
Miscellanies, 1711, p. 388 (2nd edn., 1713, p. 386).
A Collection of Original Poems, . . . *London:* . . . *Curll,* . . . *1714.*
Miscellanies. The Last Volume, 1727, p. 142 (1731, p. 225; 1733, p. 225).
Faulkner, 1735, ii. 16 (1737, ii. 13). [Ref. F.]

Mrs. Biddy Floyd was Lady Betty Germain's friend and companion.
The 'Dame *Floyd*' mentioned in 'A Ballad on the Game of Traffick' (see
p. 75) may have been her mother. Writing to Robert Hunter, 12 Jany.,
1708-9, Swift refers to the fact that the Thames was frozen over, and adds:
'Mrs. Floyd looked out with both her Eyes, and we had one Days Thaw:
but she drew in her Head, and it now freezes as hard as ever' (*Corresp.* i.
134). She was a noted beauty (*Journal to Stella,* 12 Oct., 1711; *Corresp.*
v. 57), although she had suffered from small-pox.
In Tonson's *Miscellanies* the poem is accompanied by a Latin version,

Title: TO] ON T., 1727, 1731, 1733, F.

transcribed in the *Whimsical Medley*, and reprinted in *Miscellaneous Pieces*, 1789, p. 241.

Barrett, *Essay*, 1808, p. 95, prints from the *Whimsical Medley* (i. 102) a poem, 'The Reverse (to Swift's Verses on Biddy Floyd); or Mrs. Cludd', as by Swift; but it is most unlikely to be his. The form of the title in the *Whimsical Medley* suggests that the lines were considered to be by another. Among the Harley Papers at Welbeck Abbey there are two fo. half-sheets each bearing transcripts of 'Biddy Floyd' and 'The Reverse'. One copy is endorsed 'Clud', and, in the hand of Edward Harley, '1708'; the other is endorsed by Edward Harley, 'The Receipt by M^r. Swift wth ye Answer'. The second endorsement again suggests that the 'Answer' was not regarded as Swift's. In addition 'The Reverse' was not included in the *Miscellanies*, or printed by Faulkner. See further, p. 1082.

Faulkner wrongly assigned the poem to 1707. The text is here reprinted from the *Miscellanies* of 1711.

WHEN *Cupid* did his Grandsire *Jove* intreat,
    To form some Beauty by a new Receit,
Jove sent and found far in a Country Scene,
Truth, Innocence, Good Nature, Look serene;
From which Ingredients, First the dext'rous Boy
Pickt the Demure, the Aukward, and the Coy;
The *Graces* from the Court did next provide
Breeding, and Wit, and Air, and decent Pride;
These *Venus* cleans'd from ev'ry spurious Grain
Of Nice, Coquet, Affected, Pert, and Vain.   10
Jove mix'd up all, and his best Clay imploy'd;
Then call'd the happy Composition, *Floyd*.

1 intreat,] F.   intreat 1727, 1731, 1733   5 Ingredients, First] Ingredients first, T.   Ingredients, first 1727, 1731, 1733, F.   6 Coy;] 1713   Coy: 1727, 1731, 1733, F.   8 and Air, and decent Pride;] Air, & a decent Pride W. 8 Pride;] 1713 Pride: 1727, 1731, 1733   Pride. F.   10 Pert,] Brisk, *Miscellany Poems, 1709*, W.

The title of the poem is *Cupid's Contrivance* in the *Works of Rochester and Roscommon, &c.*, published by Curll in 1709.

Apollo Outwitted.

To the Honourable Mrs. FINCH, *under her Name* of Ardelia,

Written, 1709.

Miscellanies, 1711, p. 399 (2nd edn., 1713, p. 397).
Miscellanies. The Last Volume, 1727, p. 143 (1731, p. 226; 1733, p. 226).
Faulkner, 1735, ii. 17 (1737, ii. 14). [Ref. F.]

Faulkner, and Deane Swift, *Essay*, 1755, p. 128, mistakenly assign the poem to 1707. It was written in 1709, about the same time as the lines to Mrs. Biddy Floyd. In the letter, quoted above, p. 117, in which reference is made to Mrs. Floyd, Swift says, 'I amuse myself sometimes with writing verses to Mrs. Finch' (*Corresp.* i. 135).

Mrs. Finch was Ann, daughter of Sir W. Kingsmill, and wife of Heneage Finch, afterwards fourth Earl of Winchilsea. Herself a poetess, her *Miscellany Poems* appeared in 1713. She died in 1720.

In Faulkner's edition the address reads: '*To the Honourable Mrs.* Finch, (*since Countess of* Winchelsea,) *under the Name of* Ardelia.'

Swift made one correction, l. 57, in his copy of the *Miscellanies*, 1727. The text is printed from the *Miscellanies* of 1711.

PHŒBUS now shortning every Shade,
    Up to the Northern *Tropick* came,
And thence Beheld a Lovely Maid
    Attending on a Royal Dame.

THE God laid down his Feeble Rays,
    Then lighted from his Glitt'ring Coach,
But fenc'd his Head with his own Bays
    Before he durst the Nymph approach.

UNDER those Sacred Leaves, Secure
    From common Lightning of the Skies,   10
He fondly thought he might endure
    The Flashes of *Ardeliah*'s Eyes.

    12 *Ardeliah*'s] *Ardelia*'s 1713 *and remainder*

THE Nymph who oft had read in Books,
   Of that Bright God whom Bards invoke,
Soon knew *Apollo* by his looks,
   And Guest his Business e're he Spoke.

HE in the old Celestial Cant,
   Confest his Flame, and swore by *Styx*,
What e're she would desire, to Grant,
   But Wise *Ardelia* knew his Tricks.   20

OVID had warn'd her to beware,
   Of Stroling God's, whose usual Trade is,
Under pretence of Taking Air,
   To pick up Sublunary Ladies.

HOWE'ER she gave no flat Denial,
   As having Malice in her Heart,
And was resolv'd upon a Tryal,
   To Cheat the God in his own Art.

HEAR my Request the Virgin said
   Let which I please of all the Nine   30
Attend when e'er I want their Aid,
   Obey my Call, and only mine.

BY Vow Oblig'd, By Passion led,
   The God could not refuse her Prayer;
He wav'd his Wreath Thrice o'er her Head,
   Thrice mutter'd something to the Air.

AND now he thought to Seize his due,
   But she the Charm already try'd,
Thalia heard the Call and Flew
   To wait at Bright *Ardelia*'s Side.   40

13 Nymph] 1713   Nymph, 1727 *and remainder*   16 e're] 1713   e'er 1727
and remainder   19 What e're] 1713   Whate'er 1727 *and remainder*   29
Request the Virgin said] Request, the Virgin said, 1713   Request, the Virgin
said; 1727, 1731, 1733, F.   39 Call] Call, 1727 *and remainder*   40
Bright] bright 1713 *and remainder*

ON Sight of this Celestial *Prude*,
    Apollo thought it vain to stay,
Nor in her Presence durst be Rude,
    But made his Leg and went away.

HE hop'd to find some lucky Hour,
    When on their Queen the Muses wait;
But *Pallas* owns *Ardelia*'s Power,
    For Vows Divine are kept by Fate.

THEN full of Rage *Apollo* Spoke,
    Deceitful Nymph I see thy Art,   50
And tho' I can't my gift revoke,
    I'll disappoint its Nobler Part.

LET Stubborn Pride Possess thee long,
    And be thou Negligent of Fame,
With ev'ry Muse to Grace thy Song,
    May'st thou despise a Poets Name.

OF Modest Poets thou be first,
    To silent Shades repeat thy Verse,
Till *Fame* and *Eccho* almost burst,
    Yet hardly dare one Line Rehearse.   60

AND last, my Vengeance to Compleat,
    May you Descend to take Renown,
Prevail'd on by the Thing you hate,
    A — and one that wears a Gown.

50 Nymph] Nymph, 1713, 1733   Nymph! 1727, F.   Nymph; 1731   57 thou
be] 1713, F.   be thou 1727, 1731, 1733   64 A —] 1713   A Whig, 1727,
1731, 1733, F.

44. *made his Leg*. I.e. bowed. For examples of this phrase see *O.E.D.* under *Leg*, 4.

57. *thou be first*. As noted above, this was altered by the printer in 1727 to 'be thou first'. Swift, however, in his copy of the *Miscellanies* corrected this back to 'thou be'; and this change back to the original form was followed by Faulkner in 1735. The correction is of interest, as indicative of Swift's opinion on a point of composition.

'In pity to the empty'ng Town'

Swift's autograph: Pierpont Morgan Library, New York.

Forster first called attention to this poem (*Life of Swift*, p. 228 n.), which he discovered in Swift's handwriting among the Fountaine papers at Narford, and printed five out of the six stanzas. Browning (*Poems of Jonathan Swift*, i. 54) reprinted the five stanzas under the title, 'Answer to Lines from May Fair'.

. The original, which is certainly in Swift's hand, has six stanzas. The first five, appearing on one page, are neatly written, and without correction. The concluding stanza, on another page, has two corrections in a different hand, and below is written the word 'Philovil' in a large hand, not Swift's.

Dr. Elrington Ball (*Notes and Queries*, 12 S. viii. 2) suggested that these verses may have been written by Prior; but he had never seen the original manuscript. Swift, it is true, may have been transcribing a piece not of his own composition. This, however, seems unlikely. Every other poem in Swift's hand found among the Fountaine papers was written by him. The references to Ardelia, whom he had celebrated in 'Apollo Outwitted' (see p. 119), and to Miss Worsley come naturally, and suggest a date 1708–9, when Swift appears to have been in a mood to address or exchange verses with ladies of his acquaintance, as witness also the lines 'To Mrs. Biddy Floyd', p. 117.

The poem is printed as written by Swift save for the last stanza, in which three words have been rendered illegible by corrections in another hand.

[p. 1]   In pity to the empty'ng Town
        Some God May-Fair invented,
    When Nature would invite us down,
        To be by Art prevented.

    What a corrupted Tast is ours
        When Milk-maids in mock-state
    Instead of Garlands made of Flowrs
        Adorn their Pails with Plate.

    So are the Joys which Nature yields
        Inverted in May-Fair
    In painted Cloth we look for Fields,   10
        And step in Booths for Air.

Here a Dog dancing on his Hamms
　And Puppets mov'd by Wire
Do far exceed your frisking Lambs
　Or Song of feather'd Quire.

Howe'er such Verse as yours, I grant
　Would be but too inviting
Were fair Ardelia not my Aunt,
　Or were it Worsly's writing.　　　　　20

[p. 2]　Then pray think this a lucky Hitt,
　Nor e'er expect another
For honest Harry is no Witt,
　Tho' he's a younger Brother.

A
DESCRIPTION
OF THE
MORNING.

April, 1709.

The Tatler, Numb. 9. From Thursday April 28. to Saturday April 30. 1709
[Ref. *T.*]
The Whimsical Medley, i, Appendix, p. 50.
Miscellanies, 1711, p. 404 (2nd edn., 1713, p. 402).

21 Then pray] *Written above the line in place of two words scored out and illegible.
Not in Swift's hand*　　　23 honest] *Written over another word, thereby rendered
illegible, in the same hand as the correction to l. 21*

19–20. *Ardelia . . . Worsly's writing.*
Ardelia was Mrs. Finch, afterwards
Countess of Winchilsea, see p. 119.
Miss Worsley, the daughter of Sir
Robert Worsley, was married in 1710
to Lord Carteret. Swift was to meet
her again many years later, when, during the controversy over Wood's coinage, Carteret was sent to Ireland as
Lord Lieutenant. See 'An Apology
to the Lady Carteret', p. 374. The
exact meaning of the allusions in this
and the last stanza is now lost, save
that an interchange of verses had been
taking place.

Miscellanies. The Last Volume, 1727, p. 19 (1731, p. 143; 1733, p. 143).
Faulkner, 1735, ii. 43 (1737, ii. 34). [Ref. F.]

In addition to his prose contributions to Steele's *Tatler*, for which see *Prose Works*, ed. Temple Scott, vol. ix, and ed. Davis, vol. ii, Swift contributed two verse pieces, 'A Description of the Morning', and 'A Description of a City Shower', Nos. 9 and 238, April, 1709, and October, 1710. On both occasions he was in London, with an interval, July, 1709, to the end of August, 1710, spent in Ireland.

Faulkner erroneously assigns 'A Description of the Morning' to the year 1712, Deane Swift, *Essay*, 1755, p. 144, to 1710. *Miscellanies*, 1727, gives no date.

The transcript in the *Whimsical Medley* has no noteworthy variants. The text is printed from the *Miscellanies* of 1711.

NOW hardly here and there an Hackney-Coach
Appearing, show'd the Ruddy Morns Approach.
Now *Betty* from her Masters Bed had flown,
And softly stole to discompose her own.
The Slipshod Prentice from his Masters Door,
Had par'd the Dirt, and Sprinkled round the Floor.
Now *Moll* had whirl'd her Mop with dext'rous Airs,
Prepar'd to Scrub the Entry and the Stairs.
The Youth with Broomy Stumps began to trace
The Kennel-Edge, where Wheels had worn the Place. 10
The Smallcoal-Man was heard with Cadence deep,
'Till drown'd in Shriller Notes of Chimney-Sweep,
Duns at his Lordships Gate began to meet,
And Brickdust *Moll* had Scream'd through half the Street.

1 an] *T.*, 1713, 1727, 1731, 1733   a F.   2 Morns] Morn's *remainder*   3
Masters] Master's *remainder*   5 Prentice] 'Prentice *remainder*   6 Dirt,]
Street, *T.*   11 Smallcoal-Man] *T.*   Small-coal-Man 1713   Small-coal Man
1727, 1731, 1733, F.   12 Chimney-Sweep,] Chimney-Sweep: 1713   Chimney-Sweep. 1727, 1731, 1733 *Chimney-sweep. T.*, F.   13 Lordships] Lordship's *remainder*   14 the Street.] *a Street. T.*

9–10. *The Youth with Broomy Stumps
...Place. 'To find old Nails',* according
to Faulkner's note. 'Kennel', earlier
'cannel', from old French 'canel'. *Cf.*
Gay's *Trivia*, i. 15:

'For thee, the Scavinger bids Kennels
    glide
Within their Bounds.'
See also 'Description of a City Shower',
l. 53, p. 139.

The Turnkey now his Flock returning sees,
Duly let out a Nights to Steal for Fees.
The watchful Bailiffs take their silent Stands,
And School-Boys lag with Satchels in their Hands.

On the Little House by the Church Yard of Castleknock.

Faulkner, 1746, viii. 338.
Miscellanies, 1746, xi. 268 (1749, xi. 268; 1751, xiv. 237). [Refs. 1746, 1749, 1751.] *Brett's Miscellany*, 1752, ii. 200–2.
The Works of Jonathan Swift, D.D., ed. Hawkesworth, 1755, 4to, iv (1), 304.

    This poem was written in the earlier half of 1710, during a period of residence in Ireland (see note to the preceding poem). It describes a tiny building used as a vestry by Swift's friend, Archdeacon Walls, when officiating at Castleknock church, the parish church of Phoenix Park. No date is given to the poem in the early collections. Deane Swift, *Essay*, 1755, p. 144, rightly assigns it to 1710.

    In 1943 Dr. St. John Brooks acquired four volumes, i to iv, 1748–57, of *Brett's Miscellany*, a rare Dublin publication, for the contents of which Peter Brett, parish clerk and schoolmaster of Castleknock, was responsible. In vol. ii, pp. 200–2 appears a version of Swift's poem, presenting minor variants, indicated in the apparatus by B., and differing substantially in two passages from Faulkner's text. It is clear that Brett did not rely on any printed edition of the poem. The most probable conjecture is that he had access to a manuscript which for many years had been in the possession of the vicars of Castleknock. Archdeacon Walls was succeeded as vicar in 1738 by his son the Rev. Thomas Walls, who in his turn was succeeded in 1745 by the Rev. John Towers. Jemmy Dunn, appearing by name in Brett's lines, was a predecessor of Peter Brett as parish clerk of Castleknock. A likely guess may be hazarded that Brett's variants and additional lines were part of Swift's original draft, subsequently discarded by him. Faulkner, apparently, printed from a revised and abbreviated manuscript.

16 a Nights] a-Nights 1713   a-nights 1727, 1731, 1733, F.   *a' Nights T.*

  16. *to Steal for Fees.* In return for   exact fees from the prisoners.
privileges gaolers were accustomed to

The two passages which differ substantially are—
(1) For Faulkner's four lines 19–22 Brett has five lines:

> The Vicar once a week walks in,
> Waiting the Service to begin.
> Here conns his notes, and takes a Whet
> With *Dunn* his Clark, when in they get,
> Waiting until the Flock is met.

(2) After line 54 of Faulkner Brett has fourteen lines, representing four lines only, 55–8, in Faulkner. Brett reads:

> The Clerk immediately did come,
> His Name, I think, is *Jemmy Dunn*,
> And when to her he had appear'd,
> He thought the Lady had him jeer'd,
> And cries God mend me, in a Heat,
> What! Sell the Vicar's Country Seat,
> Where he comes ev'ry Week from Town,
> I would not sell it for a Crown:
> I'll sooner Preach within *Christ-Church*,
> Than leave the Vicar in the Lurch;
> Or give from him one single Brick,
> Madam, you touch me to the Quick.
> I cannot now consent to this,
> Nor give this House to little Miss.

The poem is here printed from Faulkner's edition of the *Works*, vol. viii, 1746.

WHOEVER pleaseth to enquire,
   Why yonder Steeple wants a Spire,
The gray old Fellow Poet *Joe*
The Philosophic Cause will shew.
Once, on a Time a Western Blast,
At least twelve Inches overcast,
Reckoning Roof, Weather Cock and all,
Which came with a prodigious Fall;
And tumbling topsi-turvy round
Light with its Bottom on the Ground.   10

3 Fellow] 1746, 1749, 1751   fellow, 1755

3. *Poet Joe*. Joseph Beaumont, a linen-draper and general tradesman of Trim, a friend of Swift, and remarkable for the greyness of his hair at an early age. He introduced improvements in the art of linen weaving, and Swift assisted him in pressing a claim for reward upon the Irish government. He is said to have developed a passion for abstruse mathematics, which finally deranged him. There are frequent references to him in the *Journal to Stella* and in Swift's correspondence.

For by the Laws of Gravitation,
It fell into its proper Station.
This is the little strutting Pile,
You see just by the Church-yard Stile;
The Walls in tumbling gave a Knock;
And thus the Steeple got a Shock;
From whence the neighbouring Farmer calls
The Steeple, Knock, the Vicar, *Walls*.
The Vicar once a Week creeps in,
Sits with his Knees up to his Chin;   20
Here conns his Notes, and takes a Whet,
Till the small ragged Flock is met.
A Traveller, who by did pass,
Observ'd the Roof behind the Grass;
On Tiptoe stood and rear'd his Snout,
And saw the Parson creeping out;
Was much surpriz'd to see a Crow
Venture to build his Nest so low.
A School-boy ran unto't and thought,
The Crib was down, the Blackbird caught.   30
A Third, who lost his Way by Night,
Was forc'd, for Safety, to alight,
And stepping o'er the Fabrick-roof,
His Horse had like to spoil his Hoof.
Warburton took it in his Noddle,
This Building was designed a Model,
Or of a Pigeon-house, or Oven,
To bake one Loaf, and keep one Dove in.

11 Gravitation,] 1746, 1749, 1751 gravitation 1755   11, 12] *Part of preced-*
ing para., 1755   16 got] gave B. 1755   18 creeps] walks B.   26 creep-
ing] coming B.   out;] 1746, 1749, 1755 out. 1751

18. *Walls.* The Rev. Thomas Walls,
of English origin, entered Trinity
College, Dublin, in 1693 at the age
of twenty. He became master of the
school attached to St. Patrick's Cathedral, and held it with the Arch-
deaconry of Achrony. Later he
resigned his schoolmastership and
became incumbent of Castleknock,
near Dublin. See *Corresp.* i. 69 n.3, ii.

67 n.[8], and *passim*.
35. *Warburton.* The Rev. Thomas
Warburton was Swift's curate at Laracor. He also had a school at Trim. In
1716–17 he married and obtained the
living of Magherafelt in the Diocese
of Armagh, which he held until his
death in 1736. See *Corresp.* ii. 366 n.[2];
Leslie, *Armagh Clergy*, p. 364.

Then Mrs. *Johnson* gave her Verdict,
And every one was pleas'd, that heard it: 40
All that you make this Stir about,
Is but a Still which wants a Spout.
The Rev'rend **Dr.** *Raymond* guess'd,
More probably than all the rest;
He said, but that it wanted Room,
It might have been a Pigmy's Tomb.
   The Doctor's Family came by,
And little Miss began to cry;
Give me that House in my own Hand;
Then Madam bid the Chariot stand,   50
Call'd to the Clerk in manner mild,
Pray reach that Thing here to the Child,
That Thing, I mean, among the Kale,
And here's to buy a Pot of Ale.
   The Clerk said to her in a Heat,
What? sell my Master's Country Seat?
Where he comes ev'ry Week from Town;
He wou'd not sell it for a Crown.
Poh! Fellow keep not such a Pother
In half an Hour thou'lt make another.   60
   Says *Nancy*, I can make for Miss,
A finer House ten times than this,
The Dean will give me Willow-Sticks,
And *Joe* my Apron full of Bricks.

43 *Raymond*] *Reymond remainder*   50 bid] bad *remainder*   56 What?] 1746,
1749, 1751 What! B. 1755   59 Fellow] Fellow, 1746, 1749, 1751 fellow, 1755

39. *Mrs. Johnson.* Stella. Faulkner's
note: 'A Friend of the Author's.'
43. *Dr. Raymond.* The Rev. Anthony
Raymond became rector of Trim in
1705, and thereupon resigned his fel-
lowship at Trinity College, Dublin.
He held the living till his death in
1726. In 1713 he also received the
small living of Moymet within two
miles of Trim. Before his death he
issued the prospectus of a History of
Ireland. The work was never published (*Corresp.* i. 120 n.²). Swift and
Raymond were lifelong friends.
  61. *Nancy.* 'The Waiting Woman.'
—Faulkner.

POLITICAL &
MISCELLANEOUS
POEMS
1710–1714

THE

V I R T U E S

O F

SID HAMET the MAGICIAN's

R O D.

The Virtues of Sid Hamet the Magician's Rod. . . . London, Printed: for John Morphew, near Stationers-Hall, MDCCX. Half-sheet.
The Virtues of Sid Hamet . . . London Printed, and Re-Printed in Dublin. 1710. Half-sheet. [*The Devil a Barrel better Herring* on verso.]
The Whimsical Medley, i, Appendix, p. 44. [Ref. *W.M.*]
Miscellanies, 1711, p. 411 (2nd edn., 1713, p. 409).
Miscellanies. The Last Volume, 1727, p. 81 (1731, p. 184; 1733, p. 184).
Faulkner, 1735, ii. 44 (1737, ii. 35). [Ref. F.]

Sidney Godolphin, first Earl of Godolphin, born in 1645, came of an old Cornish family. He entered public life, as M.P. for Helston, in 1668. If not brilliant, he was a sagacious and able administrator, and succeeded in holding important offices of state under Charles II, James, and William. On the accession of Queen Anne he became Lord Treasurer, 6 May, 1702; and, with the help of Marlborough, he held the reins of office for eight years. He antagonized the High Church party by his support of the Occasional Conformity Bill. The impeachment of Sacheverell, and the weariness of the country with the war, gave the Tories an opportunity of undermining his power. On 8 August, 1710, he received a note from the Queen ordering him to break his staff of office. He retired from public life, and died, two years later, in 1712.

In a letter of 10 June, 1708 (*Corresp.* i. 92), Swift, writing to Archbishop King, relates an interview he had with Godolphin to solicit the grant of the firstfruits to the clergy of Ireland. He was given to understand that a first condition must be the consent of the clergy to the repeal of the Test. Swift retired, deeply offended, and never forgave Godolphin.

In September, 1710, he had another interview with Godolphin, and reported, writing again to Archbishop King, 'a reception very unexpected . . . altogether short, dry, and morose' (*Corresp.* i. 194). Writing to Stella on the same day (*Journal to Stella,* 9 Sept., 1710) he further mentions his cold reception, and adds, 'I am almost vowing revenge'. This was after Godolphin had been dismissed from office. The revenge took the form of his lampoon, 'Sid Hamet'. For references to the piece see *Journal to Stella*, 26, 29 Sept., 1, 4, 14, 15, 20 Oct., 8, 10, 30 Nov., 14 Dec., 1710. The poem was sent to the printer on 4th of October; and on the 14th Swift wrote: 'My lampoon is cried up to the skies; but nobody suspects me for it, except Sir Andrew Fountaine.'

In the *Miscellanies* of 1711 and 1713 the poem is introduced with a note in which the hand of Swift may be seen: '*The Following Poem being judged by some to be after the Author's manner, I have ventured to Print it.*'

The *Whimsical Medley* erroneously assigns the poem to 1703; and Faulkner to 1712. *Miscellanies*, 1727, gives no date.

The text is printed from the original half-sheet.

THE *Rod* was but a harmless Wand,
While *Moses* held it in his Hand,
But soon as e'er he *lay'd it down*,
'Twas a devouring Serpent grown.

OUR great Magician, *Hamet Sid*,
Reverses what the Prophet did;
His *Rod* was honest *English* Wood,
That, senseless, in a Corner stood,
Till Metamorphos'd by his Grasp,
It grew an all-devouring Asp;   10
Would hiss, and sting, and roll, and twist,
By the meer Virtue of his Fist:
But when he *lay'd it down*, as quick
Resum'd the Figure of a Stick.

SO to Her Midnight Feasts the Hag,
Rides on a Broomstick for a Nag,
That, rais'd by Magick of her Breech,
O'er Sea and Land conveys the Witch;
But, with the Morning-Dawn, resumes
The Peaceful State of common Brooms.   20

THEY tell us something strange and odd,
About a certain Magick *Rod*,

2 Hand,] 1711, 1713   Hand; 1727, 1731, 1733, F.   6 did;] 1711, 1713   did: 1727, 1731, 1733, F.   18 Witch;] 1711, 1713   Witch: 1727, 1731, 1733, F.

5. *Hamet Sid*. The allusion is to Godolphin's Christian name of Sidney. Swift borrowed the name Sid Hamet from *Don Quixote* (chap. xlii), a book with which he was well acquainted. The rod was Godolphin's staff of office.

22. *Magick Rod*. 'The *virgula divina*, or *divining-rod*, is described to

That, bending down it's Top, divines
When e'er the Soil has Golden Mines:
Where there are none, it stands erect,
Scorning to show the least Respect.
As ready was the *Wand* of *Sid*
To *bend* where *Golden Mines* were hid;
In *Scottish* Hills found precious Ore,
Where none e'er look'd for it before;   30
And, by a *gentle Bow*, divin'd
How well a *Cully*'s Purse was lin'd:
To a forlorn and broken *Rake*,
Stood without Motion, like a Stake.

THE *Rod* of *Hermes* was renown'd
For Charms above and under Ground;
To sleep could Mortal Eye-lids fix
And drive departed Souls to *Styx*.
That *Rod* was just a Type of *Sid's*,
Which, o'er a *British* Senate's Lids,   40
Could *scatter Opium* full as well,
And drive as many *Souls to Hell*.

SID's Rod was slender, white, and tall,
Which oft he us'd to *fish* withal:
A *PLACE* was fastned to the Hook,
And many Score of *Gudgeons* took;

30 before;] 1711, 1713   before: 1727, 1731, 1733, F.   39 just a Type] *All early edns.* just the Type *W.M.* a just type Scott *and later edns.*   41 *scatter Opium*] 1711, 1713   scatter *Opium* 1727, 1731, 1733, F.   46 many Score] many a Score F.

be a forked branch of a hazel or willow, two feet and an half long: it is to be held in the palms of the hands with the single end elevated about eighty degrees; and in this position is said to be attracted by minerals and springs, so as by a forcible inclination to direct where they are to be found.' Hawkesworth, 1755.

29. *In Scottish Hills found precious Ore.* The allusion is to the Act of Union between England and Scotland. See note, p. 95. Godolphin took a prominent part in promoting the union.

32. *Cully's Purse.* A dupe, a simpleton.

35. *The Rod of Hermes.* The *caduceus* of Mercury, an emblem of divination and power over the living and the dead. With a touch of his staff the god could bring sleep to mortals.

Yet, still so happy was his Fate,
He caught his *Fish*, and sav'd his *Bait*.

    SID's Brethren of the conj'ring Tribe
A Circle with their *Rod* describe,   50
Which proves a Magical Redoubt
To keep *mischievous Spirits* out:
Sid's *Rod* was of a larger Stride,
And made a Circle thrice as wide,
Where *Spirits* throng'd with hideous Din,
And he stood there to *take them in*.
But, when th' enchanted *Rod* was *broke*,
They vanish'd in a stinking Smoak.

    ACHILLES's Scepter was of Wood,
Like *Sid*'s, but nothing near so good;   60
Tho' down from Ancestors Divine
Transmitted to the Heroes Line,
Thence, thro' a long Descent of Kings,
Came an 𝕳𝖊𝖎𝖗=𝖑𝖔𝖔𝖒, as *Homer* sings,
Tho' this Description looks so big,
That *Scepter* was a sapless Twig:
Which, from the fatal Day when first
It left the Forest where 'twas nurst,
As *Homer* tells us o'er and o'er,
Nor Leaf, nor Fruit, nor Blossom bore.   70
Sid's Scepter, full of Juice, did shoot
In Golden Boughs, and Golden Fruit,
And He, the *Dragon* never sleeping,
Guarded each fair *Hesperian* Pippin.

---

54 And] *Om.* W.M.   59 *ACHILLES*'s] 1711, 1713 *Achilles*' 1727, 1731,
1733 *ACHILLES*' F.   60 good;] 1711, 1713, 1733 good: 1727, 1731, F.
61 Tho'] Tho, 1711 Tho', 1713 That 1727, 1731, 1733 Though F.
66 Twig:] 1711, 1713 Twig; 1727, 1731, 1733, F.

---

64. *Came an Heir-loom,* ... Godolphin rose to favour with the Queen
through his alliance with Marlborough, with whom he was connected by the marriage of his only
son, Francis, to the Duke's daughter,
Henrietta Churchill, in 1698.

73. *And He, the Dragon never sleeping,* ... In the garden of the Hesperides
a dragon which never slept guarded
the golden apples which Juno gave to
Jupiter. See note, p. 154.

No *Hobby-horse*, with gorgeous Top,
The dearest in *Charles Mather*'s Shop,
Or glitt'ring Tinsel of *May-Fair*,
Could with this *Rod* of *Sid* compare.

DEAR *Sid*, then why wer't thou so mad
To break thy *Rod* like naughty Lad?   80
You should have kiss'd it in your Distress,
And then return'd it to *your Mistress*,
Or made it a *Newmarket* Switch,
And not a *Rod* for thy own Breech.
For since old *Sid* has broken this,
His next will be a *Rod in Piss*.

83 made] make 1713

76. *Charles Mather's.* 'An eminent toy-man in *Fleet-street*.'—Hawkesworth, 1755. His shop lay over against Chancery Lane. See *The Tatler*, Nos. 27, 113, 142; *The Spectator*, Nos. 328, 503, 570.

80. *To break thy Rod . . .* Godolphin was dismissed 8 August, 1710. Swift, writing to Archbishop King, 9 September, 1710, gives the following account of his removal from office: 'A letter was sent him by the Groom of the Queen's Stables, to desire he would break his staff, which would be the easiest way, both to her Majesty and him. Mr. Smith, Chancellor of the Exchequer, happening to come in a little after, my Lord broke his staff, and flung the pieces in the chimney, desiring Mr. Smith to be witness that he had obeyed the Queen's commands' (*Corresp.* i. 194). For John Smith, Chancellor of the Exchequer, see p. 163 n.

83. *a Newmarket Switch.* Godolphin was an enthusiastic patron of horse-racing. His attachment to the turf is alluded to by Swift in contributions to *The Examiner* (*Prose Works*, ix. 172, 195), and by Pope (*Moral Essays*, Epist. I. 81–6):

'Who would not praise Patritio's high desert,
His hand unstain'd, his uncorrupted heart,
His comprehensive head! all Int'rests weigh'd,
All Europe sav'd, yet Britain not betray'd.
He thanks you not, his pride is in Piquet,
New-market-fame, and judgment at a Bet.'

A
DESCRIPTION
OF A
CITY SHOWER.

October, 1710.

The Tatler, Numb. 238. From Saturday October 14. to Tuesday October 17.
1710. [Ref. *T.*]
The Whimsical Medley, ii. 323.
Miscellanies, 1711, p. 406 (2nd edn., 1713, p. 404).
Miscellanies. The Last Volume, 1727, p. 13 (1731, p. 140; 1733, p. 140).
Faulkner, 1735, ii. 39 (1737, ii. 31). [Ref. F.]

Swift was proud of this piece, regarding it as much better than his 'Description of the Morning'. There are many references to it in the *Journal to Stella*. On 10 October, 1710, he writes to say that he is engaged upon the poem, and will send it to *The Tatler*. By the 13th he has finished and sent off the verses. On the 17th they appeared. 'They say 'tis the best thing I ever writ, and I think so too. I suppose the Bishop of Clogher will show it you. Pray tell me how you like it.' On the 27th he met Rowe and Prior, who 'both fell commending my Shower beyond any thing that has been written of the kind: there never was such a Shower since Danae's, &c.' See *Journal to Stella* further under 12, 20 Oct., 2, 8, 10, 28, 30 Nov., 14 Dec., 1710.

The 1727 volume of *Miscellanies* adds to the title the words, '*In Imitation of* VIRGIL's Georg.', in which it is followed by Bathurst and Hawkesworth, but not by Faulkner.

Faulkner mistakenly assigns the poem to 1712; one issue of the *Miscellanies* of 1713, by a printer's error, to 1720. No date is given in the 1727 *Miscellanies*.

The text is printed from the *Miscellanies* of 1711.

CAREFUL Observers may fortel the Hour
   (By sure Prognosticks) when to dread a Show'r:
While Rain depends, the pensive Cat gives o'er
Her Frolicks, and pursues her Tail no more.

1 Hour] Hour, *T.*

1. *Careful Observers* . . . The first part of the poem was evidently the last in point of composition. Writing to Stella, 12 Oct., 1710, Swift says, 'I have finished my poem on the Shower, all but the beginning'.

Returning Home at Night, you'll find the Sink
Strike your offended Sense with double Stink.
If you be wise, then go not far to Dine,
You'll spend in Coach-hire more than save in Wine.
A coming Show'r your shooting Corns presage,
Old Aches throb, your hollow Tooth will rage.   10
Sauntring in Coffee-house is *Dulman* seen;
He damns the Climate, and complains of Spleen.

MEAN while the South rising with dabbled Wings,
A Sable Cloud a-thwart the Welkin flings,
That swill'd more Liquor than it could contain,
And like a Drunkard gives it up again.
Brisk *Susan* whips her Linen from the Rope,
While the first drizzling Show'r is born aslope,
Such is that Sprinkling which some careless Quean
Flirts on you from her Mop, but not so clean.   20
You fly, invoke the Gods; then turning, stop
To rail; she singing, still whirls on her Mop.
Not yet, the Dust had shun'd th' unequal Strife,
But aided by the Wind, fought still for Life;
And wafted with its Foe by violent Gust,
'Twas doubtful which was Rain, and which was Dust.

8 You'll] You F.   16 And like a Drunkard] And, like a Drunkard, *T.*
18 aslope,] 1713, 1727, 1731, 1733   aslope: *T.*, F.   23 Not yet,] 1713
Nor yet *T.*, F.   Not yet 1727, 1731, 1733

5–6. The whole poem is built on scenes and incidents observed. On 8 Nov., 1710, Swift wrote to Stella: 'I will give ten shillings a-week for my lodging; for I am almost st—k out of this with the sink, and it helps me to verses in my Shower.'

10. *Old Aches throb.* Altered by Sheridan, who is followed by later editors, to 'Old aches will throb', forgetting that *ache* was pronounced *aitch*, and *aches* as a disyllable, *aitches.* Cf. *The Tempest*, I. ii. 370:

'Fill all thy bones with aches, make thee roar.'

Hudibras, Pt. iii, c. 2, 407:
'Can by their pangs and aches find
All turns and changes of the wind.'

The earlier pronunciation of the word explains Beatrice's pun upon the letter H, *Much Ado about Nothing*, III. iv. 51. Cf. also a note by Isaac Disraeli under the heading 'Errata' in *Curiosities of Literature*, i. 81, 1866 edition.

26. *'Twas doubtful which was Rain,* ... Faulkner's edition, 1735, though quoting inaccurately, first called attention to the parallel in Garth's *Dispensary* (Canto v. 176):
' 'Tis doubtful which is Sea, and which is Sky.'

Ah! where must needy Poet seek for Aid,
When Dust and Rain at once his Coat invade;
His only Coat, where Dust confus'd with Rain,
Roughen the Nap, and leave a mingled Stain.   30

NOW in contiguous Drops the Flood comes down,
Threat'ning with Deluge this *Devoted* Town.
To Shops in Crouds the dagged Females fly,
Pretend to cheapen Goods, but nothing buy.
The Templer spruce, while ev'ry Spout's a-broach,
Stays till 'tis fair, yet seems to call a Coach.
The tuck'd-up Sempstress walks with hasty Strides,
While Streams run down her oil'd Umbrella's Sides.
Here various Kinds by various Fortunes led,
Commence Acquaintance underneath a Shed.   40
Triumphant Tories, and desponding Whigs,
Forget their Fewds, and join to save their Wigs,

28 invade;] *T.*, 1713   invade? *remainder*
29–30] Sole Coat, where Dust cemented by the Rain
           Erects the Nap, and leaves a cloudy Stain. F.
33 dagged] daggled *remainder*   42 Fewds,] Feuds, *remainder*

29–30. *His only Coat,* . . . The variant on these two lines, which first appeared in Faulkner's edition, 1735, was adopted by Hawkesworth in 1755, despite his attacks on Faulkner as an editor.

38. *While Streams run down her oil'd Umbrella's Sides.* The use of umbrellas, made of oiled silk, was at this time confined to women. Long after Queen Anne's day the use of umbrellas by men was regarded as a mark of effeminacy. Gay, *Trivia*, i. 209–12, recommends the umbrella among '*Implements proper for female Walkers*'.

'Good Huswives all the Winter's Rage despise,
Defended by the Riding-hood's Disguise;
Or underneath th' *Umbrella's* oily Shed,

Safe thro' the Wet on clinking Pattens tread.'
But for men—
'That Garment best the Winter's Rage defends,
Whose shapeless Form in ample Plaits depends;
By various Names in various Counties known,
Yet held in all the true *Surtout* alone:
Be thine of *Kersey* firm, though small the Cost,
Then brave unwet the Rain, unchill'd the Frost.'
Ib. i. 55–60.

41. *Triumphant Tories, and desponding Whigs.* The publication of the poem followed closely upon the downfall of the Whigs, and the formation of a Tory ministry with Harley and St. John in office.

Box'd in a Chair the Beau impatient sits,
While Spouts run clatt'ring o'er the Roof by Fits;
And ever and 'anon with frightful Din
The Leather sounds, he trembles from within.
So when *Troy* Chair-men bore the Wooden Steed,
Pregnant with *Greeks*, impatient to be freed,
(Those Bully *Greeks*, who, as the Moderns do,
Instead of paying Chair-men, run them thro'.)   50
Laoco'n struck the Outside with his Spear,
And each imprison'd Hero quak'd for Fear.

    NOW from all Parts the swelling Kennels flow,
And bear their Trophies with them as they go:
Filth of all Hues and Odours seem to tell
What Street they sail'd from, by their Sight and Smell.
They, as each Torrent drives, with rapid Force
From *Smithfield*, or St. *Pulchre*'s shape their Course,
And in huge Confluent join at *Snow-Hill* Ridge,
Fall from the *Conduit* prone to *Holborn-Bridge*.   60
Sweepings from Butchers Stalls, Dung, Guts, and Blood,⎫
Drown'd Puppies, stinking Sprats, all drench'd in Mud, ⎬
Dead Cats and Turnip-Tops come tumbling down the⎟
    Flood. ⎭

48 freed,] *T.* freed. 1711   freed; *remainder*   51 *Laoco'n*] *T. Laocon* 1713
Laocoon 1727, 1731, 1733, F.   55 Filth] *T.*, 1713   Filths *remainder*   56
Street] *T.*, 1713, 1727, 1731, 1733   Streets F.   56 their] the F.   62
stinking] stinging 1711   63 Dead Cats, and Turnip-Tops F.

51. *Laoco'n struck the Outside* . . .
Virgil, *Aen.* ii. 50–3.
   53. *Kennels.* See note, p. 124.
   58–60. In Sheridan, 1784, and
later editions 'or' becomes 'to', and
'Confluent' is altered to the substan-
tival form more common to-day, 'con-
fluence'. A reference to any good map
of London in the eighteenth century
will show, however, that Swift meant
'or', and pictured the garbage and
offal from the sheep and cattle pens,
then standing to the west of West
Smithfield, washing down to meet the

overflow from the neighbourhood of
St. Sepulchre's Church at Holborn
Conduit, the junction of Snow Hill
and Cow Lane, and thence falling into
the Fleet at Holborn Bridge, at which
point the stream was still navigable.
Holborn Conduit was taken down in
1746. See Harben's *Dictionary of London*, 1918.
   61–3. A note is appended to the
poem in Faulkner's edition, 1735:
'These three last lines were intended
against that licentious Manner of
modern Poets, in making three

To Mr Harlyes Surgeon

A French adventurer, calling himself the Marquis de Guiscard, who had been taken in pay by the English government, entered into correspondence with France. He was seized and brought before the Privy Council, 8 March, 1711, when, during examination, he succeeded in wounding Harley with a penknife. Swift immediately sent off an account of the affair to Archbishop King (*Corresp.* i. 238), and wrote to Stella the same evening. He also began (see *Journal to Stella*, 16 April, 1711) and gave suggestions to Mrs. Manley for completing *A True Narrative of what pass'd at the Examination of the Marquis de Guiscard*. See further Boyer's *Political State of Great Britain*, i. 269–334; Craik, *Life of Swift*, i. 276–9.

Nearly a year after the incident, 19 Feby., 1711–12, Swift wrote to Stella: 'I dined with Ld Treas^r to day . . . I told him of 4 Lines I writt extempore with my Pencil, on a bitt of Paper in his House, while he lay wounded. Some of the Servants, I suppose, made wastpaper of them; and he never had heard of them. Shall I tell them you; They were inscribed to Mr Harley's Physicians.' He then proceeds to give the four lines, writing them continuously as prose.

The bit of paper still survives among the Marquis of Bath's Portland Papers at Longleat, vol. xi. f. 59. Near the top Swift has written in pencil:

To Mr Harlyes Surgeon
On Britain Europes safety lyes
And Britain's lost if Harly dyes
Harly depends upon your skill,
Think what you save or what you kill

J

The pencil is faint, and, lower down the slip, Edward Harley copied the lines in ink.

When he recalled the lines for Stella's benefit a year later Swift got the first line wrong, in the form, 'On Europe Britain's Safety lyes', and he began the second line, 'Britain is lost'.

Rhimes together, which they call *Triplets*; and the last of the three, was two or sometimes more Syllables longer, called an *Alexandrian*. These *Triplets* and *Alexandrians* were brought in by DRYDEN, and other Poets in the Reign of CHARLES II. They were the mere Effect of Haste, Idleness, and want of Money; and have been wholly avoided by the best Poets, since these Verses were written.' In this note Swift's hand may be clearly seen; for he writes in almost the same terms to Thomas Beach, in a letter dated 12 April, 1735 (*Corresp.* v. 162), soon after Faulkner's edition of the *Works* appeared.

A transcript of the lines, inaccurate, appears in the same volume at Long-leat, f. 76ᵛ·; and there are transcripts in the British Museum, Lansdowne 852. f. 53, and Harley 7316. p. 76. Swift's lines were printed by Nichols in his *Select Collection of Poems*, 1780–2, iv. 306; but they have not hitherto been gathered with his verse.

Guiscard's attack was followed by an outpouring of verse in Harley's honour (Longleat, xi. ff. 53–8). In 1765, in his additions to the *Works*, Deane Swift printed a Latin epigram on the incident composed by Atter-bury (sm. 8vo. xvii. 120). Cf. also British Museum, Add. MS. 1850. c. 10 (43), Fo. hf. sheet: 'To the Right Honourable Mr. *Harley*, On His appearing in Publick after the Wound given Him by *Guiscard*. By Jos. Trapp, M.A.'

AN

EXCELLENT NEW SONG,

BEING THE

Intended SPEECH of a famous Orator

against Peace.

An Excellent New Song, being the Intended Speech of a famous Orator against Peace. Half-sheet.
(?*The Earl of Nottingham's Speech to the Honourable House of Lords; London, printed by J. Tomson, near Covent-Garden, 1711.*)
The Whimsical Medley, i, Appendix, p. 31.
A Supplement to the Works of the Most Celebrated Minor Poets. . . . London: . . . F. Cogan, . . . 1750. Part iii. 89.
A Supplement to Dr. Swift's Works: . . . London, . . . J. Nichols, 1779.
Works, ed. Thomas Sheridan, 1784, vii. 74.

The occasion of this poem was the struggle for peace between the Tories and Whigs. Swift's masterly pamphlet in favour of the peace, *The Conduct of the Allies*, was published 27 Nov., 1711, and quickly ran through a num-ber of editions printed in London, Dublin, and Edinburgh. Before Parlia-ment re-assembled in December it was known that the Tory Earl of Nottingham had entered into an agreement with the Whigs to support their opposition to peace if they would assist him to pass his Occasional Conformity Bill. On 5 Dec. Swift wrote to Stella: 'Lord Nottingham, a famous Tory and speech-maker, is gone over to the Whig side.

... Lord-Treasurer was hinting as if he wished a ballad was made on him, and I will get up one against to-morrow.' It was printed the next day. On the 7th Parliament met. The Speech from the Throne was definitely pacific in tone. Marlborough supported Nottingham's amendment in the House of Lords, which was carried by a small majority. In the House of Commons the same evening the ministerial majority in favour of peace exceeded a hundred. The situation was difficult and dangerous; but Oxford calmly waited his time. Marlborough's popularity was waning; on 30 Dec. he was dismissed from all his offices; and on the 31st a majority was secured in the House of Lords by the creation of twelve new peers.

The Earl of Nottingham (1647–1730), nicknamed Dismal from his swarthy complexion, was further satirized by Swift in *Toland's Invitation to Dismal*, see p. 161, and in the prose broadside *A Hue and Cry after Dismal*.

The poem was not reprinted during Swift's lifetime. In 1750 Cogan included it in his miscellany; and it was one of the pieces collected by Nichols in his *Supplement*, 1779. Dr. Ball, *Swift's Verse*, p. 118, was the first to note and suggest that 'some version of the speech' may have been 'printed by a sham name'. In the *Journals of the House of Lords*, 15 Dec., 1711, it appears that: 'Complaint being made to the House, of a Paper printed and published, contrary to a Standing Order of this House, intituled, "*The Earl of* Nottingham's *Speech to the Honourable House of Lords*; London, printed by J. Tomson, *near* Covent-Garden, 1711".

'And the said Title being read:

'Lords Committees were appointed, to inquire who is the Author, Printer, and Publisher of the said Paper.'

A week later, on Saturday, 22 December, the committee reported that the paper had been 'printed by a sham Name', and 'by the Oath of *Sarah Vickers*, it appears to have been printed by *Andrew Hind*, living in *Peterborough-Court*, near *Fleet-Street*'.

It was ordered that Andrew Hind should be taken into custody. On Saturday, 19 January, 1711–12, he was reprimanded and discharged.

Was this untraced piece a pirated edition of Swift's poem?

There is a contemporary transcript (from the printed half-sheet?) at Welbeck Abbey showing a few insignificant variants. The only marked difference occurs at l. 52, which reads: 'I'le neither regard any figures or Tropes'.

The text is printed from the original half-sheet.

A N Orator *dismal* of *Nottinghamshire*,
　　　Who has forty Years let out his Conscience to
　　　hire,
Out of Zeal for his Country, and *want of a Place*,
Is come up, *vi & armis*, to *break the* Q—'s *Peace*.

He has vamp't an old Speech, and the Court to their
   sorrow,
Shall hear Him harangue against PRIOR to Morrow.
When once he begins, he never will flinch,
But repeats the same Note a whole Day, like a *Finch*.
I have heard all the Speech repeated by *Hoppy*.
And, *mistakes to prevent*, I *have obtain'd a Copy*.   10

The SPEECH.

WHereas, *Notwithstanding*, I am in great Pain,
   To hear we are making a Peace without *Spain*;
But, *most noble Senators*, 'tis a great Shame
There should be a Peace, while I'm *Not in game*.
The D— shew'd me all his fine House; and the D—s
From her Closet brought out a full Purse in her
   Clutches
I talk'd of a *Peace*, and they both gave a start,
His G— swore by —, and her G— let a F—t:
My *long old-fashion'd Pocket*, was presently cramm'd;
And sooner than Vote for a Peace I'll be d—nd.   20
But, some will cry, *Turn-Coat*, and rip up old Stories,
How I always pretended to be for the *Tories:*

5 Speech,] 1750   speech; 1779   15 D— ... D—s] Duke ... Dutchess 1750
16 Clutches] Clutches, 1750   clutches: 1779   18 by —,] by G—d, 1779

6. *Shall hear Him harangue against*
PRIOR . . . In July, 1711, Prior was
sent on a secret mission to Paris in an
attempt to negotiate terms of peace.
To the embarrassment of the ministry
he and his two companions were de-
tained at Deal upon their return; and,
to hide the affair in a cloud of dust,
Swift wrote his *New Journey to Paris.*
See *Prose Works*, ed. Temple Scott, v.
187–205; ed. Davis, iii. 207–18. *Cf.*
p. 268 n.

8. *Finch*. The family name of Lord
Nottingham.
9. *repeated by Hoppy*. Perhaps the
same as the Rt. Hon. Edward Hopkins, who went to Ireland later as chief
secretary to the Duke of Grafton. See
Gulliveriana, p. 61, 'Epilogue to
Hoppy's Benefit-Night'; and notes to
'Billet to the Company of Players',
p. 306.
15. *The D— . . . and the D—s*. The
Duke and Duchess of Marlborough.

2973.1   O

I answer; the Tories were in my good Graces,
Till all my *Relations* were put into *Places*.
But still I'm in Principle ever the same,
And will quit my best Friends, while I'm *Not in game*.

When I and some others subscribed our Names
To a Plot for expelling my Master K. *James*;
I withdrew my Subscription by help of a *Blot*,
And so might discover, or gain by the Plot: 30
I had my Advantage, and stood at Defiance,
For *Daniel* was got from the Den of the Lions:
I *came in* without Danger; and was I to blame?
For rather than *hang*, I would be *Not in game*.

I swore to the *Q—* that the *Pr—* of *H—r*
During Her Sacred Life, should never come over:
I made use of a *Trope*; that *an Heir to invite*,
Was like keeping her Monument always in sight.
But when I thought proper, I alter'd my Note;
And in Her own hearing I boldly did Vote,   40
That Her *M—* stood in great need of a *Tutor*,
And must have an *old*, or a *young Coadjutor:*
For why; I would fain have put all in a Flame,
Because, for some Reasons, I was *Not in game*.

Now my new *Benefactors* have *brought me about*,
And I'll Vote against Peace, *with Spain*, or *without:*
Tho' the *Court* gives my *Nephews*, and *Brothers*, and *Cousins*,
And all my whole Family, Places by Dozens;
Yet since I know where a *full Purse* may be found,
And hardly pay Eighteenpence Tax in the Pound: 50

23] *N.P.* 1750   35 *Pr—* of *H—r*] *Prince* of *Ha—er* 1750   41 Her
M—] her Majesty 1750

27. *When I and some others . . .*
Swift's charge against Nottingham of
double-dealing in his attitude toward
James II appears to have no founda-
tion. He was slow to change, slow to
accept the revolution settlement, but

once having accepted it was loyal.
32. *Daniel.* Nottingham's Christian
name.
35. *Pr— of H—r.* Prince of Hanover.

Since the *Tories* have thus disappointed my Hopes,
And will neither regard my *Figures* nor *Tropes*;
I'll *Speech* against *Peace* while *Dismal*'s my Name,
And be a *true Whig*, while I am *Not in game*.

The W - - ds—r Prophecy.

The W - - ds—r Prophecy. . . . Printed in the Year, 1711. Broadside.
(There are three editions of this broadside, two in which the prophecy is
set partly in black and partly in roman letter, but in differing type, and
one in which the prophecy is wholly in roman letter. The text is the
same.)
Faulkner, 1762, x. 266; 1763, xi. 358.
Works, 1762, xiv. 161; 1764, 4to, vii (2), 150, 8vo, xiv. 263. (Ed. by W.
Bowyer, assisted by J. Nichols.)
Works, ed. Sheridan, 1784, vii. 76.

    This fierce attack upon the Duchess of Somerset forms part of the story
of the struggle for and against peace with France. Swift and his friends
wished to see the Whig Duchess of Somerset removed from court favour
and influence.
    The subject of Swift's satire was Elizabeth, Baroness Percy (1667–1722),
only surviving daughter and sole heiress of Josceline Percy, eleventh and
last Earl of Northumberland, who died in 1670. Her early life was
chequered and adventurous. When only a girl she was married, in 1679, to
Henry Cavendish, Earl of Ogle, who died in the following year. In 1681
she married Thomas Thynne of Longleat, a man of wealth, friend of the
Duke of Monmouth, and the Issachar of Dryden's *Absalom and Achitophel.*
Repenting of the match, and before the marriage was consummated, the
bride fled to the protection of Lady Temple at The Hague. A few months
later, in February, 1681–2, Thynne was assassinated by friends of a rival
suitor, Count Königsmark, who was brought to trial, but acquitted. Four
months after the murder of Thynne, on 30 May, 1682, his widow was
married to Charles Seymour, sixth Duke of Somerset. Later the Duchess
became a favourite with Queen Anne; and, as an active Whig, incurred

1–54] The transcript in *The Whimsical Medley*, Cogan's reprint, 1750, and
Nichols, 1779, are all taken directly from the half-sheet edition, and contain no
variants beyond modernization and more careful punctuation.

Swift's hostility. See *D.N.B.* li. 297; *Notes and Queries*, 1 S. v. 269, also 78, 115, 183, 256; and 1 S. vi. 374.

There are references to 'The Windsor Prophecy' in the *Journal to Stella* on 23, 24, 26, 27 Dec., 1711, and 4 Jany., 1711–12. It was printed on the 24th of December, but barely published in the ordinary course, at least by Swift's account, for on the 26th Mrs. Masham asked him to stop it for fear of angering the Queen. And on the 4th of January he wrote, 'it is not published here, only printed copies given to friends'. The story is open to suspicion. The 'Prophecy' got abroad, and was twice reprinted in broadside form, whether by the first or by piratical printers. It is not unlikely that Swift made no more than a pretence of stopping publication. In 1733 he could no longer remember writing the poem (*Letters of Swift to Ford*, ed. D. Nichol Smith, p. 163).

Swift (see 'The Author upon Himself', p. 192 n.) attributed his disfavour with the Queen to *A Tale of a Tub*, and to the Duchess of Somerset's resentment of 'The Windsor Prophecy'. Sheridan, *Life of Swift*, 1784, pp. 95, 148–50, adopts this story.

Swift's statement, *Journal to Stella*, 24 Dec., 1711, that, 'it is somewhat in the same manner with that of Merlin in the Miscellanies', suggests that one of the black letter printings is the first edition of the piece.

The text is printed from one of the black letter broadsides. Faulkner's and the London editions of the *Works* show no variants save a few unimportant points of punctuation and spelling.

ABOUT three Months ago at *W--nd-r*, a poor Knight's Widow was buried in the Cloysters. In digging the Grave, the Sexton struck against a small Leaden Coffer, about half a Foot in length, and four Inches wide. The poor Man expecting he had discovered a Treasure, opened it with some difficulty; but found only a small Parchment, rolled up very fast, put into a Leather Case; which Case was tied at the top, and sealed with a St. *George*, the Impression on black Wax, very rude and *Gothick*. The Parchment was carried to a Gentleman of Learning, who found in it the following Lines, written in a black Old *English* Letter, and in the Orthography of the Age, which seems to be about Two hundred Years ago. I made a shift to obtain a Copy of it; but the Transcriber, I find, hath in many Parts alter'd the Spelling to the Modern way. The Original, as I am informed, is now in the Hands of the Ingenious Dr. *W*——, F.R.S. where, I suppose, the Curious will not be refused the Satisfaction of seeing it.

The Lines seem to be a sort of Prophesie, and written in Verse, as old Prophesies usually are, but in a very Hobling kind of Measure. Their Meaning is very dark, if it be any at all; of which the Learned Reader can judge better than I: However it be, several Persons were of Opinion, that they deserved to be Published, both as they discover somewhat of the Genius of a former Age, and may be an Amusement to the present.

𝕸𝖍𝖊𝖓 𝖆 𝖍𝖔𝖑𝖕 𝖇𝖑𝖆𝖈𝖐 Suede, 𝖙𝖍𝖊 Son 𝖔𝖋 Bob,
𝕸𝖎𝖙𝖍 𝖆 Saint 𝖆𝖙 𝖍𝖎𝖘 𝕮𝖍𝖎𝖓, 𝖆𝖓𝖉 𝖆 Seal 𝖎𝖓 𝖍𝖎𝖘 𝕱𝖔𝖇;
𝕾𝖍𝖆𝖑𝖑 𝖓𝖔𝖙 𝖘𝖊𝖊 𝖔𝖓𝖊 𝕹𝖊𝖜 𝖄𝖊𝖆𝖗𝖘-𝖉𝖆𝖕 𝖎𝖓 𝖙𝖍𝖆𝖙 𝖄𝖊𝖆𝖗,
𝕿𝖍𝖊𝖓 𝖑𝖊𝖙 𝖔𝖑𝖉 Englond 𝖒𝖆𝖐𝖊 𝖌𝖔𝖔𝖉 𝕮𝖍𝖊𝖆𝖗:
Windsor 𝖆𝖓𝖉 Bristow 𝖙𝖍𝖊𝖓 𝖘𝖍𝖆𝖑𝖑 𝖇𝖊
𝕵𝖔𝖕𝖓𝖊𝖉 𝖙𝖔𝖌𝖊𝖙𝖍𝖊𝖗 𝖎𝖓 𝖙𝖍𝖊 Low-Countree.
𝕿𝖍𝖊𝖓 𝖘𝖍𝖆𝖑𝖑 𝖙𝖍𝖊 𝖙𝖆𝖑𝖑 𝖇𝖑𝖆𝖈𝖐 Daventry Bird
𝕾𝖕𝖊𝖆𝖐 𝖆𝖌𝖆𝖎𝖓𝖘𝖙 𝕻𝖊𝖆𝖈𝖊 𝖗𝖎𝖌𝖍𝖙 𝖒𝖆𝖓𝖕 𝖆 𝕸𝖔𝖗𝖉;
𝕬𝖓𝖉 𝖘𝖔𝖒𝖊 𝖘𝖍𝖆𝖑𝖑 𝖆𝖉𝖒𝖎𝖗𝖊 𝖍𝖎𝖘 𝖈𝖔𝖓𝖕𝖓𝖌 𝕸𝖎𝖙𝖙,
𝕱𝖔𝖗 𝖒𝖆𝖓𝖕 𝖌𝖔𝖔𝖉 Groats 𝖍𝖎𝖘 𝕿𝖔𝖓𝖌𝖚𝖊 𝖘𝖍𝖆𝖑𝖑 𝖘𝖑𝖎𝖙𝖙: 10
𝕭𝖚𝖙 𝖘𝖕𝖎𝖌𝖍𝖙 𝖔𝖋 𝖙𝖍𝖊 Harpy 𝖙𝖍𝖆𝖙 crawls on all four,
𝕿𝖍𝖊𝖗𝖊 𝖘𝖍𝖆𝖑𝖑 𝖇𝖊 𝕻𝖊𝖆𝖈𝖊, 𝖕𝖆𝖗𝖉𝖎𝖊, 𝖆𝖓𝖉 𝕸𝖆𝖗 𝖓𝖔 𝖒𝖔𝖗𝖊.
𝕭𝖚𝖙 Englond 𝖒𝖚𝖘𝖙 𝖈𝖗𝖕 𝖆𝖑𝖆𝖈𝖐 𝖆𝖓𝖉 𝖜𝖊𝖑𝖑 𝖆 𝖉𝖆𝖕,
𝕴𝖋 𝖙𝖍𝖊 Stick 𝖇𝖊 𝖙𝖆𝖐𝖊𝖓 𝖋𝖗𝖔𝖒 𝖙𝖍𝖊 dead Sea.

1–6. *When a holy black Suede,* ... The allusions in these lines are to Dr. John Robinson, 1650–1723, who, *c.* 1680, was appointed chaplain to the English embassy at the Swedish court, where he remained more than twenty-five years. In 1709 he was appointed Dean of Windsor, Bishop of Bristol 1710, and Lord Privy Seal in 1711, preferments indicated by the words, 'Saint ... Seal ... Windsor ... Bristow'. He was, further, appointed first English plenipotentiary at the peace conference at Utrecht. Thus in his person the Deanery of Windsor and Bishopric of Bristol were 'Joyned together in the Low-Countree'. The allusion in line 3 is explained by the fact that the New Style, which was in use over a large part of the Continent, was not adopted in Great Britain and Ireland till 1752. The Bishop, leaving England at the end of December, O.S., arrived in Utrecht to find New Year's Day past by the New Style.

7. *Daventry Bird*. The Earl of Nottingham.

11. *Harpy*. The Duke of Marlborough.

14. *If the Stick be taken from the dead Sea.* Harley's wand of office. His second title was Lord Mortimer.

And dear Englond, if ought I understond,
Beware of Carrots from Northumberlond.
Carrots sown Thyn a deep root may get,
If so be they are in Sommer set:
Their Conyngs mark thou, for I have been told,
They Assassine when young, and Poison when old.
Root out these Carrots, O Thou, whose Name
Is backwards and forwards always the same;
And keep close to Thee always that Name,
Which backwards and forwards is allmost the same.
And Englond wouldst thou be happy still,
Bury those Carrots under a Hill.

CORINNA.

Miscellanies. The Last Volume, 1727, p. 226 (1731, p. 281; 1733, p. 281).
Faulkner, 1735, ii. 51 (1737, ii. 40). [Ref. F.]
Miscellanies, 1742, iv. 178.

The poem, as first printed in 1727, bears no date. Faulkner, in 1735, assigned it to 1712; but 1711 is probably correct. The subject of these lines is sufficiently indicated. Hawkesworth, in 1755, was the first to append a footnote, naming Mrs. Manley. It is difficult to divine the reason for Swift's attack.

16. *Carrots from Northumberlond.* The Duchess of Somerset, who had red hair. *Cf.* the reference to her, p. 195, in 'The Author upon Himself':
'From her red Locks her Mouth with Venom fills.'

17. *Thyn.* Thomas Thynne.

19. *Their Conyngs mark thou.* Count Königsmark.

21–2. ANNA, *i.e.* the Queen.

23–6. MASHAM. Lady Masham, whose maiden name was Abigail Hill (see l. 26), daughter of Francis Hill, was first cousin of the Duchess of Marlborough, by whose influence she was appointed bedchamber woman to Queen Anne. She gradually supplanted the Duchess in the Queen's favour; and became, through Harley's agency, an intermediary between the Queen and the Tory party. In 1707 she was privately married to Samuel Masham, groom of the bedchamber to Prince George of Denmark, to the great indignation of the Duchess of Marlborough when the fact was discovered. Through the influence of his wife Samuel Masham was one of the twelve Tory peers created in 1712 (see note, p. 142). He took the title, Baron Masham of Oates. Lady Masham was regarded by Swift with great friendliness and esteem. See Swift's *Corresp. passim*; *Prose Works*, ed. Temple Scott, v. 365 n. and *passim*.

For Mrs. Mary de la Rivière Manley, 1663–1724, see *D.N.B.* xxxvi. 35. The daughter of Sir Roger Manley, she was early led into a bigamous relationship with her cousin, John Manley. Thereafter she led a life of more than questionable morality. For some years she was mistress of Swift's friend, Alderman Barber. Her literary career, if also shady, brought her fame and some success. In *The New Atalantis* (1709) she satirized notable Whigs of the day; and in the same character wrote *Memoirs of Europe* (1710), and *Court Intrigues* (1711), besides plays, political pamphlets, and other pieces.

It is uncertain when Swift came to know Mrs. Manley personally. Writing to Addison, 22 August, 1710 (*Corresp.* i. 190), he refers to his reading of her *Memoirs of Europe* in terms which suggest that she was unknown to him. In the *Journal to Stella*, 14 Dec., 1710, he comments on Stella's mis-spelling of a word, and adds, 'let me have no more of that; 'tis the author of the Atlantis's spelling', by which it may be supposed he had seen manuscript or letters written by her. On 4 Jany., 1710–11, he writes, 'I dined with people that you never heard of, nor is it worth your while to know; an authoress and a printer'. The authoress was probably Mrs. Manley; and Swift's acquaintance with her may well have taken place at the end of 1710. His references to her are not many; but, whether in the *Journal* or in his *Correspondence*, are kindly. See his mention of her illness, *Journal*, 28 Jany., 1711–12.

The Tatler, No. 63, 1–3 September, 1709, which has been attributed to Swift, contains an attack upon Mrs. Manley as 'Epicene, the writer of Memoirs from the Mediterranean'. But it is most improbable that this paper came from Swift's hand (Craik, *Life of Swift*, i. 255 n.[3]; *Corresp.* i. 166 n.[7], 190 n.[4]).

In 1711 Mrs. Manley succeeded Swift as editor of *The Examiner*. In the same year he employed her to write *A True Narrative of what pass'd at the Examination of the Marquis de Guiscard*, and gave her hints for *A True Relation of the several Facts and Circumstances of the Intended Riot and Tumult on Queen Elizabeth's Birth-day*, and *A Learned Comment upon Dr. Hare's Excellent Sermon*. See *Journal to Stella*, 3 Nov., 1711; *Prose Works*, ed. Temple Scott, v. 171–2.

In view of these facts 'Corinna' is difficult to explain. The last stanza of the poem, with its reference to Mrs. Manley's *Memoirs of Europe*, shows that it could not have been written before 1710.

The text is printed from the *Miscellanies* of 1727.

THIS Day, (the Year I dare not tell,)
   Apollo play'd the Midwife's Part,
Into the World *Corinna* fell, .
   And he endow'd her with his Art.

1–32] The stanza divisions are not commonly observed in the Bathurst and trade editions, 1742, and later.

But *Cupid* with a *Satyr* comes;
  Both softly to the Cradle creep:
Both stroke her Hands, and rub her Gums,
  While the poor Child lay fast asleep.

Then *Cupid* thus: This little Maid
  Of Love shall always speak and write;   10
And I pronounce, (the *Satyr* said)
  The World shall feel her scratch and bite.

Her Talent she display'd betimes;
  For in twice twelve revolving Moons,
She seem'd to laugh and squawl in Rhimes,
  And all her Gestures were Lampoons.

At six Years old, the subtle Jade
  Stole to the Pantry-Door, and found
The Butler with my Lady's Maid;
  And you may swear the Tale went round.   20

She made a Song, how little Miss
  Was kiss'd and slobber'd by a Lad:
And how, when Master went to p--,
  Miss came, and peep'd at all he had.

At twelve, a Wit and a Coquette;
  Marries for Love, half Whore, half Wife;
Cuckolds, elopes, and runs in Debt;
  Turns Auth'ress, and is *Curll's* for Life.

Her Common-Place-Book all gallant is,
  Of Scandal now a *Cornucopia*;   30
She pours it out in an *Atlantis*,
  Or *Memoirs* of the *New Utopia*.

17 old,] 1731, F.   old 1733, 1742   29-32] *Om.* F.

14. *For in twice twelve.* Corrected
by Swift in his own copy of the *Miscellanies* to 'For, in a few'.
28. *Curll's for Life.* For the dis-
reputable bookseller, Edmund Curll,
see p. 394 n.; *D.N.B.* xiii. 327; and *The
Unspeakable Curll*, Ralph Straus, 1927.
31. ... *in an Atlantis.* The reference
is to Mrs. Manley's *New Atalantis*

(1709). In Bathurst's 1742 edition
altered to 'in an *Atalantis*', following
Mrs. Manley's spelling. Hawkesworth, in 1755, altered to 'in *Atalantis*'.

32. *Or Memoirs of the New Utopia.*
Mrs. Manley's *Memoirs of Europe*
(1710).

A

F A B L E

OF THE

Widow and her Cat.

A Fable of the Widow and her Cat. . . . Printed for John Morphew, near Stationers-Hall, 1712. Half-sheet.
A Fable of the Widow and her Cat. . . . London, Printed for Philpot near Charing-Cross, 1711. Broadside.
A Fable of the Widow and her Cat. . . . Printed in the Year MDCCXII. Broadside. Another edition, . . . Printed in the Year 1712.
A Fable of the VVidovv and her Cat. . . . London Printed; And Re-printed in [Dublin?]. Broadside.
Political State of Great Britain, Jany. 1711–12, iii. 13.
Supplement to Dr. Swift's Works, Ed. J. Nichols, 1779.

This piece is printed with some hesitation. The evidence is strong, however, that Swift had a hand in it.

On 21 Dec., 1711, an accusation of embezzlement was brought against Marlborough by the Commissioners appointed to examine the public accounts. On the 30th the Queen dismissed Marlborough from all his appointments 'that the matter might take an impartial examination'. A few days later was published 'A Fable of the Widow and her Cat', turning upon these incidents, and attacking the Duke of Marlborough. Swift's author ship was, from the first, assumed, or suspected. The poem was reprinted by Abel Boyer in his *Political State of Great Britain* for January, 1711–12, with a prefatory note: 'One of the Writers of the *Examiner,* who had constantly pursued the Duke with merciless Fury, and profligate Malice, did on this Occasion publish the following FABLE of the WIDOW AND HER CAT.' The words clearly point to Swift. On the 31st of the same month a poem in reply appeared, espousing Marlborough's cause, under the title, *When the Cat's away, the Mice may Play. A Fable. Humbly inscribed to Dr. Swift.* Swift refers to it in the *Journal to Stella,* on the day of publication: 'A poem is come out to-day inscribed to me, by way of a flirt; for it is a Whiggish poem, and good for nothing.' It is clear, therefore, that 'A Fable of the Widow and her Cat' was immediately ascribed to Swift, and that he did not directly dispute the attribution. It may be assumed, moreover, with more than a degree of probability, that his mention of an unnamed poem in the *Journal*, under the 4th of January, is a reference to this piece. 'I was in the city to-day, and dined with my printer, and gave him a ballad made by several hands, I know not whom. I believe Lord-Treasurer had a finger in it; I added three stanzas; I suppose Dr. Arbuthnot had the greatest share.' It may be added also that, in the *Biographia Britannica*, p. 3444, the 'Fable of the Widow and her Cat' is attributed to Swift and Prior in conjunction.

In his *Supplement*, 1779, Nichols printed both 'The Widow and her Cat' and 'When the Cat's away, the Mice may Play'; but with a footnote: 'This and the following Fable are not positively ascribed to *Swift*. They are very much in the manner of *Prior*.' They were reprinted by him in *A Select Collection of Poems*, 1780–82, iv. 50–5. See also *The Writings of Matthew Prior*, ed. A. R. Waller, ii. 380–4. But 'When the Cat's away, the Mice may Play' cannot possibly have been written by Prior, who was a diplomatic agent of the Tory ministry.

Dr. Elrington Ball assumes (*Swift's Verse*, p. 125) that Swift's words, under the 4th of January, refer to a ballad entitled, 'An Excellent new Song, Call'd The Trusty and True English-man' (see p. 1096). His reason for this attribution is not stated. It may be because the British Museum copy of this folio half-sheet ballad bears the inscription in a contemporary hand, '2. Jan. 17$\frac{11}{12}$ Ag^t y^e Whiggs'. But this date refers more probably to publication than to composition; and, in that case, cannot be reconciled with Swift's statement in the *Journal*, for the ballad of which he speaks was only handed to the printer on the 4th of January. The suggestion had previously been made, but purely as a guess, by Aitken, *Life and Works of Arbuthnot*, p. 43.

On the whole the evidence is in favour of Swift having played some part in the composition of 'A Fable of the Widow and her Cat'. See further an excellent note by Sir Charles Firth, *Review of English Studies*, 1925, i. 456.

The poem excited attention. In addition to the reply already noted, two others, at least, were printed, *The Fable of the Shepherd and his Dog*, which appeared on the 28th of January, and *The Fable of the Housewife and her Cock*.

Four editions of 'A Fable of the Widow and her Cat' appeared in rapid succession. The folio half-sheet printed by Morphew, and dated 1712, was almost certainly the first. The broadside edition without a printer's name, dated 1712, and the broadside 'Printed for Philpot', and dated 1711, were probably pirated editions of a popular piece.

Abel Boyer's reprint in the *Political State of Great Britain* was taken from one of the broadsheet editions, and contains only insignificant compositor's variants.

The text is printed from the half-sheet edition published by Morphew. There are no verbal variants between the broadsheet editions and reprints.

I.

A WIDOW kept a Favourite Cat,
    At first a gentle Creature;
    But when he was grown Sleek and Fat,
With many a Mouse, and many a Rat,
    He soon disclos'd his Nature.

II.

The *Fox* and He were Friends of old,
    Nor cou'd they now be parted;
They Nightly slunk to rob the Fold,
Devour'd the Lambs, the Fleeces sold,
    And Puss grew Lion-hearted.   10

III.

He scratch'd her Maid, he stole the Cream,
    He tore her best lac'd Pinner;
Nor Chanticleer upon the Beam,
Nor Chick, nor Duckling 'scapes, when *Grim*
    Invites the *Fox* to Dinner.

IV.

The Dame full wisely did Decree,
    For fear He shou'd dispatch more,
That the false Wretch shou'd worry'd be:
But in a sawcy manner He
    Thus Speech'd it like a *L—re*.   20

1. *A Widow kept a Favourite Cat.*
The Widow is Queen Anne; the Cat is
Marlborough.
6. *The Fox.* The Earl of Godolphin.
See *Prose Works*, x. 27, and notes, p. 131.
20. . . . *like a L—re.* Nicholas Lechmere, first Baron Lechmere, 1675–
1727. Called to the Bar, 1698. M.P.
successively for Appleby, Cocker-
mouth, and Tewkesbury. Solicitor-
General, 1714–18; Attorney-General,
1718–20. Raised to the peerage as
Baron Lechmere of Evesham, 1721.
In *The Examiner*, No. 26, Jany. 18–25,
1710–11, Swift suggests him as a
possible champion of the freethinkers
and Deists. He enjoyed a reputation
as an orator.

V.

"Must I, against all Right and Law,
  "Like Pole-Cat vile be treated?
"I! who so long with Tooth and Claw
"Have kept Domestick Mice in awe,
  "And Foreign Foes defeated!

VI.

"Your Golden Pippins, and your Pies,
  "How oft have I defended?
"'Tis true, the Pinner which you prize
"I tore in Frolick; to your Eyes
  "I never Harm intended.   30

VII.

"I am a Cat of Honour——Stay,
  Quo' She, no longer parly;
Whate'er you did in Battle slay,
By Law of Arms became your Prey,
  I hope you won it fairly.

VIII.

Of this, we'll grant you stand acquit,
  But not of your Outrages:
Tell me, Perfidious! Was it fit
To make my Cream a PERQUISITE,
  And Steal to mend your Wages?   40

IX.

So flagrant is Thy Insolence,
  So vile Thy Breach of Trust is;
That longer with Thee to Dispense,
Were want of Pow'r, or want of Sense:
  Here, *Towzer!*——Do Him Justice.

21–30, and the first six words of l. 31, printed in italics by Boyer and by the 1712, n.p. broadside.

26. *Your Golden Pippins*. An allusion to the golden apples guarded by a dragon in the garden of the Hesperides. It may be noted, as some evidence in favour of Swift's hand in the present poem, that in 'Sid Hamet', written only fifteen months earlier, he refers to the 'Hesperian Pippin'. See p. 134 and note.

45. *Towzer!* The watch-dog, Parliament.

The Fable of Midas.

The Fable of Midas. . . . *Printed for John Morphew near Stationers-Hall,*
   1712. Half-sheet.
The Fable of Midas. . . . *Printed in the Year, 1711.* Half-sheet.
Transcript by Stella; Manuscript Volume in the possession of the Duke of
   Bedford, Woburn Abbey. [Ref. S.]
Faulkner, 1735, ii. 93 (1737, ii. 74). [Ref. F.]
Miscellanies, 1735, v. 1 (1736, v. 1; 1745, 1749, v. 1; 1751, x. 1).
The Works of Jonathan Swift, D.D., ed. Hawkesworth, 1755, 4to edn.
   iv (1), 2.

This satire on the Duke of Marlborough was published on 14 February,
1711/12. On that day Swift wrote to Stella: 'To-day I published the
Fable of Midas, a Poem, printed in a loose half sheet of Paper. I know
not how it will sell; but it passd wonderfully at our Society to-night; and
Mr Sec^ty read it before me the other night to Ld T^r, at Ld Mashams,
where they equally approved of it. Tell me how it passes with you.'
   On the preceding 30th December Marlborough had been deprived of
all his appointments, a course which gave even Swift some apprehension.
Despite his inveterate hostility to the Duke, and injustice to his character,
he could write of him not ungenerously (see *Journal to Stella,* 6 Jan.,
1712/13); and he averred that on many occasions he had prevented hard
things being said of him (*Corresp.* ii. 39). The Duke's love of money chiefly
excited Swift's dislike. In *The Examiner,* No. 28, Feby. 1–8, 1710/11, he
addressed to Marlborough, as Marcus Crassus, a withering condemnation
of avarice. His remark on Macky's character of the Duke is a terse, 'De-
testably covetous' (*Prose Works,* ed. T. Scott, x. 273); and in a note to
Burnet's *History of his own Time* he dismisses Marlborough as, 'A composition of perfidiousness and avarice' (*Prose Works,* x. 359).
   See also the 'Satirical Elegy on the Death of a Famous General',
p. 295.
   This is one of the poems transcribed by Stella in the manuscript volume
now in the possession of the Duke of Bedford at Woburn Abbey. She
evidently copied from the printed half-sheet, which she follows even to
small detail.
   The poem was not reprinted in the four-volume Pope and Swift *Miscellanies,* 1727–32, and first reappeared in Faulkner's edition, 1735.
   The text is printed from the original half-sheet.

MIDAS, we are in Story told,
Turn'd ev'ry thing he touch't to *Gold*:
He *chip't* his *Bread*, the Pieces round
Glitter'd like Spangles on the Ground:
A Codling e'er it went his Lip in,
Would strait become a *Golden* Pippin:
He call'd for Drink, you saw him Sup
Potable Gold in *Golden Cup*.
His empty Paunch that he might fill,
He suck't his Vittels thro' a Quill;   10
Untouch't it pass't between his Grinders,
Or't had been happy for *Gold-finders*.
He cock't his Hat, you would have said
Mambrino's Helm adorn'd his Head.
Whene'er he chanc'd his Hands to lay,
On Magazines of *Corn* or *Hay*,
Gold ready Coin'd appear'd, instead
Of paultry *Provender* and *Bread*:
Hence we are by wise Farmers told,
Old Hay *is equal to old* Gold;   20
And hence a Critick deep maintains,
We learn't to weigh our *Gold* by *Grains*.
   This *Fool* had got a *lucky Hit*,
And People fancy'd he had *Wit*:
Two Gods their Skill in Musick try'd,
And both chose *Midas* to decide;
He against *Phebus* Harp decreed,
And gave it for *Pan*'s oaten Reed:

3 *Bread*,] *Bread*; F., 1735, 1745   4 Glitter'd] S., F. 1755 Glitter'd, 1735,
1745   7 Drink,] Drink; F., 1735, 1745   15 lay,] lay F., 1735, 1745,
1755   27, 54 *Phebus*] S., F. *Phœbus* 1735

1. *Midas*, . . . For the fable of Midas, king of Phrygia, to whom Dionysus granted the power of turning all he touched to gold, see Ovid, *Met.* xi. 85 ff.
14. *Mambrino's Helm. Orlando Furioso*, Canto i, st. 28. See also *Don Quixote*, chap. 36.

25. *Two Gods their Skill in Musick try'd*, . . . In a musical contest between Apollo and Pan, Midas decided for the latter, whereupon Apollo changed his ears to those of an ass, which the king attempted to conceal beneath a high Phrygian cap.

The God of Wit to shew his Grudge,
Clap't *Asses* Ears upon the Judge,   30
A goodly pair, erect and wide,
Which he could neither *Gild* nor hide.
     And now the Virtue of his *Hands*,
Was lost among *Pactolus* Sands,
Against whose Torrent while he Swims,
The *Golden* Scurf peels off his Limbs:
Fame spreads the News, and People travel
From far, to gather *golden* Gravel;
Midas, expos'd to all their Jears,
Had lost his *Art*, and kept his *Ears*.   40
THis Tale inclines the gentle Reader,
    To think upon a certain *Leader*,
To whom from *Midas* down, descends
That Virtue in the Fingers ends:
What else by *Perquisites* are meant,
By *Pensions*, *Bribes*, and *three per Cent?*
By *Places* and *Commissions* sold,
And turning *Dung* it self to *Gold?*
By starving in the midst of Store,
As t'other *Midas* did before?   50
     None e'er did modern *Midas* chuse,
Subject or Patron of his Muse,
But found him thus their Merit Scan,
That *Phebus* must give Place to *Pan:*
He values not the Poet's Praise,
Nor will exchange His *Plumbs* for *Bays:*
To *Pan* alone rich Misers call,
And there's the Jest, for *Pan* is *ALL:*

30 Judge,] Judge; F., 1735, 1745   42 *Leader*,] Leader; F., 1735, 1745
43 To whom] 1745, 1755   To whom, F., 1735   46 *per Cent?*] F., 1735
per Cent, 1745   *per cent*, 1755   47 sold,] sold; F., 1735, 1745   51
chuse,] chuse F., 1735, 1745, 1755   57 alone] 1755   alone, F., 1735, 1745

34. *Pactolus Sands.* Midas washed away his fatal gift in the Pactolus, whose sands were ever after rich in gold.
   45. *What else by Perquisites . . . For*   the charges of embezzlement and corruption brought against Marlborough see above, p. 151, notes to 'A Fable of the Widow and her Cat'.

Here *English* Wits will be to seek,
Howe'er, *'tis all one in the* Greek.   60
   Besides, it plainly now appears,
Our *Midas* too has *Asses* Ears;
Where every Fool his Mouth applies,
And whispers in a thousand Lies;
Such gross Delusions could not pass,
Thro' any Ears but of an *Ass.*
   But *Gold* defiles with frequent Touch,
There's nothing *fouls* the Hands so much:
And Scholars give it for the Cause,
Of *British Midas* dirty Paws;   70
Which while the *Senate* strove to scower,
They washt away the *Chymick* Power.
While He his utmost Strength apply'd,
To Swim against this *Pop'lar Tide*,
The *Golden* Spoils flew off apace,
Here fell a *Pension*, there a *Place*:
The *Torrent*, merciless, imbibes
Commissions, *Perquisites*, and *Bribes*,
By their own Weight sunk to the Bottom;
Much good may do 'em that have caught 'um.   80
And *Midas* now neglected stands,
With *Asses Ears*, and *dirty Hands.*

62 has] F., 1735, 1745   hath 1755   67 Touch,] Touch; F., 1735, 1745
73] *N.P.* 1735, 1736, 1745, 1755   75 apace,] apace; F., 1735, 1745,
1755   78 *Bribes*,] *Bribes*; F., 1735, 1745   80 *do 'em*] 1755   *do
'em*, F., 1735, 1745

  72. *They washt away the Chymick*   of inquiry Marlborough was deprived
Power. As a result of the commission   of his command and all his offices.

ATLAS.

writt. 1712

TO THE

EARL OF OXFORD, - - -

Swift's autograph: Lord Rothschild's Library, No. 2260.
Transcript by Stella; Manuscript Volume in the possession of the Duke of
Bedford, Woburn Abbey. [Ref. S.]
Miscellanies. The Last Volume, 1727, p. 87 (1731, p. 188; 1733, p. 188).
[Ref. 1727.]
Faulkner, 1735, ii. 48 (1737, ii. 38). [Ref. F.]
Miscellanies, 1742, iv. 85.

The strong Tory government of 1710 had scarcely been formed before
differences arose between Harley and St. John, which were steadily
accentuated, until Swift, in despair, retired to Letcombe in June, 1714,
where he wrote his comment upon the situation, *Some Free Thoughts upon
the Present State of Affairs* (*Prose Works*, ed. T. Scott, v. 391–415).
According to Swift, *Memoirs relating to that Change in the Queen's Ministry*
(*Prose Works*, v. 389), the first misunderstanding began with Guiscard's
attempt upon Harley in March, 1711. St. John affected to believe that the
blow was intended for him. Harley, however, got all the suffering, and
the credit. See also *Prose Works*, vol. viii, ed. Davis and Ehrenpreis.

'Atlas' was probably written about a year after that event. Dr. Ball
notes the connexion in thought of a passage in the *Journal to Stella*,
4 March, 1711–12, where, speaking of Oxford, Swift says that he 'cannot
do all himself, and will not employ others: which is his great Fault'. Swift,
Stella's transcript, Faulkner, and Deane Swift, *Essay*, 1755, p. 158, all
assign the poem to 1712. No date is given in the 1727 *Miscellanies*.

Stella gives the title as: 'Atlas. | To the Earl of Oxford. | Writ AD. 1712.'
The textual variants of her transcript show that she was copying from a
manuscript.

The text is printed from Swift's autograph, which, starting immediately
below the title, occupies the recto and one-quarter of the verso of the first
leaf of two, and is followed by a note in Pope's handwriting: 'This is the
Original, in Dr Swift's hand. A. Pope.'

ATLAS we read in antient Song
Was so exceeding tall and Strong,
He bore the Skyes upon his Back
Just as a Porter does his Pack
But, as a Porter overpresst
Unloads upon a Stall to rest
Or when he can no longer stand
Desires some Friend to lend a Hand
So Atlas, lest the pondrous Sphears
Should sink and fall about his Ears   10
Got Hercules to bear the Pile
That he might take his Rest awhile,
Yet Hercules was not so strong,
Nor could have borne it half so long.
 All Statesmen are in this Condition,
 And Atlas is a Politician
 A Premier Minister of State
 Alcides, one of second Rate.
 Suppose then Atlas ne'er so wise,
 Yet when the Weight of Kingdoms lyes   20
 Too long upon his single Shoulders
 He must sink down, or find Up-holders

1 Atlas] S.   *Atlas,* 1727, F., 1742   3 Skyes] S.   Skies 1727, F., 1742
4 Porter] S.   Pedlar 1727, F., 1742   5 Porter] S.   Pedlar 1727, F., 1742
8 some Friend] S.   a Friend 1727, F., 1742   12 take his Rest] S.   sit and
rest 1727, F., 1742   14 borne] S. born 1727, F., 1742   15 All] S.
Great 1727, F., 1742   18 Alcides,] S.   *Alcides* 1727, F., 1742   20 lyes] S.
lies 1727, F., 1742   22 He must sink down,] S.   Sink down he must, 1727,
F., 1742

T--l--nd's Invitation to *DISMAL*, to Dine with the CALVES-HEAD Club.

Imitated from Horace, *Epist. 5. Lib.* 1.

T—l—nd's Invitation to Dismal, to Dine with the Calves-Head Club.
Broadside. (There is also a second broadside edition, similar in appearance, but a different setting, possibly an Edinburgh reprint. There is a copy in the National Library of Scotland.)
Transcript by Stella; Manuscript Volume in the possession of the Duke of Bedford, Woburn Abbey. [Ref. S.]
Transcript in B.M. Add. MS. 32683.
Deane Swift's *Essay on the Life of Swift*, 1755, p. 228. [Ref. Deane Swift.]
Works, ed. Deane Swift, 1765, 4to edn., viii (2), 230; large 8vo, xvi. 357; sm. 8vo, xvii. 211. [Ref. 1765.]
Faulkner, 1765, xiii. 357.   Sheridan, 1784, vii. 79.

This lampoon upon the Earl of Nottingham (see p. 141) is mentioned by Swift, *Journal to Stella*, 1 July, 1712: 'Have you seen Toland's Invitation to Dismal? How do you like it? But it is an Imitation of Horace, and perhaps you don't understand Horace.' He also refers to it again under the 17th of July.

It was advertised in *The Examiner* as 'Lately Publish'd' (for the price of one penny) from 26 June to 31 July, when the advertisements cease. Although the broadside bears no printer's name, it was almost certainly printed by Morphew, who published *The Examiner*.

For John Toland, 1670–1722, the deist and speculative writer, see *D.N.B.* lvi. 438. His attack on orthodox religion, *Christianity not Mysterious* (1696), was ordered to be burnt. Later he became an active pamphleteer in support of the Whig party. In this satire Swift represents Lord Nottingham, the Tory, Churchman, and champion of the clergy, invited to join with Whigs and republicans in commemorating the execution of Charles I as a tyrant.

The Calves' Head Club was an association instituted in disrespect to the memory of Charles I. A calf's head formed a prominent part of the meal at annual dinners held on the 30th of January, the date of the King's execution. The original broadside edition is dated at the foot of the text, '*January* 29'. This is not the date of composition, but part of the text, representing the eve of the annual celebration.

For a bitter attack on the club see *The Secret History of the Calves-Head*

Club: Or, The Republican Unmasked (1703), an anonymous pamphlet,
which ran through many editions in the reign of Anne, and is reprinted
in the *Harleian Miscellany*. The association gradually expired after the
restoration; but the *Gentleman's Magazine*, v. 105, gives an account of
a riot following a meeting held under the name of the club in 1735.
This, however, may have been a hoax.

The poem was not included in any of the collections published during
Swift's lifetime. It was reprinted by Deane Swift, *Essay*, 1755, who says
that it was written on a hint from Oxford 'that he wished a ballad was
made on the E. of ✱✱✱'.

Stella's transcript shows no verbal variants, although a number of differences in punctuation; and the proper names are written in full. She has
not written in the date, '*January* 29', nor copied the Latin at the foot of
the poem. It is not improbable, therefore, that she was copying from a
manuscript.

The text is printed from the original broadside.

I F, dearest 𝕯𝖎𝖘𝖒𝖆𝖑, you for once can Dine
   Upon a single Dish, and Tavern Wine,
   T—l—nd to you this Invitation sends,
To eat the *CALVES-HEAD* with your trusty Friends.
Suspend a while your vain ambitious Hopes,
Leave hunting after Bribes, forget your Tropes:
To morrow We our *Mystick Feast* prepare,
Where Thou, our latest *Proselyte*, shalt share:
When We, by proper Signs and Symbols tell,
How, by *Brave Hands*, the *Royal TRAYTOR* fell;   10
The Meat shall represent the *TYRANT*'s Head,
The Wine, his Blood, *our Predecessors* shed:
Whilst an *alluding* Hymn some Artist sings,
We toast Confusion to the Race of Kings:

    S I potes archiacis conviva recumbere lectis,
      Nec modica cœnare times olus omne patella:
    Supremo te sole domi, Torquate, manebo.
    ✱   ✱   ✱   ✱   ✱   ✱   ✱

    Mitte leves spes, & certamina divitiarum,
    Et Moschi causam: Cras nato Cæsare festus
    Dat veniam somnumque dies: impune licebit
    Æstivam sermone benigno tendere noctem.
    ✱   ✱   ✱   ✱   ✱   ✱   ✱

*Spelling and typographical usage are modernized in Deane Swift's reprint, and
in 1765. In 1765, with the exception of line 26, proper names are printed in full.*

    12 shed:] shed, S., Deane Swift   shed; 1765

At Monarchy we nobly shew our Spight,
And talk *what Fools call Treason* all the Night.
  Who, by Disgraces or ill Fortune sunk,
Feels not his Soul enliven'd when he's Drunk?
Wine can clear up *G - - d - - lph - - n*'s cloudy Face,
And fill *J—ck Sm—th* with Hopes to keep his Place; 20
By Force of Wine ev'n *Sc - - rb - - r - - w* is Brave,
Hal - - grows more Pert, and *S - - mm - - rs* not so
  Grave:

> Quid non ebrietas designat? operta recludit;
> Spes jubet esse ratas; in prælia trudit inermem:

19. *G--d--lph--n's cloudy Face.* For Sidney Godolphin, first Earl of Godolphin, see p. 131.

20. *J—ck Sm—th.* John Smith, 1655–1723, sat as member of parliament for several constituencies from 1678 to the year of his death. He was a strong Whig, and friend of Godolphin, with whom he resigned office (*Corresp.* i. 194); Speaker of the House of Commons, 1705–8; Chancellor of the Exchequer, 1708–10. In his copy of Macky's *Characters* Swift wrote, 'I thought him a heavy man'.

21. *Sc--rb--r--w.* Richard Lumley, first Earl of Scarborough, d. 1721. A descendant of an ancient family, he was created Baron Lumley in 1681; Viscount Lumley, 1689; and Earl of Scarborough, 1690. He saw active service as a soldier in England, Flanders, and Ireland. His troop of horse captured the Duke of Monmouth after the battle of Sedgemoor; and he fought at the battle of the Boyne. He retired from active service in 1697. He was of the privy council; but held no office under Anne.

Nichols in his reprint of Swift's *Letter to a Whig Lord* (*Supplement*, 1779) suggests that it may have been addressed to Scarborough; but this is doubtful (*Prose Works*, ed. T. Scott, v. 238).

22. *Hal - -.* Henry Boyle. He is re-ferred to also in lines 33 and 38, in the latter as '*Harry*', the name by which he is mentioned in Swift's *Examiner*, No. 18, 30 Nov., 1710. From 1708 to 1710 he was principal Secretary of State. In 1714, on the accession of George I, he was raised to the peerage as Baron Carleton. Against Macky's characterization of Boyle, Swift wrote: 'Had some very Scurvy Qualities, particularly avarice.'

22. *S--mm--rs.* John, Lord Somers, was born in 1651. Of comparatively humble origin, he raised himself by his own abilities. He distinguished himself as one of the counsel for the seven bishops in 1688; and was active in asserting the abdication of James II. After holding office as Solicitor-General, and Lord Keeper, he was raised to the peerage in 1697 as Baron Somers of Evesham, and became Lord Chancellor. He was one of the four Whig Lords impeached by the House of Commons in 1701 for their share in the partition treaties. Swift's *Contests and Dissensions between the Nobles and Commons* was written at this time in defence of Somers, who appears in the pamphlet as Aristides. His authorship of the piece led to the friendship of Somers, to whom, later, he dedicated *A Tale of a Tub.* As late as 1708 Somers attempted to secure the Bishopric of Waterford for Swift; and also

Wine can give P—rt—d Wit, and Cl - - v - - nd Sense,
M - - t - - g - - e Learning, B - - lt - - n Eloquence:
Ch—ly, when Drunk, can never lose his *Wand*,
And L - - nc - - n then imagines he has Land.

Sollicitis animis onus eximit; addocet artes.
Fœcundi calices quem non fecere disertum ?
Contracta quem non in paupertate solutum ?

recommended him to Lord Wharton, who was going to Ireland as Lord-Lieutenant. But estrangement from Somers, as from other Whig friends, followed Swift's secession to the Tories. In later years, when annotating Macky's *Characters*, he described him as possessed of 'all excellent qualifications except virtue'. The characteristic which he attributes to Somers in this satire had evidently made an impression on Swift, for in his *Memoirs relating to the Queen's Ministry*, he speaks of 'the formality of his nature' (*Prose Works*, v. 380).

23. *P—rt—d Wit, and Cl--v--nd Sense*. William Bentinck, when page of honour to William of Orange, won that prince's lifelong affection and esteem. He was employed by William on confidential missions, and accompanied him to England, where he was created Baron Cirencester, Viscount Woodstock, and Earl of Portland. He was impeached in 1701 with Somers, Orford, and Halifax; and appears in the *Contests and Dissensions* as Phocion. His abilities were not remarkable. 'As great a Dunce as ever I knew,' Swift wrote of him in his copy of Macky's *Characters*. Charles Fitzroy, natural son of Charles II by Barbara Villiers, Duchess of Cleveland, succeeded to the title on the death of his mother in 1709.

24. *M--t--g--e*. Charles Montagu, first Earl of Halifax, whose friendship Swift also won by his *Contests and Dissensions*, in which he appears as Pericles and Alcibiades. A gradual

estrangement between the two may be traced in the *Journal to Stella*. He entered Parliament in 1689, and quickly showed a genius for finance. From 1694 to 1699 he was Chancellor of the Exchequer. In 1700 he was created Baron Halifax of Halifax; and, on the accession of George I, Viscount Sunbury and Earl of Halifax. He died the next year, 1715. He was a generous patron of letters, and Swift's comment on him (*Prose Works*, x. 275) is hardly justified. See also p. 481 n.

24. *B--lt--n*. The second Duke of Bolton and seventh Marquis of Winchester, who succeeded his father in 1699. During the reign of Queen Anne he held no distinguished office; but he was Lord-Lieutenant of Ireland from 1717 to 1719. He died in 1722.

25. *Ch—ly*. Hugh, created first Earl of Cholmondeley in 1706. In 1708 he was appointed Treasurer of the Household, an office from which he was dismissed in April, 1713, for opposing the ratification of the Treaty of Utrecht. He was, however, reappointed to the same office in the following year, and held it till his death in 1724. Swift held him in great dislike, and described him in his copy of Macky's *Characters* as 'Good for nothing as far as I ever knew'.

26. *L--nc--n*. Henry Clinton, seventh Earl of Lincoln, 1684–1728. In 1708 he was appointed a Lord of the Bedchamber to George, Prince of Denmark. He held several minor offices under George I.

My Province is, to see that all be right,
Glasses and Linnen clean, and Pewter bright;
From our *Mysterious Club* to keep out Spies,
And *Tories* (dress'd like Waiters) in Disguise.   30
You shall be coupled as you best approve,
Seated at Table next the Men you love.
S—nd—d, Or—rd, B—l, and R—ch—d's Grace
Will come; and H - - - mp - - - n shall have W - - - p - - - l's
    Place.

       Hæc ego procurare & idoneus imperor, & non
       Invitus; ne turpe toral, ne sordida mappa
       Corruget nares, ne non & cantharus & lanx
       Ostendat tibi te; ne fidos inter amicos
       Sit qui dicta foras eliminet: ut coeat par
       Jungaturque pari, Brutum tibi Septimiumque,

33. *S—nd—d.* Charles Spencer, 1674–1722, third Earl of Sunderland, an extreme Whig who had been dismissed in 1710 from the office of Secretary of State. He married Anne, daughter of Marlborough, in 1700. His political career was thwarted by an unattractive temper. Founded the famous library at Althorp.

33. *Or—rd.* Edward Russell, 1653–1727, Earl of Orford, the famous admiral. On three occasions he held office as First Lord of the Admiralty. A Whig in politics, he appears in Swift's *Contests and Dissensions* both as Miltiades and Themistocles.

33. *R—ch—d's Grace.* Charles Lennox, 1672–1723, first Duke of Richmond, natural son of Charles II by Louise de Keroualle, Duchess of Portsmouth. His daughter married the third Earl of Berkeley, son of the Lord Justice to whom Swift was attached as chaplain in Ireland (see pp. 61–2). The Duke was dismissed by Swift as 'A shallow Coxcomb' (Macky's *Characters*).

34. *H---mp---n.* Richard Hampden, son and heir of the John Hampden who committed suicide in 1696. He succeeded his father in the possession of his estates. He was, on several occasions from 1700 to his death in 1728, M.P. for Wendover; he also represented Buckinghamshire more than once; and, for a period, Berwick-on-Tweed. See G. Lipscomb's *History of Bucks.*, 1847, ii, pp. 265 ff., 478–9. On 20 March, 4 George I, he was appointed Treasurer of the Navy, an office he held till 20 Oct., 1720, when, owing to speculation in the South Sea scheme, a deficiency in his accounts was discovered. See also *Hist. MSS. Commission, Bath MSS.* i. 222, *Portland MSS.* vii. 429, 431; references in the *Wentworth Papers*, ed. J. J. Cartwright, 1883; and Boyer's *Political State of Great Britain*, 1712, iii. 408.

34. *W---p---l's Place.* In 1708 Walpole was appointed Secretary at War, and in 1710 Treasurer of the Navy. On party grounds he was, however, accused of 'high breach of trust and notorious corruption' in the discharge of his duties, expelled the House on 17 January, 1712, and sent to the Tower. See *Journal to Stella* under 16 January, 1711–12.

Wh—n, unless prevented by a Whore,
Will hardly fail, and there is room for more:
But I love Elbow-room when're I drink,
And honest *Harry* is too apt to stink.
Let no pretence of Bus'ness make you stay,
Yet take one Word of Counsel by the way: 40
If *Gu—rn—y* calls, send word you're gone abroad;
He'll teaze you with King *Charles* and Bishop *Laud*,
Or make you Fast, and carry you to Prayers:
But if he will break in, and walk up Stairs,
Steal by the Back-door out, and leave him there;
Then order *Squash* to call a Hackney Chair.   *January* 29.

> Et nisi cœna prior potiorque puella Sabinum
> Detinet, assumam, locus est & pluribus umbris:
> Sed nimis arcta premunt olidæ convivia capræ.
> Tu quotus esse velis rescribe: & rebus omissis,
> Atria servantem postico falle clientem.

41 calls,] S.   call, Deane Swift, 1765

35. *Wh—n.* Thomas Wharton, the first Marquis of Wharton (1648–1715). The son of a puritanical father, he became an unabashed profligate. He possessed, however, marked ability; and throughout a long public career remained a consistent Whig. He took an active part in inviting the Prince of Orange over in 1688, and was a favourite with William throughout his reign in England. On the accession of Queen Anne he was dismissed from his posts, but continued his public activities. In 1708 he went to Ireland as Lord-Lieutenant, and took Addison as his secretary. In *The Examiner*, No.

18, 30 November, 1710, Swift attacked Wharton, under the name of Verres, and held up to scorn his government of the country. A few days later he published what he himself described as 'a damned libellous pamphlet', his *Short Character of His Ex. T. E. of W.* During the latter years of Queen Anne's reign Wharton was a vigorous opponent of the Tory government.

41. *Gu—rn—y.* Heneage Finch, brother of 'Dismal', Lord Nottingham. He was created Baron Guernsey in 1703, and Earl of Aylesford in 1714.

Peace and Dunkirk;

BEING AN

Excellent New Song upon the Surrender of Dunkirk *to General* Hill.

To the Tune of, *The King shall enjoy his own again.*

Peace and Dunkirk; Being an Excellent New Song upon the Surrender of Dunkirk to General Hill. . . . London, Printed in the Year, 1712. Broadside.
A Supplement to Dr. Swift's Works: . . . London: . . . J. Nichols, 1779.
Works, ed. Thomas Sheridan, 1784, vii. 81.

The broadside was advertised as 'Just Publish'd' in *The Examiner* of the dates July 3–10, 10–17, 17–24, 24–31, 1712. Swift mentions it in the *Journal to Stella* on the 17th of July.

Major-General John Hill was a brother of Abigail Hill, later Lady Masham, the supplanter of the Duchess of Marlborough in Anne's favour. He was made a page to the Queen, and, through Marlborough's influence, received a commission in the army in 1703. He commanded a brigade at Almanza, 1707; and was wounded at Mons in 1709. In 1711 he was placed in command of an expedition dispatched to attack the French settlements in America, which failed with heavy losses. He was appointed governor of Dunkirk, of which he took possession on 19 July, 1712, not many days after the publication of *Peace and Dunkirk.*

As Lady Masham was greatly esteemed by Swift, he was on friendly terms with her brother. In November, 1711, Hill was elected a member of the dining society of wits and men of interest to which Swift belonged. In the *Journal to Stella,* 18 September, 1712, Swift refers to a snuff-box, 'the finest that ever you saw', presented to him by Hill; and, further, mentions dining with him and his two sisters, Lady Masham and Mrs. Hill, on 27 December, 1712. See also *Corresp.* i. 336–9.

The text is printed from the original broadside. In 1733 Swift declared that he could not remember this poem (*Letters of Swift to Ford,* ed. D. Nichol Smith, p. 163).

SPIGHT of *Dutch* Friends and *English* Foes,
  Poor *Britain* shall have Peace at last;
Holland got Towns, and we got Blows,
  But *Dunkirk*'s ours, we'll hold it fast:
    We have got it in a String,
    And the 𝔚𝔥𝔦𝔤𝔰 may all go Swing,
For among good Friends, I love to be plain;
    All their false deluded Hopes,
    Will, or ought to end in Ropes;
But the QUEEN *shall enjoy Her own again.*   10

II.

Sunder—*d*'s run out of his Wits,
  And 𝔇𝔦𝔰𝔪𝔞𝔩 double-𝔇𝔦𝔰𝔪𝔞𝔩 looks;
Whar—*n* can only Swear by Fits,
  And strutting *Hal*— is off the Hooks;
    Old *Godol*—*n* full of Spleen,
    Made *false Moves*, and lost his QUEEN;
Harry look'd fierce, and shook his ragged Mane:
    But a Prince of high Renown,
    Swore he'd rather lose a *Crown*,
Than the QUEEN *should enjoy Her own again.*   20

III.

Our Merchant Ships may cut the Line,
  And not be snapt by Privateers,

---

1 Spight . . .] *Nichols's text, 1779, followed the original broadside, from which it varies only in typographical usage, in punctuation, and in one printer's error.*

2. *Poor Britain shall have Peace at last.* When Swift's broadside was published the secret negotiations which had been progressing between England and France had led to a cessation of hostilities. The demolition of the fortress of Dunkirk was a condition demanded by England. The Treaty of Utrecht was not finally confirmed till the spring of the following year.

11. *Sunder—d's.* For Charles Spencer, third Earl of Sunderland, see p. 165 n.

12. *Dismal.* The Earl of Nottingham. See pp. 141–2.

13. *Whart—n.* For Thomas Wharton, first Marquis of Wharton, see p. 166 n.

14. *Hal—.* Henry Boyle. Referred to again as Harry in line 17. See p. 163 n.

15. *Godol—n.* For Lord Godolphin see p. 131.

And Commoners who love good Wine,
   Will drink it now as well as Peers:
      Landed-Men shall have their Rent,
      Yet our Stocks rise *Cent. per Cent*,
The *Dutch* from hence shall no more Millions drain;
      We'll bring on us no more Debts,
      Nor with Bankrupts fill *Gazetts*,
And the QUEEN *shall enjoy Her own again.*   30

IV.

The Towns we took ne'er did us good,
   What signify'd the *French* to beat?
We spent our Mony and our Blood,
   To make the *Dutch*-men proud and great:
      But the Lord of *Oxford* Swears,
      Dunkirk never shall be theirs,
The *Dutch*-hearted 𝔚𝔥𝔦𝔤𝔰 may rail and complain;
      But true *English* Men will fill,
      A good Health to Gen'ral *Hill*,
For the QUEEN *now enjoys Her own again.*   40

Part of the SEVENTH EPISTLE
of the FIRST BOOK of
H O R A C E
IMITATED.

Part of the Seventh Epistle of the First Book of Horace Imitated: And Address'd to a Noble Peer. London: Printed for A. Dodd, at the Peacock without Temple-Bar. 1713. Price 3 d. 4to. pp. 12 (2nd edn., 1713; 3rd edn., 1713).

   Title] Stella *has* 'Imitation of Horace | to Lord Oxford. A.D. 1713.'

The Seventh Epistle of the first Book of Horace Imitated. . . . *Dublin: Reprinted for John Henly, Bookseller in Castle-sttreet, 1713.* 4to. pp. 4. [Ref. D.]

Political State of Great Britain, November, 1713, vi. 340.

Transcript by Stella; Manuscript Volume in the possession of the Duke of Bedford, Woburn Abbey. [Ref. S.]

The Whimsical Medley, i. 238. [Ref. *W.M.*]

Miscellaneous Works, Comical & Diverting: . . . *London, Printed by Order of the Society de propagando, &c.* M.DCC.XX. p. 411.

Miscellanies in Prose and Verse. The Fourth Edition, . . . *Dublin:* . . . *S. Fairbrother,* . . . 2721 [1721], p. 232.

Miscellanies, . . . *The Fourth Edition.* . . . *London:* [Curll] . . . 1722. p. 197.

Miscellanies. The Last Volume. 1727, p. 21 (1731, p. 145; 1733, p. 145). Faulkner, 1735, ii. 100 (1737, ii. 79). [Ref. F.]

This poem, addressed to Oxford, was written by Swift on his return to England after his installation as Dean of St. Patrick's; and was published 23 October, 1713.

The text is printed from the first edition. Parallels from the original of Horace, printed as footnotes in the early editions, have been omitted.

Henly's reprint has some obvious mistakes, followed by Stella, the *Whimsical Medley,* and Fairbrother's edition of the *Miscellanies.* Absence of reference to Fairbrother's *Miscellanies* indicates agreement with Henly's reprint. The *Political State of Great Britain* follows Dodd's London edition.

There is a transcript in a clerical hand, evidently from the first edition, among the manuscripts of the Marquis of Bath, *Portland Papers,* xvii. ff. 133–5.

H ARLEY, the Nation's great Support,
Returning home one Day from Court,
(His Mind with Publick Cares possest,
All *Europe's* Bus'ness in his Breast)
Observ'd a *Parson* near *Whitehall,*
Cheapning old Authors on a Stall.
The Priest was pretty well in case,
And shew'd some Humour in his Face;
Look'd with an easie, careless Mien,
A perfect Stranger to the Spleen;   10
Of Size that might a Pulpit fill,
But more inclining to sit still.

3, 4] *Om. brackets* D., S., 1720

MY LORD, who (if a Man may say't)
Loves Mischief better than his Meat,
Was now dispos'd to crack a Jest;
And bid Friend *Lewis* go in quest
(This *Lewis* is a Cunning Shaver,
And very much in *HARLEY*'s Favour)
In quest, who might this *Parson* be,
What was his Name, of what Degree;   20
If possible, to learn his Story,
And whether he were *Whig* or *Tory?*
   Lewis his Patron's Humour knows;
Away upon his Errand goes,
And quickly did the Matter sift,
Found out that it was Dr. *S—t:*
A Clergyman of special Note,
For shunning those of his own Coat;
Which made his Brethren of the Gown
Take care betimes to run him down: 30
No Libertine, nor Over-nice,
Addicted to no sort of Vice;
Went where he pleas'd, said what he thought,
Not Rich, but ow'd no Man a Groat;
In State-Opinions *a-la Mode*,
He hated *Wh—n* like a Toad;
Had giv'n the *Faction* many a Wound,
And Libell'd all the *Junta* round;
Kept Company with Men of Wit,
Who often father'd what he writ;   40

13 if] as D. *In Stella's transcript* 'as' *is corrected to* 'if'   14 Meat,] 1720,
1722, 1727, F. Meat; D., S.   16 quest] Quest. D., S., 1720 quest, 1722,
1727 quest; F.   24 goes,] 1720, 1722, 1727 goes S. goes; F. goes: D.
26 *S—t:*] F. Swift. S. *Swift:* 1720, 1722, 1727   30 betimes] 1720, 1722,
1727, F. by time D., S., *W.M.* in time 1721   36 *Wh—n*] D., S., 1727
Wharton 1720, 1722, F.   38 *Junta*] 1720, 1722, F. *Juncto* D. Juncto S.
Junto 1727

13. (*if a Man may say't*). In Stella's transcript 'as' is scored out, and 'if' written above the line. Forster conjectured that the correction was in Swift's hand, but this is not the case.

It seems probable that Stella was copying from Henly's Dublin reprint.
  16. *Lewis.* See p. 199 n.
  36. *Wh—n.* Thomas Wharton, first Marquis of Wharton, see p. 166 n.

His Works were hawk'd in ev'ry Street,
But seldom rose above a Sheet:
Of late indeed the Paper-*Stamp*
Did very much his Genius cramp;
And, since he could not spend his Fire,
He now intended to Retire.
    Said *HARLEY*, I desire to know
From his own Mouth, if this be so?
Step to the Doctor straight, and say,
I'd have him Dine with me to Day.   50
S—t seem'd to wonder what he meant,
Nor wou'd believe MY LORD had sent;
So never offer'd once to stir,
But coldly said, *Your Servant, Sir.*
Does he refuse me? *HARLEY* cry'd:
He does, with Insolence and Pride.
Some few Days after *HARLEY* spies
The Doctor fasten'd by the Eyes,
At *Charing-Cross*, among the Rout,
Where painted Monsters are hung out.   60
He pull'd the String, and stopt his Coach,
Beck'ning the Doctor to approach.
    S—t, who could neither fly nor hide,
Came sneaking to the Chariot-side,
And offer'd many a lame Excuse;
He never meant the least Abuse—

46 He now intended] 1720, 1722, 1727, F.   Is now contented D., S., *W.M.*
48 so?] 1720, 1722, 1727   so; D., S.   so: F.   51 *S—t*] D., F.   Swift S.
Swift 1720, 1722, 1727   52 wou'd] 1720, 1722   cou'd D., S.   would 1727,
F.   55 refuse me? *HARLEY* cry'd:] 1722, 1727   refuse me Harley cry'd?
D., S.   refuse me? HARLEY cry'd. F.   60 are hung out.] dangle out.
F.   61 his] the D., S.   63 *S—t*,] F.   Swift S.   *Swift*, 1720, 1722,
1727   63 could] would S.   wou'd D., *W.M.*   64 to the Chariot-side,]
by the Chariots Side; D., S.   to the Chariot side, 1720   to the Chariot Side,
1722, 1727, F.

43. *Paper-Stamp.* The Newspaper Stamp Duty was imposed as the most 'effectual way of suppressing libels' and attacks on the government. An Act was passed by Parliament, 10 June, 1712, to come into force on the 1st of August, by which all newspapers printed on a half-sheet, or less, were to be taxed a halfpenny, a penny if on a whole sheet and not more. See *Journal to Stella*, 31 Jany., 1711, 19 July, 7 Aug., 1712.

My Lord—The Honour you design'd—
Extremely proud—but I had din'd—
I'm sure I never shou'd neglect—
No Man alive has more Respect—   70
Well, I shall think of that no more,
If you'll be sure to come at *Four.*
The Doctor now obeys the Summons,
Likes both his Company and Commons;
Displays his Talent, sits till Ten,
Next Day invited, comes agen;
Soon grows Domestick, seldom fails
Either at Morning, or at Meals;
Came early, and departed late:
In short, the Gudgeon took the Bait: 80
MY LORD wou'd carry on the Jest,
And down to *Windsor* takes his Guest.
S—t much admires the Place and Air,
And longs to be a *Canon* there;
In Summer round the Park to ride,
In Winter—never to reside.
A *Canon!* that's a Place too mean:
No, Doctor, you shall be a *Dean;*
Two Dozen *Canons* round your Stall,
And you the Tyrant o'er them all: 90
You need but cross the *Irish* Seas,
To live in Plenty, Power and Ease.
Poor *S—t* departs, and, what is worse,
With borrow'd Money in his Purse;

67–70] *Rom. and quotes* 1720   69 *I'm sure*] 1720, 1722, 1727, F.   I am
sure— D., S.   72, 73] *In quotes* 1727, F.   75 Ten,] Ten; D., S., 1727,
F. ten, 1720, 1722   79 Came . . . departed] *Corrected to* 'Comes . . . departeth'
by Swift *in his copy of Faulkner,* 1737, *vol. ii*   83 *S—t*] F., D.   Swift S.
Swift 1720, 1722, 1727   93 *S—t*] D., F.   Swift S.   *Swift* 1720, 1722, 1727
93 departs, and, what is worse,] 1720   departed, and what's worse, S.
departed, and what is worse, D., 1721   departs; and, what is worse, 1722,
1727, F.

94. *With borrow'd Money . . .* Swift   Stearne, his predecessor (see *Corresp.* ii.
found that on taking possession of   124, 147), and the expenses of installa-
his Deanery he incurred liability to   tion were burdensome. Furthermore,

Travels at least a Hundred Leagues,
And suffers numberless Fatigues.
 Suppose him, now, a *Dean* compleat,
Devoutly lolling in his Seat;
The Silver Virge, with decent Pride,
Stuck underneath his Cushion-side: 100
Suppose him gone through all Vexations,
Patents, Instalments, Abjurations,
First-Fruits and Tenths, and Chapter-Treats,
Dues, Payments, Fees, Demands and Cheats,
(The wicked Laity's contriving,
To hinder Clergymen from thriving);
Now all the Doctor's Money's spent,
His Tenants wrong him in his Rent;
The Farmers, spightfully combin'd,
Force him to take his Tythes in kind;   110

†*The Dean's Agent, a French-man.* And †*Parvisol* discounts Arrears,
By Bills for Taxes and Repairs.

 Poor *S——t*, with all his Losses vext,
Not knowing where to turn him next;
Above a Thousand Pounds in Debt,
Takes Horse, and in a mighty Fret
Rides Day and Night at such a Rate,
He soon arrives at *HARLEY*'s Gate;
But was so dirty, pale and thin,
Old *Read* would hardly let him in.   120
 Said *HARLEY*, Welcome Rev'rend Dean!
What makes your Worship look so lean?

98 Devoutly] Demurely F. 99 The] And D., S., 1721 104 Cheats,]
. . . Cheats. 1727, F. 109 combin'd,] 1720, 1722, 1727, F. combine,
D., S. 110 kind;] 1720 K S. Kind; 1722, 1727, F. 113 *S——t,*]
F. Swift S. *Swift,* 1720, 1722, 1727 121 Dean!] 1720, 1722 Dean,
D., S. Dean; 1727, F. 122 lean?] 1720 *and remainder* Lean; D., S.

Queen Anne's last Ministry fell before
redeeming its promise to assist him with
a gift of a thousand pounds.

111. *Parvisol.* Isaiah Parvisol was
Swift's steward and tithe-collector. He
is frequently mentioned in the *Journal
to Stella,* and in Swift's correspondence

from 1708 onward. The references are
nearly always in a spirit of irritation or
contempt; and for a time he seems to
have been dismissed (*Corresp.* ii. 164–
6, 179, 182, 203, 271). He died in
Swift's service, 1718.

120. *Old Read.* Harley's porter.

Why sure you won't appear in Town,
In that old Wig and rusty Gown!
I doubt your Heart is set on Pelf
So much, that you neglect your Self.
What! I suppose now Stocks are high,
You've some good Purchase in your Eye;
Or is your Money out at use?—

    Truce, good MY LORD, I beg a Truce!   130
The Doctor in a Passion cry'd;
Your Raillery is misapply'd:
I have Experience dearly bought,
You know I am not worth a Groat:
But you resolv'd to have your Jest,
And 'twas a Folly to Contest:
Then since you now have done your worst,
Pray leave me where you found me first.

124 Gown!] 1720   Gown. D., S.   Rusty-Gown? 1722   Gown? 1727, F.
127 What!] 1720, 1722, 1727   What? F.   129 use?—] use, D., S.   use.—
1720   Use?— 1722, 1727, F.   133 I have Experience] Experience I have
F.   135 you] you'r D., S.   135, 136]
                 But it's a Folly to contest,
                 When you resolve to have your Jest; F.
137 Then] And F.
Stella *marks only two paragraph divisions, at lines 87 and 97. Minor variations in paragraphing in early editions have not been noted.*

To LORD HARLEY,
since Earl of OXFORD, on his
MARRIAGE.

Written in the Year M DCC XIII.

Works of Jonathan Swift, ed. Deane Swift, 1765, 4to, viii (2), 146; 8vo, xvi. 252.
Faulkner, 1765, xiii. 270.
Works, ed. Sheridan, 1784, vii. 140.

   This poem was addressed by Swift to Lord Harley, only son of the first Earl of Oxford, Lord Treasurer, upon his marriage, 31 August, 1713, to Lady Henrietta Cavendish Holles, daughter and sole heiress of John, Duke of Newcastle. Swift was supposed to have assisted in the negotiations and also in arrangements for the division of the Duke's inheritance between her and Lord Pelham, the male heir. See *Corresp.* ii. 183, where Erasmus Lewis describes the apportionment of the Duke of Newcastle's estate consequent upon the marriage (*cf. Portland MSS.* v. 324). Bolingbroke, writing to Swift, 1 Jany., 1721-2, sarcastically described the marriage as the ultimate end of Oxford's administration (*Corresp.* iii. 113).
   In the *Journal to Stella*, 8 November, 1711, Swift writes: 'Lord Harley is a very valuable young gentleman; and they say the girl is handsome, and has good sense, but red hair,' a less glowing account of the couple than he gives in the verses.
   The text is printed from the *Works*, 1765.

AMONG the numbers who employ
Their tongues and pens to give you joy,
Dear Harley, gen'rous Youth, admit
What friendship dictates more than wit.

   Forgive me, when I fondly thought
(By frequent observation taught)
A spirit so inform'd as yours
Could never prosper in amours.
The God of Wit, and Light, and Arts,
With all acquir'd and nat'ral parts,   10

Whose harp could savage beasts enchant,
Was an unfortunate gallant.
Had Bacchus after Daphne reel'd,
The Nymph had soon been brought to yield;
Or, had Embroider'd Mars pursu'd,
The Nymph would ne'er have been a prude.
Ten thousand footsteps, full in view,
Mark out the way where Daphne flew.
For such is all the sex's flight,
They fly from learning, wit, and light: 20
They fly, and none can overtake
But some gay coxcomb, or a rake.

How then, dear Harley, could I guess
That you should meet, in love, success?
For, if those antient Tales be true,
Phœbus was beautiful as you:
Yet Daphne never slack'd her pace,
For wit and learning spoil'd his face.
And, since the same resemblance held
In gifts, wherein you both excell'd,   30
I fancy'd ev'ry nymph would run
From you, as from Latona's son.

Then where, said I, shall Harley find
A virgin of superior mind,
With wit and virtue to discover,
And pay the merit of her Lover?

This character shall Ca'ndish claim,
Born to retrieve her sex's fame.
The chief among that glitt'ring crowd,
Of titles, birth, and fortune proud,   40
(As fools are insolent and vain)
Madly aspir'd to wear her chain:
But Pallas, guardian of the Maid,
Descending to her Charge's aid,

18. *Mark out the way where Daphne flew.* Ovid, *Met.* i. 452.

Held out Medusa's snaky locks,
Which stupify'd them all to stocks.
The Nymph, with indignation, view'd
The dull, the noisy, and the lewd:
For Pallas, with celestial light,
Had purify'd her mortal sight;   50
Shew'd her the Virtues all combin'd,
Fresh blooming, in young Harley's mind.

Terrestrial nymphs, by formal arts,
Display their various nets for hearts:
Their looks are all by method set,
When to be prude, and when coquette;
Yet, wanting skill and pow'r to chuse,
Their only pride is to refuse.
But, when a Goddess would bestow
Her love on some bright youth below,   60
Round all the earth she casts her eyes;
And then, descending from the skies,
Makes choice of him she fancies best,
And bids the ravish'd youth be bless'd.

Thus the bright Empress of the Morn
Chose, for her spouse, a mortal born:
The Goddess made advances first,
Else what aspiring hero durst?
Tho', like a virgin of fifteen,
She blushes when by mortals seen;   70
Still blushes, and with speed retires,
When Sol pursues her with his fires.

Diana thus, Heav'n's chastest queen,
Struck with Endymion's graceful mien,
Down from her silver chariot came,
And to the Shepherd own'd her flame.

65. *Thus the bright Empress of the Morn* . . . Aurora, enamoured of Tithonous, carried him away and espoused him.

69–72. According to Scott, *Memoirs,* p. 196 n., these four lines, erased by the author, were restored by Deane Swift.

Thus Ca'ndish, as Aurora bright,
And chaster than the Queen of Night,
Descended from her sphere to find
A Mortal of superior kind.   80

THE
FIRST *ODE*
OF THE
SECOND BOOK
OF
HORACE
PARAPHRAS'D:

And Address'd to *Richard St - - le*, Esq;

*The First Ode of the Second Book of Horace Paraphras'd: And Address'd to
Richard St - - le, Esq; . . . London: Printed for A. Dodd, at the Peacock
without Temple-Bar. 1714. Price 3d.* 4to, pp. 11. (In some copies the
date on the title-page is 1713.)
The First Ode . . . Dublin: Reprinted for John Henly, . . . 1714.
A Supplement to Dr. Swift's Works, ed. Nichols, 1776 and 1779.
Works, ed. Sheridan, 1784, vii. 129.

The poem has an almost unmistakable faithfulness to Swift's style in
satirical and polemical verse; and its omission from the earlier collections
and miscellanies may have been due to his desire to bury this episode in his
relationship to Steele, or to a hesitancy on account of its political references.
    For an account of the quarrel between Steele and Swift, arising first from
the pages of the *Examiner* and *Guardian* in April–May, 1713, and con-
tinuing in a personal correspondence shortly before Swift left for Ireland to
be installed as Dean of St. Patrick's, see Aitken's *Life of Steele*, i. 378 ff.,
and *Prose Works*, ed. Temple Scott, v. 276–82. After Swift's return the
misunderstanding was embittered by a war of political pamphlets between
the two. In September appeared Steele's *Importance of Dunkirk Considered,*

to which Swift retorted vigorously in October with *The Importance of the Guardian Considered.* Meanwhile, during the latter part of the year, 22nd October onward, Steele's forthcoming pamphlet, *The Crisis,* was heralded by successive announcements. Swift, seizing upon the tedious absurdity of repeated pompous advertisements and protracted delay, printed the present poem, ridiculing Steele and his promised pamphlet. It appeared on the 6th or 7th of January, 1713–14 (*Daily Courant,* 5 and 7 Jany., *Post-Boy,* 5–7 Jany., *Mercator,* 2–4 Jany.). On the 19th of January *The Crisis* was, at length, published. Swift's destructive rejoinder, *The Publick Spirit of the Whigs,* came out on the 23rd of February. See further Aitken's *Life of Steele,* i. 399–409, ii. 3–23; *Prose Works,* v. 311–12.

The poem was first printed with the collected *Works* of Swift by Nichols. The text is printed from a copy of the first edition. The Latin parallels, which appeared as footnotes to the original edition, are not reprinted.

D ICK, thour't resolv'd, as I am told,
 Some strange *Arcana* to unfold,
And with the help of *Buckley's* Pen
To vamp the *good Old Cause* again,
Which thou (such *Bur—t's* shrewd Advice is)
Must furbish up and Nickname *CRISIS.*
Thou pompously wilt let us know
What all the World knew long ago,
(Ere since Sir *William G—e* was May'r,
And *HAR—Y* fill'd the *Commons* Chair)   10
That we a *German* Prince must own
When *A—N* for Heav'n resigns Her Throne.
But more than that, thou'lt keep a rout
With—who is *in*—and who is *out,*
Thou'lt rail devoutly at the *Peace,*
And all its secret *Causes* trace,

3. *Buckley's Pen.* Samuel Buckley was the publisher of *The Crisis.* He also published *The Spectator,* and was associated with Steele's ventures for some years. In 1714 Buckley succeeded Charles Ford as editor of *The London Gazette* (*Letters of Swift to Ford,* ed. Nichol Smith, p. xv). He died in 1741.

5. *such Bur—t's shrewd Advice is.* Gilbert Burnet, Bishop of Salisbury.

In *The Publick Spirit of the Whigs* Swift refers to Steele as a 'Writer, who either affects, or is commanded of late to copy after the Bishop of *Sarum'.* *Prose Works,* ed. Temple Scott, v. 321.

9. *Sir William G—e.* Sir William Gore served as Lord Mayor in 1702.

10. *HAR—Y fill'd the Commons Chair.* Harley was Speaker of the House, 1701–5.

The *Bucket-play* 'twixt Whigs and Tories,
Their ups and downs, with fifty Stories
Of *Tricks*, the Lord of *Ox—d* knows,
And *Errors* of our *Plenipoes*.   20
Thou'lt tell of *Leagues* among the Great
Portending ruin to our State,
And of that dreadful **coup d'eclat*,   * *Vide En-*
Which has afforded thee much Chat,   *glishman,*
The Q—n (*forsooth, Despotick*) gave   No. 36.
Twelve *Coronets*, without *thy* leave!
A Breach of Liberty, 'tis own'd,
For which no Heads have *yet* atton'd!
Believe me, what thou'st undertaken
May bring in Jeopardy thy Bacon,   30
For Madmen, Children, Wits and Fools
Shou'd never meddle with Edg'd Tools.
But since thou'rt got into the Fire,
And canst not easily retire,
Thou must no longer deal in *Farce*,
Nor pump to cobble wicked Verse;
Untill thou shalt have eas'd thy Conscience,
Of Spleen, of Politicks and Nonsense,
And when thou'st bid adieu to Cares,
And settled *Europe's Grand* Affairs,   40
'Twill then, perhaps, be worth thy while
For *Drury-lane* to shape thy Stile:

This is said to be the Plot of a Comedy with which Mr. St--le has long threatned the Town.

"To make a pair of Jolly Fellows,
"The Son and Father, join to tell us,
"How Sons may safely disobey,
"And Fathers never shou'd say nay,
"By which wise Conduct they grow Friends
"At last—and so the Story ends.

23. *that dreadful coup d'eclat.* In *The Examiner* for 18–21 Dec., 1713, it was said of Marlborough that 'he once made a *Coup d'Ecclat,* for placing himself at the Head of a *Stratocracy*'. In Steele's *Englishman,* No. 36, 26 December, the passage is quoted, and twice again in the same paper reference is made to the phrase '*Coup d'Eclat*'.

26. *Twelve Coronets.* See p. 142.

43–8. The marginal note appeared in the original. Nichols observes, 'In some particulars it would apply to "The Conscious Lovers",' Steele's last comedy, produced at Drury Lane in 1722.

Vide
Tatlers.

When first I knew thee, *Dick*, thou wert
Renown'd for Skill in *Faustus* Art,   50
Which made thy Closet much frequented
By buxom Lasses—Some repented
Their luckless Choice of Husbands—others,
Impatient to be like their Mothers,
Receiv'd from thee profound Directions
How best to settle their Affections;
Thus thou, a Friend to the Distress'd,
Didst in thy calling do thy best.

But now the *Senate* (if things *hit*
And thou at *Stockbridge* wert not *bit*)   60
Must feel thy Eloquence and Fire,
Approve thy Schemes, thy Wit admire,
Thee with *Immortal Honours* crown,
Whilst *Patr'ot-like* thou'lt strut and frown.

What, tho' by Enemies 'tis said,
The *Lawrel*, which adorns thy Head;
Must one Day come in competition,
By vertue of some sly *Petition:*
Yet *Mum* for that, hope still the best,
Nor let such Cares disturb thy Rest.   70

Methinks I hear thee loud, as Trumpet,
As Bagpipe shrill, or Oyster-Strumpet,
Methinks I see thee, spruce and fine,
With Coat embroider'd richly shine,
And dazzle all the *Idol-Faces*
As thro' the *HALL* thy Worship paces:
(Tho' this I speak but at a venture,
Supposing thou hast *Tick* with *Hunter*)

50. *Renown'd for Skill in Faustus
Art.* Tatler No. 2, 'I am an adept in
astrological speculations'. Steele also
interested himself in chemistry, and
had a laboratory at Poplar.
51. *thy Closet much frequented* . . . In

his character of Bickerstaff Steele was
accustomed in *The Tatler* to give advice to anxious females.
60. *Stockbridge.* In 1713 Steele was
elected M.P. for Stockbridge. See
Aitken, *Life of Steele,* i. 395 ff.

Methinks I see a *black-guard Rout*
Attend thy Coach, and hear them shout   80
In Approbation of thy Tongue,
Which (in their Stile) is *purely hung*.
Now, now you carry all before ye,
Nor dares one *Jacobite* or *Tory*
Pretend to answer one Syl - - lable,
Except the Matchless Hero *Abel*.
What tho' her *Highness* and her *Spouse*
In *Ant—rp* keep a frugal House,
Yet not forgetful of a Friend
They'll soon enable thee to spend,   90
If to *Macc - - rt - - y* thou wilt toast,
And to his *Pious Patron*'s *Ghost*.
Now manfully thou'lt run a Tilt
"On *Popes*, for all the Blood they've spilt,
"For Massacres, and Racks, and Flames,
"For Lands enrich'd by crimson Streams,
"For Inquisitions taught by *Spain*,
"Of which the Christian World complain.

    Dick, we agree—all's true, thou'st said,
As that my Muse is yet a Maid,   100
But, if I may with freedom talk,
All this is foreign to thy Walk:
Thy *Genius* has perhaps a knack
At trudging in a beaten Track,
But is for *State-Affairs* as fit,
As mine for Politicks and Wit.

86. *the Matchless Hero Abel*. Abel Roper, 1665–1726, a vigorous journalist. He was connected with *The Post-Boy* (a Tory newspaper started by him in 1695) till about 1714.

88. *In Ant—rp keep a frugal House*. Marlborough resided in Antwerp for a time, after he had been dismissed from his offices at the end of 1711.

91. *Macc - - rt - - y*. General Maccartney, second to Lord Mohun in his duel with the Duke of Hamilton. He was accused of murderously stabbing the Duke, and fled to Holland. In 1716 he surrendered to justice, was tried for murder, and convicted of manslaughter. He was, thereupon, restored to his military rank. For an account of the duel see *Journal to Stella*, 15 Nov., 1712. The '*Pious Patron*'s *Ghost*' refers to Mohun, who was a strong Whig.

94–8. A gibe at Steele's political style.

Then let us both in time grow wise,
Nor higher, than our Talents, rise,
To some snug Cellar let's repair
From Dunns and Debts, and drown our Care; 110
Now quaff of honest Ale a Quart,
Now venture at a Pint of Port,
With which inspir'd we'll club each Night
Some tender Sonnet to indite,
And with *Tom D'urf - - y*, *Phill - ps*, *D - - nnis*,
Immortalize our *Dolls* and *Jenneys*.

JEUX D'ESPRIT
OF THE
SCRIBLERUS CLUB

Manuscripts of the Marquis of Bath, Portland Papers, vol. xiii. ff. 66, 67, 82, 84.
Letters, ed. Hawkesworth, 1766, 4to, x. 205.
Swiftiana, 1804, i. 109.
Works, ed. Scott, 1814, xvi. 128.
Works of Alexander Pope, Elwin and Courthope, 1871–89, viii. 225 n.[2].
Life and Works of John Arbuthnot, G. A. Aitken, 1892, p. 56 n.
Correspondence, ed. F. Elrington Ball, ii, Appendix vii.

An association belonging to the winter of 1713/14, formed by Pope, Swift, Arbuthnot, and Gay, with Parnell as an occasional visitor, was given the name of the Scriblerus Club. See R. J. Allen's *Clubs of Augustan London*, pp. 260 ff. In his edition of Swift's correspondence, 1766, Hawkesworth printed some disjointed verses (II–V below) passing between members of the Club and Lord Oxford, in which Oxford was invited to take part in the gatherings. I have not been able to trace the manuscripts used by Hawkesworth.

Further Scriblerus verses are preserved among the manuscripts of the Marquis of Bath at Longleat. Among these Hawkesworth's pieces are only represented by a transcript of IV written on the first two pages of a sheet

115. *And with Tom D'urf--y, Phill-ps, D--nnis*. Tom D'Urfey, the popular writer of burlesque and song; Ambrose Philips, the poet, friend of Addison and Steele, some years later, when in Ireland, incurred Swift's ridicule; John Dennis, the critic, and enemy of Pope.

folded to two quarto leaves. The names appended to this transcript, which are not autograph signatures, have, with the exception of that of Gay, been scribbled over in ink. Hawkesworth does not give the signatures, and has some verbal variants. This piece was also printed by Aitken, *Life of Arbuthnot*, p. 56 n. It is here printed from the Longleat transcript.

The series, so far as it has been preserved, seems to begin with Swift. Among the Longleat manuscripts is a folded sheet, making two quarto leaves, addressed on the verso of the second leaf, 'To the Lord High Treasurer'. On the recto of the first leaf are six lines (I) in Swift's autograph, dated below by Lord Oxford: 'Marc. 20: 1713/14'. These lines were printed in Elwin and Courthope's *Pope*, viii. 225 n.[2]. They are here reprinted as written by Swift.

The most interesting of the Scriblerus manuscripts preserved at Longleat is number VI, hitherto unprinted. On one side of a small quarto leaf, verso blank, are written five invitations to Oxford of two lines each, severally in the autographs of Pope, Swift, Parnell, Arbuthnot, and Gay. The leaf is undated.

I

THE Doctor and Dean, Pope, Parnell and Gay
In manner submissive most humbly do pray,
That your Lordship would once let your Cares all
    alone
And Climb the dark Stairs to your Friends who have
    none:
To your Friends who at least have no Cares but to
    please you
To a good honest Junta that never will teaze you.

From the Doctor's Chamber
past eight.

II

April 14, 1714. Back Stairs, past Eight.
IN a summons so large, which all clergy contains,
I must turn *Dismal*'s convert, or part with my brains,
Should I scruple to quit the back stairs for your blind ones,
Or refuse your true juncto for one of—

I. By 'the Doctor's Chamber' is meant the room occupied by Arbuthnot in his capacity as physician to the Queen.

II. These lines, although headed 'Gay' by Hawkesworth, are clearly an answer by Oxford to an invitation received. Dr. Ball, changing the order, prints them as an answer to IV. Dismal was Lord Nottingham.

III

The following is their answer to his lordship, chiefly written by the Dean.

LET not the whigs our tory club rebuke;
Give us our earl, the devil take their duke.
Ouædam quæ attinent ad Scriblerum,
Want your assistance now to clear 'em.
One day it will be no disgrace,
In *Scribler* to have had a place.
Come then, my lord, and take your part in
The important history of *Martin*.

IV

A Pox of all Senders
For any Pretenders
Who tell us these troublesome stories,
In their dull hum-drum key
Of Arma Virumque
Hannoniae qui primus ab oris.

A fig too for H—r
Who prates like his Grand mere
And all his old Friends would rebuke
In spite of the Carle
Give us but our Earle,   10
And the Devil may take their Duke.

Then come and take part in
The Memoirs of Martin,

IV. 1 of] on 1766   7 A fig too for H—r] A pox too on *Hanmer*, 1766
12 And the] The 1766

III. The allusions in line 2 are to Lord Oxford and the Duke of Marlborough.
IV. 6. *Hannoniae.* 'The duchy of *Hainault*.—Hawkesworth. The allusion is to the scene of Marlborough's campaigns. At this time the return of the Duke was generally expected. He arrived in England 2 August 1714.
7. *H—r.* Sir Thomas Hanmer, although a strong Tory, declared himself trenchantly in the House upon the danger to the Protestant succession under Oxford's administration.
14. *Martin.* Martinus Scriblerus.

Lay by your White Staff & gray Habit,
    For trust us, friend Mortimer
    Should you live years forty more
Haec olim meminisse juvabit.
      by order of yᵉ Club
          A. Pope
          J. Gay
          J. Swift
          J. Arbuthnot
          T. Parnel

V

More Lines of Humour, by Lord Treasurer.

         April 14, 1714.

I honour the men, Sir,
    Who are ready to answer,
When I ask them to stand by the queen;
    In spite of orâtors,
    And blood-thirsty praters,
Whose hatred I highly esteem.
    Let our faith's defender
    Keep out ev'ry pretender,
And long enjoy her own;
    Thus you four, five,   10
    May merrily live,
Till faction is dead as a stone.

VI

My Lord, forsake your Politick Utopians,
To sup, like Jove, with blameless Ethiopians.
                   Pope.

IV. 15 by] down 1766

IV. 16. *friend Mortimer.* Harley was raised to the peerage as Earl of Oxford
and Mortimer.

In other Words, You with the Staff,
Leave John of Bucks, come here and laugh.
                                        Dean.

For Frolick Mirth give ore affairs of State,
To night be happy, be to morrow great.
                                        Parnell

Give Clans your money, us your smile
your Scorn to T—end & Ar—ile
                                        Doctor

Leave Courts, and hye to simple Swains,
Who feed *no* Flock Upon *no* Plains
                                        Gay.

VI. An initial before Parnell's signature is heavily blotted out. The names in Arbuthnot's couplet should be filled in as 'Townshend & Argyle'. Gay had trouble with his couplet. He first wrote 'come', struck this through, and wrote 'hye' beyond it. In the second line 'feed' and 'Flock' have each a final 's' struck out.

THE

FAGGOT.

Written in the Year 1713, *when the* QUEEN'S *Ministers
were quarrelling among themselves.*

Faulkner, 1735, ii. 97 (1737, ii. 77).
Miscellanies, . . . Volume the Fifth, 1735, p. 5 (1736, v. 5; 1745, v. 7).
[Ref. 1735.]
Vol. IV. of the Miscellanies . . . Dublin, . . . Samuel Fairbrother, . . . 1735.
p. 8.
Works of Jonathan Swift, D.D., ed. Hawkesworth, 1755, 4to, iv (1), 7.

This poem was first printed by Faulkner in 1735. On the 13th of June, 1713, Swift was in Dublin, and installed Dean of St. Patrick's. On the 29th of August he left Dublin; and on the 9th of September he was back in London. He found the Tory leaders at variance. The extreme Tories suspected Oxford, whose moderation disturbed them. Bolingbroke, pressing for power, was adopting a more hostile attitude.

Swift's poem may have been written in the latter part of 1713; but it seems not unlikely that it was composed upon a hint conveyed in a letter written to him by the Duchess of Ormonde, 24 April, 1714: 'I hope our friends will . . . .remember the story of the Arrows, that were very easily broke singly, but when tied up close together, no strength of man could hurt them' (*Corresp.* ii. 133).

At an earlier date Swift addressed a remonstrance in verse to Harley on the same subject. *Cf.* 'Atlas: or, the Minister of State', p. 159, and Swift's pamphlet, *Some Free Thoughts upon the Present State of Affairs* (*Prose Works*, ed. Temple Scott, v. 393–415; ed. Davis, viii. 73–98).

The text is printed from Faulkner's edition of 1735.

O Bserve the dying Father speak:
  Try Lads, can you this Bundle break;
Then, bids the youngest of the Six,
Take up a well-bound Heap of Sticks.
They thought it was an old Man's Maggot;
And strove by Turns to break the Faggot:
In vain: The complicated Wands
Were much too strong for all their Hands.
See, said the Sire, how soon 'tis done:
Then, took and broke them one by one.   10
So strong you'll be, in Friendship ty'd;
So quickly broke if you divide.
Keep close then Boys, and never quarrel.
Here ends the Fable and the Moral.

  This Tale may be apply'd in few Words
To Treasurers, Controllers, Stewards,
And others, who in solemn Sort
Appear with slender Wands at Court:
Not firmly join'd to keep their Ground,
But lashing one another round: 20
While, wise Men think they ought to fight
With *Quarter*-staffs instead of *White*;
Or Constable with *Staff* of Peace,
Should come and make the Clatt'ring cease;

9 done:] 1745, 1755   done? 1735   done! 1736   21 While,] While 1735, 1736, 1745, 1755

Which now disturbs the Queen and Court,
And gives the *Whigs* and Rabble Sport.

IN History we never found
The Consul's Fasces were unbound;
Those *Romans* were too wise to think on't,
Except to lash some grand Delinquent.   30
How would they blush to hear it said,
The Prætor broke the Consul's Head;
Or, Consul in his Purple Gown,
Came up, and knock't the Prætor down.

COME Courtiers: Every Man his Stick:
Lord-Treasurer; for once be quick:
And, that they may the closer cling,
Take your blue Ribbin for a String.
Come trimming *Harcourt*; bring your Mace;
And squeeze it in, or quit your Place: 40
Dispatch; or else that Rascal *Northey*,
Will undertake to do it for thee:
And, be assur'd, the Court will find him
Prepar'd to *leap o'er Sticks*, or bind 'em.

34 down.] down? 1735, 1736, 1745, 1755   41 Rascal *Northey*,] R—l *N*—,
1735   R—l *N*— 1736   R—l *Northey* 1745   rascal *Northey* 1755

38. *Take your blue Ribbin* . . . The
blue ribbon of the Order of the Garter
with which Oxford was invested in
1712. Scott notes, in a comment on
this poem (*Memoirs*, 1814, p. 205),
that, while naming others, 'with infinite delicacy the poet omitted all
mention of Bolingbroke'.

39. *trimming Harcourt*. Simon Harcourt, first Viscount Harcourt, 1661 ?–
1727; *D.N.B.* xxiv. 322. A successful barrister. M.P. for various constituencies. Created Baron Harcourt,
1711; Lord Chancellor 1713–14. Probably called 'trimming *Harcourt*' by
Swift because he considered that his
judicial temper would be useful in

allaying the disputes between Oxford
and Bolingbroke. See *Corresp.* ii.
31 n.².

41. *Rascal Northey*. Sir Edward
Northey, 1652–1723. He was knighted
in 1702. Attorney-General 1701–7,
and again 1710–18, on the second occasion succeeding Harcourt when the
latter was appointed Lord Keeper.
Faulkner's note observes of him,
'*brought in by the Lord* Harcourt; *yet
very desirous of the Great Seal*'.

44. *leap o'er Sticks*. Compare Swift's
description of court diversions in Lilli-
put, *Gulliver's Travels*, Part I, chap.
iii.

To make the Bundle strong and safe,
Great *Ormonde* lend thy Gen'ral's Staff:
And, if the *Crosier* could be cramm'd in,
A Fig for *Lechmere*, *King*, and *Hambden*.
You'll then defy the strongest *Whig*,
With both his Hands to bend a Twig;   50
Though with united Strength they all pull,
From *Sommers* down to *Craigs* and *Walpole*.

THE

AUTHOR upon Himself.

*A few of the first Lines were wanting in the Copy
sent us by a Friend of the Author's from* London.

Faulkner, 1735, ii. 343 (1737, ii. 129).
Miscellanies, . . . *Volume the Fifth,* 1735, p. 54 (1736, v. 54; 1745, v. 10;
1749, v. 10; 1751, x. 9).
Works of Jonathan Swift, D.D., ed. Hawkesworth, 1755, 4to, iv (1), 10.

On Monday, 31 May, 1714, Swift, in despair at the growing enmity
between Oxford and Bolingbroke, left London, and, apparently, reached
Letcombe on 3 June (*Portland MSS.,* vii. 186) on a visit to the rector, the

46. *Great Ormonde* . . . After the
Tory party had succeeded in securing
the dismissal of Marlborough, the
Duke of Ormonde, whose sympathies
were pronouncedly Jacobite, was, in
1712, appointed commander-in-chief
and captain-general.

47. *if the Crosier* . . . *I.e.* the support
of the Church.

48. *Lechmere.* See p. 153 n.

48. *King.* Peter King, a man of
humble birth, became Recorder of
London and was knighted in 1708.
He was, with Lechmere, one of the
managers at the trial of Sacheverell,
1710. In 1714 he was appointed Chief

Justice of the Common Pleas. In
1725 he was created Baron King of
Ockham; and later in the same year
became Lord Chancellor.

48. *Hambden.* See p. 165 n.

52. *Sommers.* For Lord Somers see
p. 163 n.

52. *Craigs.* James Craggs, 1657–
1721, a man of business, M.P. for
Grampound 1702–13, pursued various
activities, including that of agent for
the Duchess of Marlborough. He was
joint Postmaster-General, 1715–20. In
1721 he was implicated in the South
Sea Company scandal. See p. 287 n.

Rev. John Geree. On the 8th we find him writing from the rectory to Esther Vanhomrigh (*Corresp.* ii. 142). On the 8th of August, after the Queen's death, he announced to Archdeacon Walls his intention of setting out for Ireland on the 16th (*Corresp.* ii. 227); on the 12th he told Ford, 'I sett out early on Monday next for Ireland' (*Letters of Swift to Ford*, ed. Nichol Smith, p. 52); and on the 15th he wrote to Oxford, 'I set out to-morrow morning' (*Corresp.* ii. 236). His stay at Letcombe thus extended from the 3rd of June to the 16th of August, 1714; and, as the poem clearly shows, it was during this period that these verses on himself were written.

A note to the last line of the poem, in Faulkner's edition, runs: '*The Author retired to a Friend in* Berkshire, *ten Weeks before the* Qu— *died; and never saw the Ministry after.*' This is not quite accurate, for Anne died on Sunday, 1st of August; but it places the poem correctly, despite the mistaken statement in the same edition, 'Written in the Year 1713'. The wrong dating has been followed by later editors.

The Rev. John Geree, Swift's host during these weeks, was a native of Farnham, near Moor Park, and is said to have lived 'in Sir William Temple's family' (*Portland MSS.*, vii. 186). In the *Journal to Stella*, 10 May, 1712, Swift writes: 'Did I tell you that young Parson Geree is going to be married, and asked my advice when it was too late to break off?' Thereupon he busied himself on behalf of the improvident young clergyman. 'Lord-Keeper promised me yesterday the first convenient Living to poor Mr. Geree, who is married, and wants some Addition to what he has' (*Journal to Stella*, 22 Dec., 1712). Geree had been a fellow of Corpus Christi College, Oxford, and was presented by his College to the living of Letcombe Bassett, Berkshire. Thither Swift sent him a present of wine in April, 1714 (*Corresp.* ii. 134). Geree wrote to thank him, as also for his good offices with the Lord Chancellor, which, however, had produced nothing so far. He mentioned also the school he had opened at the rectory.

All communication between Swift and Geree seems to have been broken off after the Letcombe visit, till the latter wrote once more to the Dean (from Letcombe) in 1736 (*Corresp.* v. 334) recommending a Captain Scroggs to his attention, and submitting some translations of Horace. In 1734 Geree had been appointed a Canon of Hereford. He died in 1761.

Swift's poem, as first printed by Faulkner, 1735, shows a number of blanks which are easily supplied with the exception of those in l. 1 and ll. 53, 54. In the Harvard College Library is preserved a copy of Orrery's *Remarks* annotated by himself, MS. Eng. 218. 14. Opposite his observations on p. 48 about Sharp, Archbishop of York, Orrery has written:

'In Volume the 2ᵈ. Page 129ᵗʰ. Is a very severe poem, that evidently proves the violence of *Swift's* resentment, The two first Lines may be read thus,

> By an old redhair'd, murd'ring Hag pursued,
> A crazy Prelate, and a royal Prude.

'And again in Page 131st, Line of the same Poem, The Asterisks are to be thus filled up,
'Now Madam Coningsmark her vengeance vows,
On *Swift's* reproaches for her murdered spouse.'

The volume and page references are to Faulkner's edition. Printed editions have left the blank in l. 1, and supplied that in l. 53, if at all, with 'angry Somerset'. Orrery's reading, which may well represent Swift's intention, casts an additional slur on the Duchess.

It may be noted that in Orrery's manuscript 'Madam Coningsmark' is written above a word heavily scored out, which appears to be 'Coningsmark'.

The text of the poem is here printed from Faulkner's edition of 1735.

* * * * * * * *
* * * * * * *
* * * * * * *
* * * * * * * *

BY an —— —— —— pursu'd,
A Crazy Prelate, and a Royal Prude.
By dull Divines, who look with envious Eyes,
On ev'ry Genius that attempts to rise;
And pausing o'er a Pipe, with doubtful Nod,
Give Hints, that Poets ne'er believe in God.
So, Clowns on Scholars as on Wizards look,
And take a Folio for a conj'ring Book.

S— had the Sin of Wit no venial Crime;
Nay, 'twas affirm'd, he sometimes dealt in Rhime: 10

1 By an —] 1735, 1736, 1745   By an old 1737, 1755   2 A crazy Prelate,
and a Royal Prude.] 1737   A crazy P—, and a R— Prude. 1735, 1736, 1745

The footnotes to this poem, appearing in Faulkner's edition of the *Works*, are typically in Swift's manner, and may have been written by him. They are here inserted, with blanks completed, and distinguished by an F. The introductory note, stating that a few lines are missing, is probably a literary pretence.

1. For the reading probably intended, see introductory notes.

2. '*Dr.* Sharpe, *Archbishop of* York.' —F. '*Her late Majesty.*'—F. Swift attributed the refusal of the Queen to give him preferment in England to the opposition of Dr. John Sharp, Archbishop of York, and to the hatred of the Duchess of Somerset. The former represented the author of *A Tale of a Tub* as unfit for a seat on the episcopal bench; the latter was infuriated by the *Windsor Prophecy*, see p. 145. See also Orrery, *Remarks*, 1752, p. 48; King, *Political and Literary Anecdotes*, 1818, p. 60. Sharp, who had been suspended by James II for preaching sermons reflecting on Roman Catholicism, was installed Dean of Canterbury in 1689, and promoted to the Archbishopric of York in 1691.

Humour, and Mirth, had Place in all he writ:
He reconcil'd Divinity and Wit.
He mov'd, and bow'd, and talk't with too much Grace;
Nor shew'd the Parson in his Gait or Face;
Despis'd luxurious Wines, and costly Meat;
Yet, still was at the Tables of the Great.
Frequented Lords; *saw those that saw the Queen*;
At *Child*'s or *Truby*'s never once had been;
Where Town and Country Vicars flock in Tribes,
Secur'd by Numbers from the Lay-men's Gibes;   20
And deal in Vices of the graver Sort,
Tobacco, Censure, Coffee, Pride, and Port.

BUT, after sage Monitions from his Friends,
His Talents to employ for nobler Ends;
To better Judgments willing to submit,
He turns to Pol[it]icks his dang'rous Wit,

AND now, the publick Int'rest to support,
By *Harley* S— invited comes to Court.
In Favour grows with Ministers of State;
Admitted private, when Superiors wait: 30
And, *Harley*, not asham'd his Choice to own,
Takes him to *Windsor* in his Coach, alone.
At *Windsor* S— no sooner can appear,
But, *St. John* comes and whispers in his Ear;
The Waiters stand in Ranks; the Yeomen cry,
Make Room; as if a Duke were passing by.

Now *Finch* alarms the Lords; he hears for certain,
This dang'rous Priest is got behind the Curtain:
Finch, fam'd for tedious Elocution, proves
That S— oils many a Spring which *Harley* moves.   40

18. *At Child's or Truby's* . . . 'A
Coffee-house and Tavern near St.
Paul*'s, much frequented by the Clergy*.'
—F. Both in St. Paul's Churchyard.
Cf. p. 171:
'A Clergyman of special Note,
For shunning those of his own Coat.'

34. *But, St. John comes* . . . 'Then
Secretary of State, now Lord Boling-
broke, *the most universal Genius in*
Europe.'—F.

37. *Finch*. '*Late Earl of* Nottingham,
*who made a Speech in the House of Lords
against the Author*.'—F. See p. 141.

W— and *Ayslaby*, to clear the Doubt,
Inform the Commons, that the Secret's out:
"A *certain* Doctor is observ'd of late,
"'To haunt a *certain* Minister of State:
"From whence, with half an Eye we may discover,
"'The Peace is made, and *Perkin* must come over.
York is from *Lambeth* sent, to shew the Queen
A dang'rous Treatise writ against the Spleen;
Which by the Style, the Matter, and the Drift,
'Tis thought could be the Work of none but *S*——   50
Poor *York!* the harmless Tool of others Hate;
He sues for Pardon, and repents too late.

    Now, —— —— her Vengeance vows
On *S*—'s Reproaches for her —— ——
From her red Locks her Mouth with Venom fills:
And thence into the Royal Ear instills.
The Qu— incens'd, his Services forgot,
Leaves him a Victim to the vengeful *Scot*;

41 *W*— and *Ayslaby*,] *W*— and *A*— 1735, 1736   *W*—*e* and *Ayslaby*, 1737
W— and *Aslabie* 1745   *Walpole* and *Aislabie* 1755   47] *N.P.* 1736, 1745,
1751, 1755

41. *W*— and *Ayslaby*. The initial
letter veils an allusion to Walpole.
*'Those two made Speeches in the House
of Commons against the Author, although
the latter professed much Friendship for
him.'*—F. John Aislaby was then
M.P. for Ripon.
    48. *A dang'rous Treatise. A Tale of a
Tub.*
    52. *He sues for Pardon.* '*It is known
that his Grace sent a Message to the
Author, to desire his Pardon, and that
he was very sorry for what he had said
and done.'*—F. Archbishop Sharp
died in 1714, before Swift wrote these
lines; and it may be surmised that his
request for pardon was of recent date.
It is significant that, Sharp being
dead, Swift's friend, John Barber,
addressed a letter to him at Letcombe, in which he said: 'Lord

Bolingbroke told me last Friday, that
he would reconcile you to Lady Somerset, and then it would be easy to set you
right with the Queen' (3 Aug., 1714;
Corresp. ii. 212). The Queen, however, had already died on Sunday, 1st
August.
    53, 54. See introductory notes; also
notes to 'The Windsor Prophecy',
pp. 145–6.
    58. . . . *the vengeful Scot.* '*The Pro-
clamation was against the Author of a
Pamphlet, called,* The publick Spirit of
the Whigs, *against which the* Scotch
Lords complained.'—F. *The Publick
Spirit of the Whigs,* published 23 Feby.,
1714, was Swift's rejoinder to Steele's
Whig pamphlet, *The Crisis.* The Scots
peers, who had been contemptuously
attacked, took action. Morphew, the
publisher, and Barber, the printer,

Now, through the Realm a Proclamation spread,
To fix a Price on his devoted Head.　　　　　　　　　60
While innocent, he scorns ignoble Flight;
His watchful Friends preserve him by a Sleight.

　By *Harley*'s Favour once again he shines;
Is now caress't by Candidate Divines;
Who change Opinions with the changing Scene:
Lord! how were they mistaken in the Dean!
Now, *Delawere* again familiar grows;
And, in *S - - - - t*'s Ear thrusts half his powder'd Nose.
The *Scottish* Nation, whom he durst offend,
Again apply that *S—* would be their Friend.　　　　70

　By Faction tir'd, with Grief he waits a while,
His great contending Friends to reconcile.
Performs what Friendship, Justice, Truth require:
What could he more, but decently retire?

were taken into custody; and a reward of £300 was offered for the discovery of the author. Oxford, however, shielded Swift, and secretly sent him £100 to reimburse the publisher and printer.

67. *Delawere.* '*Lord* Delawere, *then Treasurer of the Houshold, always caressing the Author at Court. But during the Tryal of the Printers before the House of Lords, and while the Proclamation hung over the Author, his Lordship would not seem to know him, till the Danger was past.*'—F. John West, sixth Baron De La Warr, 1687–1723; Treasurer of the Chamber,

1713–14. In a copy of Macky's *Characters*, Swift described him as, 'Of very little sense but formall, and well stockt with the low kind of lowest Politicks'.

69, 70. '*The* Scotch *Lords treated and visited the Author more after the Proclamation than before, except the Duke of* Argyle, *who would never be reconciled.*'—F.

74. '*The Author retired to a Friend in* Berkshire, *ten Weeks before the Queen died; and never saw the Ministry after.*' —F. See introductory notes to the poem.

HORACE, *Lib*. 2. *Sat*. 6.

PART of it imitated.

Transcript by Stella; Manuscript Volume in the possession of the Duke of Bedford, Woburn Abbey. [Ref. S.]

Miscellanies. The Last Volume, 1727, p. 33 (1736, p. 146; 1742, iv. 53). Faulkner, 1735, ii. 108 (1737, ii. 86). [Ref. F.]

An Imitation of the Sixth Satire of the Second Book of Horace. Hoc erat in Votis, &c. The first Part done in the Year 1714, By Dr. Swift. The latter Part now first added, And never before Printed. London: ... B. Motte ... C. Bathurst ... J. and P. Knapton ... MDCCXXXVIII. F°.

Works of Jonathan Swift, D.D., ed. Hawkesworth, 1755, 4to, iii (2), 47.

Swift's imitation of Horace's 'Hoc erat in votis' was also written at Letcombe. Writing to Ford, 3 August, 1714, Swift informed him that he had finished the poem; and Ford in reply from London, 5 August, asked him to send it, or 'bring it up' himself; but Swift considered it 'not yet sufficiently corrected' (*Letters of Jonathan Swift to Charles Ford*, ed. D. Nichol Smith, pp. 44, 48, 50).

The poem, as first printed in 1727, and as reprinted in successive editions of Swift's verse, ran to 112 lines. Stella's transcript added two lines, which were not included in any edition till that of Browning, 1910, who followed a collation by Forster. They were, presumably, rejected by Swift when he was supplying Pope with copy for the *Miscellanies*.

The last eight lines of the poem, as printed in 1727, have been attributed to Pope, and certainly read as if an addition to the poem. As, however, they appear in Stella's transcript, and as they were left standing by Swift in his own copy of Faulkner, they may be accepted as his.

In 1738 the poem was published in folio (pp. iv+23) extended to 221 lines. In this version Latin and English face each other. The additional matter has generally been attributed to Pope, but it may be questioned whether he did not make some use of lines written by Swift. On the verso of the 1738 title (see above) appears an 'Advertisement' stating that the piece is by Swift, but in 'no way meant to interfere with the *Imitations* of Horace by Mr. *Pope*', for 'His Manner, and that of Dr. *Swift* are so entirely different, that they can admit of no Invidious Comparison'.

The version of 1738 follows that of 1727 for the first eight lines. Then come 20 lines, 9–28, which are new. These seem to be an addition by Swift, and not by Pope. Lord Bathurst, writing to Swift, 5 Oct., 1737 (*Corresp.* vi. 45), says: 'That very pretty epistle which you writ many years ago to Lord Oxford is printed incorrectly. I have a copy, of which I send you a transcript, ... you will find that you left off without going through with the epistle.' He then refers to the fable of the country and city mouse, which closes the poem in Pope's version, and enjoins Swift to complete his imitation. The original of this letter, which is preserved in the British Museum, is endorsed: 'Oct^br. 5. 1737 | Ld Bathurst. | Answ^d Oc^tr 8th | 1737. | And addition | to the Poem | of I often wished. | 20 lines added.' These lines are almost certainly 9–28, which, on this external evidence, coupled with the internal evidence of style, may be attributed to Swift. Lord Bathurst, it is clear, was sending Swift a manuscript copy of Pope's version, and, it may be surmised, at Pope's instigation, who, doubtless, was anxious to note the result. This was in October, 1737. In March, 1738 (see Griffith, *Alexander Pope: A Bibliography*, No. 479), Pope published the poem in its extended form, which included, as well as his own matter, twenty new lines from Swift's pen.

These twenty lines, 9–28, are followed by ll. 9–112 of the 1727 version, thus becoming, in 1738, ll. 29–132. Then follow ll. 133–221, consisting, for the most part, of the fable of the country and the city mouse, which are by Pope.

According to Pope (*Spence's Anecdotes*, ed. Singer, 1820, p. 257), Swift did not think the extension 'at all a right imitation of his style'.

I have printed the poem as it appeared in *Miscellanies. The Last Volume*, 1727, inserting within square brackets those twenty lines of the 1738 version which I consider to be by Swift.

> I Often wish'd, that I had clear
> For Life, six hundred Pounds a Year,
> A handsome House to lodge a Friend,
> A River at my Garden's End,
> A Terras Walk, and half a Rood
> Of Land set out to plant a Wood.
>
> Well, now I have all this and more,
> I ask not to increase my Store,
> [But here a Grievance seems to lie,
> All this is mine but till I die;
> I can't but think 'twould sound more clever,
> To me and to my Heirs for ever.

1 I Often] I've often 1738

5. *A Terras Walk* . . . See Delany, *Observations*, 1754, p. 286. At Laracor Swift planted a piece of about half a rood with elms, where they continued many years, till the proprietor, for it was 'no part of Swift's glebe', removed them. Swift refers to this act of destruction, writing to Bolingbroke, 14 Sept., 1714 (*Corresp.* ii. 240).

If I ne'er got, or lost a groat,
By any *Trick*, or any *Fault*;
And if I pray by Reason's rules,
And not like forty other Fools:
As thus, "Vouchsafe, Oh gracious Maker!
"To grant me this and t'other Acre:
"Or if it be thy Will and Pleasure
"Direct my Plow to find a Treasure:"
But only what my Station fits,
And to be kept in my right wits.
Preserve, Almighty Providence!
Just what you gave me, Competence:
And let me in these Shades compose
Something in Verse as true as Prose;
Remov'd from all th' ambitious Scene,
Nor puff'd by Pride, nor sunk by Spleen.]
But should be perfectly content,
Could I but live on this side *Trent*;   10
Nor cross the *Channel* twice a Year,
To spend six Months with *Statesmen* here.

I must by all means come to Town,
'Tis for the Service of the Crown.
"*Lewis*; the *Dean* will be of Use,
"Send for him up, take no Excuse.
The Toil, the Danger of the Seas;
Great Ministers ne'er think of these;
Or let it cost Five hundred Pound,
No matter where the Money's found;   20

9 But should be] S., 1736, 1742, 1755 And should be F. In short I'm 1738
10 Could I but] S., F. Cou'd I but 1736, 1742 Let me but 1738   17
Toil,] Toyle, S.   19 Five hundred Pound,] a hundred Pound S.

If I ne'er got . . . See *Works of Pope*, Elwin and Courthope, 1881, iii. 405 n.3. 'These lines (13–28) are not in the Imitation as printed in the Miscellanies. They have evidently been added by Pope.' This is inaccurate. The additional lines, shown above in square brackets, number twenty (9–28), and (see notes above) they are from Swift's hand.

15. *Lewis.* Erasmus Lewis, secretary to Harley, 1704, later to Lord Dartmouth. *D.N.B.* xxxiii. 175.

19. *Five hundred Pound.* The allusion is to Swift's expenses in entering upon the Deanery of St. Patrick's.

It is but so much more in Debt,
And that they ne'er consider'd yet.

"Good Mr. *Dean* go change your Gown,
"Let my Lord know you're come to Town.
I hurry me in haste away,
Not thinking it is Levee-Day;
And find his Honour in a Pound,
Hemm'd by a triple Circle round,
Chequer'd with Ribbons blew and green;
How should I thrust my self between?   30
Some Wag observes me thus perplext,
And smiling, whispers to the next,
"I thought the *D* - - - *n* had been too proud,
"To justle here among a Crowd.
Another in a surly Fit,
Tells me I have more Zeal than Wit,
"So eager to express your Love,
"You ne'er consider whom you shove,
"But rudely press before a Duke.
I own, I'm pleas'd with this Rebuke,   40
And take it kindly meant to show
What I desire the World should know.

I get a Whisper, and withdraw,
When twenty Fools I never saw
Come with Petitions fairly pen'd,
Desiring I would stand their Friend.

This, humbly offers me his Case - - -
That, begs my Interest for a Place - - -
A hundred other Men's Affairs
Like Bees, are humming in my Ears.   50
"To morrow my Appeal comes on,
"Without your Help the Cause is gone - - -
The Duke expects my Lord and you,
About some great Affair, at Two - - -

"Put my Lord *Bolingbroke* in Mind,
"To get my Warrant quickly signed:
"Consider, 'tis my first Request. - - -
Be satisfy'd, I'll do my best: - - -
Then presently he falls to teize,
"You may for certain, if you please;   60
"I doubt not, if his Lordship knew - - -
"And Mr. *Dean*, one Word from you - - -

'Tis (let me see) three Years and more,
(*October* next, it will be four)
Since HARLEY bid me first attend,
And chose me for an humble Friend;
Would take me in his Coach to chat,
And question me of this and that;
As, "What's a-Clock?" And, "How's the Wind?
"Whose Chariot's that we left behind?   70
Or gravely try to read the Lines
Writ underneath the Country *Signs*;
Or, "Have you nothing new to day
"From *Pope*, from *Parnel*, or from *Gay?*
Such Tattle often entertains
My Lord and me as far as *Stains*,
As once a week we travel down
To *Windsor*, and again to Town,
Where all that passes, *inter nos*,
Might be proclaim'd at *Charing-Cross*.   80

68 And question] Or question S.   72] *After 72 S. inserts two lines for
which there is no other authority:*

> And mark at Brentford how they Spell
> Hear is good *Eal* and *Bear* to *cell*;

74] To shew from Parnel, Pope, and Gay? S.   79 passes, *inter nos*,] F.,
1736, 1738, 1742   passes *inter nos* S., 1755

62. *one Word from you* - - - See a letter from Swift to Mrs. Howard, 9 July, 1727 (*Corresp.* iii. 405), where he speaks of the general belief 'that a word of mine to you would do anything'.

63. *three Years and more,* . . . Swift was privately introduced to Harley, 4 Oct., 1710. See *Journal to Stella.*

74. *From Pope,* . . . Members of the Scriblerus Club. See p. 184.

80. *Charing-Cross.* Royal proclamations are read at Charing Cross.

Yet some I know with Envy swell,
Because they see me us'd so well:
"How think you of our Friend the *Dean?*
"I wonder what some People mean;
"My Lord and he are grown so great,
"Always together, *tête à tête:*
"What, they admire him for his Jokes - - -
"See but the Fortune of some Folks!
There flies about a strange Report
Of some Express arriv'd at Court;   90
I'm stopt by all the Fools I meet,
And catechis'd in ev'ry Street.
"You, Mr. *Dean* frequent the Great;
"Inform us, will the Emp'ror treat?
"Or do the Prints and Papers lye?
Faith Sir, you know as much as I.
"Ah Doctor, how you love to jest?
"'Tis now no Secret - - I protest
'Tis one to me. - - "Then, tell us, pray
"When are the Troops to have their Pay?   100
And, though I solemnly declare
I know no more than my *Lord Mayor,*
They stand amaz'd, and think me grown
The closest Mortal ever known.

Thus in a Sea of Folly tost,
My choicest Hours of Life are lost:
Yet always wishing to retreat;
Oh, could I see my Country Seat.
There leaning near a gentle Brook,
Sleep, or peruse some antient Book;   110
And there in sweet Oblivion drown
Those Cares that haunt the Court and Town.

87 "What, they] 1736, 1738, 1742, 1755   What! they S.   "What? they F.
89] *N.P.* S., F., 1738   90 some Express] mighty News S.   97 jest?] F., 1736,
1738, 1742 jest! S., 1755   106 choicest] sweetest S.   112 the Court] a Court F.

94. *will the Emp'ror treat?* The   Ministry was negotiating the Treaty
Emperor of Austria was ignored and   of Utrecht.
kept in the dark while the English

In SICKNESS.

Written soon after the Author's coming to live in Ireland,
upon the Queen's Death, October 1714.

Faulkner, 1735, ii. 356 (1737, ii. 133).
Miscellanies, . . . Volume the Fifth, 1735, p. 65 (1736, v. 65; 1745, v. 14;
1751, x. 13).
Works of Jonathan Swift, D.D., ed. Hawkesworth, 1755, 4to, iv (1), 13.

Swift left Letcombe for Ireland on 16 August, 1714, and arrived in
Dublin on the 24th (*Letters of Swift to Ford,* ed. Nichol Smith, p. 60). He
was despondent at the turn of political events, sick at heart on parting from
his English friends, and assailed by lampoons. Among these squibs may be
named *An Hue and Cry after Dr. S—t,* which appeared before he left
Letcombe, *A farther Hue and Cry after Dr. S—t,* and *Essays, Divine,
Moral, and Political: . . . By the Author of the Tale of a Tub.* His personal
prospects, further, were endangered by his association with a fallen party.

The earliest surviving letter written by Swift, after his return to Ireland,
is addressed to Ford (Nichol Smith, *op. cit.,* p. 60), and the next to Bolingbroke, 14 Sept., 1714. His subsequent letters are filled with melancholy
and disappointment.

Writing to Pope, early in September, Arbuthnot mentions a letter from
Swift which has been lost (*Life and Works of John Arbuthnot,* G. A.
Aitken, p. 81). On 19 October Arbuthnot wrote to the Dean describing
the general supersession of his political friends (*Corresp.* ii. 245). It was
probably after the receipt of this letter, with Arbuthnot specially in mind,
that Swift composed the lines 'In Sickness'. There is every reason to
believe Faulkner's date, 'October', to be correct.

The text is printed from Faulkner's edition of 1735.

'TIS true,—then why should I repine,
  To see my Life so fast decline?
But, why obscurely here alone?
Where I am neither lov'd nor known.
My State of Health none care to learn;
My Life is here no Soul's Concern.
And, those with whom I now converse,
Without a Tear will tend my Herse.

3 alone?] 1735, 1736, 1745 alone, 1751, 1755   4 known.] 1735, 1736
known? 1745, 1751, 1755

Remov'd from kind *Arbuthnot*'s Aid,
Who knows his Art but not his Trade;   10
Preferring his Regard for me
Before his Credit or his Fee.
Some formal Visits, Looks, and Words,
What meer Humanity affords,
I meet perhaps from three or four,
From whom I once expected more;
Which those who tend the Sick for pay
Can act as decently as they.
But, no obliging, tender Friend
To help at my approaching End,   20
My Life is now a Burthen grown
To others, e'er it be my own.

YE formal Weepers for the Sick,
In your last Offices be quick:
And spare my absent Friends the Grief
To hear, yet give me no Relief;
Expir'd To-day, entomb'd To-morrow,
When known, will save a double Sorrow.

9. *kind Arbuthnot's Aid*. John Arbuthnot, b. 1667, after taking his medical degree at St. Andrews, removed to London. The accident of being called to attend on Prince George of Denmark led to his appointment as physician-extraordinary to Queen Anne, 1705. He was associated with the wits of the day, and formed a close friendship with Swift for whose ailments he prescribed. In addition to medical and scientific works he wrote a number of witty political and literary satires, of which the best-known is the *History of John Bull* (1712). A man of unblemished character, he was held in almost universal regard. He died in 1735. See *Life and Works*, G. A. Aitken, 1892; *John Arbuthnot*, Lester M. Beattie, 1935.

MISCELLANEOUS

A N D

PERSONAL POEMS
1715–1723

The FABLE of the BITCHES.

Wrote in the Year 1715, on an attempt to repeal the Test Act.

Faulkner, 1762, x. 308; 1763, xi. 406.
Works, 1762, xiv. 184.
Works, 1764, 4to, vii (2), 170; 8vo, xiv. 290.

This poem was first attributed to Swift by Faulkner in 1762/3, and re-printed in the continuation of the London edition of the *Works* edited by Bowyer, and published by the trade in the same year.

Swift was throughout life bitterly opposed to relieving Catholics and Dissenters from the disabilities they suffered under the Test Act. His first pamphlet on the subject, *A Letter from a Member of the House of Commons in Ireland to a Member of the House of Commons in England,* was written in 1708, and included by him in his first collected *Miscellanies,* 1711. When, in 1732–3, a renewed attempt was made in Ireland to repeal the Test Act, the several tracts published by him show that his opinions had in no way been chastened by the passage of time. See *Prose Works,* ed. Temple Scott, iv. 3–106. See also 'The Tale of a Nettle', p. 1084; and notes on the poem, '*On the Words*—Brother Protestants, and Fellow Christians', p. 809.

'This piece', says Dr. Elrington Ball, 'seems to have been occasioned by the proceedings of the General Assembly of the Church of Scotland in May and the correspondence that ensued' (*Swift's Verse,* pp. 150–1).

The text is printed from Faulkner's volume of 1762.

A BITCH that was full pregnant grown,
   By all the Dogs and Curs in Town;
Finding her ripen'd Time was come,
Her Litter teeming from her Womb,
Went here and there, and ev'ry where,
To find an easy Place to lay-her.

AT length to *Musick*'s House she came,
And begg'd like one both blind and lame;
"My only Friend, my Dear," said she,
"You see 'tis meer Necessity,   10
"Hath sent me to your House to whelp,
"I'll dye, if you deny your Help.

7. *Musick's House.* '*The Church of* England.'—Faulkner.

WITH fawning Whine, and rueful Tone,
With artful Sigh and feigned Groan,
With couchant Cringe, and flattering Tale,
Smooth *Bawty* did so far prevail;
That *Musick* gave her Leave to litter,
But mark what follow'd,—Faith she bit her.

WHOLE Baskets full of Bits and Scraps,
And Broth enough to fill her Paps,   20
For well she knew her num'rus Brood,
For want of Milk, wou'd suck her Blood.

BUT when she thought her Pains were done,
And now 'twas high Time to be gone;
In civil Terms,—"My Friend," says she,
'My House you've had on Courtesy;
"And now I earnestly desire,
"That you wou'd with your Cubbs retire:
"For shou'd you stay but one Week longer,
"I shall be starv'd with Cold and Hunger."   30

THE Guest reply'd,—"My Friend, your Leave,
"I must a little longer crave;
"Stay till my tender Cubs can find,
"Their Way—for now you see they're blind;
"But when we've gather'd Strength, I swear,
"We'll to our Barn again repair."

THE Time pass'd on, and *Musick* came,
Her Kennel once again to claim;
But, *Bawty*, lost to Shame and Honour,
Set all her Cubs at once upon her;   40
Made her retire, and quit her Right,
And loudly cry'd—a Bite, a Bite.

16. *Bawty*. 'Bawty, (*the Name of a Bitch in* Scotch,) *alludes to the Kirk*.'— Faulkner.

42. *a Bite*. A slang term in common use at the time denoting a hoax, or sell.

The M O R A L .

Thus did the *Grecian* Wooden Horse,
Conceal a fatal armed Force;
No sooner brought within the Walls,
But *Illium*'s lost, and *Priam* falls.

T O

The Earl of *O X F O R D*, Late Lord Treasurer.   Sent to him when he was in the Tower, before his Tryal.

Out of HORACE.

Written in the Year 1716.

Faulkner, 1735, ii. 348 (1737, ii. 135).
Miscellanies, . . . Volume the Fifth, 1735, p. 58 (1736, v. 58; 1745, v. 15; 1751, x. 14).
Works of Jonathan Swift, D.D., ed. Hawkesworth, 1755, 4to, iv (1), 14.

George I arrived at Greenwich on the 29th of September, and was crowned at Westminster on the 31st of October, 1714. A Parliament, mainly composed of Whigs, met in March, 1715; and a committee was appointed to inquire into Jacobite intrigues. Bolingbroke and Ormonde fled the country; and, in July, Oxford was thrown into the Tower. After he had lain there nearly two years he petitioned the House of Lords, who fixed 13 June, 1717, for his trial. The Commons requested a postponement to the 24th, which was agreed; but later followed a fierce dispute on procedure between the two Houses. On 1 July Oxford was acquitted of all charges by the Upper House. On the 15th of that month he was, however, at the instigation of the Commons, expressly excluded from the King's act of grace.

On the 19th of July, 1715 (*Corresp.* ii. 293), Swift wrote a noble and dignified letter to Oxford in the Tower, whither he had been committed on the 9th. On the 15th of June, 1717, Erasmus Lewis wrote to inform Swift

that Oxford's trial was fixed for 'Monday next come sennight'. He wrote
again on the 18th in case the Dean should 'have any thoughts of coming
over'. On the 2nd of July he wrote that 'Lord Oxford's impeachment was
discharged'; and on the 9th Swift wrote to congratulate Oxford.

The poem was first printed by Faulkner in 1735, and assigned to the
year 1716, a date which is presumably correct, for the tenor of the piece
suggests that it was written during Oxford's long wait in the Tower, and not
in immediate urgency before the trial took place.

In early editions the poem is merely stated to be 'Out of Horace'. The
original parallel is Bk. III, Ode II.

The text is printed from Faulkner's 1735 edition.

HOW blest is he, who for his Country dies;
Since Death pursues the Coward as he flies.
The Youth, in vain, would fly from Fate's Attack,
With trembling Knees, and Terror at his Back;
Though Fear should lend him Pinions like the Wind,
Yet swifter Fate will seize him from behind.

VIRTUE repuls't, yet knows not to repine;
But shall with unattainted Honour shine;
Nor stoops to take the *Staff*, nor lays it down,
Just as the Rabble please to smile or frown.   10

VIRTUE, to crown her Fav'rites, loves to try
Some new unbeaten Passage to the Sky;
Where *Jove* a Seat among the Gods will give
To those who die, for meriting to live.

NEXT, faithful Silence hath a sure Reward:
Within our Breast be ev'ry Secret barr'd:
He who betrays his Friend, shall never be
Under one Roof, or in one Ship with me.
For, who with Traytors would his Safety trust,
Lest with the Wicked, Heaven involve the Just?   20
And, though the Villain 'scape a while, he feels
Slow Vengeance, like a Blood-hound at his Heels.

2 flies.] flies! 1755

9. *Nor stoops to take the Staff.* The white staff of the Lord Treasurer's office.

Ad AMICUM Eruditum
THOMAM SHERIDAN.

Scripsit *Oct. Ann. Dom.* 1717.

The Whimsical Medley, iii. 354.
Faulkner, 1735, ii. 475 (1737, ii. 387).
Miscellanies, . . . Volume the Fifth, 1735, p. 153 (1736, v. 153; 1745,
v. 16).
Works of Jonathan Swift, D.D., ed Hawkesworth, 1755, 4to, iv (1), 15.
Essay on the Earlier Part of the Life of Swift, Barrett, 1808, p. 155.
Works, ed. Scott, 1814, x. 572.

This epistle was first printed by Faulkner in 1735. According to Orrery,
Remarks, 1752, p. 130, Swift took special pride in these Latin verses (see
below, p. 316, notes on 'Carberiæ Rupes').
    The poem was transcribed, from a manuscript copy, into *The Whimsical
Medley,* together with a jesting introductory letter in English:

'To Mr. Tho: Sheridan

Rev^{d:} and learned S^{r.},
    I am Teacher of English for a want of a better to a poor Charity School
in the lower end of St. Thomas Street, but in my time I have been a Virgilian,
tho' I am now forc'd to teach English wch. I understood less than my own
Native Language, or even than Latin it self; therefore I made bold to send y^u
the inclosed, the Fruit of My Muse, in hopes it may qualify me for the
honnour of being one of your most inferior Ushers, if you will Vouchsafe to
send me an Answer, direct it to me next door but one to the Harrow, on the
left hand in Crocker's Lane.

I am y^{rs.}
Rev^{d.} S^{r.} to Command,
Pat: Reyly.

Scribimus indocti doctique poemata passim. Horat:'

    Barrett, in his *Essay,* 1808, printed this letter, together with other trifles
which passed between Sheridan and Swift, taken from *The Whimsical
Medley.* In consequence some modern editors have, most inappropriately,
included Swift's Latin epistle among the 'Trifles'. These verses were far
otherwise regarded by him.
    The text is printed from Faulkner's edition of the *Poetical Works,* 1735.

DELICIÆ *Sheridan* Musarum, dulcis amice,
Sic tibi propitius Permessi ad flumen *Apollo*
Occurrat, seu te mimum convivia rident;
Æquivocosve sales spargis, seu ludere versu
Malles; dic, *Sheridan*, quisnam fuit ille Deorum,

1. *Sheridan.* The acquaintance between Swift and Sheridan may only have begun in the year to which this poem was assigned by Faulkner. Temple Scott, *Prose Works*, xi. 152, states that they became acquainted in 1713, when Swift came over to Ireland to be installed Dean of St. Patrick's. But there is no evidence of this. See *Corresp.* iii. 19 n.¹. Further, in *The History of the Second Solomon*, Swift refers to verses lampooning him, written by Sheridan 'in three months after their acquaintance'. These verses clearly rankled with Swift, for they prompted his lines to Delany (see p. 214) belonging to October, 1718. It is incredible that Sheridan should have satirized the Dean in 1713, or that Swift should have carried the particular memory for five years.

Thomas Sheridan, for whom see further *D.N.B.* lii. 86, was born in 1687, and came of an Irish family of some distinction (see Sichel's *Sheridan*, i. 215–17). He had a measure of the genius which marked the family for generations. He was the father of Thomas Sheridan, 1719–88, Swift's biographer, and grandfather of the famous Richard Brinsley Sheridan.

Sheridan entered Trinity College, Dublin, in 1707, took his B.A. in 1711, and M.A. in 1714. He possessed real gifts as a schoolmaster (see Orrery, *Remarks*, 1752, p. 84), but ruined his career by improvidence and bad management. Through Swift's influence with Carteret, Sheridan was appointed one of the chaplains to the Lord Lieutenant, and, in 1725, was presented to the living of Rincurran, in the county of Cork (*Letters of Swift*

to Ford, ed. Nichol Smith, p. 122). Hardly had he been instituted before he gave offence by preaching, on the 1st of August, the anniversary of the accession of the House of Hanover, a sermon from the text, 'Sufficient unto the day is the evil thereof'. Lord Carteret was informed of the fact by a certain Richard Tighe (see pp. 772–3), and as, in any event, Sheridan came of a family known for its Jacobite leanings, he was struck off the list of chaplains (see *Prose Works*, ed. Temple Scott, vii. 241–3).

For many years an intimate friendship subsisted between Sheridan and Swift, and pasquinades, riddles, verse trifles passed continually from one to the other. Just before Sheridan's death the friendship was broken. Swift took offence at having his attention called to growing signs of avarice. Sheridan was informed that his presence was no longer welcome at the Deanery. He died in poverty in 1738. See further on the relations of Swift and Sheridan, *Corresp.* vi, Appendix VIII, pp. 210–12.

For a verse criticism of Sheridan by Swift see the poem sent to Delany in November, 1718 (p. 214). *The History of the Second Solomon* (*Prose Works*, xi. 152–8), first printed by Deane Swift in 1765, and assigned to the year 1729, contains an ungracious picture of his friend by Swift. After Sheridan's death, however, Swift made amends with his *Character of Doctor Sheridan* (*Prose Works*, xi. 161–3), also first printed by Deane Swift.

Sheridan collaborated with Swift in writing *The Intelligencer* (1728). He

Quæ melior natura orto tibi tradidit artem
Rimandi genium puerorum, atq; ima cerebri
Scrutandi? Tibi nascenti ad cunabula *Pallas*
Astitit; & dixit, mentis præsaga futuræ,
Heu puer infelix! nostro sub sydere natus;   10
Nam tu pectus eris sine corpore, corporis umbra;
Sed levitate umbram superabis, voce cicadam:
Musca femur, palmas tibi Mus dedit, ardea crura.
Corpore sed tenui tibi quod natura negavit;
Hoc animi dotes supplebunt; teq; docente,
Nec longum Tempus, surget tibi docta juventus,
Artibus egregiis animas instructa novellas.
Grex hinc Pœonius venit, ecce, *salutifer* orbi.
Ast, illi causas orant; his infula visa est
Divinam capiti nodo constringere mitram.   20

    NATALIS te horæ non fallunt signa; sed usq;
Conscius, expedias puero seu lætus *Apollo*
Nascenti arrisit; sive illum frigidus horror
Saturni premit, aut septem inflavere triones.

    QUIN tu altè penitusq; latentia semina cernis,
Quæq; diu obtundendo olim sub luminis auras
Erumpent, promis; quo ritu saepè puella
Sub cinere hesterno sopitos suscitat ignes.

    TE Dominum agnoscit quocunq; sub aere natus;
Quos indulgentis nimium custodia matris   30
Pessundat: Nam sæpè vides in stipite matrem.

---

13 ardea] 1737, 1755   Ardea 1735, 1736, 1745   18] *In place of l. 18 'The Whimsical Medley' has the following two lines:*

        Hinc strenuus prodit Dux, hinc Neptunia proles,
        Pœonis hinc proles venit, ecce salutifer Orbi.

may have written some of the coarse pieces commonly ascribed to Swift, including *The Wonderful Wonder of Wonders* (Scott, *Works*, 1814, xiii. 457). The lines on Delville (see p. 1107) have been attributed to him. His verses on Ballyspellin (see p. 438), and other pieces, received replies from Swift. See also notes p. 1012.

    For Mrs. Sheridan see 'A Portrait from the Life', p. 954.

AUREUS at ramus venerandæ dona Sibyllæ,
Æneæ sedes tantùm patefecit Avernas:
Sæpè puer, tua quem tetigit semel aurea virga,
Cœlumq; terrasq; videt, noctemq; profundam.

To *Mr.* DELANY.

Swift's autograph: Forster Library, South Kensington (541).
Works, ed. Deane Swift, 1765, 4to, viii (2), 170; 8vo, xvi. 285. [Ref. 1765.]
Faulkner, 1765, xiii. 297.
Works, ed. Sheridan, 1784, vii. 152.

In the Forster Library, South Kensington, is preserved a letter from Swift to Delany, accompanying a copy of these verses neatly written in the Dean's hand. The letter is dated 'Nov^br. 10th. 1718|9 in the morning.', and the four pages of verses, on one folded sheet, are dated, at the foot of the last page, 'Oct^br. 10th. 1718|9 in the morning.' For the letter see *Corresp.* iii. 18.

Swift had not long been acquainted with Sheridan (for whom see p. 212 n.) when a piece of badinage by that irrepressible jester wounded his feelings. In *The History of the Second Solomon*, stated by Deane Swift to have been written in 1729, Swift says: 'In three months' time Solomon, without the least provocation, writ a long poem, describing that person's muse to be dead, and making a funeral solemnity with asses, owls, &c., and gave the copy among all his acquaintance.' The letter accompanying Swift's lines requests Delany to regard the poem as confidential, 'else I may be thought a Man who will not take a Jest'. Swift also suggested that Sheridan should receive a hint that he had transgressed 'all the Rules of Raillery'.

Delany (*Observations*, 1754, pp. 17, 18) quotes ll. 1, 2, 5–8, from memory, and not quite accurately, stating they were the only lines he remembered, and that he was 'assured, the person they were address'd to, burnt the original in a fit of mortification: and kept no copy'. This implies that the original manuscript, or a copy, reached Sheridan. In Delany's opinion the verses were among the 'genteelest' ever written by Swift.

Swift's acquaintance with Delany appears to have begun no earlier than the year in which this poem was written. Patrick Delany was, at the time, a Junior Fellow of Trinity College, Dublin. He enjoyed a reputation both as a scholar and a preacher. Lord Carteret, when Lord Lieutenant, held him in esteem, and, in 1727, made him Chancellor of Christ Church Cathedral. In addition he received the College living of Derryvullen. But his tastes were extravagant, and in 1729 he addressed a rhyming epistle to Carteret soliciting further preferment, for which he was ridiculed by Swift and Sheridan (see pp. 470 ff.). In 1730 he was appointed Chancellor of St. Patrick's, and in 1744 Dean of Down. His *Observations upon Lord Orrery's Remarks* (1754) was a defence of Swift. He died in 1768. See Ball's *Hist. of County Dublin*, Part vi, 129 ff.

The text is printed from Swift's holograph. Deane Swift evidently used a revised copy.

[p. 1]   To You, whose Virtues I must own
With shame, I have too lately known;
To you, by Art and Nature taught
To be the Man I long have sought,
Had not ill Fate, perverse and blind,
Plac'd you in Life too far behind;
Or what I should repine at more,
Plac'd me in Life too far before;
To you the Muse this Verse bestows,
Which might as well have been in Prose;   10
No Thought, no Fancy, no Sublime,
But simple Topicks told in Rime.
    Three Gifts for Conversation fit
Are Humor, Raillery and Witt:
The last, as boundless as the Wind;
Is well conceiv'd thô not defin'd;
For, sure, by Wit is onely meant
Applying what we first Invent:
What Humor is, not all the Tribe
Of Logick-mongers can describe;   20
Here, onely Nature acts her Part,
Unhelpt by Practice, Books, or Art.
For Wit and Humor differ quite,
That gives Surprise, and this Delight:

13 Three Gifts] Talents 1765   14 Raillery and] breeding, sense, and 1765
17 onely] chiefly 1765   18 Applying what we first] Applying well what we 1765   21 onely Nature] nature only 1765

5–8. *Had not ill Fate, . . .* Delany,   '*Oh why did fate perverse and blind,*
Observations, 1754, p. 18, quotes these   *Place you in life so far behind?*
four lines from memory in the form of   *Or, what I should repine at more,*
questions: *Place me in life so far before?*'

Humor is odd, grotesque, and wild,
Onely by Affectation spoild,
Tis never by Invention got,
Men have it when they know it not.
   Our Conversation to refine
True Humor must with Wit combine: 30
From both, we learn to Railly well;
Wherein French Writers most excell:
[p. 2] Voiture in various Lights displays
That Irony which turns to Praise,
His Genius first found out the Rule
For an obliging Ridicule:
He flatters with peculiar Air
The Brave, the Witty, and the Fair;
And Fools would fancy he intends
A Satyr where he most commends.   40
   But as a poor pretending Beau
Because he fain would make a Show,
Nor can afford to buy gold Lace,
Takes up with Copper in the Place;
So, the pert Dunces of Mankind
Whene're they would be thought refin'd,
Because the Diff'rence lyes abstruse
'Twixt Raillery and gross Abuse,
To show their Parts, will scold and rail,
Like Porters o'er a Pot of Ale.   50
   Such is that Clan of boist'rous Bears
Always together by the Ears;
Shrewd Fellows, and arch Wags, a Tribe
That meet for nothing but to gibe;

30 True Humor must with Wit] Humour and wit must both 1765   32
Wherein French Writers most] Wherein sometimes the French 1765   43
Nor can afford to buy gold] Nor can arrive at silver 1765   46 Whene're]
Whene'er 1765   47 Because the Diff'rence lyes] As if the diff'rence lay
1765   51] *No break* 1765   51 that] the 1765

33. *Voiture*. Vincent Voiture, 1598–1648, poet and letter-writer, found patrons in Richelieu and Louis XIII. He was a wit, a courtier, a favourite with the other sex, and an original member of the Academy. Swift possessed a Paris and a Brussels edition of his works (*Dean Swift's Library*, H. Williams, p. 65).

Who first Run one another down,
And then fall foul on all the Town;
Skilld in the Horse-laugh and dry Rub,
And calld by Excellence, *the Club*:
I mean your Butler, Dawson, Car,
All special Friends, and allways jarr.   60
    The mettled and the vicious Steed
Do not more differ in their Breed,
Nay, Voiture is as like Tom Lee,
As Rudeness is to Repartee.
[p. 3]   If what You said, I wish unspoke,
'Twill not suffice, it was a Joke.
Reproach not tho in jest, a Friend
For those Defects he cannot mend;
His Lineage, Calling, Shape or Sense
If nam'd with Scorn, gives just Offence.   70
    What Use in Life, to make Men frett?
Part in worse humor than they met?
Thus all Society is lost,
Men laugh at one another's Cost;
And half the Company is teazd
That came together to be pleasd:
For all Buffoons have most in View
To please themselves by vexing You

62 Do not more differ] Differ as little 1765   71 frett ?] fret, 1765   78]
After l. 78 Deane Swift and later editors print ll. 87–94, with variants. Swift first wrote the lines in this position, scored them out, and, with some change, placed them as in the text.

59. *Butler, Dawson, Car.* These three were figures well known in Dublin society. Brinsley Butler (referred to by Swift as 'Prince Butler' in *The Publick Spirit of the Whigs,* and *Corresp.* ii. 242, iii. 49) became second Lord Newtown-Butler and first Viscount Lanesborough. He was a friend and correspondent of Joshua Dawson, sometime Under-Secretary at Dublin Castle (see *Corresp.* i. 178 n.4). Dr. Charles Carr was Dawson's son-in-law. In 1716 he was appointed Bishop of

Killaloe.
    63. *Tom Lee.* Two brothers, James ('Jemmy') and Tom Leigh, are frequently mentioned in the *Journal to Stella.* The former was a Westmeath landlord with a passion for London life; the latter was a clergyman whose formal ways particularly excited Swift's dislike. See also p. 968 n.
    69. In Swift's manuscript the words 'His Person, Family or Sense' are scored out.

When Jests are carryd on too far,
And the loud Laugh proclaims the War;   80
You keep Your Countenance for shame
Yet still you think your Friend to blame.
And thô men cry, they love a Jest,
Tis but when others stand the Test,
For would you have their Meaning known?
They love a Jest—when 'tis their own.
[p. 4]   You wonder now to see me write
So gravely, where the Subject's light.
Some part of what I here design
Regards a Friend of yours and mine,   90
Who full of Humor, Fire and Wit,
Not allways judges what is fit;
But loves to take prodigious Rounds,
And sometimes walks beyond his Bounds.
You must, although the Point be nice,
Venture to give him some Advice.
Few Hints from you will set him right,
And teach him how to be polite.
Let him, like you, observe with Care
Whom to be hard on, whom to spare: 100
Nor indiscreetly to suppose
All Subjects like Dan Jackson's Nose.

80 proclaims] begins 1765   83 And] For, 1765   86 when] that 1765
88 where the Subject's light.] on a subject light; 1765   91 Who full of
Humor, Fire and Wit,] Who, neither void of sense nor wit, 1765   92 Not
allways] Yet seldom 1765
93–4]   But sallies oft beyond his bounds,
               And takes unmeasurable rounds. 1765
95] *N.P.* 1765   96 Venture to give him some] Bestow your friend some
good 1765   97 Few Hints] One hint 1765   99 Let] Bid 1765   101
Nor indiscreetly] Nor, indistinctly, 1765

90. *a Friend. I.e.* Sheridan.
99. 'Bid' altered by Swift to 'Let'.
102. *Dan Jackson's Nose.* The Rev.
Daniel Jackson, a cousin of the Grattans (for whom see notes pp. 314, 741).
His brother, the Rev. John Jackson,
held the living of Santry, within a few
miles of Dublin, where his grandfather

and father before him had been vicars.
Daniel Jackson's large nose was a
subject of jest in the circle of Swift's
friends. It is mentioned in several
verse trifles written about this time.
See pp. 984 n., 990 ff., and B. W.
Adams, *History of Santry*, 1883, pp. 5,
68–70.

To study the obliging Jest,
By reading those who teach it best.
For Prose, I recommend Voiture's,
For Verse, (I speak my Judgment) Yours:
He'll find the Secret out from thence
To Rime all day without Offence;
And I no more shall then Accuse
The Flirts of his ill-mannerd Muse.   110
   If he be Guilty, you must mend him,
If he be innocent, defend him.

A quiet Life, and a good Name
To &c. Writ A.D. 1719

Transcript by Stella; Manuscript Volume in the possession of the Duke of
  Bedford, Woburn Abbey.
Faulkner, 1735, ii. 349 (1737, ii. 178). [Ref. F.]   [[Ref. 1735, &c.]
Miscellanies, ...Volume the Fifth, 1735, p. 59 (1736, v. 59; 1745, v. 62).
Read's Weekly Journal. April 12, 1735. *The St. James's Evening Post*.
  April 10–12, 1735.
The Muse in Good Humour: Or, A Collection of Comic Tales, ... *Printed for
  F. Noble*, ... 1751, 6th edn., p. 171.

Stella's transcript is the earliest form in which this poem has been preserved. Whether she was copying from a printed sheet or manuscript, she
did not give that part of the title which is supplied by Faulkner: '*To a
Friend, who married a Shrew*.' Stella assigned the piece to 1719. Faulkner
says vaguely: 'Written about the YEAR 1724.' Stella's date may be accepted
with a doubt.

Although the details are not wholly relevant matter of fact, it is possible
that Swift had Sheridan and his wife in mind. See pp. 954–5.

The poem is printed from Stella's transcript.

    Nell scolded in so loud a Din
That Will durst hardly venture in;
He mark't the Conjugall Dispute,
Nell roar'd incessant, Dick sate mute:

   1 Din] Din. F., 1735, 1736, 1745

But when He saw his Friend appear
Cry'd bravely, Patience, good my Dear.
At sight of Will she bawl'd no more,
But hurry'd out, and clapp't the Dore.
   Why Dick! the Devil's in thy Nell
Quoth Will; thy House is worse than Hell: 10
Why, what a Peal the Jade has rung,
Damn her, why don't you Slit her Tongue?
For nothing else will make it cease,—
Dear Will, I suffer this for Peace;
I never quarrell with my Wife,
I bear it for a quiet Life
Scripture you know exhorts us to it,
Bids us to seek Peace and ensue it.
   Will went again to visit Dick
And entring in the very nick,   20
He saw Virago Nell belabor
With Dick's own Staff his Peacefull Neighbor,
Poor Will, who needs must interpose,
Receiv'd a brace or two of Blows.
   But now, to make my Story Short
Will drew out Dick to take a Quart,
Why Dick, thy Wife has dev'lish Whims:
Ods buds, why don't you break her Limbs:
If she were Mine, and had such Tricks,
I'd teach her how to handle Sticks: 30
Z—ds I would ship her for Jamaica
And truck the Carrion for Tobacca,
I'd send her far enough away—
Dear Will, but, what would People say?
Lord! I should get so ill a Name,
The Neighbors round would cry out Shame.
   Dick suffer'd for his Peace and Credit,
But who believ'd him when he said it:

9 Nell] *Nell,* F., 1735, 1736, 1745   11 rung,] rung! F., 1735, 1736, 1745
16 Life] Life. F., 1735, 1736, 1745   19 Dick] *Dick*; F., 1735, 1736, 1745
28 Limbs:] Limbs? F., 1735, 1736, 1745   32 Tobacca,] *Tobacco*; F.,
1735, 1736 *Tobacco:* 1745   38 it:] it? F., 1735, 1736, 1745

Can he who makes himself a Slave
Consult his Peace, or Credit save?   40
Dick found it by his ill Success
His Quiet small, his Credit less;
Nell serv'd him at the usu'll Rate
She stun'd, and then she broke his Pate.
And what he thought the hardest Case,
The Parish jear'd him to his Face:
Those Men who wore the Breeches least
Call'd him a Cuckold, Fool, and Beast,
At home, he was pursu'd with Noise,
Abroad, was pester'd by the Boys,   50
Within, his wife would break his Bones,
Without, they pelted him with Stones,
The Prentices procur'd a Riding
To act his Patience, and her chiding.
    False Patience, and mistaken Pride!
There are ten thousand Dicks beside;
Slaves to their Quiet and good Name,
Are us'd like Dick, and bear the Blame.

P H I L L I S,
Or, the Progress of Love.
Written A.D. 1719.

Transcript by Stella: Manuscript Volume in the possession of the Duke of Bedford, Woburn Abbey.
Miscellanies. The Last Volume, 1727, p. 236 (1731, p. 287; 1733, p. 287; 1736, p. 267; 1742, iv. 183; 1751, vii. 167).
Faulkner, 1735, ii. 120 (1737, ii. 96). [Ref. F.]
The Muse in Good Humour. Or, a Collection of Comic Tales, . . . Printed for J. Noble, . . . 1744. p. 18.
Works of Jonathan Swift, D.D., ed. Hawkesworth, 1755, 4to, iii (2), 158.

    This and the following two poems are related in title, conception, and, apparently, in date. The first two were included in Stella's volume of transcripts; all three first appeared in print in the *Miscellanies* of 1727. As between Stella and the printed text the variants are few and unimportant in the 'Progress of Love'; but five of Stella's stanzas in the 'Progress of Beauty' were omitted in the printed version. It is clear that these stanzas belonged to the original draft. An omission, in the latter poem, between lines 60 and 61 of the printed version is evident, and Stella's stanza supplies it. These stanzas were either deleted by Swift, or possibly by Pope as editor of the *Miscellanies*.

No date of composition is given for these three poems in the *Miscellanies*, 1727. Stella assigns both the 'Progress of Love' and the 'Progress of Beauty' to 1719. All three probably belong to 1719–20. Faulkner gives 1716 for the 'Progress of Love', but this is almost certainly wrong, and, possibly, only a printer's error.

This and the following poem are printed from Stella's transcripts. Swift made one annotation to the 'Progress of Love', l. 35, in his copy of the *Miscellanies*.

Stella spells 'Phillis', the printed version '*Phyllis*' throughout.

> Desponding Phillis was endu'd
> With ev'ry Talent of a Prude,
> She trembled when a Man drew near;
> Salute her, and she turn'd her Ear:
> If o'er against her you were plac't
> She durst not look above your Wast;
> She'd rather take you to her Bed
> Than let you see her dress her Head;
> In Church you heard her thrô the Crowd
> Repeat the Absolution loud;   10
> In Church, secure behind her Fan
> She durst behold that Monster, Man:
> There practic'd how to place her Head,
> And bit her Lips to make them red:
> Or on the Matt devoutly kneeling
> Would lift her Eyes up to the Ceeling,
> And heave her Bosom unaware
> For neighb'ring Beaux to see it bare.
>   At length a lucky Lover came,
> And found Admittance from the Dame.   20
> Suppose all Partyes now agreed,
> The Writings drawn, the Lawyer fee'd,

9 heard] 1727, 1731, 1733, F. hear 1736, 1742, 1751, 1755   19] *No break*
1731, 1733, 1736, 1742, 1751, 1755   20 from] to *printed version*

The Vicar and the Ring bespoke:
Guess how could such a Match be broke.
See then what Mortals place their Bliss in!
Next morn betimes the Bride was missing,
The Mother scream'd, the Father chid,
Where can this idle Wench be hid?
No news of Phil. The Bridegroom came,
And thought his Bride had sculk't for shame,   30
Because her Father us'd to say
The Girl had such a Bashfull way.
    Now, John the Butler must be sent
To learn the Way that Phillis went;
The Groom was wisht to saddle Crop,
For John must neither light nor stop;
But find her where so'er she fled,
And bring her back, alive or dead.
See here again the Dev'l to do;
For truly John was missing too: 40
The Horse and Pillion both were gone
Phillis, it seems, was fled with John.
Old Madam who went up to find
What Papers Phil had left behind,
A Letter on the Toylet sees
To my much honor'd Father; These:
('Tis always done, Romances tell us,
When Daughters run away with Fellows)
Fill'd with the choicest common-places,
By others us'd in the like Cases.   50
That, long ago a Fortune-teller
Exactly said what now befell her,

24 broke.] broke ? *printed version*   29 Phil.] *Phil!* 1727, 1755   *Phyl!* 1731,
1733, F., 1736, 1742, 1751   34 Way] Road *printed version*   36 nor]
or 1727   39] *N.P.* 1727 *and remainder*   43] *N.P.* 1727 *and remainder*
50 Cases.] Cases; 1727, 1731, 1733, F. Cases! 1736, 1742, 1751   51–72]
In quotes, printed version

35. *The Groom was wisht* . . . In his   wrote at the foot of the page, 'A
own copy of the *Miscellanies* Swift   trades-men's Phrase'. In Faulkner's
underlined the word 'wish'd' and   edition the word is printed in italics.

And in a Glass had made her see
A serving-Man of low Degree:
It was her Fate; must be forgiven;
For Marriages are made in Heaven:
His Pardon begg'd, but to be plain,
She'd do't if 'twere to do again.
Thank God, 'twas neither Shame nor Sin,
For John was come of honest Kin: 60
Love never thinks of Rich and Poor,
She'd beg with John from Door to Door:
Forgive her, if it be a Crime,
She'll never do't another Time,
She ne'r before in all her Life
Once disobey'd him, Maid nor Wife.
One Argument she summ'd up all in,
The Thing was done and past recalling:
And therefore hop'd she would recover
His Favor, when his Passion's over. 70
She valued not what others thought her;
And was—His most obedient Daughter.
  Fair Maidens all attend the Muse
Who now the wandring Pair pursues:
Away they rode in homely Sort
Their Journy long, their Money short;
The loving Couple well bemir'd,
The Horse and both the Riders tir'd:
Their Vittells bad, their Lodging worse,
Phil cry'd, and John began to curse; 80
Phil wish't, that she had strained a Limb
When first she ventur'd out with him.
John wish't, that he had broke a Leg
When first for her he quitted Peg.
  But what Adventures more befell 'um
The Muse has now not time to tell 'um.
How Jonny wheadled, threatned, fawnd,
Till Phillis all her Trinkets pawn'd:

How oft she broke her marriage Vows
In kindness to maintain her Spouse;   90
Till Swains unwholsome spoyld the Trade,
For now the Surgeon must be paid;
To whom those Perquisites are gone
In Christian Justice due to John.
     When Food and Rayment now grew scarce
Fate put a Period to the Farce;
And with exact Poetick Justice:
For John is Landlord, Phillis Hostess;
They keep at Stains the old blue Boar,
Are Cat and Dog, and Rogue and Whore.   100

THE
PROGRESS of BEAUTY

Written A D: 1719

Transcript by Stella: Manuscript Volume in the possession of the Duke of
Bedford, Woburn Abbey.
Miscellanies. The Last Volume, 1727, p. 247 (1731, p. 293; 1733, p. 293;
     1736, p. 273; 1742, iv. 188; 1751, vii. 172).
Faulkner, 1735, ii. 131 (1737, ii. 105). [Ref. F.]
Works of Jonathan Swift, D.D., ed. Hawkesworth, 1755, 4to, iii (2), 163.

     See notes to the preceding poem. Faulkner gives 1720 as the date of this
poem.
     It is possible that Swift adopted his title from the well-known poem by
George Granville, Lord Lansdown, which first appeared in Charles
Gildon's *New Miscellany of Original Poems*, 1701.
     The text is printed from Stella's transcript. In Swift's copy of Faulkner,
vol. ii, 1737, three printer's errors, l. 2, 'Streams', l. 84 (100) omission of
'but', l. 93 (109) 'moves', are corrected. These slips do not appear in the
1735 edition.

92 Surgeon] 1727, 1731, 1733, F., 1736   Surgeons 1742, 1751   surgeons 1755
99 Stains the old blue Boar,] *Staines*, the *Old Blue Boar*, 1727, 1731, 1733
Staines, the *old blue boar*, F.   *Staines*, the *Old Blue-Boar*, 1736, 1742, 1751
Staines the *Old Blue Boar*, 1755

When first Diana leaves her Bed
Vapors and Steams her Looks disgrace,
A frouzy dirty colour'd red
Sits on her cloudy wrinckled Face.

But by degrees when mounted high
Her artificiall Face appears
Down from her Window in the Sky,
Her Spots are gone, her Visage clears.

'Twixt earthly Femals and the Moon
All Parallells exactly run;   10
If Celia should appear too soon
Alas, the Nymph would be undone.

To see her from her Pillow rise
All reeking in a cloudy Steam,
Crackt Lips, foul Teeth, and gummy Eyes,
Poor Strephon, how would he blaspheme!

The Soot or Powder which was wont
To make her Hair look black as Jet,
Falls from her Tresses on her Front
A mingled Mass of Dirt and Sweat.   20

Three Colours, Black, and Red, and White,
So gracefull in their proper Place,
Remove them to a diff'rent Light
They form a frightfull hideous Face,

For instance; when the Lilly slipps
Into the Precincts of the Rose,
And takes Possession of the Lips,
Leaving the Purple to the Nose.

So Celia went entire to bed,
All her Complexions safe and sound,   30
But when she rose, the black and red
Though still in Sight, had chang'd their Ground.

17–20] *Om. printed version*   23 Light] scite, 1755 *followed by later editors*
25 slipps] skips *printed version*   31 the black and red] White, Black, and
Red, *printed version*

The Black, which would not be confin'd
A more inferior Station seeks
Leaving the fiery red behind,
And mingles in her muddy Cheeks.

The Paint by Perspiration cracks,
And falls in Rivulets of Sweat,
On either Side you see the Tracks,
While at her Chin the Conflu'ents met.   40

A Skillfull Houswife thus her Thumb
With Spittle while she spins, anoints,
And thus the brown Meanders come
In trickling Streams betwixt her Joynts.

But Celia can with ease reduce
By help of Pencil, Paint and Brush
Each Colour to it's Place and Use,
And teach her Cheeks again to blush.

She knows her Early self no more,
But fill'd with Admiration, stands,   50
As Other Painters oft adore
The Workmanship of their own Hands.

Thus after four important Hours
Celia's the Wonder of her Sex;
Say, which among the Heav'nly Pow'rs
Could cause such wonderfull Effects.

Venus, indulgent to her Kind
Gave Women all their Hearts could wish
When first she taught them where to find
White Lead, and Lusitanian Dish.   60

Love with White lead cements his Wings,
White lead was sent us to repair
Two brightest, brittlest earthly Things
A Lady's Face, and China ware.

37–44] *Om. printed version*   52] *Italics* F.   56 wonderfull Effects.]
marvellous Effects ? *printed version*

Swift's Poems

She ventures now to lift the Sash,
The Window is her proper Sphear;
Ah Lovely Nymph be not too rash,
Nor let the Beaux approach too near.

Take Pattern by your Sister Star,
Delude at once and Bless our Sight,   70
When you are seen, be seen from far,
And chiefly chuse to shine by Night.

In the Pell-mell when passing by,
Keep up the Glasses of your Chair,
Then each transported Fop will cry,
G—d d—m me Jack, she's wondrous fair.

But, Art no longer can prevayl
When the Materialls all are gone,
The best Mechanick Hand must fayl
Where Nothing's left to work upon.   80

Matter, as wise Logicians say,
Cannot without a Form subsist,
And Form, say I, as well as They,
Must fayl if Matter brings no Grist.

And this is fair Diana's Case
For, all Astrologers maintain
Each Night a Bit drops off her Face
When Mortals say she's in her Wain.

While Partridge wisely shews the Cause
Efficient of the Moon's Decay,   90
That Cancer with his pois'nous Claws
Attacks her in the milky Way:

But Gadbury in Art profound
From her pale Cheeks pretends to show
That Swain Endymion is not sound,
Or else, that Mercury's her Foe.

73–6] *Om. printed version*

89. *Partridge*. See p. 97 n.   1704, was an astrologer of note and a
93. *Gadbury*. John Gadbury, 1627–   busy writer. *D.N.B.* xx. 345.

But, let the Cause be what it will,
In half a Month she looks so thin
That Flamstead can with all his Skill
See but her Forehead and her Chin.　　100

Yet as she wasts, she grows discreet,
Till Midnight never shows her Head;
So rotting Celia stroles the Street
When sober Folks are all a-bed.

For sure if this be Luna's Fate,
Poor Celia, but of mortall Race
In vain expects a longer Date
To the Materialls of Her Face.

When Mercury her Tresses mows
To think of Oyl and Soot, is vain,　　110
No Painting can restore a Nose,
Nor will her Teeth return again.

Two Balls of Glass may serve for Eyes,
White Lead can plaister up a Cleft,
But these alas, are poor Supplyes
If neither Cheeks, nor Lips be left.

Ye Pow'rs who over Love preside,
Since mortal Beautyes drop so soon,
If you would have us well supply'd,
Send us new Nymphs with each new Moon.　　120

110 To think of Oyl and Soot, is vain,] To think of Black-head Combs is vain;
printed version　　113–16] *Om. printed version*

99. *Flamstead*. John Flamsteed, 1646–1719, first astronomer royal.

THE
PROGRESS
OF
POETRY.

Miscellanies. The Last Volume, 1727, p. 243 (1731, p. 291; 1733, p. 291;
1736, p. 271; 1742, iv. 187; 1751, vii. 170).
Faulkner, 1735, ii. 129 (1737, ii. 103).
Works of Jonathan Swift, D.D., ed. Hawkesworth, 1755, 4to, iii (2), 161.

Faulkner is the only authority for the date of this poem. In his 1735
edition he gives it as, 'Written in the Year 1720'. In his 1737 edition the
word 'in' is altered to 'about'; but in 1744 he returned to 'in'.
The text is printed from the *Miscellanies* of 1727.

THE Farmer's Goose, who in the Stubble,
   Has fed without Restraint, or Trouble;
Grown fat with Corn and Sitting still,
Can scarce get o'er the Barn-Door Sill:
And hardly waddles forth, to cool
Her Belly in the neighb'ring Pool:
Nor loudly cackles at the Door;
For Cackling shews the Goose is poor.

   But when she must be turn'd to graze,
And round the barren Common strays,   10
Hard Exercise, and harder Fare
Soon make my Dame grow lank and spare:
Her Body light, she tries her Wings,
And scorns the Ground, and upward springs,
While all the Parish, as she flies,
Hear Sounds harmonious from the Skies.

   Such is the Poet, fresh in Pay,
(The third Night's Profits of his Play;)

His Morning-Draughts 'till Noon can swill,
Among his Brethren of the Quill: 20
With good Roast Beef his Belly full,
Grown lazy, foggy, fat, and dull:
Deep sunk in Plenty, and Delight,
What Poet e'er could take his Flight?
Or stuff'd with Phlegm up to the Throat,
What Poet e'er could sing a Note?
Nor *Pegasus* could bear the Load,
Along the high celestial Road;
The Steed, oppress'd, would break his Girth,
To raise the Lumber from the Earth.   30

But, view him in another Scene,
When all his Drink is *Hippocrene*,
His Money spent, his Patrons fail,
His Credit out for Cheese and Ale;
His Two-Year's Coat so smooth and bare,
Through ev'ry Thread it lets in Air;
With hungry Meals his Body pin'd,
His Guts and Belly full of Wind;
And, like a Jockey for a Race,
His Flesh brought down to Flying-Case: 40
Now his exalted Spirit loaths
Incumbrances of Food and Cloaths;
And up he rises like a Vapour,
Supported high on Wings of Paper;
He singing flies, and flying sings,
While from below all *Grub-street* rings.

A N

E L E G Y

On the much lamented Death of Mr. *Demar*,
the Famous rich Man, who died the *6th* of
this Inst. *July*, 1720.

*An Elegy On the much lamented Death of Mr. Demar, the Famous rich Man,
who died the 6th of this Inst. July, 1720.* Fo. Broadside.
An Elegy . . . Mr. Joseph Demar, . . . who died in Dublin . . . Fo. Broadside,
St. James's Post, July 20, 1720. [*Journal.*]
Weekly Journal: or, British Gazeteer, Saty., July 23, 1720. [Ref. *Weekly*
*A Defence of English Commodities. . . . To which is Annexed, An Elegy upon
the much lamented Death of Mr. Demar, . . . Printed at Dublin: And Re-
printed at London, by J. Roberts in Warwick-Lane. MDCCXX.* p. 25.
[Ref. 1720.]
Pinkethman's Jests: Or, Wit Refined. . . . London: . . . 1721, 2nd part,
p. 121.
*Miscellanies, written By Jonathan Swift, D.D. . . . The Fourth Edition.
London: Printed in the Year M.DCC.XXII.* (Curll.) p. 194.
Miscellanies. The Last Volume, 1727, p. 286 (1731, p. 318; 1733, p. 318).
Epitaph only.
Gulliveriana, 1728, p. 82. [Ref. *Gull.*]
*The Drapier's Miscellany. . . . Dublin: Printed by and for James Hoey, . . .
1733.* p. 26 (30). [Ref. 1733.]
Faulkner, 1735, ii. 137 (1737, ii. 109). [Ref. F.]
*A Collection of Poems, &c. Omitted in the Fifth Volume of Miscellanies in
Prose and Verse. London: . . . Charles Davis, . . . MDCCXXXV.* p. 433.
[Ref. 1735.]

There are two broadside editions of this piece, both probably printed in
Dublin. They are modelled on the pattern of the ordinary broadside elegies
of the day. At the foot of the 'Elegy' is a mourning rule, and below appears
'The Epitaph'. A heavy mourning border surrounds the whole. No place,
date, or printer.

Within the same month, July, 1720, the poem was reprinted in the London *Weekly Journal: or, British Gazetteer*; and in the same year in *A Defence
of English Commodities* as 'By the AUTHOR of *the Art of Punning*'. In the
Pope and Swift *Miscellanies* the Epitaph only appears. Faulkner prints the

two; and the supplement to the Fifth Volume of *Miscellanies*, 1735, prints
both. In the Bathurst editions of Swift's *Works* the 'Elegy' and the
'Epitaph' commonly appear in separate volumes.

The following note appears in Scott's edition, 1814, xiv. 120: 'My late
regretted friend, Mr. Cooper Walker, favoured me with the following
notices concerning this elegy: "The subject was John Demar, a great merchant in Dublin, who died 6th July, 1720. Swift, with some of his usual
party, happened to be in Mr. Sheridan's, in Capel Street, when the news
of Demar's death was brought to them; and the elegy was the joint composition of the company".' As John Cooper Walker was not born till 1761
the story can be accepted only with reserve. It is not improbable, however,
that Swift was only in part responsible for the poem. The Pope and Swift
Miscellanies of 1727 print the Epitaph only. Delany, *Observations*, 1754,
p. 53, says: 'The writing an elegy upon Demar, was a subject started, and
partly executed in company, Swift, and Stella, and a few friends
present. Every one threw in their hint, and Stella added her's as follows.' He then quotes ll. 31–4. Hawkesworth repeated this statement in
his *Life* of Swift (1755, 4to, i. 42). It is not unlikely, judging by style, that
the 'Elegy' may have been a piece of patchwork; and the 'Epitaph' is most
suggestive of Swift's manner. Of Stella's part in the poem Scott (i. 271)
observes, 'if she really wrote the last verse in the epitaph on Demar the
usurer, she wrote by far the best lines in the poem'. He was evidently
labouring under a mistake about the lines attributed to her.

The correspondent who forwarded the 'Elegy' to *The Weekly Journal:
or, British Gazetteer* professed to have known 'Deamur' for 'upward of
50 Years'. He gives him a high character for kindliness and generosity. 'I
look upon his Death to be one of the greatest Losses Ireland cou'd labour
under, . . . The Death of Mr. Demur [*sic*] produc'd the following Elegy,
written by the Celebrated Author of the Art of Punning.'

Joseph Damer, or Demar, was born in England in 1630, and served with
the Parliamentary forces as a commander of horse. At the restoration he
deemed it safer to retire to France; and, later, selling some of his English
property, bought land in Ireland. He set up as a usurer in Dublin, with his
offices at the London Tavern. He died, unmarried, at the age of ninety.
See Gilbert's *Hist. of the City of Dublin*, i. 65–7.

The text is here printed from one of the broadside editions. The words
'This Inst.' are generally omitted from the title in later editions.

K Now all Men by these Presents, Death the Tamer
By *Mortgage* hath secur'd the *Corps* of *Demar*;
Nor can *four hundred thousand sterling Pound*
Redeem him from his *Prison* under Ground.
His Heirs might well of all his Wealth possest,
Bestow to bury him one Iron Chest.

2 *Demar*;] Demur; *Weekly Journal*   Damer; *Gull.*

Pluto the god of Wealth, will joy to know
His faithful Steward, in the Shades below.
He walk'd the Streets, and wore a Thread-bare Cloak;
He Din'd and Sup'd at Charge of other Folk,   10
And by his Looks, had he held out his Palms,
He might be thought an Object fit for Alms.
So to the Poor if he refus'd his Pelf,
He us'd 'em full as kindly as himself.
    Where'er he went he never saw his *Betters*,
Lords, *Knights* and *Squires* were all his humble Debtors.
And under *Hand* and *Seal* the *Irish* Nation
Were forc'd to own to him their *Obligation*.
    He that cou'd once have half a Kingdom bought,
In half a Minute is not worth one Groat;   20
His *Coffers* from the *Coffin* could not save,
Nor all his Int'rest keep him from the Grave.
A golden Monument would not be Right,
Because we wish the Earth upon him Light,
    Oh *London Tavern*! Thou hast lost a Friend,
Tho' in thy Walls he ne'er did Farthing spend,
He *touch'd* the *Pence* when others *touch'd the Pot*;
The Hand that sign'd the Mortgage paid the Shot.
    Old as he was, no vulgar known Disease
On him could ever boast a Pow'r to seize;   30
But as his Gold he weigh'd, grim Death in spight,
Cast in his Dart which made three Moydores Light.

14–15] 1720 *and early edns. space between paras.*   20 one Groat;] 1720, 1733
a Groat; 1722, *Gull.*, F.   a Groat. 1735

25. *Oh London Tavern!* Faulkner, 1737 (not 1735), has a footnote: 'A *Tavern* in Dublin, *where Mr. Demar kept his Office*.' Taverns were commonly used for the transaction of affairs, and given as business addresses. Scott (1814) adds: 'Mr. Walker found this note in the diary of a deceased friend: "As I passed through Smith-field (Dublin), I saw the house, No. 34, in which the remarkable John Demar, the usurer, lived and died. He was buried in the S.W. corner of St. Paul's church-yard.—No tombstone for many years." ' See also Horace Walpole's letter to Montagu, 22 Oct. 1766 (Yale edn. of *Correspondence*, *Montagu*, ii. 233).

28. *paid the Shot. I.e.* reckoning. See *O.E.D.*, Shot iv.

32. *Moydores.* Also spelled moidore. A Portuguese gold coin current in England during the first half of the eighteenth century, and accepted at

And as he saw his darling *Money* fail,
Blew his last Breath to sink the lighter Scale.
   He who so long was *Currant* 'twould be strange
If he shou'd now be *cry'd down* since his *Change*
   The *Sexton* shall green Sods on thee bestow.
Alas the *Sexton* is thy *Banker* now!
A dismal *Banker* must that *Banker* be,
Who gives no *Bills*, but of *Mortality*.   40

The EPITAPH.

BEneath this verdant *Hillock* lies
   Demar the *Wealthy*, and the *Wise*.
His *Heirs* for *Winding-Sheet* bestow'd
His *Money-Bags* together sow'd.
And that he might securely Rest,
Have put his *Carcass* in a *Chest*.
The very *Chest*, in which they say
His *other Self*, his *Money* lay.
And if his *Heirs* continue kind,
To that dear *Self* he left behind;   50
I dare believe that Four in Five
Will think his *better Half* alive.

a value between 27*s.* and 28*s.* Later   sum of 27*s.*
the word survived as a name for the

43, 44] *Om.* 1727, F., 1735   45 And that he might securely Rest,] 1720
And, that . . . 1722, 1733   And that he might, . . . *Gull.*   His *Heirs,* that he
might safely rest, 1727, 1731, F., 1735   47 The] 1720, 1722, 1727, 1733, F.
That Gull.   52 *Half*] Self F., 1735

AN
Excellent new SONG on a seditious Pamphlet.

To the Tune of Packington's Pound.

Written in the Year 1720.

Faulkner, 1735, ii. 358 (1737, ii. 126).
Miscellanies, ... *Volume the Fifth,* 1735, p. 67 (1736, v. 67; 1745, v. 36; 1751; x. 33).
Works of Jonathan Swift, D.D., ed. Hawkesworth, 1755, 4to, iv (1) 29.

Swift's *Proposal for the Universal Use of Irish Manufacture* (*Prose Works,* ed. Temple Scott, vii. 11; ed. Davis, ix. 13–22) appeared in April, or May, of 1720. The result was an outcry upon what was characterized as a seditious pamphlet. Edward Waters, the printer, was prosecuted. The jury returned a verdict of not guilty. Lord Chief Justice Whitshed refused to accept this verdict, sent the jury back nine times, and kept them eleven hours. In August, 1721, the Duke of Grafton arrived in Dublin as Lord Lieutenant; and the matter ended in the grant of a *noli prosequi*. For Swift's account of this affair see his letter to Sir Thomas Hanmer, 1 Oct., 1720 (*Corresp.* iii. 64), his letter to Pope, 10 Jany., 1722 (*Corresp.* iii. 115), and his *Proposal that all the Ladies and Women of Ireland should appear constantly in Irish Manufactures* (*Prose Works,* vii. 193).

William Whitshed had been appointed Chief Justice of the King's Bench in Ireland on the accession of George I. Despite his behaviour at the trial of Waters he appears to have been a man of probity, who was held in general respect. He also acted as judge at Harding's trial; and Swift never forgave him. See 'Whitshed's Motto on his Coach', 'Verses on the Upright Judge' (pp. 347–50), the lines in 'Verses on the Death of Doctor Swift' (pp. 569–70), and Ball, *Judges in Ireland,* ii. 189 *et passim*.
The text is printed from Faulkner's edition.

BROCADO's, and Damasks, and Tabbies, and Gawses,
  Are by *Robert Ballentine* lately brought over;
With Forty Things more: Now hear what the Law says,
  Whoe'er will not were them, is not the King's Lover.

4 were] wear *remainder*

Tho' a Printer and Dean
Seditiously mean
Our true *Irish* Hearts from old *England* to wean;
We'll buy *English* Silks for our Wives and our Daughters,
In Spight of his Deanship and Journeyman *Waters*.

II.

In *England* the Dead in Woollen are clad, 10
  The Dean and his Printer then let us cry Fye on;
To be cloath'd like a Carcass would make a Teague
    mad,
  Since a living Dog better is than a dead Lyon,
      Our Wives they grow sullen
      At wearing of Woollen,
  And all we poor Shopkeepers must our Horns
    pull in.
Then we'll buy *English* Silks, *&c.*

III.

Whoever our Trading with *England* would hinder,
  To *inflame* both the Nations do plainly conspire;
Because *Irish* Linen will soon turn to Tinder; 20
  And Wool it is greasy, and quickly takes Fire.
      Therefore I assure ye,
      Our noble Grand Jury,
  When they saw the Dean's Book they were in a great
    Fury:
They would buy *English* Silks for their Wives, *&c.*

10. *In England the Dead in Woollen are clad.* In 1667, the eighteenth year of Charles II, according to the reckoning used, an Act was passed, to encourage the wool trade, decreeing that dead bodies should be buried in woollen, and in 1678 an amending Act ordering that an affidavit of burial in wool should be entered in the register. This enactment remained on the statute book till 1815.

24. *Dean's Book.* Swift's pamphlet, *A Proposal for the Universal Use of Irish Manufacture.*

IV.

This wicked Rogue *Waters*, who always is sinning,
   And before *Corum Nobus* so oft has been call'd,
Henceforward shall print neither Pamphlets nor Linnen,
   And, if Swearing can do't, shall be swingingly mawl'd:
     And as for the Dean,   30
     You know whom I mean,
If the Printer will peach him, he'll scarce come off clean.
Then we'll buy *English* Silks for our Wives and our
    Daughters,
In Spight of his Deanship and Journeyman *Waters*.

The Run upon the Bankers.

Written A:D: 1720.

Transcript by Stella; Manuscript Volume in the possession of the Duke
of Bedford, Woburn Abbey.
*The Run upon the Bankers, and, The South-Sea Detected. . . . Cork: Printed
by Samuel Terry, . . . 1721. Fo. Broadside.*
Faulkner, 1735, ii. 208 (1737, ii. 122). [Ref. F.]
*A Collection of Poems, &c. Omitted in the Fifth Volume of Miscellanies in
Prose and Verse. London: . . . Charles Davis, . . . MDCCXXXV.* p. 436.
[Ref. 1735.]
Miscellanies, 1736, v. 208 (1745, v. 27).

No copy of a Dublin broadside edition of this piece has been traced,
although it is probable that the Cork broadside was printed from a Dublin
issue. Faulkner introduces the poem with the enigmatic note: '*This Poem
was printed some Years ago, and it should seem by the late Failure of two
Bankers to be somewhat prophetick, it was therefore thought fit to be reprinted.*'
Stella gives the date 1720, and this is probably correct. Dr. Elrington Ball
(*Swift's Verse,* p. 157) calls attention to a remark by Swift in a letter to
Vanessa under date 18 October, 1720: 'Conversation is full of nothing
but South Sea, and the ruin of the kingdom, and scarcity of money.'
(*Corresp.* iii. 68.) The poem may well be connected with events of that

27 *Corum Nobus*] 1735, 1737   *Coram nobis* 1736   *Corum nobus* 1745, 1751, 1755

27. *Corum Nobus.* The spelling is intended to represent vulgar and colloquial
pronunciation.

time. See, further, notes on the next poem, the imitation of Horace
addressed to Archbishop King.
     The text is printed from Stella's transcript. The only verbal variant of
the Cork broadside is the omission of 'a' in l. 37.

The bold Encroachers on the Deep,
Gain by Degrees huge Tracts of Land,
'Till Neptune with a Gen'ral Sweep
Turns all again to barren Strand.

The Multitude's Capricious Pranks
Are said to represent the Seas,
Breaking the Bankers and the Banks,
Resume their own when e'er they please.

Money, the Life-blood of the Nation,
Corrupts and stagnates in the Veins,   10
Unless a proper Circulation
Its Motion and its Heat maintains.

Because 'tis Lordly not to pay,
Quakers and Aldermen, in State,
Like Peers, have Levees ev'ry Day
Of Duns, attending at their Gate.

We want our Money on the Nail;
The Banker's ruin'd if he pays;
They seem to act an Ancient Tale,
The Birds are met to strip the Jays.   20

Riches, the Wisest Monarch sings,
Make Pinions for themselves to fly,
They fly like Bats, on Parchment Wings,
And Geese their silver Plumes supply.

In the early collected editions the stanzas are numbered in Roman figures; and
many words are in italics   1 on] F., 1745   of 1735, 1736   3 a] one F.,
1735, 1736, 1745   17 want] F., 1745   count 1735, 1736

14. *Quakers* . . . Quakers refused to   21. *Riches, the Wisest Monarch*
pay tithes for the support of what they   *sings* . . . Solomon, Proverbs xxiii. 5:
regarded as a hireling ministry. In   'For riches certainly make themselves
consequence consistent members of the   wings; they fly away as an eagle
sect were distrained for the amount due.   toward heaven.'

No Money left for squandring Heirs!
Bills turn the Lenders into Debters,
The Wish of Nero now is Theirs,
That, they had never known their Letters.

Conceive the Works of Midnight Hags,
Tormenting Fools behind their Backs;   30
Thus Bankers o'er their Bills and Bags
Sit squeezing Images of Wax.

Conceive the whole Enchantment broke,
The Witches left in open Air,
With Pow'r no more than other Folk,
Expos'd with all their Magick Ware.

So Pow'rful are a Banker's Bills
When Creditors demand their Due;
They break up Counters, Doors, and Tills,
And leave his emty Chests in View.   40

Thus when an Earthquake lets in Light
Upon the god of Gold and Hell,
Unable to endure the Sight,
He hides within his darkest Cell.

As when a Conj'rer takes a Lease
From Satan for a Term of Years,
The Tenant's in a Dismal Case
When e'er the bloody Bond appears.

38 When] Where F., 1735, 1736, 1745   39 Counters,] 1745   Counter, F.,
1735, 1736   40 his emty] the empty F., 1735, 1736, 1745   43 Sight,]
F., 1745   Light, 1735, 1736

27. *The Wish of Nero.* Suetonius, *Lib.* vi. 10: 'Et quum de supplicio cujusdam capite damnati, ut ex more subscriberet, admoneretur: *Quam vellem*, inquit, *nescire litteras.*'

32. *Sit squeezing Images of Wax.* Alluding to the common use of wax images in witchcraft. These, if melted before the fire, or otherwise damaged, were supposed to transfer the injury to absent enemies.

48. *bloody Bond.* 'These contracts were always supposed to be signed with blood.'—*Hawkesworth.*

A baited Banker thus desponds,
From his own Hand foresees his Fall,   50
They have his Soul who have his Bonds,
'Tis like the Writing on the Wall.

How will the Caitiff Wretch be scar'd
When first he finds himself awake
At the last Trumpet, unprepar'd,
And all his Grand Account to make?

For in that Universall Call
Few Bankers will to Heav'n be Mounters:
They'll cry, Ye Shops, upon us fall
Conceal, and cover us, Ye Counters.   60

When Other Hands the Scales shall hold,
And They in Men and Angels Sight
Produc'd with all their Bills and Gold,
Weigh'd in the Ballance, and found Light.

Part of the 9th ODE *of the 4th* BOOK *of* HORACE, *address'd to Doctor* WILLIAM KING, *late Lord Arch-Bishop of* Dublin.

Paulùm sepultae, &c.

Miscellaneous Poems, By Several Hands. Published by D. Lewis. . . .
  London: Printed by J. Watts. M DCC XXX. p. 49. [Ref. 1730.]
Faulkner, 1746, viii. 179.
Miscellanies, 1746, xi. 226 (1751, xiv. 206).
The Story of the Injured Lady. . . . London, Printed for M. Cooper, . . .
  MDCCXLVI. p. 63. *Brett's Miscellany,* 1752, ii. 206.
Works of Jonathan Swift, D.D., ed. Hawkesworth, 1755, 4to, iv (1), 275.
Works, ed. Sheridan, 1784, vii. 151.

52. Daniel v. 25 ff.

The date, 1718, assigned to the poem by Sheridan, in his edition of the *Works*, 1784, although incorrect, has been accepted by later editors.

Since the days when Swift had been sent by Archbishop King as his agent in England, to solicit the remission of the first-fruits, a coolness had sprung up between the two upon Swift's joining the Tory party. The first sign of re-awakened cordiality, apart possibly from the present poem, was Swift's letter to King of the 28th of September, 1721 (*Corresp.* iii. 100). This was due to King's sympathy with Swift's Irish patriotism. After six years of silence, following upon his retirement to Ireland in 1714, Swift appeared again as a political pamphleteer with his *Proposal for the Universal Use of Irish Manufacture*, 1720. This was an attack upon the monopolizing acts passed in the reign of William III, prohibiting the export of woollen goods from Ireland, except into England and Wales. The effect of these statutes upon Irish manufactures was disastrous (see *Prose Works*, vii. 13–30; Scott, vii. 15–17). In 1720 a project was put forward by the Earl of Abercorn, Viscount Boyne, Sir Ralph Gore, and others, for the establishment of a National Bank in Ireland, with a capital of £500,000 for the purpose of making advances to merchants at low rates of interest. The proposals were not without merit, but Swift associated the scheme with moneyed Whig interests and stock-jobbers; and there was a very general opposition to the whole plan. The scheme was approved by the King in July, 1721; but eventually rejected by both Houses of the Irish Parliament in December of the same year. See *Journals of the House of Commons of Ireland*, iii, Part I, pp. 253, 256–7, 283, 289; *Journals of the House of Lords of Ireland*, ii. 711–13, 716, 720. For tracts in opposition to the bank project attributed to Swift or his friends see *Prose Works*, ed. Davis, ix. 281–311.

Writing to Archbishop King on the 28th of September, 1721, Swift says: 'I hear you are likely to be the sole opposer of the bank, . . . Bankrupts are always for setting up banks; how then can you think a bank will fail of a majority in both Houses?' (*Corresp.* iii. 101). He was, as the event proved, mistaken.

Other versions of the same ode, (1) addressed to Lord Carteret, (2) addressed to Humphry French, Lord Mayor of Dublin, have been attributed to Swift—see pp. 1132–3.

The first printing of these lines appears to have been in the second volume of Lewis's *Miscellaneous Poems*, 1730. There is no attribution of authorship. Faulkner included the poem in Swift's *Works* in 1746. The text is here reprinted from Faulkner.

VIRTUE conceal'd within our Breast
　　Is Inactivity at best:
But, never shall the Muse endure
To let your Virtues lye obscure,

Or suffer Envy to conceal
Your Labours for the Publick Weal.
Within your Breast all Wisdom lyes,
Either to govern or advise;
Your steady Soul preserves her Frame
In good and evil Times the same.   10
Pale Avarice and lurking Fraud
Stand in your sacred Presence aw'd;
Your Hand alone from Gold abstains,
Which drags the slavish World in Chains.

Him for an happy Man I own,
Whose Fortune is not overgrown;
And, happy he, who wisely knows
To use the Gifts, that Heav'n bestows;
Or, if it please the Powers Divine,
Can suffer Want, and not repine.   20
The Man, who Infamy to shun,
Into the Arms of Death would run,
That Man is ready to defend
With Life his Country, or his Friend.

The Description of an *Irish-Feast*, translated almost literally out of the Original *Irish*.

Translated in the Year 1720.

Faulkner, 1735, ii. 295 (1737, ii. 300).
Miscellanies, ... Volume the Fifth, 1735, p. 14 (1736, v. 14; 1745, v. 31;
  1751, x. 28).
Works of Jonathan Swift, D.D., ed. Hawkesworth, 1755, 4to, iv (1), 25.

This ballad is commonly held to celebrate a great feast, which long lived
in memory, given by the O'Rourke, who rebelled against the English in

11 Avarice] 1730   Avarice, *remainder*   15 an] 1730   a *remainder*

1580. The Irish poem was, however, composed in the first or second decade of the eighteenth century, and was probably a skit on some O'Rourkes, *circa* 1710.

The original *Pléaraca na Ruarcach* is attributed to Hugh MacGauran (*flor. circa* 1712). It was set to music by the Irish bard, Carolan (J. C. Walker's *Historical Memoirs of the Irish Bards*, 1786). According to Wilson's *Swiftiana*, ii. 19–23, Swift, while staying at a country house near Cavan, was furnished with a literal translation by MacGauran himself. The evidence for this story is slight, but it need not be dismissed as impossible.

For bibliographical and other details relating to *Pléaraca na Ruarcach* see 'A Rare Book of Irish and Scottish Gaelic Verse', by Séamus Ó Casaide, in *Publications of the Bibliographical Society of Ireland*, iii. No. 6, 1928.

The Irish poem runs to 96 lines. Swift translated ll. 1–40 and 45–72 of the full Irish text. The text, not complete, with Swift's translation, appeared in the second edition, 1781, and also in the re-issue, 1782, of Charles Vallancey's *Grammar of the Iberno-Celtic, or Irish Language*. Charles Henry Wilson published the Irish text with an English verse translation of his own in his rare *Poems Translated from the Irish Language into the English*, 1782. Scott, in his edition of Swift's *Works*, 1814, xiv. 135–41, gives the original Irish, Wilson's translation of ll. 41–4, and a spirited translation by himself of ll. 73–96.

The text of Swift's translation is printed from Faulkner's edition of 1735.

O ROURK's noble Fare
    Will ne'er be forgot,
By those who were there,
    Or those who were not.
His Revels to keep,
    We sup and we dine,
On seven Score Sheep,
    Fat Bullocks and Swine.
Usquebagh to our Feast
    In Pails was brought up,   10
An Hundred at least,
    And a Madder our Cup.

9 *Usquebagh*] 1735   *Usquebaugh* 1736, 1737, 1745, *and remainder*

9. *Usquebagh*. Usually spelled *usque-*   water of life. *Uisge*, water, whisky.
baugh. From Irish *uisge-beatha*,   12. *Madder*. '*Wooden Vessel*.'—

O there is the Sport,
    We rise with the Light,
In disorderly Sort,
    From snoring all Night.
O how was I trick't,
    My Pipe it was broke,
My Pocket was pick't,
    I lost my new Cloak.   20
I'm rifled, quoth *Nell*,
    Of Mantle and Kercher,
Why then fare them well,
    The De'el take the Searcher.
Come, Harper, strike up,
    But first by your Favour,
Boy, give us a Cup;
    Ay, this has some Savour:
O *Rourk*'s jolly Boys
    Ne'er dream't of the Matter,   30
Till rowz'd by the Noise,
    And musical Clatter,
They bounce from their Nest,
    No longer will tarry,
They rise ready drest,
    Without one *Ave Mary*.
They dance in a Round,
    Cutting Capers and Ramping,
A Mercy the Ground
    Did not burst with their stamping.   40
The Floor is all wet
    With Leaps and with Jumps,
While the Water and Sweat,
    Splish, splash in their Pumps.

---

17 trick't,] 1737 trick't? 1735 trick't! 1736, 1745, 1751, 1755   23 well,]
well. Faulkner 1735

Faulkner. Also 'meadar', 'mether'.   22. *Kercher*. A form of kerchief. A
From the Irish *meadar*, a square,   cloth used by women to cover the
wooden drinking vessel.   head.

Bless you late and early,
   Laughlin O Enagin,
By my Hand, you dance rarely,
   Margery Grinagin.
Bring Straw for our Bed,
   Shake it down to the Feet,   50
Then over us spread,
   The winnowing Sheet.
To show, I don't flinch,
   Fill the Bowl up again,
Then give us a Pinch
   Of your Sneezing; *a Yean.*
Good Lord, what a Sight,
   After all their good Cheer,
For People to fight
   In the Midst of their Beer: 60
They rise from their Feast,
   And hot are their Brains,
A Cubit at least
   The Length of their Skeans.
What Stabs and what Cuts,
   What clatt'ring of Sticks,
What Strokes on Guts,
   What Bastings and Kicks!
With Cudgels of Oak,
   Well harden'd in Flame,   70
An hundred Heads broke,
   An hundred struck lame.
You Churle, I'll maintain
   My Father built *Lusk,*

60 Beer:] 1737   Beer? 1735, 1736, 1745, *and remainder*   67 Guts,] the
Guts, 1735, 1736, 1737, 1745, *and remainder*

48. Here Swift left four lines of the original untranslated. Wilson's version runs:
   'Here's to you, dear mother.
    I thank you, dear Pat;
   Pitch this down your throat.
    I'm the better of that.'
56. *a Yean.* '*Another* Irish *Name for*

a Woman.'—Faulkner.
  64. *Skeans.* '*Daggers, or short Swords.*'—Faulkner.
  74. *Lusk.* A village thirteen miles north by east of Dublin, once a place of some ecclesiastical importance. The original says Boyle, Sligo, and Galway.

The Castle of *Slain,*
   And *Carrickdrumrusk:*
The Earl of *Kildare,*
   And *Moynalta,* his Brother,
As great as they are,
   I was nurs'd by their Mother.   80
Ask that of old *Madam,*
   She'll tell you who's who,
As far up as *Adam,*
   She knows it is true,
Come down with that Beam,
   If Cudgels are scarce,
A Blow on the Weam,
   Or a Kick on the A——se.

75 *Slain,*] 1735, 1736, 1745, 1751, 1755   *Slane,* 1737

75. *The Castle of Slain.* Slane Castle on the River Boyne, co. Meath.

76. *Carrickdrumrusk.* Cara Droma Rúisg, now Carrick-on-Shannon.

77. *The Earl of Kildare.* The reference is possibly to Gerald Fitzgerald, the eleventh Earl of Kildare, who died in 1585.

80. *Mother.* 'It is the custom in *Ireland* to call nurses foster-mothers; their husbands foster-fathers; and their children foster-brothers or foster-sisters; and thus the poorest claim kindred to the richest.' — Hawkesworth.

The last twenty-four lines of the original poem were not translated by Swift. In *Swiftiana,* ii. 23, Charles Wilson's translation of these stanzas is given. Scott, xiv. 140 n., gives the following more spirited version:

Who kick'd up this dust?
   Cried one of the clergy;
Bolting up like a post,
   Come be quiet, I charge ye.

He brought no holy water,
   The riot to charm;
But a switch, for the matter
   Scarce so thick as his arm.

While he deem'd them all quell'd,
   This churchman so able,
By a back-stroke was fell'd,
   Like a log on the table.

Next up got a friar
   To appease these rude members;
But was pitched cross the fire
   With his breech on the embers.

While loudly he hollowed,
   'Would you match you with me,
Who my studies have followed
   At Rome beyond sea,

While you thrum'd old ballads,
   Sitting squat like a boor;
With potatoes for sallads,
   In the bog of Shiemoor?

The BUBBLE

Swift's autograph. Lord Rothschild's Library, No. 2265.

Transcript by Stella; Manuscript Volume in the possession of the Duke of Bedford, Woburn Abbey. [Ref. Stella.]

The Bubble: A Poem. London, Printed for Benj. Tooke, . . . and Sold by J. Roberts, . . . M.DCC.XXI. [Ref. R.]

The Bubble: A Poem. . . . London: Printed for Ben. Tooke, . . . And Re-printed in Dublin, 1721. [Ref. D.]

The Bubble: . . . Printed for Benj. Tooke: And are to be Sold at John Paton's Shop in the Parliament-Closs. 1721. [Ref. P.]

A Miscellaneous Collection of Poems, Songs and Epigrams. By several Hands. Published by T. M. Gent. . . . Dublin: Printed by A. Rhames, 1721. ii. 147. [Ref. T.M.] [*the Year 1720.*

The Bubblers Medley, or a Sketch of the Times Being Europes Memorial for Miscellaneous Poems, Original and Translated, By Several Hands. . . . Published by Mr. Concanen. . . . London: Printed for J. Peele, . . . MDCCXXIV. p. 148. [Ref. C.]

A New Collection of Poems on Several Occasions. By Mr. Prior, and Others. . . . London: Printed for Tho. Osborne, . . . MDCCXXV. p. 94.

Miscellanies. The Last Volume, 1727. p. 185 (1731, p. 255; 1733, p. 255; Faulkner, 1735, ii. 147 (1737, ii. 136). [Ref. F.] [1742, iv. 153).

A Supplement to Dr. Swift's Works, 1779. (Notes.)

Works, ed. Sheridan, 1784, vii. 192.

The textual history of this poem is complicated. A copy in Swift's hand has been preserved among the Ford papers, now Lord Rothschild. This holograph is closely written in double column. The poem carries no title. It was sent to Swift's friend, Ford, in London, addressed:

> 'To Charles Ford Esqr,
> at His Lodgings at the
> blue Perewig in Pell-Mell
> London.'

Swift's covering letter, written at the end of the manuscript, is dated 'Dec^br. 15th. 1720'. The London postmark shows that Ford did not receive it before the 26th of December. It was, however, advertised in *The Daily Courant* and *The Post-Boy* as published on 3 Jany., 1720–1. Three weeks later it was advertised in *The Evening Post,* Jany. 24–6, with the quotation of two stanzas, the 48th and the last.

Swift directed Ford to send the copy to the printer without revealing the authorship of the poem. As the original survives, with other Ford letters and manuscripts, it is clear that Ford sent the printer a transcript, and that the poem was published by Roberts in seven or eight days. The title, 'The Bubble', was, presumably, chosen by Ford. It appeared anonymously; but the two stanzas printed later in *The Evening Post* were said to be by Swift.

The text published by Roberts follows the manuscript closely. Two marked differences are 'Garr'way's' for 'GARR'WAY' (l. 153), and 'Bone' instead of 'Bones' (l. 204). In this form the poem extends to fifty-five stanzas.

In the same year ten of the stanzas appeared in a piece called *The Bubblers Medley, or a Sketch of the Times Being Europes Memorial for the Year 1720*. They are, in order, reckoning by the 55-stanza version of the poem, nos. 35, 36, 37, 38, 39, 17, 42, 26, 28, and 55. See *Catalogue of Prints and Drawings in the British Museum. Division I. Political and Personal Satires*, ii. 412 (No. 1610). Again, in 1721, in both instances with the addition of two stanzas, the 9th and 10th, it was printed in a Dublin edition, and in *A Miscellaneous Collection of Poems, Songs and Epigrams*, edited by 'T. M. Gent.', also published in Dublin. In the single publication a quotation from Virgil appears on the title; in the collection it is prefixed to the poem.

The next appearance of the poem in print, as far as we now know, is in Concanen's collection of *Miscellaneous Poems*, 1724, where it is attributed to Swift. The Latin quotation heads the poem, and there are 57 stanzas. The poem was included in a London miscellany of 1725, *A New Collection of Poems*, published by Osborne. The Latin quotation is prefixed, and there are 57 stanzas. The text agrees with the Dublin and Concanen versions, and it is needless to show its readings in the apparatus.

In the Dublin collection edited by 'T. M. Gent.' there are several marked variants from Swift's manuscript, and from the printed versions. In l. 116 (108 of the text here printed), 'T.M.' reads 'sink' for 'sunk'; l. 143 (135), 'the' for 'this'; l. 191 (183), 'by' for 'in'; l. 214 (206), 'Those' for 'These'; l. 222 (214), 'these' for 'those'.

Stella heads her transcript of the poem in the Woburn volume:

'The Bubble.
Printed in Ireland A:D: 1720.'

She omits the Latin quotation. She was copying, presumably, as her heading implies, from the separate Dublin edition, or she may have been using the copy of a manuscript supplied to the printer of that edition, for she does not follow the 'T.M.' readings. Two important variants appear in her transcript for the first time—l. 33, 'Five hundred' for 'Two hundred'; and l. 180, 'Pallace-Roofs' for 'Castle-Roofs'. The latter reading was adopted in the *Miscellanies* of 1727; and both by Faulkner in 1735.

In *Miscellanies. The Last Volume*, 1727, the poem was completely revised. The title was changed to 'The *South-Sea*. 1721'; the Latin quotation was removed to the end; and thirteen of the fifty-seven stanzas (13, 17, 27, 28, 29, 30, 39, 42, 43, 50, 51, 52, 53) were omitted. There are only two distinctive new readings: ll. 14 and 16 are transposed; and 'at last', in l. 139, becomes 'and scarce'.

The *Miscellanies* were edited by Pope; but during the summer of 1727 Swift was staying with Pope at Twickenham, and it is unlikely that such extensive alterations were made without Swift's cognizance. It is also noteworthy that Swift made no annotations against 'The *South-Sea*' in his own copy of the *Miscellanies*. Nevertheless he may have been deterred by the amount of correction necessary, for that version can hardly be considered his last thought for the poem. His interest in Faulkner's edition of the *Works*, 1735, is manifest, and Faulkner restored eleven out of the thirteen rejected stanzas, the exceptions being 17 and 29. The title becomes 'Upon the South-Sea Project.' Swift made no corrections in his copy of Faulkner.

The additional stanzas included by Faulkner were not noted by the editor of *Miscellanies, In Prose and Verse. Volume the Fifth*, 1735; and Bathurst and the London trade editions continued to print 44 stanzas only. The omission of the thirteen stanzas was pointed out by Nichols, *Supplement*, 1779; they were included by Sheridan in his edition of the *Works*, 1784, and by all subsequent editors.

The poem was first printed from Swift's manuscript by Professor D. Nichol Smith, *Letters of Jonathan Swift to Charles Ford*, 1935, pp. 182–92.

Dr. Elrington Ball, *Swift's Verse*, p. 160, presumes that Swift took a hint for his concluding stanzas from Prior's letter to him of 28 Feby., 1720–1: 'I am tired with politics, and lost in the South Sea. The roaring of the waves, and the madness of the people, were justly put together' (*Corresp.* iii. 74). But the poem had then been in print several weeks. It is more probable that Prior's remark was prompted by the poem.

For an account of the South Sea project and its collapse see Lecky, *History of England in the Eighteenth Century*, i. 321–3, and *The South Sea Bubble*, by Viscount Erleigh, 1933.

The text is printed from Swift's manuscript. No note is taken of variations in punctuation, &c., unless of significance.

[p. 1]   Ye wise Philosophers explain
What Magick makes our Money rise
When dropt into the Southern Main,
Or do these Juglers cheat our Eyes?

1–220] *Save for two words, the only variations from Swift's manuscript in Roberts's edition are in spelling, punctuation, or typographical usage. These have not been noted in the tables of variants. In the printed editions ll. 1 & 3, 2 & 4 are ranged with each other.*   D., T.M., C. *prefix as a motto:*

    Apparent rari nantes in gurgite vasto:
    Arma virum, tabulæque & Troia gaza per undas. Virg.

1727, F., 1742, *and others place these lines at the end of the poem.*

Put in Your Money fairly told;
Presto be gone—Tis here ag'en,
Ladyes, and Gentlemen, behold,
Here's ev'ry Piece as big as ten.

Thus in a Basin drop a Shilling,
Then fill the Vessel to the Brim,   10
You shall observe as you are filling
The pond'rous Metal seems to swim;

It rises both in Bulk and Height,
Behold it mounting to the Top,
The liquid Medium cheats your Sight,
Behold it swelling like a Sop.

In Stock three hundred thousand Pounds;
I have in view a Lord's Estate,
My Mannors all contig'ous round,
A Coach and Six, and serv'd in Plate: 20

Thus the deluded Bankrupt raves,
Puts all upon a desp'rate Bett,
Then plunges in the *Southern* Waves,
Dipt over head and Ears—in Debt.

So, by a Calenture misled,
The Mariner with Rapture sees
On the smooth Ocean's azure Bed
Enamell'd Fields, and verdant Trees;

With eager Hast he longs to rove
In that fantastick Scene, and thinks   30

14 mounting to the Top,] R., D., T.M., Stella, C.   swelling like a Sop!
1727, F.   16 swelling like a Sop.] R., D., T.M., Stella, C.   mounted to
the Top! 1727, F.   17 Pounds;] Pound; 1727, 1742, &c.

25. *Calenture.* An old term of | board ships. Sailors afflicted with it
Spanish origin (*calentura*) denoting a | were subject to delirium during which
form of tropical fever occurring on | they flung themselves into the sea.

It must be some enchanted Grove,
And in he leaps, and down he sinks.

Rais'd up on Hope's aspiring Plumes,
The young Advent'rer o'er the Deep
An Eagle's Flight and State assumes,
And scorns the middle Way to keep:

On *Paper* Wings he takes his Flight,
With *Wax* the *Father* bound them fast,
The *Wax* is melted by the Height,
And down the towring Boy is cast: 40

A Moralist might here explain
The Rashness of the *Cretan* Youth,
Describe his Fall into the Main,
And from a Fable form a Truth:

[col. 2]   His *Wings* are his *Paternall Rent*,
He melts his *Wax* at ev'ry Flame,
His Credit sunk, his Money spent,
In Southern *Seas he leaves his Name.*

Inform us, You that best can tell,
Why in yon dang'rous Gulph profound   50
Where hundreds and where thousands fell,
Fools chiefly float, the *Wise* are drown'd.

32] *After l. 32* D., T.M., Stella, C., 1727, F., 1742, *&c. insert two additional stanzas:*

Two hundred Chariots just bespoke
Are sunk in these devouring Waves,
  The Horses drown'd, the Harness broke,
And here the Owners find their Graves.

Like *Pharaoh,* by *Directors* led,
They with their *Spoils* went safe before,
  His Chariots tumbling out the Dead
Lay shatter'd on the *Red-Sea* Shore.

In the first line of these two stanzas Stella, F., *read* 'Five Hundred'.   38
Father] *Feather* T.M.   41–4] *Om.* 1727, 1742, *&c.; restored* F.   52
drown'd.] R., D., T.M., Stella, C.   drown'd? 1727, F., 1742, *&c.*

42. *Cretan Youth.* Icarus, son of Dædalus, flew with his father from Crete to escape the wrath of Minos. The heat of the sun melted the wax holding his wings, and he fell into the sea. Ovid, *Met.* viii. 183 ff.

So have I seen from *Severn*'s Brink
A Flock of *Geese* jump down together,
Swim where the Bir[d] of Jove would sink,
And swimming ne[ver] wet a Feather.

But I affirm, 'tis false in Fact,
Directors better know their Tools,
We see the Nation['s] Credit crackt,
Each Knave hath [ma]de a thousand Fools. 60

One Fool may f[r]om another win,
And then get off with Money stor'd,
But if a *Sharper* once comes in,
He throws at all, and sweeps the Board.

As Fishes on each other prey
The great ones swall'wing up the small
So fares it in the *Southern* Sea
But Whale *Directors* eat up all.

When *Stock* is high they come between,
Making by second hand their Offers, 70
Then cunningly retire unseen,
With each a Million in his Coffers.

So when upon a Moon-shine Night
An Ass was drinking at a Stream,
A Cloud arose and stopt the Light,
By intercepting e[v]'ry Beam;

The Day of Judgment will be soon,
Cryes out a Sage among the Croud,
An Ass hath swallow'd up the Moon,
The Moon lay safe behind the Cloud. 80

Each poor *Subscriber* to the Sea
Sinks down at once, and there he lyes,
Directors fall as well as they,
Their Fall is but a Trick to rise:

57–60] *Om.* 1727, F., 1742, *&c.*   63 comes] gets P.

So Fishes rising from the Main
Can soar with moistned Wings on high,
The Moysture dry'd they sink again,
And dip their Fins again to fly.

[p. 2]   Undone at Play, the Femal Troops
Come here their Losses to retrieve,   90
Ride o'er the Waves in spacious Hoops,
Like *Lapland* Witches in a Sieve:

Thus *Venus* to the Sea descends
As Poets fein; but where's the Moral?
It shews the Queen of Love intends
To search the Deep for Pearl and Coral.

The Sea is richer than the Land,
I heard it from my Grannam's Mouth,
Which now I clearly understand,
For by the Sea she meant the *South*.   100

Thus by *Directors* we are told,
Pray Gentlemen, believe your Eyes,
Our Ocean's cover[d o]'er with Gold,
Look round about [h]ow thick it lyes:

We, Gentlemen, a[re] Your Assisters,
We'll come and hol[d] you by the Chin,
Alas! all is not Go[l]d that glisters;
Ten thousand sunk by leaping in.

97–104] *Om.* 1727, 1742, *&c.*; *restored* F.   105–8] *Om.* 1727, F., 1742, *&c.*
108 sunk] sink T.M.

85. *So Fishes* . . . The exact nature of the flight of some species of fishes is hardly as described by Swift. The genus Exocœtus (*Flying Herrings*), including forty known species, and the genus Dactylopterus (*Flying Gurnards*), of which three species are known, are both capable of rapid flight above water for considerable distances. The fins are distended like a parachute, and not moved like the wings of birds or bats.

92. *Lapland Witches.* Lapland witches, or, more properly, wizards, were famous from early times. References to Lapland witches became frequent in English literature after the publication of the *Historia de Gentibus Septentrionalibus* of Olaus Magnus in 1555.

Oh! would these Patriots be so kind
Here in the Deep to *wash their Hands*,   110
Then like *Pactolus* we should find
The Sea indeed had *golden Sands.*

A Shilling in the *Bath* You fling,
The Silver takes a nobler Hue,
By Magick Virtue in the Spring,
And seems a Guinnea to your View:

But as a Guinnea will not pass
At Market for a Farthing more
Shewn through a multiplying Glass
Than what it allways did before;   120

So cast it in the *Southern* Seas,
And view it through a *Jobber*'s Bill,
Put on what Spectacles You please,
Your Guinnea's but a Guinnea still.

One Night a Fool into a Brook
Thus from a Hillock looking down,
The *Golden* Stars for Guinneas took,
And *Silver Cynthia* for a Crown;

The Point he could no longer doubt,
He ran, he leapt into the Flood,   130
There sprawl'd a while, at last got out,
All cover'd o'er with Slime and Mud.

[col. 2]   Upon the Water cast thy Bread
And after many Days thou'lt find it,
But Gold upon this Ocean spred
Shall sink, and leave no mark behind it.

109–12] *Om.* 1727, 1742, *&c.*; *restored* F.   109 these] R., D., T.M., Stella,
C.   those F.   131 at last] R., D., T.M., Stella, C.   and scarce 1727, F.,
1742, *&c.*   133, 134] *In italics* F.   135 this] the T.M.   136]
'behind' *written above* 'find' *struck out*

111. *Pactolus.* See p. 157 n.   133. *Upon the Water* ... Ecclesiastes xi. 1.

There is a Gulph where thousands fell,
Here all the bold Advent'rers came,
A narrow Sound, though deep as Hell,
CHANGE-ALLY is the dreadfull Name;   140

Nine times a day it ebbs and flows,
Yet He that on the Surface lyes
Without a Pilot seldom knows
The Time it falls, or when 'twill rise.

Subscribers here by thousands float,
And justle one another down,
Each padling in his leaky Boat,
And here they fish for Gold and drown:

*Psalm
107.

Now bury'd in the Depth below,
Now mounted up to Heav'n again,   150
They reel and stagger too and fro,
At their Wits end like drunken Men.

*Coffee
House
in Cha-
nge-Al-
ly.

Mean time secure on *GARR'WAY Clifts
A savage Race by Shipwrecks fed,
Ly waiting for the foundred Skiffs,
And strip the Bodyes of the Dead.

But these, you say, are factious Lyes
From some malicious Tory's Brain,
For, where Directors get a Prize,
The *Swiss* and *Dutch* whole Millions drain.   160

---

140 CHANGE-ALLY] *'Change-Alley* 1727, F., 1742, &c.   145–9] *Om.* 1727,
1742, &c.; *restored* F.   153 GARR'WAY] D., Stella, C., 1727, F., 1742,
&c. *Garr'way's* R., T.M.   157–64] *Om.* 1727, 1742, &c.; *restored* F.

140. *Change-Ally.* So called from
being opposite to the Royal Exchange.
149. *Now bury'd* . . . Psalm cvii. 26,
27.
153. *Garr'way Clifts.* Garraway's,
Jonathan's, and other celebrated
coffee-houses stood in Change Alley.

The original proprietor of Garraway's
coffee-house was Thomas Garway, a
tobacconist and coffee-man, and tea
was first sold in England at his house.
During the South Sea Bubble Garraway's became a centre of business
transactions. It was closed in 1866.

Thus when by Rooks a Lord is ply'd,
Some Cully often wins a Bett
By vent'ring on the cheating Side,
Tho not into the Secret let.

While some build Castles in the Air,
Directors build 'em in the Seas;
Subscribers plainly see 'um there,
For Fools will see as Wise men please.

Thus oft by Mariners are shown,
Unless the Men of *Kent* are Ly'rs,   170
Earld Godwin's Castles overflown,
And Castle roofs, and Steeple Spires.

Mark where the Sly *Directors* creep,
Nor to the Shore approach too nigh,
The Monsters nestle in the Deep
To seise you in your passing by:

[p. 3]   Then, like the Dogs of *Nile* be wise,
Who taught by Instinct how to shun
The Crocodile that lurking lyes,
Run as they drink and drink and run.   180

Antæus could by Magick Charms
Recover Strength whene'er he fell,
Alcides held him in his Arms,
And sent him *up in Air* to Hell.

172 Castle roofs,] R., D., T.M., C. Pallace-Roofs, Stella, 1727, F., 1742, &c.
183 in] by T.M.

171. *Earld Godwin's Castles* . . . According to tradition the present Goodwin Sands were once a fertile island belonging to Earl Godwin. After the Conquest these estates were given to the abbot of St. Augustine at Canterbury. He allowed the sea wall to fall into disrepair, and the island was submerged. Geologists, however, are sceptical. See G. B. Gattie's *Memorials of the Goodwin Sands* (1890).

181. *Antæus*. Son of Terra and Neptune. He received new strength from his mother as often as he touched ground. Hercules, in combat with him, squeezed him to death in the air. Lucan, *Pharsalia*, iv. 590 ff.

Directors thrown into the Sea
Recover Strength and Vigor there,
But may be tam'd another way,
Suspended for a while in Air.

Directors; for tis you I warn,
By long Experience we have found   190
What Planet rul'd when you were born;
We see you never can be drown'd:

Beware, nor over-bulky grow,
Nor come within your Cullyes Reach,
For if the Sea should sink so low
To leave you dry upon the Beach,

You'll ow Your Ruin to your Bulk;
Your Foes already waiting stand
To tear you like a foundred Hulk
While you ly helpless on the Sand: 200

[col. 2]   Thus when a Whale hath lost the Tide
The Coasters crowd to seise the Spoyl,
The Monster into Parts divide,
And strip the Bones, and melt the Oyl.

Oh, may some *Western* Tempest sweep
These *Locusts* whom our Fruits have fed,
That Plague, *Directors*, to the Deep,
Driv'n from the *South*-Sea to the *Red.*

May He whom Nature's Laws obey,
Who *lifts* the Poor, and *sinks* the Proud,   210
Quiet the Raging of the Sea,
And *Still the Madness of the Crowd.*

189–204] *Om.* 1727, 1742, *&c.; restored* F.   201] *At the top of col. 2, p. 3 of
MS., before l. 201*
                              You'll ow your Ruin to your
                              Thus when a whale hath lost
crossed out   204 Bones,] Bone, *Printed editions and* Stella   206
These] Those T.M.

But never sh[all our is]le have Rest
Till those devour[ing] *Swine* run down,
(*The Devils leavi[ng] the Possess't*)
And *headlong i[n] the Waters drown.*

The Nation t[oo] too late will find
Computing all th[eir] Cost and Trouble,
Directors Promi[ses] but Wind,
South-Sea at best [a m]ighty BUBBLE.   220

Written on the Deanery Window of St. PATRICK'S, Dublin.

By Dr. DELANY.

Transcript in the possession of the Duke of Portland, Welbeck Abbey.
  [Ref. W.]
Two contemporary transcripts (hands unknown) in the possession of Lord
  Mount Temple, Broadlands, Romsey, Hants. [Ref. Ashley (1) and
Transcript in the British Museum, Harley 7316, pp. 146–7.   [(2).]
Transcript in the Gilbert Collection, Dublin.
Miscellaneous Poems, Original and Translated, By Several Hands. . . .
  Published by Mr. Concanen. . . . London: *Printed for J. Peele,* . . .
  MDCCXXIV. p. 137.
Miscellanies in Prose and Verse. . . . *By Jonathan Swift, D.D. and Alex-*
  ander Pope, Esq; . . . *London Printed, and Re-printed in Dublin, By and*
  for Sam. Fairbrother, . . . 1728. ii. 167. [Ref. 1728.]
A New Miscellany In Prose and Verse. . . . London: *Printed for T. Read,*
  . . ., MDCCXLII. p. 62.
Faulkner, 1746, viii. 322. [Ref. 1746.]
The Story of the Injured Lady. . . . London, *Printed for M. Cooper,* . . .
  MDCCXLVI. p. 60. (Printed from and follows Faulkner.)
Observations upon Lord Orrery's Remarks. [Delany], 1754, p. 182. [Ref.
  Delany.]

    An interchange of four poetical pieces between Delany and Swift took
place in January and February, 1721 (see below, 'Apollo to Dean Swift',
l. 29, and 'News from Parnassus', l. 1). Delany, with suggestions from

214 those] these T.M.   217 too too] R. then too D., T.M., Stella, C., 1727,
F., 1742, &c.

Stella, began by writing two sets of verses on a window of the Deanery, in the first comparing Swift's domestic economy with that of his predecessor, in the second alleging that Swift chose Apollo, his patron, as host in his house, fobbing off with wit and wine those that came 'expecting to dine'. Swift responded with the long poem 'Apollo to Dean Swift', of which an autograph is now in the Pierpont Morgan Library, New York. To this Delany replied with 'News from Parnassus'; and Swift closed the group with 'Apollo's Edict'. The fifth and last poem may have been written later—see p. 271 n.

The first three poems were printed in Concanen's *Miscellaneous Poems*, 1724, the first two duly attributed to Delany, the third to Swift. In Fairbrother's Dublin reprint (1728) of the London *Miscellanies in Prose and Verse* (1727) the three poems were added, at the end of vol. ii, to those contained in the London edition. No author is named for the first two, the third is assigned to Swift. In 1735 Faulkner printed 'Apollo to the Dean' apart from the two pieces leading up to it; and in 1746 he added these two (without note or reference to Swift's reply) as cut on the Deanery windows '*by two of the* Dean's *Friends*'. Delany, in his *Observations*, 1754, prints the first two poems, but makes no claim to have composed them, and he gives the first two lines of 'Apollo to the Dean', which he describes as 'genteel, and finely imagined'. It may be added that the first two pieces were included, as by Delany, in *A Collection of Epigrams*, published by J. Walthoe in 1727.

'Apollo to the Dean', in Swift's autograph, is preserved in the Pierpont Morgan Library, New York; and it was one of the poems transcribed by Stella. At Welbeck Abbey there is a contemporary transcript of the two sets of window verses and of 'Apollo to the Dean' on a folio sheet folded to make two leaves, endorsed 'Transcribed'. In the library at Broadlands there are two separate transcripts of the three poems in differing hands. In the main these three manuscripts agree with each other against Concanen's printed version. There is also a transcript of the three poems in one of the Harley miscellanies in the British Museum. Save for quite insignificant differences the text agrees with the Welbeck MS. There are also transcripts of the three poems in the Gilbert Collection, Dublin.

Delany's poem, 'News from Parnassus', in reply to 'Apollo to the Dean', appeared in newspapers in 1721; and in 1724 it was reprinted in Concanen's miscellany, but at a later point in the volume, without indication of authorship or any reference to the three poems with which it was connected. It was printed by Nichols in his *Supplement*, 1779, as 'Occasioned by "Apollo to the Dean"'. Swift's response, 'Apollo's Edict', was first printed in Dublin as a two-leaf quarto pamphlet; and next in *Gulliveriana*, 1728, with a footnote reference to 'News from Parnassus'.

The three poems are printed from Concanen's *Miscellaneous Poems*.

Swift's autograph was not the manuscript which lay before Stella, although she follows closely in detail every surviving line of Swift's script. Her transcript, however, other transcripts, and Concanen have 108 lines against the 86 of the Morgan manuscript. After line 50 Swift's autograph has four lines heavily blotted out, and lines 51 to 72, as here printed, do not appear.

VERSES ON THE DEANERY WINDOW
By DELANY

ARE the Guests of this House still doom'd to be cheated?
  Sure, the Fates have decreed, they by Halves should be
    treated.
In the Days of good *John*, if you came here to dine,
You had Choice of good Meat, but no Choice of good Wine.
In *Jonathan*'s Reign, if you come here to eat,
You have Choice of good Wine, but no Choice of good Meat.
O *Jove*, then how fully might all Sides be bless'd,
Would'st Thou but agree to this humble Request;
Put both Deans in one, or if that's too much Trouble,
Instead of the Dean, make the Dean'ry double.   10

A N O T H E R,
By the SAME.

As above—five manuscripts.
Miscellaneous Poems . . . Concanen. p. 138.
Miscellanies in Prose and Verse. . . . Fairbrother. ii. 168. [Ref. 1728.]
Faulkner, 1746, viii. 321. [Ref. 1746.]
The Story of the Injured Lady, p. 59. (Printed from and follows Faulkner.)
Observations [Delany], 1754, p. 183. [Ref. Delany.]

3 Days] Day 1746   4 Choice . . . Choice] *store . . . choice* Delany   4 but]
Om. Ashley (2), 1728, 1746, Delany   4 no] not Ashley (2)   5 Reign,]
days, Delany   6 Choice . . . Choice] *choice . . . store* Delany   6 but] *Om.*
W., Ashley (2), 1728, 1746, Delany   8 Would'st] Wou'd W., Ashley (1)
8 agree] *comply* Delany   10 Dean,] Deans, W., Ashley (1) and (2), 1728,
1746, Delany

1–10. Faulkner, 1746, prints this poem after, not before, the next.

3. *John*. Delany, *Observations*, p. 182, says: 'SWIFT'S predecessor, Doctor JOHN STERN, was very hospitable: but not much distinguished for taste, either in wine, or victuals; plenty was all that he regarded.' John Sterne, 1660–1745, was Dean of St. Patrick's, 1702–12. He was successively Bishop of Dromore, 1713, and of Clogher, 1717. Swift and he were on friendly terms. On Swift's housekeeping, see also p. 954.

A Bard, on whom *Phœbus* his Spirit bestow'd,
Resolv'd to acknowledge the Bounty he ow'd;
Found out a new Method at once of confessing,
And making the most of so mighty a Blessing:
To the God he'd be grateful, but Mortals he'd chouse.
By making his Patron preside in his House;
And wisely foresaw this Advantage from thence,
That the God must in Honour bear most of th' Expence:
So the Bard he finds Drink, and leaves *Phœbus* to treat
With the Thoughts he inspires, regardless of Meat: 10
Hence they that come hither, expecting to dine,
Are always fob'd off, with Sheer-Wit, and Sheer-Wine.

A P O L L O,

T O

Dean *S W I F T*.

By HIMSELF.

Swift's autograph: Pierpont Morgan Library, New York. [Ref. S.]
Transcript by Stella; Manuscript Volume in the possession of the Duke
of Bedford, Woburn Abbey. [Ref. Stella.]
Transcript in the possession of the Duke of Portland, Welbeck Abbey.
[Ref. W.]
Two transcripts at Broadlands, Romsey, Hants. [Ref. Ashley (1) and (2).]
Transcripts in the British Museum, Harley 7316, pp. 147–51, and
Add. MS. 31152. fol. 8 ff.
Transcript in the Gilbert Collection, Dublin.
Miscellaneous Poems. . . . Concanen. p. 140.
Miscellanies in Prose and Verse. . . . Fairbrother. ii. 169. [Ref. 1728.]
Faulkner, 1735, ii. 180 (1737, ii. 117). [Ref. F.]

2 Resolv'd to acknowledge] Resolving t'acknowledge 1746   5 chouse.]
chouse, 1728, 1746, Delany   7 thence,] hence, 1728   8 must] wou'd 1746
would Delany

Title] *In* Stella, *the* Ashley MSS., *and edns. later than* Concanen, *becomes*
'Apollo to the Dean'. Stella *and* Faulkner *give the date 1720.* Fairbrother
adds to the title, 'By D-- S--'.

RIght Trusty, and so forth; We let you to know,
We are very ill us'd by you Mortals below;
For, first, I have often by Chymists been told,
Tho' I know nothing on't, 'tis I that make Gold;
Which when you have got, you so carefully hide it,
That since I was born, I hardly have spy'd it;
Then, it must be allow'd, whenever I shine,
I forward the Grass, and ripen the Vine:
To me the good Fellows apply for Relief,
Without whom they could get neither Claret nor Beef; 10
Yet their Wine and their Victuals, those curmudgeon
Lubbards
Lock up from my Sight in Pantries and Cupboards:
That I have an ill Eye, they wickedly think,
And taint all their Meat, and sour all their Drink.
But thirdly and lastly, it must be allow'd,
I alone can inspire the poetical Crowd;
This is gratefully own'd by each Boy in the College,
Whom if I inspire, 'tis not to my Knowledge;
This every Pretender to Rhyme will admit,
Without troubling his Head about Judgment or Wit: 20
These Gentlemen use me with Kindness and Freedom,
And as for their Works, when I please I may read 'em;
They lie open on Purpose, on Counters and Stalls,
And the Titles I view, when I shine on the Walls:
But a Comrade of yours, that Traytor *Delany*,
Who I, for your Sake, have us'd better than any;
And of my meer Motion, and special good Grace,
Intended in Time to succeed to your Place;
On *Tuesday* the Ninth, seditiously came,
With a certain false Traitress, one *Stella* by Name, 30

4 'tis] it is S., Stella, W., 1728, F.   7 whenever] wherever W., Ashley (2)
8 and ripen] and I ripen S., Stella, F.   10 could] S., Stella, 1728, F.   can
W., Ashley (1) and (2)   11 those] these 1728, F.   12 Pantries] 1728
Cellars S., Stella, F.   14] W., Ashley (1) and (2) *om. second* 'all'   18 'tis]
1728   it is S., Stella, F.   19 to Rhyme] to Rhime 1728, F.   in Rhime W.,
Ashley (1) and (2)   in Rime S., Stella   26 Who] Whom S., Stella, W.,
Ashley (1) and (2), 1728, F.   28 to your] in your S., Stella, 1728, F.   to
this Ashley (1) and (2)   in this W.   29 Ninth] tenth S., Stella, Ashley (2)
Tenth Ashley (1), 1728, F.   tenth he W.

To the Dean'ry House, and on the *North* Glass,
Where for fear of the Cold, I never can pass;
Then and there, *Vi & Armis*, with a certain Utensil,
Of Value five Shillings, in *English* a Pencil;
Did maliciously, falsly, and traiterously write,
Whilst *Stella* aforesaid stood by with the Light;
My Sister has lately depos'd upon Oath,
That she stopt in her Course to look on them both;
That *Stella* was helping, abetting and aiding,
And still as he writ, stood smiling and reading;			40
That her Eyes were as bright as our self at Noon-Day;
But her graceful black Locks, were all mingled with
  Grey,
And by the Description I certainly know,
'Tis the Nymph that I courted some ten Years ago;
Whom, when I with the best of my Talents endu'd,
On her Promise of yielding, she acted the Prude;
That some Verses were writ with felonious Intent,
Direct to the *North*, where I never yet went;
That the letters appear'd revers'd on the Pane,
But in *Stella*'s bright Eyes were plac'd right again;			50
Wherein she distinctly could read ev'ry Line,
And presently guess'd that the Fancy was mine;
She can swear to the Person, whom oft she has seen,
At Night between *Cavan-street* and *College-Green*:
Now you see why his Verses so seldom are shown,
The Reason is plain, they are none of his own;
And observe while you live, that no Man is shy
To discover the Goods he came honestly by:

36 Whilst] While S., Stella, W.   38 on] at S., Stella, 1728, F.   41 our self] my self S., Stella, W., Ashley (1) and (2), 1728, F.   42 all] *Om.* S., Stella, W., Ashley (1) and (2), 1728, F.   44 'Tis the Nymph that I] S., Stella, 1728, F. Tis ye same Nymph I W., Ashley (1) and (2)   45 Whom,] S., Stella Who, 1728, F.   47 writ] written W.   48 never yet went;] never once went; S., Stella   never went; W., Ashley (1) and (2), 1728, F.   49 revers'd on] reverse thro' S., Stella, 1728, F.   50 were] S., Stella they were 1728, F.   52 guess'd that the] guesst the Stella guess'd the 1728, F.   53, 54] *Om.* F.   53 Person,] Parson, Stella, 1728   58 came] Stella, 1728, F. comes W., Ashley (1) and (2)

37. *My Sister.* Diana.   53. *She can swear to the Person,* . . . *I.e.* Delany.

If I light on a Thought, he will certainly steal it,
And when he has got it, finds Ways to conceal it;　60
Of all the fine Things he keeps in the Dark,
There's scarce one in ten, but what has my Mark;
And let them be seen by the World if he dare,
I'll make it appear that they're all stol'n Ware:
But as for the Poem he writ on your Sash,
I think I have now got him under my Lash;
My Sister transcrib'd it last Night, to his Sorrow,
And the Publick shall see't, if I live 'till to Morrow;
Thro' the *Zodiack* around, it shall quickly be spread,
In all Parts of the Globe, where your Language is read;　70
He knows very well I ne'er gave a Refusal,
When he ask'd for my Aid, in the Forms that are usual:
But the Secret is this; I did lately intend
To write a few Verses on you as my Friend;
I study'd a Fortnight, before I could find,
As I rode in my Chariot, a Thought to my Mind;
And resolv'd the next Winter, for that is the Time,
When the Days are at shortest, to put it in Rhyme;
Till then it was lock'd in my Box at *Parnassus*;
When that subtle Companion, in hopes to surpass us,　80
Conveys out my Paper of Hints by a Trick,
For I think in my Conscience he deals with *Old Nick*;
And from my own Stock, provided with Topicks,
He gets to a Window beyond both the *Tropicks*;
There out of my Sight, just against the *North-Zone*,
Writes down my Conceits, and then calls them his own:
And you like a Booby, the *Bubble* can swallow;
Now who but *Delany* can write like *Apollo?*

60 finds] Stella　　find 1728, F.　　64 that they're] they are Stella, W.,
Ashley (1) and (2), 1728, F.　　65 your] the W., Ashley (1) and (2)　　70
your] the W., Ashley (1) and (2)　　77 And] I Ashley (1)　　78 put]
get S., Stella, W., Ashley (1) and (2), 1728, F.　　80 that] this Ashley (1) and
(2)　then W.　　82] *In round brackets* Ashley (1), Stella, F.　　83 own] old
W., Ashley (1) and (2)　　85 just against] S., Stella, 1728, F.　　against W.,
Ashley (2)　beyond Ashley (1)　　86 then] *Om.* S., Stella, W., Ashley (1)
and (2), 1728, F.　　87 Booby,] Cully, S., Stella, W., Ashley (1) and (2),
1728, F.　　88 Now] For Ashley (1)　　88 can write] that writes S., Stella,
1728, F.

High Treason by Statute! But here you object,
He only stole Hints; the Verse is correct; 90
Tho' the Thought be *Apollo*'s, 'tis finely express'd;
So a Thief steals my Horse, and then gets him well
    drest;
Now, whereas the said Criminal seems past Repentance,
We *Phœbus* think fit to proceed to his Sentence;
Since *Delany* has dar'd, like *Prometheus* his Sire,
To climb to our Region, and thence to steal Fire;
We order a Vulture, in Shape of the *Spleen*,
To prey on his Liver, but not to be seen:
And we order our Subjects, of every Degree,
To believe all his Verses were written by me; 100
And under the Pain of our highest Displeasure,
To call nothing his, but the Rhyme and the Measure.
And lastly for *Stella*, just out of her Prime,
I am too much reveng'd already by Time;
In return to her Scorn, I send her Diseases,
And will now be her Friend whenever she pleases;
And the Gifts I bestow'd her, will find her a Lover,
Tho' she lives 'till she's Grey as a Badger all over.

N E W S *from* Parnassus.

By DELANY

The Weekly Journal: or, British Gazetteer, 25 March, 1721.
Miscellaneous Poems . . . Concanen. p. 215.
A Supplement to Dr. Swift's Works: . . . J. Nichols, 1779.

89 Statute!] Statute: S., Stella Statutes. 1728 Statute. F.   90 the Verse] but
the Verse S., Stella, W., Ashley (1) and (2), 1728, F.   91 be] is Ashley (1)
92 then gets him] has him S., Stella, W., 1728, F.   95 has] hath Stella
95 *Prometheus* his] Prometheus's W.   96 thence] Stella, F.   there S., W.,
Ashley (1) and (2), 1728   98 but] S., Stella, 1728, F. and W., Ashley (1)
and (2)   101, 102] *Om.* Ashley (1)   104 reveng'd already] Already re-
venged W.   105 to] 1728, F. of S., Stella   105 send] sent S., Stella, F.
cure 1728   106 And] 1728 But Stella, F.   108 'till she's] 1728 till she's
Stella to be F.   108. The last two words, 'all over', are written large by
Swift and underlined.

*P*Arnassus, *February* the twenty-seventh,
   The *Poets* assembled here on the Eleventh;
   Conven'd by *Apollo*, who gave them to know,
He'd have a *Vicegerent* in his Empire below;
But declar'd that no *Bard* shou'd this Honour inherit,
'Till the rest had agreed he surpass'd them in Merit:
Now this you'll allow was a difficult Case,
For each *Bard* believ'd he had a Right to the Place;
So finding the Assembly grow warm in Debate,
He put 'em in Mind of his *Phaeton*'s Fate: 10
'Twas urged to no Purpose, the Dispute higher rose,
Scarce *Phœbus* himself cou'd their Quarrels compose.
'Till at length he determin'd that every *Bard*
Shou'd (each in their Turn) be patiently heard.

   First, one who believ'd he excell'd in Translation,
Founds his Claim on the Doctrine of *Transmigration*:
"Since the Soul of great *Milton* was given to me,
"I hope the Convention will quickly agree—
Agree, quoth *Apollo*, from whence is this Fool?
Is he just come from reading *Pythagoras* at School?   20
Begone, Sir, you've got your Subscriptions in Time,
And giv'n in Return neither Reason nor Rhyme.

   To the *next*, says the God, tho' now I won't chuse you,
I'll tell you the Reason for which I refuse you;

---

4 *Vicegerent*] Viceregent 1779   9 the Assembly] th' assembly 1779   14 their]
his 1779   16 of *Transmigration*:] of man's transmigration: 1779

---

10. *Phaeton's Fate.* Phaethon, the son of Phœbus, attempting to drive his father's chariot, lost control of the horses, threatening the world with universal conflagration. Zeus destroyed him with a thunderbolt, and his corpse fell into the river Eridanus.

15. *First, one who believ'd he excell'd in Translation.* The reference is to Joseph Trapp, 1679–1747, who was first professor of poetry at Oxford, 1708–18. Apart from mediocre verse, and translations, of which the most ambitious was his translation of the *Æneid* into blank verse, he was a High Church pamphleteer, and achieved reputation as a preacher. Swift thought little of his abilities. He described him to Stella (*Journal*, 7 Jany., 1710–11) as 'a sort of pretender to wit, a second-rate pamphleteer for the cause, whom they pay by sending him to Ireland'. Trapp had then just been appointed chaplain to Sir Constantine Phipps, Lord Chancellor of Ireland. But in July, 1712, Swift got him made chaplain to Bolingbroke (*Journal*, 17 July), and was on friendly terms with him in 1714 (*Letters of Swift to Ford*, ed. Nichol Smith, pp. 15, 17).

Love's Goddess has oft to her Parent complain'd,
Of my fav'ring a *Bard* who her Empire disdain'd,
That at my Instigation a Poem you writ,
Which to Beauty and Youth prefer'd Judgment and Wit;
That to make you a Laureat I gave the first Voice,
Inspiring the *Britons* t'approve of my Choice.   30
Jove sent her to me her Power to try;
The Goddess of *Beauty* what God can deny?
She forbids your Preferment, I grant her Desire,
Appease the fair Goddess, you then may rise higher.

The *next* that appear'd, had good Hopes of succeeding,
For he merited much for his Wit and his Breeding.
'Twas wise in the *Britons* no favour to shew him,
He else might expect they shou'd pay what they owe him.
And therefore they prudently chose to discard
The Patriot, whose Merits they wou'd not reward: 40
The God with a Smile bid his Fav'rite advance,
You were sent by *Astrea* her Envoy to *France*.
You bent your Ambition to rise in the *State*,
I refuse you, because you cou'd stoop to be great.

Then a *Bard*, who had been a successful Translator,
"The Convention allows me a Versificator.

Says *Apollo*, you mention the least of your Merit,
By your Works it appears you have much of my Spirit;
I esteem you so well, that to tell you the Truth,
The greatest Objection against you's your Youth;   50
Then be not concern'd you are now laid aside,
If you live you shall certainly one Day preside.

Another, low bending, *Apollo* thus greets,
"'Twas I taught your Subjects to walk thro' the Streets.

25 Parent] parents 1779.   41 bid] bade 1779

35. *The next that appear'd, . . .* Prior.
The allusion in l. 42 is to his secret
diplomatic mission to France in 1711,
on returning from which he was de-
tained by the English customs officials,
an incident which led to Swift's
fictitious *New Journey to Paris*
(*Prose Works*, v. 188). Cf. p. 143 n.

45. *Then a Bard, who had been a
successful Translator.* Pope; with
reference to his translation of the
Iliad. The *Odyssey* came later.

53. *Another, low bending, . . .* Gay;
alluding to his *Trivia: or, the Art of
Walking the Streets of London.*

You taught 'em to walk, why they knew it before,
But give me the *Bard* that can teach them to soar;
Whenever he claims his Right, I'll confess
Who lately attempted my Style with Success;
Who writes like *Apollo*, has most of his Spirit,
And therefore 'tis just I distinguish his Merit;   60
Who makes it appear by all he has writ,
His Judgment alone can set Bounds to his Wit;
Like *Virgil* correct, with his own Native Ease,
But excels ev'n *Virgil* in elegant Praise;
Who admires the Ancients, and knows 'tis their due,
Yet writes in a Manner entirely new;
Tho' none with more Ease their Depths can explore,
Yet whatever he wants he takes from my Store;
Tho' I'm fond of his Virtues, his Pride I can see,
In scorning to borrow from any but me;   70
'Tis owing to this, that like *Cynthia*, his Lays
Enlighten the World by reflecting my Rays.
This said, the whole Audience soon found out his Drift,
The Convention was summon'd in Favour of *Sw—t*.

Apollo's Edict.

Apollo's Edict; 4 pp. 4to, no imprint or date.
Gulliveriana, 1728, p. 50. [Ref. 1728.]
Poems on Several Occasions. London: Printed for C. Rivington [Mary Barber] . . . 1734, p. 105. See note, pp. 355–6.
Vol. IV. of the Miscellanies . . . Dublin, Printed by and for Samuel Fairbrother, . . . 1735. p. 164. [Ref. 1735.]
A Supplement to Dr. Swift's Works: . . . J. Nichols, 1779.
See note on p. 355.

IRELAND is now our royal Care,
We lately fix'd our *Viceroy* there:
How near was she to be undone,
Till pious Love inspir'd her Son?

56 soar;] *soar.* 1779   71 'Tis] It is 1779   74 *Sw—t.*] SWIFT. 1779
4 Son?] 1728, 1735   Son! 1779

2. *Viceroy*. See above, 'News from Parnassus', l. 4, p. 267.

What cannot our *Vicegerent* do,
As *Poet* and as *Patriot* too?
Let his Success our Subjects sway
Our Inspirations to obey,
And follow where *he* leads the Way:
Then study to correct your Taste,   10
Nor *beaten* Paths be longer trac'd.

No Simile shall be begun,
With *rising* or with *setting* Sun:
And let the *secret Head of* Nile
Be ever banish'd from your Isle.
When wretched Lovers live on Air,
I beg you'll the *Camelion* spare.
And when you'd make an Heroe grander,
Forget he's like a *Salamander*.
No Son of mine shall dare to say,   20
Aurora usher'd in the Day,
Or ever name the *milky Way*.
You all agree, I make no doubt,
Elijah's Mantle's worn out.
The *Bird of Jove* shall toil no more,
To teach the humble *Wren* to soar.
Your tragick Heroes shall not rant,
Nor Shepherds use *poetick Cant*:
Simplicity alone can grace,
The Manners of the rural Race,   30
Theocritus and *Philips* be,
Your guides to *true* Simplicity.
When *Damon's Soul shall take its Flight*,
Tho' Poets have the second Sight,
They shall not see a *Trail of Light*:

10 Taste,] Taste; 1728, 1735   taste; 1779   17 spare.] spare; 1728, 1735,
1779   18 an] a 1728, 1735, 1779   24 *Mantle's*] *Mantle* is 1728, 1735
mantle is 1779   27] *No break* 1728, 1779

19. *Salamander*. See Swift's attack   Salamander', p. 82.
on Lord Cutts, 'Description of a   31. *Philips*. Ambrose Philips, whose

Nor shall the *Vapour upwards rise*,
Nor a *new Star* adorn the Skies:
For who can hope to place one there,
As glorious as *Belinda's Hair?*
Yet if his Name you'd eternize   40
And must exalt him to the Skies:
Without a *Star* this may be done,
So *TICKELL* mourn'd his *ADDISON*.

If *ANNA's* happy Reign you praise,
Pray not a word of *Halcyon Days*.
Nor let my Votaries show their Skill
In apeing Lines from *Cooper's Hill*;
For know I cannot bear to hear,
The Mimickry of *deep yet clear*.

When e'er my *Viceroy* is address'd,   50
Against the *Phœnix* I protest.
When Poets soar in youthful Strains,
No *Phaeton* to *hold the Reins*.

36 *Vapour*] 1728, 1735 *vapours* 1779   49 *deep yet clear.*] *deep, yet clear.*
1728, 1735, 1779   52] *No break* 1728, 1735, 1779

pastorals excited the ridicule of Pope. He supported the government in the *Free-thinker*, and was rewarded in 1724 with a secretaryship to Archbishop Boulter in Ireland. The diction of complimentary addresses composed by him at this period was satirized by Henry Carey in 'Namby-Pamby', and in Dublin parodies, some of which, including 'A Poem upon Rover' and 'A Christmas Box for Namby Pamby', have been attributed to Swift. *Cf.* pp. 1124–6.

34–9. *Tho' Poets . . . Cf. The Rape of the Lock*, v. 123–32.

43. *So TICKELL mourn'd his ADDISON.* Thomas Tickell, 1686–1740, Addison's friend and biographer, incurred Pope's enmity by issuing, at the same time as Pope, a translation of the first book of the *Iliad*. This feeling was not shared by Swift, who probably scarcely knew Tickell, until he came

over to Ireland in 1724 as secretary to Lord Carteret, when friendly relations were established between them. The reference in this line is to Tickell's elegy, 'On the Death of Mr. Addison'. Tickell's edition of Addison's *Works*, to which the elegy was prefixed, was not, however, published till 2 October, 1721. 'Apollo's Edict' may therefore have been composed in the latter part of 1721, or ll. 40–43 may have been a later addition, or Swift may have seen the elegy in manuscript.

49. *The Mimickry of deep yet clear.* The allusion is to the well-known lines of Sir John Denham's poem, 'Cooper's Hill':

'Though deep yet clear, though gentle yet not dull;
Strong without rage, without o'er-flowing full.'

When you describe a lovely Girl,
No Lips of *Coral* Teeth of *Pearl*.
Cupid shall ne'er mistake another
However beauteous for his Mother:
Nor shall his Darts at random fly
From Magazeen in *Cælia*'s Eye.
With Women Compounds I am cloy'd,　　　60
Which only pleased in *Biddy Floyd*:
For foreign Aid what need they roam,
Whom Fate has amply bless'd at home?
Unerring Heav'n, with bounteous Hand,
Has form'd a Model for your Land;
Whom *Jove* endow'd with ev'ry Grace,
The Glory of the *Granard* Race;
Now destin'd, by the Powers divine,
The Blessing of *another Line*:
Then wou'd you paint a *matchless* Dame,　　　70
Whom you'd consigne to endless Fame?
Invoke not *Citherea*'s Aid,
Nor borrow from the *Blew-ey'd* Maid,
Nor need you on the *Graces* call,
Take Qualities from *DONEGAL*.

59 Magazeen] Magazine 1728, 1735, 1779　　　60] *No break* 1779　　　70
Then wou'd you] Then, would you 1728, 1735　　When would you 1779
71 Fame?] 1728, 1735　fame; 1779

61. *Biddy Floyd.* See p. 117.
64–75. These twelve lines refer to Catherine, only daughter of Arthur, first Earl of Granard. She married, in 1685, Arthur Chichester, third Earl of Donegal, who was killed near Barcelona, 1706, fighting under the command of Peterborough. She died in 1743, and was buried at Carrickfergus (Lodge, *Peerage of Ireland*, i. 338–40). The last twelve lines of 'Apollo's Edict' were perhaps printed separately, at the time, as a tribute to her. They were reprinted, as

'VERSES *upon the late Countess of* DONEGAL, *who died in the Year* 1743' in the small miscellany of Swift pieces, entitled *The Story of the Injured Lady,* 1746, p. 67, and also in Cogan's *Supplement to the Works of Dr. Swift,* 1752, p. 125. In the Pierpont Morgan Library, New York, there is a manuscript copy of these lines, headed 'On yᵉ late Countess of Donegal. Published upon her Ladyship's interment in her family vault at Garrick-fergus by Dean Swift'. See p. 1143.

AN

EPILOGUE,

To be spoke at the

THEATRE-ROYAL

This present Saturday being *April* the 1st.   In the
Behalf of the Distressed *WEAVERS*.

Stella's transcript; Manuscript Volume in the possession of the Duke of
Bedford, Woburn Abbey. [Ref. Stella.]
An Epilogue [as above] ... *Dublin Printed by J. W.* F°. Broadside.
*An Epilogue, As it was spoke by Mr. Griffith at the Theatre-Royal On Satur-
day the First of April. In the Behalf of the Distressed Weavers.*
        [Printed on the verso of *A Prologue, spoke by Mr. Elrington At
        the Theatre-Royal On Saturday the First of April. In the
        Behalf of the Distressed Weavers. ... ... Dublin Printed
        by John Harding.*] F°. Hf. sheet. [Ref. *Hf. Sheet.*]
An Epilogue: ... *Limerick Printed by Andrew Welsh.* Fo. Broadside.
St. James's Post, 10–12 April, 1721.
Weekly Journal: or, British Gazetteer, 15 April, 1721.
Gentleman's Journal, 15 April, 1721.
Weekly Journal, or Saturday's Post, 13 May, 1721.
Miscellanies, Written By Jonathan Swift, D.D. ... *The Fourth Edition.
London: Printed in the Year M.DCC.XXII.* ... p. 192.
Miscellaneous Poems, ... *Published by Mr. Concanen,* 1724, p. 208.
Miscellanies. The Last Volume, 1727. p. 283 (1731, p. 316; 1733, p. 316).
The Drapier's Miscellany. ... *Dublin: Printed by and for James Hoey,* ...
1733. p. 6. [Ref. 1733.]
Faulkner, 1735, ii. 172 (1737, ii. 146). [Ref. F.]

    The weaving industry in Ireland had been severely crippled by English
legislation; and, in the earlier part of 1721, unemployment, poverty, and
suffering became acute. Distress in Dublin was also due to speculation in
the South Sea funds. Archbishop King estimated that the number of
families in the weaving trade in dire want was nearly seventeen hundred,
and the number of persons six thousand (*Corresp.* iii. 75 n.[2]). The
government ordered £100 for relief purposes; collections were made in
the churches; and a play, realizing £73, was given for the benefit of
distressed weavers. The play chosen for performance was *Hamlet* (*Gentleman's Journal,* 15 April, 1721). A special prologue and epilogue were
written for the occasion.
    The prologue, beginning 'Great Cry and Little Wool', was written by

Sheridan, the epilogue by Swift. Both exhorted ladies to the wearing of
Irish woollen. An anonymous 'Answer' appeared, ridiculing the vain
attempt to displace silk and cotton as materials of feminine attire. The
'Prologue', 'Epilogue', and 'Answer' were reprinted together by Concanen
in 1724. Faulkner and the London trade editions printed the 'Epilogue'
only. Nichols, in his *Supplement*, 1779, reprinted the 'Prologue' and
'Answer'.

Sheridan's 'Prologue' and Swift's 'Epilogue' appeared, in the first
instance, as folio broadsides, and also together on opposite sides of a folio
half-sheet. They were almost immediately reprinted in several London newspapers. The *St. James's Post* and *The Gentleman's Journal* attributed the
'Epilogue' to Swift, although the broadside made no mention of the author.
Concanen, also, assigned the pieces to Sheridan and Swift respectively.

The 'Epilogue' is one of the poems transcribed by Stella. She heads it
'Epilogue for the Weavers | Written A.D. 1721.'

The 'Prologue' was spoken by Thomas Elrington, for whom see
D.N.B. xvii. 332. He flourished 1688–1732, was Deputy Master of the
Revels, Steward of the King's Inns, and Chief of his Majesty's Company of
Comedians in Ireland. The 'Epilogue' was spoken by Thomas Griffith,
well known on the Dublin stage during the early part of the eighteenth
century. In 1736, heavily in debt, he appealed to Swift for help (*Corresp.*
v. 304).

The text is printed from the original broadside from which the Limerick
broadside was reprinted.

W HO dares affirm this is no pious age,
  When Charity begins to tread the Stage:
  When Actors who at best are hardly Savers,
  Will give a Night of Benefit to Weavers.
Stay—But let me see how finely will it Sound,
Imprimis: From his Grace a Hundred pound.
Peers, Clergy, Gentry, all are Benefactors;
And then Comes in the Item of the Actors.
Item the Actors, freely gave a Day,
The Poet had no more who made the Play.   10

2 Stage:] Stella, 1722, 1724   Stage? 1727, 1733, F.   4 Weavers.] Stella,
1733   Weavers? 1722, 1724, 1727, F.   5 But] 1724   *om.* Stella, 1722,
1727, 1733, F.   5 Sound,] Stella, 1724   Sound: 1722   Sound! 1727, F.
6 a] Stella, 1722, 1724, 1727   an 1733, F.

6. *From his Grace* . . . Archbishop   *the Play.* The play was *Hamlet.*
King.   Shakespeare, being dead, had no more
10. *The Poet had no more who made*   days to give.

But whence this Wonderous Charity, in Play'rs,
They learnt it not at Sermons or at pray'rs.
Under the Rose since here are none but friends;
To own the truth we have some private Ends.
Since Waiting Women like Exacting Jades,
Hold up the prices of their Old *Brocades*.
We'll dress in *Manufactures*, made at home?
Equip our KINGS, and *Generalls* at the Comb.
We'll Rigg in Meath-Street, *Egypt's* hauty *Queen*,
And *Anthony* shall Court her in *Ratteen*.   20
In *blew shalloon*, shall *Hanniball* be Clad,
And *Scipio*, trail an *Irish purple Plad*.
In Drugget drest of Thirteen Pence a Yard,
See *Philip's* Son amidst his *Persian* Guard;
And proud *Roxana* fir'd with jealous Rage,
With fifty Yards of Crape, shall sweep the Stage.
In short our Kings and Princesses within,
Are all resolv'd the Project to begin;
And you, our Subjects, when you here resort,
Must Imitate the Fashion of the Court.   30

O! Cou'd I see this Audience Clad in *Stuff*,
Tho' Moneys scarce we shou'd have Trade enough;
But *Chints*, *Brocades*, and *Lace* take all away,
And scarce a Crown is left to see the Play:
Perhaps you wonder whence this Friendship Springs,
Between the *Weavers* and us Play-House Kings.

11 Play'rs,] Stella   Players; 1724   Play'rs? 1722, 1727, F.   12 not] sure
Hf. sheet   14 To own the truth] *In round brackets* 1722, 1724, 1727, F.
15, 16] *Om. Hf. sheet*, 1724   17 home?] home Stella   Home, 1722, 1733
home; 1724, 1727, F.   19 We'll] Will 1733   19 in] Stella, 1722, 1727,
1733, F.   from 1724   23 Thirteen] 1722, 1727, F.   Thirty Stella, 1724,
Hf. sheet, 1733   32 Moneys] Money's Stella *and remainder*   34 the Play:]
Stella, 1722   the Play. 1724   a Play: 1727, F., 1733   35] *N.P.* 1724

17. Faulkner's 1737 edition of the   *famous for Woollen Manufactures.'*—
Works, vol. ii, reads 'Well dress'd' in   Faulkner.
this line. In Swift's copy of the   21. *In blew shalloon.* A woollen
volume a pencil note corrects back to   stuff chiefly used for linings. From
'We'll dress'.   Châlons-sur-Marne, an early place of
18. *at the Comb.* '*A Street in* Dublin   manufacture.

But Wit and Weaving had the same beginning,
Pallas first taugh[t] us Poetry and Spinning;
And next Observe how this Alliance fits,
For *Weavers* now are just as poor as Wits;   40
Their Brother Quill-Men Workers for the Stage,
For sorry *Stuff*, can get a Crown a Page;
But *Weavers* will be Kinder to the *Players*,
And Sell for Twenty Pence a Yard [of] theirs;
And to your knowledge there is often less in,
The *Poets* Wits, than in the *Players* Dressing.

THE

J O U R N A L.

The Journal. [? 1721] Broadside.
Baker's News; or, the Whitehall Journal, January, 1722–3.
The Weekly Journal: or, British Gazetteer, 19 January, 1722–3.
Manuscript copy, in an unidentified hand, sent to Lady Giffard from
   Ireland, and endorsed by Lady Giffard, 'Dr. Swift's Verses'. Formerly
   in the possession of the Rev. John Longe, Yelverton Rectory, Norfolk.
   [Ref. G.]
Miscellanea. The Second Volume. . . . *London: Printed in the Year*, 1727.
   p. 85.
Gulliveriana, 1728, p. 13.
Miscellanies. The Third Volume, 1732, p. 20.
Faulkner, 1735, ii. 174 (1737, ii. 156). [Ref. F.]
Miscellanies, 1742, iv. 226.

From June to October, in 1721 (*Letters of Swift to Ford*, ed. Nichol
Smith, pp. 93, 95 n.[1]), Swift was staying at Gaulstown House, which lay
between the town of Trim and Woodbrooke, the seat of Knightley Chetwode, to whom, possibly, was due his introduction to Baron Rochfort,
the owner of Gaulstown. Robert Rochfort (for whom see also *D.N.B.*
xlix. 74), a member of the Irish Bar, was, after the accession of William,
chosen a commissioner of the Great Seal of Ireland, and accompanied the
King from London to the Boyne (*Corresp.* ii. 257 n.[6]). Disapproving,
however, of concessions to the Roman Catholics, he went into opposition.

39 next] 1722, 1727, 1733, F.   pray Stella, 1724, *Hf. sheet*   46 Wits,]
1724   Wit, Stella, 1722, 1727, 1733, F.

In 1695 he became Attorney-General of Ireland, and Speaker of the Irish House of Commons. From 1707 to 1714 he was Chief Baron of the Exchequer; but, as a strong Tory, was deprived of this office on the accession of George I.

Gaulstown House, which has now been replaced, was given by Lord Chief Baron Rochfort to his eldest son, George, on that son's marriage to Lady Betty Moore, youngest daughter of the Earl of Drogheda. The interchange of verses was a favourite amusement between Swift, George, and the younger son John Rochfort (see pp. 965 ff.).

Gaulstown House was satirically described in verses written by Delany, and printed in *Whartoniana*, 1727, i. 30.

'The Journal', and later, 'A Soldier and a Scholar', 1732, led to some criticism of Swift for abusing the hospitality of his friends (*Corresp.* iii. 141; iv. 303). In *Gulliveriana*, pp. 11, 12, 20, Swift, as '*Dean Celer*', is attacked for repaying 'so rudely, the Hospitality of his Friend'. A broadside poem (n.p. or d.) called 'A Letter of Advice to the Revd. D—r D—la—y', has the lines:

> If you presume too far, you miss that end,
> For the like Cause lost *Sw—t* his *Galls-town* Friend.

Percival, Dean of Emly, was, not unnaturally, nettled at Swift's description of himself and his wife in 'The Journal', and retorted with 'A Description In Answer to the Journal', which appeared in Dublin, 1722, on the verso of a half-sheet, on the recto of which Swift's poem was printed. 'A Description' was reprinted by Scott, *Works*, 1814, i. 272 n.

Swift's poem, descriptive of Gaulstown and the house-party, during his stay there in 1721, was probably composed in the autumn towards the end of his visit (see line 51). It is possible, however, that the printed broadside did not appear till the following year, for it was not reprinted in the London newspapers till January, 1723. Faulkner says, 'Written in the YEAR 1723'.

In the broadside edition the title of the poem is 'The Journal'; and this title is followed in Curll's *Miscellanea*, 1727, and in *Gulliveriana*, 1728. In the Pope and Swift *Miscellanies* volume of 1732 the title becomes 'The Country Life', and this title is followed in the Bathurst and trade editions. Faulkner, 1735, called the poem 'The Part of a Summer, at the House of *George Rochfort*, Esq;'.

In the possession of the Rev. John Longe at Yelverton Rectory, Norfolk, were papers which had come down from Sir William Temple's family. Among them was a transcript of this poem, not in Swift's hand. This transcript is now in Lord Rothschild's Library, No. 2266. The manuscript is folded. On the back is written 'To the Lady Giffard', together with an endorsement, 'Dr. Swift's Verses' in Lady Giffard's hand. Swift broke off all intercourse with Lady Giffard in 1709, in consequence of a difference which sprang up between them after the publication of the third part of Temple's *Memoirs*. At a later date, when Swift was in London, she made advances, but only to be repulsed. It is not improbable, however, that the transcript of the poem reached her from Ireland.

This is one of the poems corrected by Swift in his own copy of the *Miscellanies*, 1727–32. His corrections number seven, and are marked 'S.' in the apparatus.

The text is printed from the broadside edition.

THALIA, tell in sober Lays,
How *George*, *Nim*, *Dan*, *Dean* pass their Days;
And shou'd our *Galls-town* Wit grow fallow,
Yet, *Neget quis Carmina Gallo*.
Here (by the Way) by *Gallus* mean I,
Not *Sheridan*, but friend *Delany*.
Begin, my Muse, first from our Bowers,
We issue forth at different Hours;
At Seven, the *Dean* in Night-gown drest,
Goes round the House to wake the rest: 10
At Nine, grave *Nim* and *George* Facetious,
Go to the *Dean* to read *Lucretius*.
At Ten, my Lady comes and Hectors,
And kisses *George*, and ends or Lectures:

3–6] *Om.* 1732, F., 1742   4 *Gallo*.] Gallo; G.   *Gallo?* 1727, 1728   7 Muse, first] Muse; First, 1727, 1732   Muse. First 1728   Muse. First, F.   Muse; First 1742

2. *How George, Nim, Dan, Dean pass their Days.* George, for whom see introductory notes above, was the eldest son of the Lord Chief Baron Rochfort. 'Nim', or 'Nimrod', a nickname given to the Baron's second son, John, on account of his fondness for hunting. He was M.P. for Bally-shannon. When in Dublin he was frequently at the Deanery. He was named by Stella one of her executors; and he was selected a member of the Lunacy Commission appointed, in 1742, to inquire into the state of Swift's mind. 'Dan' was the Rev. Daniel Jackson whose large nose was a constant subject of ridicule in verse

trifles passing between the Dean, the Grattans, and the Rochforts, pp. 990 ff.
4. *Neget quis Carmina Gallo.* Virgil, *Ecl.* x. 3. Gaius Cornelius Gallus, whose poems have been lost. He was prefect of Egypt; and one of Virgil's oldest friends.
12. *Go to the Dean to read Lucretius.* References to Lucretius in Swift's writings show him to have been a favourite and well-known author, although, curiously enough, his library only contained one edition of the poet's works.
13. *At Ten, my Lady . . .* George Rochfort's wife, Lady Betty, for whom see introductory notes above.

And when she has him by the Neck fast,
Hawls him, and scolds us down to Breakfast.
We squander there an Hour and more,
And then all hands, Boys, to the Oar
All, Heteroclit *Dan* except,
Who neither time nor order kept.   20
But by peculiar Whimseys drawn,
Peeps in the Ponds to look for Spawn:
O'er sees the Work, or *Dragon* rowes,
Or spoils a Text, or mends his Hose.
Or—but proceed we in our *Journal*,
At Two or after we return all,
From the four Elements assembling,
Warn'd by the Bell, all Flocks come trembling,
From Airy Garrets some descend,
Some from the Lakes remotest end.   30
My Lord and *Dean*, the Fire forsake;
Dan leaves the Earthly Spade and Rake,
The Loyt'res quake, no Corner hides them,
And Lady *Betty* soundly chides them.
Now Water's brought, and Dinner done,
With Church and King, the Lady's gone;
Not reckoning half an hour we pass,
In talking ore a moderate Glass.
Dan growing drowsy like a Thief,
Steals off to dose away his Beef,   40

15 when] as 1728   17 and] G., 1727, 1728   or 1732, F., 1742   19 Hetero-
clit] G., S. Heteroctil Broadside, 1732, 1742 Heteroctil, 1727 *Heteroclite* 1728
heteroclite F.   20 neither] 1727, 1728, 1732, 1742 Never G., S., F.   23
O'er sees] Or sees G. O'er-sees 1728 O'ersees 1727, 1732, F., 1742   24 spoils]
mars F.   28 Flocks] 1727 folkes G. Folks 1728, 1732, F., 1742   31, 32 forsake
... Rake,] forsakes ... Rakes G.   33 quake, no Corner] quakes no Corners G.
35 Dinner] 1728 Dinners G.   Dinner's 1727, 1732, F., 1742   Now Water
brought and Dinner done; S.   37, 38] *In round brackets* 1732, F., 1742

19. *Heteroclit.* In the seventeenth and
eighteenth centuries the word 'heteroclite' was of fairly common use, as
applied to persons and things, in the
sense of eccentric, exceptional, ab-
normal.

23. *Dragon.* In the *Dramatis Per-*

sonae prefixed to the poem in *Gulliveriana* the allusion is explained as 'the
Boat's Name on the Canal'. Faulkner's
footnote (1735) is '*My Lord Chief
Baron's smaller Boat*'.

31. *My Lord.* Lord Chief Baron
Rochfort.

And this must pass for reading *Hammond*:
While *George*, and *Dean*, go back to Gammon.
George, *Nim* and *Dean*, set out at Four,
And then again, Boys, to the Oar.
But when the Sun goes to the Deep,
Not to disturb him in his Sleep;
Or make a rumbling o'er his Head,
His Candle out, and he a Bed.
We watch his Motions to a Minute,
And leave the Flood when he goes in it: 50
Now stinted in the short'ning Day,
We go to Pray'rs, and then to play
Till Supper comes, and after that,
We sit an hour to drink and chat.
'Tis late, the old and younger Pairs,
By *Adam* lighted walk up stairs:
The weary *Dean* goes to his Chamber,
And *Nim* and *Dan* to Garret clamber:
So when this Circle we have run,
The Curtain falls, and we have done.   60
I might have mention'd several facts,
Like *Episodes* between the Acts;
And tell who loses, and who wins,
Who gets a Cold, who break their Shins.
How *Dan* caught nothing in his Net,
And how his Boat was over set,

42 back to Gammon.] goe to bagammon G.   go to Back-Gammon. 1727,
1732, F., 1742 go to *Back-gammon*; 1728   46–8] *In round brackets* 1732, F.,
1742   50 leave] Leaves G.   51 stinted] Shooted G.   56 walk] walks
1742 57 weary] Wary G.   58 to Garret] to their Garrets G.   60 we have]
all is F.   61] *N.P.* 1728, 1732, F., 1742   63 And tell] Att which G.   64
break] 1728   breaks G., 1727, 1732, F., 1742   65 nothing] *nothing* F.
66 how] *Om.* G.   66 his] 1728 the 1727, 1732, F., 1742

41. *Hammond.* Henry Hammond, the divine, who was elected a fellow of Magdalen College, Oxford, in 1625. Later he received various ecclesiastical preferments of which he was deprived for loyalty to Charles I. Hammond's sister was Sir William Temple's mother; and Temple owed to him his early education. The works by which he is chiefly remembered are his *Practical Catechism* (1644), and his *Paraphrase and Annotations on the New Testament* (1653). He died in 1660. His life was written by John Fell, Bishop of Oxford.

56. *Adam.* The Butler.

For brevity I have retrench'd,
How in the Lake the *Dean* was drench'd:
It would be an Exploit to brag on,
How Valiant *George* rode o'er the *Dragon*;   70
How steady in the Sterne he sat,
And sav'd his Oar, but lost his Hat.
How *Nim*, no Hunter 'ere could match him,
Still brings us Hares when he can catch them:
How skilfully *Dan* mends his Nets,
How Fortune fails him when he sets:
Or how the *Dean* delights to vex
The Ladys, or Lampoon the Sex.
I might have told how oft *Dean Per—l*
Displays his Pedantry unmerciful,   80
How haughtily he lifts his Nose,
To tell what ev'ry School Boy knows:
And with his Finger on his Thumb,
Explaining strikes opposers Dumb;

68 the Lake] a Lake G.   71 Sterne] storm G.   Storm 1728, F.   Stern
1727, 1732, 1742   73] ... (no Hunter e'er could match him,) 1732, F., 1742
74 us] in 1728   78 or] and F.   78] ... and Lampoon their Sex. 1728
79 how oft] him how G.   79, 80] *Om.* 1732, F., 1742   81 haughtily he
lifts] haughty he lifts up G.   haughtily he cocks 1728   Or how our Neighbour
lifts his Nose 1732, F., 1742   83 And] Then 1732, 1742   84 Explaining]
Explaining, 1727, 1728, 1732, F., 1742

68. *How in the Lake the Dean was drench'd*. The Giffard MS. has a side-note 'D. Swift fell out of ye Boat into ye Cannall'.

79. *Dean Per—l*. The name is given in full in the Giffard MS., in the *Miscellanea* of 1727, and in *Gulliveriana*. In the *Miscellanies* of 1732 ll. 79 and 80 were omitted, and l. 81 altered to avoid offence. William Percival, Archdeacon of Cashel, was, in 1713, elected Prolocutor of the Irish Lower House of Convocation, an appointment for which Swift hoped. Later he became Dean of Emly. As noted above, he replied to Swift's satire with 'A Description In Answer to the Journal', in which he ridiculed the mean character of Swift's housekeeping at the Deanery (*cf.* p. 261 n.) and the nature of his conversation. Swift refers to this piece in a letter to Robert Cope of 9 October, 1722: 'Dean Percival has answered the other Dean's journal in Grub Street, justly taxing him for avarice and want of hospitality. Madam Percival absolutely denies all the facts, insists that she never made candles of dripping, that Charley never had the chincough, etc.' (*Corresp.* iii. 141). Nichols, in a note to this letter, as printed in his *Supplement*, 1779, restores the full text of the relevant passage in Swift's poem, which, since 1732, had been printed in the revised version.

And how his Wife that Female Pedant,
But now there need no more be said on't,
Shews all her Secrets of House keeping,
For Candles, how she trucks her Driping;
Was forc'd to send three Miles for Yest,
To brew her Ale, and raise her Paste: 90
Tells ev'ry thing that you can think of,
How she cur'd *Charley* of the Chincough;
What gave her Brats and Pigs the Meazles,
And how her Doves were kill'd by Weezles:
How Jowler howl'd, and what a fright
She had with Dreams the other Night.
But now, since I have gone so far on,
A word or two of Lord Chief *Baron*;
And tell how little weight he sets,
On all Whig Papers, and Gazets: 100
But for the Politicks of Pue,
Thinks ev'ry Syllable is true;
And since he owns the King of *Sweden*
Is dead at last without evading.
Now all his hopes are in the *Czar*,
Why *Muscovy* is not so far,
Down the black Sea, and up the Streights,
And in a Month he's at your Gates:
Perhaps from what the Packet brings,
By *Christmas* we shall see strange things.   110

85 And] 1727   Nor G., 1728   Or 1732, F., 1742   86] *In round brackets*
1727, 1732, F., 1742   91 you] She G. she 1728   92 *Charley*] Tommy
1732, F., 1742   93 Brats] Brat G.   96 with] in 1728   97] *N.P.* 1732,
F., 1742   104 evading.] Invading G. Invading; 1728 evading, 1727,
1732, 1742 evading; F.   106 Why] Why, 1727 Why! 1728 "Why, 1732,
F., 1742   106–10] *Within quotation marks* 1732, F., 1742   108 your]
the G.   109 the] 1727, 1732, F., 1742 this G., 1728

92. *Charley*. Dean Percival's son.
Faulkner's reading, '*Tommy*', is corrected back to '*Charley*' in Swift's
copy of Faulkner, vol. ii, 1737, but,
apparently, not in his hand.

101. *Pue*. *I.e. Pue's Occurrences*, a
daily paper started in Dublin in 1700,
by Richard Pue, on Tory principles.

Pue died in 1758. The paper, however,
continued to 1792. See Gilbert's
Hist. of the City of Dublin, i. 172–5.

103. *King of Sweden*. Charles XII,
who was killed, 11 December, 1718,
by a stray musket-ball at the siege of
Frederikshald.

Why shou'd I tell of Ponds and Drains,
What Carps we met with for our pains:
Of Sparrows tam'd, of Nuts innumerable,
To Choak the Girls, or consume the Rabble;
But you, who are a Scholar, know
How transient all things are below:
How prone to change in human life,
Last Night arriv'd *Clem* and his Wife.
This Grand Event half broke our Measures,
Their Reign began with cruel Seizures;   120
The *Dean* must with his Quilt supply,
The Bed in which these Tyrants lie:
Nim lost his Wig-block, *Dan* his Jordan,
My Lady says she can't afford one;
George is half scar'd out of his Wits,
For *Clem* gets all the dainty bits.
Henceforth expect a different survey,
This House will soon turn topsy turvey;
They talk of further Alterations,
Which causes many Speculations.   130

111] *N.P.* F.   112 met] 1727, 1732, F., 1742   meet G., 1728   113
of] G., 1728   *om.* 1727   and 1732, F., 1742   114 or consume] or to
consume G.   consume 1727, 1728   and to consume-a-Rabble. 1732, 1742
and to consume a Rabble? F.   116 all things are] G., 1727, 1728, F.   are all
Things 1732, *corrected by* Swift *to* all Things are   are all things 1742   117
in] G., 1727   is 1728, 1732, F., 1742   119 half] G., 1727, 1728, 1732,
1742   hath S., F.   123 Wig-block,] Wigg Box G.   Wig-Block, 1727,
1732, F., 1742   *Wig-box*, 1728   124] *In round brackets* 1732, F., 1742
126 dainty] 1727, 1728, 1732, 1742   Tiny G.   tiny S., F.

118. *Clem.* In *Gulliveriana* he is   *town*'. See *Corresp.* ii. 280 n.[6]. Clement
described as 'Mr. Barry, chief   Barry, a distant cousin of Lord Santry,
Favourite and Governour of *Galls-*   lived near Dublin.

A quibbling E L E G Y on the Worshipful Judge *B O A T*.

Faulkner, 1735, ii. 331 (1737, ii. 167).
Miscellanies, . . . Volume the Fifth, 1735, p. 43 (1736, v. 43; 1745, v. 52).

Godfrey Boate, a Judge of the King's Bench, was joined in 1720 with Lord Chief Justice Whitshed in the trial of Edward Waters, the printer of Swift's pamphlet, *A Proposal for the Universal Use of Irish Manufactures* (see p. 236). He would, therefore, incur Swift's hostility. Dr. Ball (*Swift's Verse*, p. 164) suggests, further, that 'the origin of the satire is possibly to be found in the fact that Boate was connected with Swift's great friend Knightly Chetwode, through Chetwode's wife, and as in his will he recommends his executor to compel Chetwode to make a settlement, it may be opined that their relations were not too cordial'. Through her mother Mrs. Chetwode was a niece of Judge Boate.

Boate died in 1721; his will was proved on November the 17th; the composition of Swift's elegy may be placed in the latter part of the year. Faulkner, who first printed the poem, assigned it to 1723, which is unlikely to be correct.

The text is printed from Faulkner's edition of the *Works*, 1735.

TO mournful Ditties, *Clio*, change thy Note,
  Since cruel Fate hath *sunk* our Justice *Boat*;
Why should he *sink* where nothing seem'd to press?
His *Lading* little, and his *Ballast* less.
Tost in the *Waves* of this *tempestuous* World,
At length, his *Anchor* fixt, and *Canvas* furl'd,
To *Lazy-Hill* retiring from his Court,
At his *Ring*'s-*End* he *founders* in the *Port*.
With *Water* fill'd he could no longer *float*,
The common Death of many a stronger *Boat*.   10

2 *Boat*;] 1737   *B—t*; 1735, 1736   *Boat.* 1745

7, 8. *Lazy-Hill . . . Ring's-End.* 'Two *Villages near the Sea, where Boatmen and Seamen live*.'—Faulkner. Rings-end is a seaside village, from the seventeenth to the nineteenth century the chief place for embarking and disembarking the passenger traffic of Dublin. See Ball's *History of Dublin*, Pt. II, pp. 33–42.

9. *With Water fill'd . . .* '*It was said he dy'd of a Dropsy*.'—Faulkner. An allusion also to the trial of Waters.

A Post so fill'd, on Nature's Laws entrenches;
Benches on *Boats* are plac't, not *Boats* on *Benches*.
And yet our *Boat*, how shall I reconcile it?
Was both a *Boat*, and in one Sense a *Pilat*.
With ev'ry *Wind* he *sail'd*, and well could *tack:*
Had many *Pendents*, but abhor'd a *Jack*.
He's gone, although his Friends began to hope
That he might yet be lifted by a *Rope*.

Behold the awful *Bench* on which he sat,
He was as *hard*, and pond'rous *Wood* at that: 20
Yet, when his *Sand* was out, we find at last,
That, Death has *overset* him with a *Blast*.
Our *Boat* is now *sail'd* to the *Stygian* Ferry,
There to supply old *Charon*'s leaky Wherry:
Charon in him will ferry Souls to Hell;
A Trade, our *Boat* had practic'd here so well.
And, *Cerberus* hath ready in his Paws,
Both *Pitch* and *Brimstone* to fill up his *Flaws*;
Yet, spight of Death and Fate, I here maintain
We may place *Boat* in his old *Post* again.   30
The Way is thus; and well deserves your Thanks:
Take the three strongest of his broken Planks,
Fix them on high, conspicuous to be seen,
Form'd like the Triple-Tree near *Stephen*'s-Green;
And, when we view it thus, with Thief at End on't,
We'll cry; look, here's our *Boat*, and there's the *Pen-*
dent.

---

14 *Pilat.*] *Pilot.* 1735, 1736, 1737, 1745   26 had] 1737   hath 1735,
1736, 1745

16. *Had many Pendents, but*
abhor'd a Jack. A pendent, pendant,
or pennant is a tapering flag; a jack
is a distinguishing flag, especially one
flown from the jack-staff at the bow.
Cf. 'Union-Jack'. Further 'Jack' was
a 'Cant Word for a Jacobite'.—
Faulkner.
   26. Faulkner's note is, '*In hanging*
People as a Judge'.
   34. *Stephen's-Green.* '*Where the*
Dublin *Gallows stands.*'—Faulkner.

The EPITAPH.

HERE lies *Judge* Boat *within a Coffin.*
Pray gentle-Folks forbear your Scoffing.
A Boat *a Judge! yes, where's the Blunder?*
A wooden *Judge is no such Wonder.*   40
And in his Robes, you must agree,
No Boat *was better* deckt *than He.*
'Tis needless to describe him fuller.
In short, he was an able Sculler.

The B A N K thrown down.

To an Excellent New TUNE.

  Although this ballad has not hitherto been included in any edition of Swift's works there seems good reason to believe that it came from his hand. His opposition to proposals for the establishment of a National Bank in Ireland has been stated on p. 242. 'The Bank thrown down' is certainly not unworthy of him; the movement and style are reminiscent of his manner; the references to Demar and the South Sea are suggestive; and it was printed as a broadside by Harding. Ball (*Swift's Verse*, p. 164) accepted the ballad as undoubtedly by Swift. It is therefore here printed, with some hesitation, as probably authentic.

  The ballad evidently belongs to December, 1721, when the scheme for a National Bank was finally rejected by both Houses of the Irish Parliament, or to the beginning of 1722.

  The text is given as it appears on the original broadside, copies of which may be found in the British Museum, 839. m. 23 (93); Trinity College, Dublin, Press A. 7. 6 (2); the Gilbert Collection, Dublin, Newenham Pamphlets, 1 (28); Rothschild, No. 2069.

39 *Blunder?*] 1735, 1736, 1745   *Blunder!* 1737

44. *Sculler.* Faulkner's footnote may be attributed to Swift:—'Query, *Whether the Author meant* Scholar, *and wilfully mistook?*'

PRay, what is this BANK of which the Town Rings?
  The BANKS of a River I know are good Things,
But a Pox o' those BANKS that choak up the SPRINGS.
  Some Mischief is Brewing, the Project smells Rank,
  To shut out the *River* by raising the BANK.

The DAMS and the WEIRS must all be your own,
You get all the FISH, and others get none,
We look for a SALMON, you leave us a *Stone*.
  But Thanks to the HOUSE, the Projectors look blank,
  And Thanks to the MEMBERS that Kickt down the
  BANK.   10

This BANK is to make us a New Paper Mill,
This Paper they say, by the Help of a Quill,
The whole Nations Pockets with Money will fill.
  But we doubt that our Purses will quickly grow lank,
  If nothing but Paper comes out of this BANK.

'Tis happy to see the whole Kingdom in *Rags*,
For *Rags* will make *Paper*, and Pa-ba-ba-brags,
This Paper will soon make us richer than *Crags*.
  From a bo-bo-bo-Boy he pursues his old Hank,
  And now he runs mad for a ba-ba-ba-BANK.   20

Oh! then but to see how the *Beggars* will Vapour,
For Beggars have *Rags* and Rags will make Paper,
And Paper makes Money, and what can be cheaper?
  Methinks I now see them so jovial and crank,
  All riding on Horseback to *Hell* and the BANK.

But the *Cobler* was angry, and swore he had rather
As they did in old Times, make Money of *Leather*,
For then he could *Coyn* and could *Cobble* together;
  And then he could pay for the Liquor he drank
  With the Scrap of a *Sole*, and a Fig for the BANK.   30

18. *Crags*. James Craggs, 1657–
1721, a man of humble origin, who,
entering the household of Marlborough, reached position and wealth.
In 1715 he became joint postmaster-
general with Charles, fourth Lord
Cornwallis. He was involved in the
South Sea Company, though not a
director, and died, under suspicion
of suicide, 16 March, 1721. His estate
was valued at one million and a half.
See p. 191 n.

By a Parliament Man when the *Farmer* was told,
That *Paper* would quickly be dearer than *Gold*,
He wonder'd for how much an Inch 'twould be Sold:
 Then Plodding, he thought on a whimsical Prank
 To turn to small Money a Bill on the BANK.

For nicely computing the Price by Retail,
He found he could purchase Two Tankards of Ale
With a Scrap of Bank Paper the Breadth of his Nail;
 But the *Tapster* well Cudgell'd him both Side and
  Flank,
 And made him to Curse the poor innocent BANK. 40

The Ghost of old *D—mer*, who left not his Betters,
When it heard of a BANK appear'd to his Debtors,
And lent them for Money the *Backs* of his Letters:
 His Debtors they wonder'd to find him so frank,
 For *old Nick* gave the Papers the *Mark* of the BANK.

In a *Chancery* Bill your Attorney engages,
For so many Six-pences, so many *Pages*,
But Six-pence a *Letter* is monstrous high Wages:
 Those that dropt in the *South-Sea* discover'd this
  Plank,
 By which they might Swimmingly *land* on a BANK. 50

But the *Squire* he was cunning and found what they
  meant,
That a Pack of sly Knaves should get fifty per Cent,
While his Tenants in *Paper* must pay him his Rent:
 So for their *Quack-Bills* he knows whom to thank,
 For those are but *Quacks*, who *mount* on a BANK.

41. *D—mer*. See 'Elegy on Demar', p. 232.

The Progress of Marriage. Jany. 1721-2

Swift's autograph; Forster Collection, South Kensington (No. 517).
Works of Jonathan Swift, ed. Deane Swift, 1765, 4to, viii (2), 218; 8vo, xvi. 343. [Ref. 1765.]
Faulkner, 1765, xiii. 346. [Ref. F.]

What appears to be the first draft of this poem, with many corrections and interlineations, is preserved in the Forster collection. It is written on three folded half-sheets. The wrapper is blank on the inner side. On the front recto Swift has written the title and date: 'Progress of Marriage Jan. 1721–2.' On the back verso of wrapper the title appears twice and the date once. The text of the poem occupies eight pages. An attempt has been made, so far as is possible apart from facsimile reproduction, to present the author's corrections.

The marriage satirized was that of Dean Pratt to Lady Philippa Hamilton. Pratt died 5 Dec., 1721. He had only been married about twelve months. Writing to Knightley Chetwode, 9 Dec., 1721, Swift comments on Pratt's intention of setting up town and country establishments, and 'great equipages'. He adds, 'What a ridiculous thing is man' (*Corresp.* iii. 108).

Benjamin Pratt entered Trinity College, Dublin, while Swift was an undergraduate there. He was a man of considerable fortune, was elected a fellow, and became Provost in 1710. He was accomplished and possessed musical tastes (Delany, *Observations*, p. 190). In 1717 he was appointed Dean of Down. About a year before his death he married Philippa, daughter of the sixth Earl of Abercorn. He was fond of society, something of a *bon vivant*, and incurred criticism for spending too much of his time in London instead of attending to his duties as Provost. Swift was on friendly terms with him. See also pp. 966 n., 1099.

The poem is here given from Swift's manuscript draft. The printed version of Deane Swift, 1765, shows no striking variants.

[p. 1]   Ætatis suæ fifty two
          A rich Divine began to woo
          A handsome young imperious *Girl*
          Nearly related to an Earl.

Scorings-out and first readings:
    2. reverend Dean resolved   2. grave   4. Philippa daughter

4. *Nearly related to an Earl.* Swift first wrote 'Philippa daughter to an Earl', giving the lady's real name (see introductory notes above); but,

Her Parents and her Friends consent,
The Couple to the Temple went:
They first invite the Cyprian Queen,
'Twas answerd, she would not be seen.
The Graces next, and all the Muses
Were bid in form, but sent Excuses: 10
Juno attended at the Porch
With farthing Candle for a Torch,
While Mistress Iris held her Train,
The faded Bow distilling Rain.
Then Hebe came and took her Place
But showed no more than half her Face
Whate'er these dire fore-bodings meant,
In Mirth the wedding-day was spent.
The *Wedding-day*, you take me right,
I promise nothing for the Night: 20
The Bridegroom dresst, to make a Figure,
Assumes an artificiall Vigor;
[p. 2] A flourisht Night-cap on, to grace
His ruddy, wrinckled, smirking Face,
Like the faint red upon a Pippin
Half wither'd by a Winters keeping . .
    And, thus set out this happy Pair,
The Swain is rich, the Nymph is fair;
But, which I gladly would forget,
The Swain is old, the Nymph Coquette.   30
Both from the Goal together start;
Scarce run a Step before they part;

Scorings-out and first readings:
5. The   7. first *on line, and* first *above line*   9. *Imperfectly legible*
variants struck through.   First written: And then the Graces and the Muses
14. had wet with Rain   18. Joy   18. Marriage   19. *Marriage*
24. smiling *written above* smirking, *which is not struck through*   26. with

17] *N.P.* 1765, F.   17 these] those 1765, F.   24 smirking] smiling
1765, F.   29 which] what 1765, F., *The MS. is not clear*

thinking better of it, altered her name   23. *A flourisht Night-cap. I.e.*
to Jane, and changed his text in this   flowered, ornamented.
line.

No common Ligament that binds
The various Textures of their Minds,
Their Thoughts, and Actions, Hopes, and Fears,
Less corresponding than their Years.
Her Spouse desires his Coffee soon,
She rises to her Tea at noon.
While He goes out to cheapen Books,
She at the Glass consults her Looks   40
While Betty's buzzing at her Ear,
Lord, what a Dress these Parsons wear,
So odd a Choice, how could she make,
Wish't him a Coll'nell for her Sake.

[p. 3] Then on her fingers Ends she counts
Exact to what his Age amounts,
The Dean, she heard her Uncle say
Is fifty, if he be a Day;
His ruddy Cheeks are no Disguise;
You see the Crows feet round his Eyes.   50
At one she rambles to the Shops
To cheapen Tea, and talk with Fops.
Or calls a Councel of her Maids
And Tradesmen, to compare Brocades.
Her weighty Morning Bus'ness o'er
Sits down to Dinner just at four;
Minds nothing that is done or said,
Her ev'ning *Work* so fills her Head;
The *Dean*, who us'd to dine at one,
Is maukish, and his Stomach gone;   60
In threed-bare Goun, would scarce a louse hold,
Looks like the Chaplain of the Houshold,
Beholds her from the Chaplain's Place
In French brocades and Flanders Lace;

Scorings-out and first readings:
37. The *Dean*   39. The *Dean*   41. tatling   48. sixty   49. Looks
64. silver Stuffs

41 at] in 1765, F.   42 wear,] wear! 1765, F.   43 make,] make ? 1765,
F.   48 fifty,] sixty, 1765, F.   51] *N.P.* 1765, F.   62 the Household,] his household, 1765, F.

[p. 4]   He wonders what employs her Brain;
         But never asks, or asks in vain;
         His Mind is full of other Cares,
         And in the sneaking Parsons Airs
         Computes, that half a Parish Dues
         Will hardly find his Wife in Shoes.   70
         Canst thou imagine, dull Divine,
         'Twill gain her Love to make her fine?
         Hath she no other wants beside?
         You raise Desire as well as Pride,
         Enticing Coxcombs to adore,
         And teach her to despise thee more
         If in her Coach she'll condescend
         To place him at the hinder End
         Her Hoop is hoist above his Nose,
         His odious Goun would soil her Cloaths,   80
         And drops him at the Church, to pray
         While she drives on to see the Play.
         He like an orderly Divine
         Comes home a quarter after nine,
         And meets her hasting to the Ball,
         Her Chairmen push him from the Wall:
         He enters in, and walks up Stairs,
         And calls the Family to Prayrs,
[p. 5]   Then goes alone to take his Rest
         In bed, where he can spare her best.   90
         At five the Footmen make a Din,
         Her Ladyship is just come in,
         The Masquerade began at two,
         She stole away with much ado,
         And shall be chid this afternoon
         for leaving company so soon;

Scorings-out and first readings:
74. To feed her want [?]
                    77, 78. If by a more than usuall Grace
                            She leads him in her Chariot Place
80. For fear his Goun should   84. three quarters   87. The Dean gets
in,   88. Then *and* And *both struck through*

            71] *N.P.* 1765, F.   77] *N.P.* 1765, F.

She'll say, and she may truly say't
She can't abide to stay out late.

But now, though scarce a twelvemonth marry'd,
His Lady has twelve times miscarry'd,   100
The Cause, alas, is quickly guesst,
The Town has whisper'd round the Jest:
Think on some Remedy in time
You find His Rev'rence past his Prime,
Already dwindled to a Lath;
No other way but try the Bath:
For Venus rising from the Ocean
Infus'd a strong prolifick Potion,
That mixt with Achelous Spring,
The *horned* Floud, as Poets sing: 110
[p. 6] Who with an English Beauty smitten
Ran under Ground from Greece to Brittain,
The genial Virtue with him brought,
And gave the Nymph a plenteous Draught;
Then fled, and left his Horn behind
For Husbands past their Youth to find;
The Nymph who still with Passion burnd,
Was to a boiling Fountain turn'd,
Where Childless wives crowd ev'ry morn
To drink in Achilous' Horn.   120
And here the Father often gains
That Title by anothers Pains.

Scorings-out and first readings:
97. can   98. endure   100. Poor Lady Jane has thrice   101.
Town *for* Cause *struck out*   104. The *Dean,* you see, is
Struck out after 120.
                    Or bathe beneath the Cross their limbs
                    Where fruitfull Matter chiefly Swims,

100 His Lady has twelve times] Poor Lady Jane has thrice 1765, F.   109
Achelous] Achelaus Achelaus' F., 1765   120 Achilous'] Achelaus 1765
Achelaus' F.

109, 120. Acheloüs was god of the   Hercules had broken off, he received
river of that name in Epirus. In   the cornucopia of Amalthea. See
exchange for his own horn, which   Ovid, *Met. Lib.* ix.

Hither, though much against his Grain,
The *Dean* has carry'd Lady Jane
He for a while would not consent,
But vow'd his Money all was spent;
His Money spent! a clownish Reason?
And, must my Lady slip her Season?
The Doctor with a double Fee
Was *brib'd* to make the *Dean* agree   130
    Here, all Diversions of the Place
Are *proper* in my Lady's Case
[p. 7] With which she patiently complyes,
Merely because her Friends advise;
His Money and her Time employs
In musick, Raffling-rooms, and Toys,
Or in the *cross-bath* seeks an Heir
Since others oft have found one there;
Where if the Dean by chance appears
It shames his Cassock and his Years   140
He keeps his Distance in the Gallery
Till banisht by some Coxcombs Raillery;
For, it would his Character Expose
To bath among the Belles and Beaux.

    So have I seen within a Pen
Young Ducklings, fostered by a Hen;
But when let out, they run and muddle
As Instinct leads them, in a Puddle;

Scorings-out and first readings:
123, 124. *Apparently these lines originally ended* will, *and* Phil   127. *Was
ever such a foolish*   139, 140. *At first writing these lines followed line* 134

123 his] the 1765, F.   127 Reason?] reason! 1765, F.   143 it would]
'twould 1765, F.

137. *Or in the cross-bath* . . . 'On the
west side of Stall-street, and about
three hundred feet from the front of
the new baths, is the *Cross Bath*, of
a triangular form, and so denominated
from a very curious cross or pillar,
erected in it by John Earl of Melfort,
secretary of state to King James the
Second, on the Queen's conceiving
after the use of the waters.' John
Collinson's *History of Somerset*, 1791,
vol. i, *Bath*, p. 41. A plate facing
p. 315 of R. Warner's *History of
Bath*, 1801, gives an illustration of the
cross. The cross was taken down in
1783. *Cf.* also the reference in *The
Tatler*, No. 24.

The sober Hen not born to swim
With mournful Note clocks round the Brim.   150

The Dean with all his best Endeavour
Gets not an Heir, but gets a Feaver;
A Victim to the last Essays
Of Vigor in declining Days.
He dyes, and leaves his mourning Mate
(What could he less,) his whole Estate.

[p. 8]   The Widow goes through all her Forms;
New Lovers now will come in Swarms.
Oh, may I see her soon dispensing
Her Favors to some broken Ensign   160
Him let her Marry for his Face,
And only Coat of tarnish't Lace;
To turn her Naked out of Doors,
And spend her Joynture on his Whores:
But for a parting Present leave her
A rooted Pox to last for ever.

A

SATIRICAL ELEGY

On the DEATH of a late

FAMOUS GENERAL.

The Gentleman's Magazine, xxxiv. 244, May, 1764. [Ref. *G.M.*]
Works of Jonathan Swift, ed. Deane Swift, 1765, 4to, viii (2), 205;
    8vo, xvi. 327.
Faulkner, 1765, xiii. 333.

Scorings-out and first readings:
150. (*a*) Mean while stands chuckling at the Brim.   (*b*) Pining and chuckling
at the Brim.   (*c*) walks.   151. *The word* Dean *is partly struck through, but
no correction is made*   156. The best of Heirs his whole Estate

150 clocks] clucks 1765, F.   156 (What could he less,)] (What could he
less?) 1765, F.   160 Ensign] ensign! 1765, F.

This ungenerous attack on Marlborough appears first to have been printed in *The Gentleman's Magazine*, 1764. It was included in the *Works* by Deane Swift in the following year. The *Gentleman's Magazine* copy may have been obtained from Deane Swift.

The Duke died on the 16th of June, 1722. For Swift's attitude towards Marlborough see notes introductory to 'The Fable of Midas', p. 155.

The text of the poem is given as printed by Deane Swift.

HIS Grace! impossible! what dead!
Of old age too, and in his bed!
And could that Mighty Warrior fall?
And so inglorious, after all!
Well, since he's gone, no matter how,
The last loud trump must wake him now:
And, trust me, as the noise grows stronger,
He'd wish to sleep a little longer.
And could he be indeed so old
As by the news-papers we're told?   10
Threescore, I think, is pretty high;
'Twas time in conscience he should die.
This world he cumber'd long enough;
He burnt his candle to the snuff;
And that's the reason, some folks think,
He left behind *so great a s - - - k.*
Behold his funeral appears,
Nor widow's sighs, nor orphan's tears,
Wont at such times each heart to pierce,
Attend the progress of his herse.   20
But what of that, his friends may say,
He had those honours in his day.
True to his profit and his pride,
He made them weep before he dy'd.

Come hither, all ye empty things,
Ye bubbles rais'd by breath of Kings;
Who float upon the tide of state,
Come hither, and behold your fate.

3 fall?] fall, *G.M.*   8 He'd] He'll *G.M.*   10 told?] told! *G.M.*   16
s - - - k.] *stink. G.M.*

Let pride be taught by this rebuke,
How very mean a thing's a Duke;   30
From all his ill-got honours flung,
Turn'd to that dirt from whence he sprung.

Upon the horrid *Plot* discovered by *Harlequin* the B ---- of *R*—'s *French* Dog.

In a Dialogue between a *Whig* and a *Tory*.

Written in the Year 1722.

Faulkner, 1735, ii. 409 (1737, ii. 161).
Miscellanies, . . . *Volume the Fifth*, 1735, p. 197 (1736, v. 201; 1745, v. 44).

Francis Atterbury, Bishop of Rochester, was in 1722 committed to the Tower, charged with plotting for the restoration of the Stuarts. He was deprived of his ecclesiastical offices and banished the kingdom.

Towards the end of chapter vi, Part III of *Gulliver's Travels*, Swift ridicules the proceedings brought against Atterbury, and, in particular, the attempt to extract secret meanings from his correspondence. 'Artists of Dexterity' in this practice, Swift suggests, may read a reference to 'a lame Dog' to mean 'an Invader'. Atterbury received from France the present of a dog which had its leg broken on the journey. It was mentioned under feigned names in his correspondence. The poem also refers to this incident. See *The Weekly Journal: or, British Gazetteer*, 1 Sept., and *The Freeholder's Journal*, 5 Sept., 1722, which contain references to Atterbury's examination.

The poem was first printed by Faulkner in vol. ii of his edition of the *Works*, 1735. When vol. v of the Pope and Swift *Miscellanies* was printing in London in the same year it was at first either overlooked or withheld for political reasons. It does not appear in the table of contents to the volume, and is printed on two supplemental leaves at the end of the verse and just before the prose section. These leaves are signed [O 3] and [O 4], pp. *197–*200, following upon O 3 and O 4, pp. 197–200.

The text follows Faulkner's edition of 1735.

I Ask'd a *Whig* the other Night,
  How came this wicked Plot to Light:
He answer'd, that a *Dog* of late
Inform'd a Minister of State.
Said I, from thence I nothing know;
For, are not all Informers so?
A Villain, who his Friend betrays,
We style him by no other Phrase;
And so a perjur'd *Dog* denotes
Porter, and *Prendergast*, and *Oates*.   10
And forty others I could name—
    Whig. But you must know this Dog was lame.
    Tory. A weighty Argument indeed;
Your *Evidence* was *lame*. Proceed:
Come, help your *lame Dog o'er the Style.*
    Whig. Sir, you mistake me all this while:
I mean a *Dog*, without a Joke,
Can howl, and bark, but never spoke.
    Tory. I'm still to seek which *Dog* you mean;
Whether Curr *Plunket*, or Whelp *Skean*,   20

2 Light:] 1737   Light? 1735, 1736, 1745   4 Minister] 1737 M—r 1735,
1736, 1745   10 *Prendergast*,] 1735, 1736, 1745 PRENDERGAST, 1737
11] *Paragraphs divided by a space,* 1737

10. *Porter, and Prendergast, and Oates.* George Porter, once a captain in Slingsby's horse, and Thomas Prendergast, or Pendergrass, were two conspirators implicated in the plot to assassinate William III, in 1696, by waylaying his coach. Prendergast informed the government; and was summoned to an audience with the King. He was rewarded, created a baronet in 1699, and entered the army. He served with distinction, was promoted brigadier-general, and fell mortally wounded at the battle of Malplaquet. Prendergast's son, the second baronet, was, later, lampooned by Swift in 'On Noisy Tom' (see pp. 824–6); and both father and son were attacked in 'The Legion Club' (see pp. 831–2). George Porter was arrested among conspirators in the same plot, but procured his pardon by turning King's evidence. Titus Oates was the notorious perjurer and informer who concocted the story of a Popish plot to assassinate Charles II, and to seize the reins of government, 1678.

20. *Whether Curr Plunket, or Whelp Skean.* John Plunket and Skin, or Skinner, were Jacobite agents implicated in the plot for which Atterbury was brought to trial. The proceedings in the impeachment of Atterbury were directed 'against John Plunkett, George Kelly, alias Johnson, and Dr. Francis Atterbury, Bishop of Rochester, upon Bills of Pains and Penalties for a Treasonable Conspiracy'.—Howell's *State Trials*, xvi. 323. Plunket was arrested in January,

An *English* or an *Irish* Hound;
Or t'other *Puppy* that was drown'd,
Or *Mason* that abandon'd Bitch:
Then pray be free, and tell me which:
For, ev'ry Stander-by was marking
That all the Noise they made was *barking*:
You pay them well; the *Dogs* have got
Their *Dogs-heads in a Porridge-pot*:
And 'twas but just; for, wise Men say,
That, *every Dog must have his Day*.   30
Dog W— laid a Quart of *Nog* on't,
He'd either *make a Hog or Dog on't*,
And look't since he has got his Wish,
As if he had *thrown down a Dish*.
Yet, this I dare foretel you from it,
He'll soon *return to his own Vomit*.
   Whig. Besides, this horrid Plot was found
By *Neno* after he was drown'd.
   Tory. Why then the Proverb is not right,
Since you can teach *dead Dogs to bite*.   40
   Whig. I prov'd my Proposition full:
But, *Jacobites* are strangely dull.
Now, let me tell you plainly, Sir,
Our Witness is a real *Curr*,
A *Dog* of Spirit for his Years,
Has twice two Legs, two hanging Ears;

---

23 *Mason*] *Mason*, 1737, 1745   *M—n*, 1735, 1736   25 marking] 1735, 1736, 1745   marking, 1737   31 *W—*] 1745   — 1735, 1736   *W—le* 1737   38 *Neno*] 1735, 1736   *Neyno* 1737   *Neynoe* 1745

1723, brought to trial, and confined as a state prisoner in the Tower. He died in 1738. For Kelly see note on l. 47 below.

22. *Or t'other Puppy that was drown'd*. This was Philip Neynoe, named in l. 38, a clerk employed by Kelly. He was drowned while attempting to escape. *State Trials*, xvi. 326.

23. *Mason*. Elizabeth Mason was a brothel keeper to whom Christopher Layer, a great scoundrel and Jacobite conspirator, entrusted incriminating papers. Layer was betrayed, brought to trial on 21 November, 1722, condemned and executed at Tyburn, 17 May, 1723.

31. *W—*. Walpole.

His Name is *Harlequin*, I wot,
And that's a Name in ev'ry *Plot:*
Resolv'd to save the *British* Nation,
Though *French* by Birth and Education: 50
His Correspondence plainly dated,
Was all *decypher'd*, and *translated*.
His Answers were exceeding pretty
Before the secret wise Committee;
Confess't as plain as he could bark;
Then with his Fore-foot set his *Mark*.

 Tory. Then all this while have I been bubbled;
I thought it was a *Dog in Doublet:*
The Matter now no longer sticks;
For Statesmen never want *Dog-tricks.*   60
But, since it was a real *Curr*,
And not a *Dog* in Metaphor,
I give you Joy of the Report,
That he's to have a Place at C—t.

 Whig. Yes, and a Place he will grow rich in;
A Turn-spit in the R—l Kitchen.
Sir, to be plain, I tell you what;
We had Occasion for a Plot;
And, when we found the *Dog* begin it,
We guess't the *B*—'s *Foot was in it.*   70

 Tory. I own it was a dang'rous Project;
And you have prov'd it by *Dog-Logick.*

55 could] 1737, 1745 can 1735, 1736 66 R—l Kitchen.] 1737 R— K—.
1735, 1736, 1745 70 *B*—'s] *B*—'s 1735, 1736 *B*---*p's* 1737 Bishop's
1745

47. *Harlequin.* George Kelly (see
note on l. 20 above), a Non-juror,
who went by the name of James
Johnson, was entrusted with letters
from the Earl of Mar to Atterbury.
Kelly lodged with a Mrs. Barnes. A
paper found in her house mentioned a
lame dog called Harlequin dispatched
from France to a certain Mr. Illington.
Mrs. Barnes, under examination,
innocently admitted that she had
taken charge of a dog for the Bishop
of Rochester. Atterbury's part in the
treasonable correspondence was thereby confirmed, for Illington was the
name used by him in a letter to Mar,
and by Mar in his reply. See Dean
Beeching's *Francis Atterbury*, pp. 279,
294–6, and Howell's *State Trials*,
xvi. 376–7.

64. *C*—*t.* Court.
66. *R*—*l.* Royal.
70. *B*—'s. Bishop's.

Sure such Intelligence between
A *Dog* and *B*— ne'er was seen,
Till you began to change the Breed;
Your *B*—*s* all are *D*—*gs* indeed.

T H E   S T O R M ;
M I N E R V A' S Petition.

Manuscript in the Huntington Library, San Marino, California, in a
volume of manuscripts and printed broadsides (113198–259). [Ref. H.]
*Poems on Several Occasions, from Genuine Manuscripts ... London: Printed
for J. Bromage, ... 1749. p. 1.*
*A Supplement to the Works of the Most Celebrated Minor Poets.... London:
Printed for F. Cogan, ... M DCC L. iii. Pt. 3, p. 79.*
*A Supplement to the Works of Dr. Swift. London: Printed for F. Cogan,
... 1752. p. 127.*
Faulkner, 1762, x. 321; 1763, xi. 439.
Works of Dr. Jonathan Swift, 1762, xiv. 197; 4to, 1764, vii (2), 182;
8vo, 1764, xiv. 307.

Swift's satire is directed against Josiah Hort, for whom see *D.N.B.*
xxvii. 388. He was educated as a Nonconformist; but soon came over to
the Church of England. In 1709 he became chaplain to Lord Wharton
in Ireland, which paved the way to ecclesiastical preferment. He was
successively Dean of Cloyne, of Ardagh; Bishop of Ferns and Leighlin,
1721, Kilmore and Ardagh, 1727; and Archbishop of Tuam from 1742
to the year of his death, 1751.

Swift's attack was unmerited; and later he was reconciled to Hort.
See notes on 'On a Printer's being sent to Newgate', pp. 822–3.

In this poem Hort is referred to as 'Bishop *Judas*'; but it is uncertain
whether he is the subject of the poem of 1732, so named (see p. 806).
The epigram, 'On seeing a worthy Prelate go out of Church' (see p. 808)
is also directed at Hort.

The references to the recent elevation of Hort to the episcopal bench,
and to Berkeley's project for the Bermudas, fix the date of 'The Storm' at
about 1722, apart from the fact (see below) that Hort and Berkeley crossed
to England, in stormy weather, in December, 1722.

No broadside or early separate edition of the poem can be traced. It was

74 *B*—] B— 1735, 1736, 1745   *B*---*p* 1737   76 *B*—*s*] — 1735, 1736   *B*---*ps*
1737   Bishops 1745

first collected and assigned to Swift by Bromage, who professed to be
working from 'Genuine Manuscripts'. His text (and that of Cogan) was
not followed by Faulkner in 1762. Faulkner's text, followed by the London
editions, is manifestly more correct; and is here reprinted. The readings
of Bowyer (1762), editor of the London edition of the same year as
Faulkner's, are indicated only when they differ from him.

There is a manuscript copy of uncertain date and hand in the Huntington Library. This manuscript has several readings which do not appear in
any printed edition. It is probable that Swift had no intention of printing
the poem at the time of its composition owing to its libellous character. Doubtless a number of contemporary manuscript copies passed from hand to hand.

The occasion of the poem is sufficiently explained by the following
excerpt from *The Freeholder's Journal* for 12 December, 1722:

'The King's Yatch from Dublin to Chester, met with a violent Storm at
Sea, in which the Guns were thrown overboard, and the Vessel was drove
into Scotland, Dr. Hort Bishop of Leighlin and Fernes, Mr. Maddox,
Secretary to the Lords Justices of Ireland, Dr. Berkley, an Irish Dean,
together with several other Persons of Distinction, were on Board, who are
now on their Road to London.' See also *Letters . . . to and from William
Nicolson*, 1809, ii. 555.

P ALLAS, a Goddess chaste and wise,
Descending lately from the Skies,
To *Neptune* went, and begg'd in Form
He'd give his Orders for a Storm;
A Storm, to drown that Rascal —,
And she wou'd kindly thank him for't.
A Wretch! whom E - *gl* - *sh* Rogues to spite her,
Had lately honour'd with a M—tre.

THE God, who favour'd her Request,
Assur'd her he wou'd do his best: 10
But *Venus* had been there before
Pleaded the B— lov'd a W—,

1 a] the H.   3 and begg'd] to beg H.   5 —,] H— H. *and throughout H—t,
1749, 1750, 1752 and throughout*   7 A] The 1749, 1750, 1752   7 E - gl - sh
Rogues] Irish Knaves 1749 *Irish . . .* 1750, 1752   9] *No break* 1749, 1750,
1752   9 THE God,] Neptune H.   9 who favour'd] to favour 1749, 1750, 1752
11] *N.P.* 1749, 1750, 1752   12 B— . . . W—,] Bishop . . . whore, H.

7. *E - gl - sh Rogues*. The manuscript
copy from which Bromage printed in
1749 read 'Irish Knaves', which can
hardly be what Swift wrote, for one of
his characteristic complaints was the
bestowal of Irish preferments by the
Crown upon English ecclesiastics.

And had enlarg'd her Empire wide,
He own'd no Deity beside.
At Sea, or Land, if e'er you found him,
Without a Mistress, hang or drown him.
Since *B - rn - t*'s Death, the —'s Bench,
'Till — arriv'd ne'er kept a Wench;
If — must sink, she grieves to tell it,
She'll not have left one single Prelate:　　20
For to say Truth, she did intend him,
Elect of *Cyprus* in *commendam*.
And since her Birth the Ocean gave her,
She could not doubt her Uncle's Favour.

THEN *Proteus* urg'd the same Request,
But half in Earnest, half in Jest;
Said he — "Great Sovereign of the Main,
"To drown him all Attempts are vain,
"— can assume more Forms than I,
"A Rake, a Bully, Pimp, or Spy.　　30

15 At Sea, or Land, if e'er you found] By Sea and Land where e're you find
H.　　17, 18] *Om.* H.　　17 *B - rn - t*'s...—'s] *B—t*'s... Bishop's 1749, 1750,
1752　　21 For to say Truth,] For to tell truth, H.　And she must own, 1749,
1750, 1752　　22 of] for 1749, 1750, 1752　　23, 24] *Om.* H.　　25 urg'd]
made 1749, 1750, 1752　　29 "— ... Forms] He ... Shapes, 1749, 1750,
1752　　30 a Bully,] or Bully, H., 1749, 1750, 1752

17. *Since B - rn - t's Death.* Gilbert
Burnet, Bishop of Salisbury, died on
the 17th of March, 1715, about seven
years before the date of 'The Storm'.
Swift's first pamphlet, *A Discourse of
the Contests and Dissensions between
the Nobles and Commons in Athens and
Rome*, won him the notice and
friendship of Burnet; but as Swift
swung over to the Tory party the
Whiggish and latitudinarian principles
of the Bishop became obnoxious to
him. His attack on Burnet in *A
Preface to the Bishop of Sarum's
Introduction*, 1713, is one of his most
successful pieces of satirical humour.
Burnet was married three times, but the
insinuation of Swift's line was wholly
unjustified. *Cf.* pp. 1148-9.

22. *Elect of Cyprus, in commendam.*
In commendam was an ancient manner
of holding ecclesiastical benefices,
abolished in 1836. On the vacancy of
a benefice by preferment of the holder
it was *commended* by the Crown to
another, frequently the bishop of a
poorer see, until a new incumbent
was appointed. Such a living was said
to be held *in commendam*.

"Can creep, or run, can fly or swim,
"All Motions are alike to him:
"Turn him adrift, and you shall find
"He knows to sail with ev'ry Wind;
"Or, throw him overboard, he'll ride
"As well against, as with the Tide,
"But, *Pallas*, you've apply'd too late,
"For 'tis decreed by *Jove* and Fate,
"That *Ireland* must be soon destroy'd,
"And who but — can be employ'd?   40
"You need not then have been so pert,
"In sending *Bolton* to *Clonfert*.
"I found you did it by your Grinning;
"Your Business is to mind your Spinning.
"But how you came to interpose,
"In making B—s, no one knows.
"And if you must have your Petition,
"There's *Berkeley* in the same Condition;
"Look, there he stands, and 'tis but just
"If one must drown, the other must;   50

31 "Can creep, or run, can,fly or swim,] Can run, or creep, or fly, or swim, 1749,
1750, 1752   37 "But, *Pallas*, you've apply'd] And *Pallas*, you apply 1749,
750, 1752   39 soon] *Om.* H.   40 "And who but — can] And who but
H— must H.   Then who but *H—t*, should 1749, 1750, 1752   41 then have
been] therefore be 1749, 1750, 1752   42 "In] On 1749, 1750, 1752   43
found] find 1749, 1750, 1752, *and* Faulkner 1763   45 "But] And 1749, 1750,
1752   46 B—s,] Bishops, H.   46 one] man H., 1749, 1750, 1752   46–7]
Between these lines the following additional couplet appears in 1749, 1750, 1752:
              Or who regarded your Report?
              For never were you seen at Court.
47 "And] But H., 1749, 1750, 1752   48 There's] Here's 1749, 1750, 1752
49 "Look, there] Look how 1749, 1750, 1752   50 "If one must drown, the
other must;] If *H—t* must drown the *Doctor* must: 1749, 1750, 1752

41. *pert.* The word is here employed
in the sense, once common, of quick,
prompt, ready.
    42. *In sending Bolton to Clonfert.*
Theophilus Bolton, Bishop of Elphin
and Clonfert, and later Archbishop
of Cashel, should not be confused with
the John Bolton who received the
Deanery of Derry in 1700, when Swift
thought it was his due. See intro-

ductory notes to 'The Discovery',
p. 61. Theophilus Bolton won Swift's
regard by his opposition to Wood's
halfpence, and to the Bills of Residence
and Division (see notes on 'On the
Irish Bishops' and 'On the Archbishop
of Cashel and Bettesworth', pp. 801–
2, 804, 818).
    48, 52. *There's Berkeley . . . We'll give
you Berkeley for Bermudas.* George

"But, if you'll leave us B—p *Judas*,
"We'll give you *Berkeley* for *Bermudas*.
"Now, if 'twill gratify your Spight,
"To put him in a plaguy Fright,
"Although 'tis hardly worth the Cost,
"You soon shall see him soundly tost.
"You'll find him swear, blaspheme, and damn,
"And ev'ry Moment take a Dram,
"His ghostly Visage with an Air
"Of Reprobation and Despair: 60
"Or, else some hiding Hole he seeks,
"For Fear the rest shou'd say he squeeks;
"Or, as *Fitzpatrick* did before,
"Resolve to perish with his W—;
"Or, else he raves, and roars, and swears,
"And, but for Shame, wou'd say his Pray'rs.
"Or, wou'd you see his Spirits sink,
"Relaxing downwards in a St—k?
"If such a Sight as this can please ye,
"Good Madam *Pallas*, pray be easy,   70

51 you'll] you 1749, 1750, 1752   53 "Now,] But H. Or 1749, 1750, 1752
55] *In round brackets* 1749, 1750, 1752   55 'tis hardly worth] 'twill hardly
quit 1749, 1750, 1752   57 him swear,] he'll swear 1749, 1750, 1752   him
sweat, Faulkner 1763   59 ghostly] ghastly 1749, 1750, 1752   61 else]
when H., 1749, 1750, 1752   64 "Resolve] Resolv'd 1749, 1750, 1752   64
W—;] whore; H. *W—re*; 1749, 1750, 1752   65 "Or, else he raves, and
roars,] Or when he raves and roars H. Or when he raves, or roars 1749, 1750, 1752
68 "Relaxing downwards in a St—k?] . . . stink; H. Refluxing downwards,
in a Stink? 1749 . . . Stink; 1750, 1752   69 Sight] Scene 1749, 1750, 1752
70 Madam] M^rs H.

Berkeley, idealistic philosopher, and Bishop of Cloyne, possessed a rare charm of character, and was always held in the greatest esteem by Swift, although he found his writings 'too speculative' (*Corresp.* iv. 295). About 1721 Berkeley conceived the idea of establishing a college in the Bermudas for the promotion of missionary work in America; and in 1724 he crossed over to London to solicit Lord Carteret's assistance in the scheme (see Swift's amusing letter to Carteret, *Corresp.* iii. 212–13).

63. *Fitzpatrick*. '*Brigadier* FITZ-PATRICK *was drowned in one of the Packet Boats in the Bay of* Dublin, *in a great storm*.'—Faulkner. A footnote in the Huntington manuscript is more explicit: 'Brigadier Fitzpatrick drown'd with his Mistress comeing from England in the year 1696.'

"To *Neptune* speak, and he'll consent;
"But he'll come back the Knave he went."

THE Goddess, who conceiv'd an Hope,
That — was destin'd to a Rope,
Believ'd it best to condescend
To spare a Foe, to save a Friend:
But fearing *Berkeley* might be scar'd
She left him Virtue for a Guard.

B I L L E T

to the

COMPANY of PLAYERS.

Works of Jonathan Swift, ed. Deane Swift, 1765, 4to, viii (2), 159;
8vo, xvi. 269.
Faulkner, 1765, xiii. 285. [Ref. F.]

The Right Hon. Edward Hopkins came to Ireland as Chief Secretary
to the Duke of Grafton. In the autumn of 1722 he was appointed Master
of the Revels in Ireland, with an increase in the customary salary of £300
a year, which was, apparently, to be obtained from the players (*Corresp.*
iii. 152 n.[3]). The following piece was first printed and edited by Deane
Swift in 1765. It describes Hopkins's attempt to compel the company of
actors at the Smock Alley Theatre, Dublin, to pay £300 a year for licence
to act. Swift has a reference to Hopkins in the fourth of his *Drapier's
Letters*: 'And we lately saw a *Favourite Secretary* descend to be *Master
of the Revels*, which by his *Credit and Extortion* he hath made *Pretty
Considerable.*' (*Drapier's Letters*, ed. Herbert Davis, p. 74.)

In *Gulliveriana*, 1728, p. 61, is printed another piece on the same sub-

71 "To *Neptune* speak, and he'll consent;] Let *Neptune* speak, and I'll consent,
1749, 1750, 1752   72 he'll come] H— comes H.   72 Knave] Rogue 1749,
1750, 1752   73] *No break* H., 1749, 1750, 1752   73 conceiv'd an]
conceiv'd a H.   receiv'd a 1749, 1750, 1752   74 to] for 1749, 1750, 1752
75, 76] *Om.* 1752   76 To spare a Foe,] And spare a Rogue, 1749, 1750
77 But fearing *Berkeley* might] Yet fearing *Berkly* might 1749, 1750, 1752
But fearing *Berkeley* should Faulkner 1763   78 a] his 1749, 1750, 1752

ject, an 'Epilogue *to Mr.* Hoppy's *Benefit-Night, at* Smock-Alley'. A footnote says that it was 'Spoken by the *Captain,* one Evening, at the End of a private Farce, acted by Gentlemen, for their own Diversion, at *Gallstown'.* Dr. Elrington Ball (*Corresp.* iii. 152 n.[3]; *Swift's Verse,* p. 168) attributes the 'Epilogue' to John Rochfort and Swift in conjunction, during a visit of the latter to Gaulstown House at Christmas, 1722, or Easter, 1723. The poem is reprinted by Scott in his edition of Swift's *Works,* 1814, xiv. 159, with a prefatory note in which he remarks that 'it is more likely to have been written by some other among the joyous guests of the Lord Chief Baron, since it does not exhibit Swift's accuracy of numbers'. Scott is unquestionably right. See p. 1108.

Scott also prints (x. 588) another poem, 'Punch's Petition to the Ladies', in which Hopkins appears as 'Vander Hop'. He is inclined to attribute it to Sheridan. See p. 1108.

The text is printed from the *Works,* 1765.

THE inclosed Prologue is formed upon the story of the Secretary's not suffering you to act, unless you would pay him 300*l. per annum,* upon which you got a licence from the Lord Mayor to act as strollers.

The Prologue supposes, that, upon your being forbidden to act, a company of country-strollers came and hired the Play-house, and your cloaths, *&c.* to act in.

The PROLOGUE.

OUR set of strollers, wand'ring up and down,
Hearing the House was empty, came to town;
And, with a licence from our good Lord May'r,
Went to one Griffith, formerly a play'r:
Him we persuaded with a mod'rate bribe,
To speak to Elrington, and all the tribe,
To let our company supply their places,
And hire us out their scenes, and cloaths, and faces.
Is not the truth the truth? Look full on me;
I am not Elrington, nor Griffith he.　　　　10
When we perform, look sharp among our crew,
There's not a creature here you ever knew.

4, 6. *Griffith, ... Elrington.* For these two players see introductory notes to an 'Epilogue, To be spoke at the Theatre-Royal', p. 274.

The former folks were servants to the king,
We, humble strollers, always on the wing.
Now, for my part, I think upon the whole,
Rather than starve, a better man would strole.

Stay, let me see—Three hundred pounds a year,
For leave to act in town? 'Tis plaguy dear.
Now, here's a warrant; Gallants please to mark,
For three thirteens and sixpence to the clerk.   20
Three hundred pounds! Were I the price to fix,
The public should bestow the actors six.
A score of guineas, given under-hand,
For a good word or so, we understand.
To help an honest lad that's out of place,
May cost a crown or so; a common case:
And, in a crew, 'tis no injustice thought
To ship a rogue, and pay him not a groat.
But, in the chronicles of former ages,
Who ever heard of servants paying wages?   30

I pity Elrington with all my heart;
Would he were here this night to act my part.
I told him what it was to be a stroller,
How free we acted, and had no controller:
In ev'ry town we wait on Mr. May'r,
First get a licence, then produce our ware:
We sound a trumpet, or we beat a drum;
Huzza! the school-boys roar, the play'rs are come!
And then we cry, to spur the bumkins on,
Gallants, by Tuesday next we must be gone.   40
I told him, in the smoothest way I could,
All this and more, yet it would do no good.
But Elrington, tears falling from his cheeks,
He that has shone with Betterton and Weeks,

20. *three thirteens and sixpence.* By proclamation, in 1687, James II made an English shilling equivalent to thirteen pence in Ireland, and an English guinea to twenty-four shillings.

44. *Betterton and Weeks.* Thomas Betterton, 1635?–1710, who began

To whom our country has been always dear,
Who chose to leave his dearest pledges here,
Owns all your favours; here intends to stay,
And, as a stroller, act in ev'ry play:
And the whole crew this resolution takes,
To live and die all strollers for your sakes; 50
Not frighted with an ignominious name,
For your displeasure is their only shame.

A pox on Elrington's majestic tone!
Now to a word of bus'ness in our own.

Gallants, next Thursday night will be our last,
Then, without fail, we pack up for Belfast.
Lose not your time, nor our diversion miss,
The next we act shall be as good as this.

To Charles Ford Esqᵣ on his Birth-day
Janᵣʸ. 31ˢᵗ for the Year 1722–3

Ford Papers: Swift's autograph, 4 fᵒ. pages. Lord Rothschild's Lib. No. 2267.
Faulkner, 1762, x. 310; 1763, xi. 408. [Ref. F.]
Works of Dr. Jonathan Swift, 1762, xiv. 186; 1764, 4to, vii (2), 171; 8vo, xiv. 293. [Ref. 1762.]

Charles Ford, son of Edward Ford, or Forth, an officer in the army, and grandson of Sir Robert Forth, was born in Dublin on 31 January, 1681–2. He inherited a moderate fortune and the small estate of Woodpark, about eleven miles from Dublin, in co. Meath, on the road to Trim. Here he was to entertain Swift and Stella.

his stage career three years before the Restoration, was associated with Davenant's company. He distinguished himself chiefly in tragedy; and was greatly admired by nearly all his contemporaries. Robert Wilks, 1665 ?–1732, after winning popularity in Dublin, removed to London, where he was associated in turn with Drury Lane and the Haymarket. He made a great hit in the comedy of Farquhar.

Ford became one of Swift's closest and most trusted friends. He knew the Vanhomrighs well; and is frequently mentioned in the *Journal to Stella*. Swift introduced him to the Duke of Ormonde, to Harley, and to St. John; and, in 1712, procured him the office of Gazetteer (*Journal to Stella*, 1 July, 1712). Ford followed Bolingbroke to France, but returned, and later visited Rome. He was back in Dublin in the summer of 1718. During the following years he wearied of Ireland, preferring life in London, with visits of varying length to Woodpark, which he finally let in 1731. He died in London in 1743.

Delany, *Observations*, 1754, p. 97, described Ford as 'the best lay-scholar of his time, and nation'. Swift availed himself several times of his assistance in literary matters. He copied out for the press Swift's *Letter to the October Club* (*Journal to Stella*, 18 Jany., 1711–12). In 1714 he was entrusted with the manuscript of the *Free Thoughts*, which was, however, suppressed, and first published by Faulkner in 1741. Many years later Ford was employed by Swift to bring to the attention of Motte, the publisher, mistakes and falsifications in the text of his editions of *Gulliver's Travels*. There are two copies of this work with corrections in Ford's hand, one in the Forster Collection, South Kensington, and one in the Pierpont Morgan Library, New York.

The best account of Ford and of his friendship with Swift is contained in Dr. Nichol Smith's edition of the *Letters of Swift to Ford*, 1935. The present poem is there printed (pp. 193–7) for the first time from Swift's manuscript.

Sir Frederick Falkiner (*Prose Works*, ed. Temple Scott, xii. 66) assigns this poem to 1715 or 1716, and Ball (*Swift's Verse*, p. 196) to January, 1724, during the occasion of a visit to Quilca; but, as Swift's manuscript shows, the date is January, 1723. Ford seems to have come to Ireland during the summer of 1722, and to have remained there for more than twelve months (*Corresp.* iii. 151 n.²). In April–May, 1723, Swift was twice at Woodpark (*Corresp.* iii. 161).

The poem, as first printed in the *Works*, 1762/3, by Faulkner and Bowyer, appears to have been set up from a rough draft. Swift's autograph, sent to Ford, from which the text is here printed, was a fair copy. The differences between the manuscript and the 1762/3 text are numerous and interesting. Swift made three alterations in his fair copy, two of which are important. (1) In l. 44 he scored out 'torturing Engins' and wrote above it 'Informations'. (2) L. 85 as it first stood, 'Could you and I be once so wise', is struck through, and above is written 'Oh, were but You and I so wise'. (3) In l. 89 'Belcamp' is struck out and 'Cushogue' written above, with a marginal note, 'The true Name of Belcamp'.

The printed text has, l. 44, 'torturing engines', and, l. 89, 'Belcamp', without any note. In l. 85, however, the printed text has the substituted reading, which suggests that Swift wrote it thus in his first draft, then altered it in the fair copy, then altered it back again.

The text is here printed from Swift's autograph. Immaterial differences in typographical usage, as between the Dublin and London editions, are ignored in the apparatus.

[p. 1]   Come, be content, since out it must,
    For, Stella has betray'd her Trust,
    And, whisp'ring, charg'd me not to say
    That Mͬ Ford was born to day:
    Or if at last, I needs must blab it,
    According to my usuall habit,
    She bid me with a serious Face
    Be sure conceal the Time and Place,
    And not my Compliment to spoyl
    By calling This your native Soyl;   10
    Or vex the Ladyes, when they knew
    That you are turning fourty two.
    But if these Topicks should appear
    Strong Arguments to keep You here,
    We think, though You judge hardly of it,
    Good Manners must give Place to Profit.
    The Nymphs with whom You first began
    Are each become a Harridan;
    And Mountague so far decayd,
    That now her Lovers must be payd;   20
    And ev'ry Belle that since arose
    Has her Cotemporary Beaux.
    Your former Comrades, once so bright,
    With whom you toasted half the Night,
    Of Rheumatism and Pox complain,
    And bid adieu to dear Champain:
    Your great Protectors, once in Power,
    Are now in Exil, or the Tower,

13 should] shall F., 1762   15 We] I F., 1762   20 That now her Lovers must] Her Lovers now must all F., 1762   26 Champain:] Champain, F., 1762   28 Tower,] Tow'r. F., 1762

19. *And Mountague.* . . . Lady Mary Churchill, youngest daughter of the great Duke of Marlborough, celebrated for her beauty and charm. She married John Montagu, who succeeded his father, in 1709, as Marquess of Monthermer and Duke of Montagu. See l. 70.

Your Foes, triumphant o'er the Laws,
Who hate Your Person, and Your Cause,   30
[p. 2] If once they get you on the Spot
You must be guilty of the Plot,
For, true or false, they'll ne'r enquire,
But use You ten times worse than Pri'r.
    In London! what would You do there?
Can You, my Friend, with Patience bear,
Nay would it not Your Passion raise
Worse than a Pun, or Irish Phrase,
To see a Scoundrel Strut and hector,
A Foot-boy to some Rogue Director?   40
To look on Vice triumphant round,
And Virtue trampled on the Ground:
Observe where bloody Townshend stands
With Informations in his Hands,
Hear him Blaspheme; and Swear, and Rayl,
Threatning the Pillory and Jayl.
If this you think a pleasing Scene
To London strait return again,

35 London!] *London*, F., 1762   40 Director?] Director: F.   director;
1762   43 Townshend] — F., 1762   44 Informations] torturing Engines
F., 1762

34. *But use . . . than Pri'r.* In 1711
Matthew Prior was engaged in negotiations preliminary to the Treaty of
Utrecht (*cf.* Swift's *New Journey to
Paris, Prose Works*, ed. Temple Scott,
v. 187–205; ed. Davis, iii. 207–18),
and in 1712 he became plenipotentiary
at Paris. On Queen Anne's death he
was recalled, and (1715) imprisoned.
Although excepted from the Act of
Grace he was released in 1717.

43. *Townshend.* The name was represented by a dash in Faulkner and
in the 1762 London edition, and has
not before appeared in the printed
versions. Charles Townshend, second
Viscount Townshend, entered public
life as a Tory, but, falling under the

influence of Lord Somers, he seceded
to the Whigs. He negotiated the
Barrier Treaty, for which he was
afterwards voted an enemy of his
country. He obtained the confidence
of George I, who appointed him
Secretary of State. Swift's harsh
epithet has reference to Townshend's
part in the proceedings against the
negotiators of the Treaty of Utrecht,
and his severity after the insurrection
of 1715. Townshend married Walpole's sister, but later quarrelled with
his brother-in-law, retired into private
life, 1730, devoted himself to agri-
culture, and died in 1738.

44. 'Informations' written above
'torturing Engins' scored out.

Where you have told us from Experience,
Are swarms of Bugs and Hanoverians.   50
I thought my very Spleen would burst
When Fortune hither drove me first;
Was full as hard to please as You,
Nor Persons Names, nor Places knew;
But now I act as other Folk,
Like Pris'ners when their Gall is broke.
If you have London still at heart
We'll make a small one here by Art:
The Diff'rence is not much between
St James's Park and Stephen's Green;   60
And, Dawson street will serve as well
To lead you thither, as Pell-mell,
(Without your passing thro the Palace
To choque your Sight, and raise your Malice)
[p. 3] The Deanry-house may well be match't
(Under Correction) with the thatcht,
Nor shall I, when you hither come,
Demand a Croun a Quart for Stumm.
Then, for a middle-aged Charmer,
Stella may vye with your Mountharmar: 70
She's Now as handsom ev'ry bit,
And has a thousand times her Wit.
The Dean and Sheridan, I hope,
Will half supply a Gay and Pope,

50 Hanoverians.] Presbyterians. F., 1762   54 Persons Names,] Persons,
Names, F., 1762   56 Gall] Jayl F., 1762   63 (Without your passing
thro] Nor want a Passage through F., 1762   63, 64] *Om. brackets* F., 1762
70 Mountharmar:] Main-charmer, F. main charmer, 1762

56. Swift's manuscript reads 'Gall', the other draft, or copy, evidently read 'Gaol', or it was so read by the printer, who set up 'Jayl'.
60, 61. *Stephen's Green;* ... *Dawson street.* St. Stephen's Green is the largest open space in Dublin, and Dawson Street one of the chief thoroughfares. Ford's mother lived in Dawson Street.
66. *the thatcht.* The Thatched

House, in St. James's Street, was a fashionable tavern during the eighteenth century. The original building was demolished in 1814, but the Thatched House Club, a descendant of the rural inn, now stands on a neighbouring site.
68. *Stumm.* Unfermented, or partially fermented grape-juice.
70. *Mountharmar.* See note to l. 19. The printer here went wrong.

Corbet, though yet I know his Worth not,
No doubt, will prove a good Arbuthnot:
I throw into the Bargain, Jim:
In London can you equall Him?
What think you of my fav'rite Clan,
Robin, and Jack, and Jack, and Dan?   80
Fellows of modest Worth and Parts,
With chearfull Looks, and honest Hearts.
Can you on Dublin look with Scorn?
Yet here were You and Ormonde born
Oh, were but You and I so wise
To look with Robin Grattan's Eyes:
Robin adores that Spot of Earth,
That litt'rall Spot which gave him Birth,
And swears, Cushogue is to his Tast,   *The true
                                             Name of Belcamp
As fine as Hampton-court at least.   90
When to your Friends you would enhance
The Praise of Italy or France
For Grandeur, Elegance and Wit,
We gladly hear you, and submit:
But then, to come and keep a Clutter
For this, or that Side of a Gutter,

77 Jim:] *Tim*, F., 1762   79] *No break* F., 1762   85] *N.P.* F., 1762
86 To look with Robin Grattan's Eyes:] To see with *Robin Grattan's* Eyes, F.
To see with *Robert Gratton's* eyes, 1762   89 Cushogue] *Belcamp* F., 1762
91] *No break* F., 1762

75. *Corbet.* The Rev. Francis Corbet, one of the executors to Stella's will, and later a successor to Swift in the Deanery of St. Patrick's.

77. *Jim.* The Rev. James King, a Prebendary of St. Patrick's, from 1730 to 1759 vicar of St. Bride's, Dublin. Swift held him in esteem, and named him amongst his executors. See W. G. Carroll's *Succession of Clergy in S. Bride*, pp. 21–2; *Corresp.* v. 255 n.².

80. *Robin, and Jack, and Jack, and Dan?* Robert and John Grattan, and John and Daniel Jackson, with whom Swift was in the habit of exchanging verse trifles. See pp. 741 n., 965 ff.

84. *Ormonde.* James Butler, second Duke of Ormonde, who had been attainted and was living abroad. A favourite hero of the Jacobite and Tory party.

85. On Swift's correction of this line see notes introductory to the poem.

89. *Cushogue.* The earlier name of Belcamp, the home of the Grattans. See introductory notes to this poem, and p. 965. Belcamp lies five miles to the north of Dublin, to the west of the road leading to Malahide. See *Corresp.* ii. 263 n.¹. In the marginal note 'true' is written after 'Iris' struck out.

To live in this or t'other Isle,
We cannot think it worth your while.
For, take it kindly, or amiss,
The Diff'rence but amounts to this,   100
[p. 4] You bury, on our Side the Channell
In Linnen, and on Yours, in Flannell.
You, for the News are ne'r to seek,
While We perhaps must wait a Week:
You, happy Folks, are sure to meet
A hundred Whores in ev'ry Street,
While We may search all Dublin o'er
And hardly hear of half a Score.
    You see, my Arguments are Strong;
I wonder you held out so long,   110
But since you are convinc't at last
We'll pardon you for what is past.
So — let us now for Whisk prepare;
Twelvepence a Corner, if you dare.

Carberiæ Rupes in Comitatu Corgagensi *apud* Hybernicos.

Scripsit *Jun. Ann. Dom.* 1723.

Faulkner, 1735, ii. 477 (1737, ii. 389).
Miscellanies, . . . *Volume the Fifth,* 1735, p. 155 (1736, v. 155; 1745, v. 39).

Swift, on his southern journey, during the summer of 1723, after the death of Vanessa, reached the parish of Skull, in the south-west corner of

101 You] We F., 1762   104 must] may F., 1762   106 A] An F., 1762
107 search] trace F., 1762   108 And hardly hear of] Before we find out F.,
1762   113] *No break* F., 1762   113 Whisk] Whist F., 1762
    The paragraphs are divided by spaces in F., 1762

101. 'You', which puzzled Ford, is lightly struck through. Above is 'We' altered to 'They', and above this indistinct 'They' a clear 'They', all written by Ford. The printer, working from another draft, set up 'We'.

101, 102. *You bury, . . . Flannell.* See note, p. 237. A law compelling burial in woollen was passed by the Irish Parliament 31 Dec. 1733.
107. Swift altered 'we' to 'We'.
113. *Whisk.* Earlier form of 'whist'.

Cork, and these Latin verses describe the wild scenery of that extremity of Ireland.

'Carberiæ Rupes' and Swift's Latin epistle 'Ad Amicum Eruditum Thomam Sheridan' (see p. 211), together with an English version of the former by William Dunkin, were first printed by Faulkner in 1735 at the end of the *Poetical Works*. Orrery tells us that 'The Dean was extremely solicitous, that they should be printed among his works', and that 'he assumed to himself more vanity upon these two Latin poems, than upon many of his best English performances'. In Orrery's opinion, however, had they been 'the produce of any other author, they must have undergone a severe censure from Dr. SWIFT'. (*Remarks*, 1752, pp. 130, 131.) Delany, on the other hand, deemed them both 'excellent in their kinds'. He tells us, further, that Swift's over-eager curiosity in surveying the cliffs nearly led to an accident. (*Observations*, 1754, pp. 135, 136.)

The 'Contents' table of the 1735 *Miscellanies* omits the poem, although it is duly printed in the body of the work.

The text is printed from Faulkner, 1735.

ECCE ingens fragmen scopuli quod vertice summo
Desuper impendet, nullo fundamine nixum
Decidit in fluctus: maria undiq; & undiq; saxa
Horisono Stridore tonant, & ad æthera murmur
Erigitur; trepidatq; suis *Neptunus* in undis.
Nam, longâ venti rabie, atq; aspergine crebrâ
Æquorei laticis, specus imâ rupe cavatur:
Jam fultura ruit, jam summa cacumina nutant;
Jam cadit in præceps moles, & verberat undas.
Attonitus credas, hinc dejecisse Tonantem   10
Montibus impositos montes, & *Pelion* altum
In capita anguipedum cœlo jaculâsse gigantum.

SÆPE etiam spelunca immani aperitur hiatu
Exesa è scopulis, & utrinq; foramina pandit,
Hinc atq; hinc a ponto ad pontum pervia Phœbo:
Cautibus enormè junctis laquearia tecti
Formantur; moles olim ruitura supernè.
Fornice sublimi nidos posuere palumbes,
Inq; imo stagni posuere cubilia phocæ.

1 Ecce] 1735, 1736, 1745   Ecce! 1737   18 posuere] 1735, 1736, 1737
struxere 1745

SED, cum sævit hyems, & venti carcere rupto   20
Immensos volvunt fluctus ad culmina montis;
Non obsessæ arces, non fulmina vindice dextrâ
Missa Jovis, quoties inimicas sævit in urbes,
Exæquant sonitum undarum, veniente procellâ:
Littora littoribus reboant; vicinia latè,
Gens assueta mari, & pedibus percurrere rupes,
Terretur tamen, & longè fugit, arva relinquens.

GRAMINA dum carpunt pendentes rupe capellæ
Vi salientis aquæ de summo præcipitantur,
Et dulces animas imo sub gurgite linquunt.   30

PISCATOR terrâ non audet vellere funem;
Sed latet in portu tremebundus, & aera sudum
Haud sperans, Nereum precibus votisq; fatigat.

A TRANSLATION BY WILLIAM DUNKIN

Faulkner introduced this translation with the following note:

We have added a Translation of the preceding Poem, for the Benefit of our English Readers. It is done by Mr. W. Dunkin, M.A. for whom our supposed Author hath

20 & venti carcere rupto] & venti, carcere rupto, 1745   28 carpunt] 1735, 1736, 1745   carpunt, 1737

18, 19. *posuere . . . posuere*. The repetition, a fault usually corrected by Swift, passed unnoticed. In the 1745 Bathurst edition of the *Miscellanies* 'struxere' was substituted in l. 18; but Hawkesworth returned to the repetition in 1755; and he is followed by Scott and modern editors.

Mr. W. Dunkin, M.A. William Dunkin, 1709?–1765, for whom see also *D.N.B.* xvi. 203, was, apparently, at the time he translated these verses, still a student of Trinity College,

Dublin. The Dean may then have been 'unacquainted with him'. He soon, however, began to interest himself in the young man. Dunkin's aunt had bequeathed lands in Louth to the College on condition that the Board undertook the education of her nephew. Swift succeeded in having his annuity raised to £100 a year. In 1735 Dunkin was ordained; and Swift ineffectually tried to obtain for him the living of Coleraine. In 1746 he was appointed master of Portora School, *expressed a great Regard, on Account of his ingenious Performances, although unacquainted with him.*

Carbery *Rocks in the County of* Cork, Ireland.

L O! from the Top of yonder Cliff, that shrouds
Its airy Head amidst the azure Clouds,
Hangs a huge Fragment; destitute of props
Prone on the Waves the rocky Ruin drops.
With hoarse Rebuff the swelling Seas rebound,
From Shore to Shore the Rocks return the Sound:
The dreadful Murmur Heav'n's high Convex cleaves,
And *Neptune* shrinks beneath his Subject Waves;
For, long the whirling Winds and beating Tides
Had scoop'd a Vault into its nether Sides.   10
Now yields the Base, the Summits nod, now urge
Their headlong Course, and lash the sounding Surge.
Not louder Noise could shake the guilty World,
When *Jove* heap'd Mountains upon Mountains hurl'd,
Retorting *Pelion* from his dread abode,
To crush Earth's rebel Sons beneath the Load.

OFT too with hideous yawn the Cavern wide
Presents an Orifice on either Side,

3 Fragment;] 1737, 1745   Fragment! 1735, 1736   4 drops.] 1737   drops!
1735, 1736, 1745

Enniskillen, by Lord Chesterfield, who recognized his abilities. He became a D.D. in 1744.

Dunkin's poetical works, Latin and English, may be found in two large quarto volumes, posthumously published in London, 1774. His *Select Poetical Works* had been previously published in Dublin, two volumes, 8vo, 1769–70. His verse has some merit, and, at its best, approaches more nearly to Swift's style than that of any contemporary. His 'Vindication of the Libel on Dr. Delany' has often been attributed

to Swift. It is printed by Scott, *Works*, 1814, x. 559, Browning, *Poetical Works*, ii. 272, who also print another poem by him, 'Bettesworth's Exultation', x. 534, and ii. 254. In 1734 Dunkin entered upon a war of epigrams with Charles Carthy in which Swift probably took a hand (see pp. 665–72). He wrote some excellent verses to accompany the portrait of Swift painted by Bindon in 1740. (See Sir Frederick Falkiner in *Prose Works*, ed. Temple Scott, xii. 31–5.) See also pp. 1133–4.

A dismal Orifice from Sea to Sea
Extended, pervious to the God of Day: 20
Uncouthly joyn'd, the Rocks stupendous form
An Arch, the Ruin of a future Storm:
High on the Cliff their Nests the *Woodquests* make,
And Sea calves stable in the oozy Lake.

     BUT when bleak Winter with her sullen Train
Awakes the Winds, to vex the watry Plain;
When o'er the craggy Steep without Controul,
Big with the Blast, the raging Billows rowl;
Not Towns beleaguer'd, not the flaming Brand
Darted from Heav'n by *Jove*'s avenging Hand,   30
Oft as on impious Men his Wrath he pours,
Humbles their Pride, and blasts their gilded Tow'rs,
Equal the Tumult of this wild Uproar:
Waves rush o'er Waves, rebellows Shore to Shore.
The neighb'ring Race, tho' wont to brave the Shocks,
Of angry Seas, and run along the Rocks,
Now pale with Terror, while the Ocean foams,
Fly far and wide, nor trust their native Homes.

     THE Goats, while pendent from the Mountain top
The wither'd Herb improvident they crop,   40
Wash'd down the Precipice with sudden Sweep,
Leave their sweet Lives beneath th' unfathom'd Deep.

     THE frighted Fisher with desponding Eyes,
Tho' safe, yet trembling in the Harbour lies,
Nor hoping to behold the Skies serene,
Wearies with Vows the Monarch of the Main.

---

23 *Woodquests.* Wood-pigeons. A   nineteenth century, but now only
word in use from the sixteenth to the   dialectical.

The First of April:

A P O E M.

Inscrib'd to Mrs. *E. C.*

The First of April: A Poem. Inscrib'd to Mrs. E. C. Broadside; n.p. or d.

Although these charming verses have not hitherto been included in any edition of Swift's *Works* they were considered by Dr. Elrington Ball (*Swift's Verse*, p. 171) to be undoubtedly by him; and both internal and external evidence strongly support the attribution. The style and versification are in Swift's manner, and fully worthy of him; and the poem is addressed to the wife of Robert Cope, an Irish friend whom he visited on several occasions.

Robert Cope, a strong Tory in politics, had a country seat at Loughall in the county of Armagh. He sat for his county in Queen Anne's last Irish Parliament. Swift met him for the first time in London. 'I dined with three Irishmen at one Mr. Cope's lodgings; the other two were one Morris, an archdeacon, and Mr. Ford' (*Journal to Stella*, 11 Feby., 1710–11). Later he paid summer visits to Loughall, in 1717 (*Corresp.* ii. 392), 1720 probably (*Corresp.* iii. 53), and 1722 (*Letters of Swift to Ford*, ed. Nichol Smith, p. 95; *Corresp.* iii. 131 n.[1]), and, almost certainly, on other occasions. Sheridan (*Life of Swift*, 1784, p. 431) says: 'He spent a good deal of time in the north at Mr. Robert Cope's.' For an amusing tale about Cope and Swift see further Sheridan's *Life*, p. 217 n.

The recipient of these lines would be the second Mrs. Cope, a daughter of Sir William Fownes. They were probably written at some date between 1720 and 1724. On the 11th of May, 1723 (*Corresp.* iii. 161), Swift wrote a warm and friendly letter to Cope, full of compliments to him and his lady, quite in the spirit of the poem.

The text is printed from the original broadside, of which a copy is preserved in the library of the Royal Irish Academy (24. C. 32).

THIS morn the *God of Wit* and Joke,
   Thus to his *Choir of Muses* spoke;

"Go, Sisters Nine, into that Cabbin,
"Where most true Sons of *Phœbus* ha' bin.

"Each take a Child into her Care,
"There's one for each and one to spare:
"Tho' there's a Boy whom a Lord chuses,
"Who is as good as all the Muses;
"And beauteous *Bess* a diff'rent case is,
"For she belongs to all the Graces;   10
"Divide the rest, but then take care,
"Ye don't fall out about the Heir.

They dropp'd low Court'sies, One and All,
And took their Progress tow'rds *L—ll.*
Apollo laugh'd till he was sick,
That he had serv'd the Prudes a Trick.

"With due Submission to the God,
"*Thalia* said, 'tis somewhat odd,
"We all shou'd march on this Occasion,
"And not leave one for Invocation.   20
"Poets till they grow hoarse may bawl,
"And not a Muse will hear their Call:
"Besides, to me this seems a Bubble,
"'Tis all to save their Mother trouble;
"I'll warrant she's some flaunting Dame,
"Regardless of her House and Fame;
"When we come there we'll stand unseen,
"T' observe her Management within.

They peep'd, and saw a Lady there
Pinning on Coifs and combing Hair;   30
Soft'ning with Songs to Son or Daughter,
The persecution of cold Water.

---

7. *whom a Lord chuses.* A footnote to the original broadside identifies the 'Lord' as 'Anglesey'. He would be Arthur Annesley, fifth Earl of Anglesey, and Viscount Valentia. Like his brother, the fourth Earl, he was a strong supporter of the Tory party, and this fostered a friendship with Swift and Robert Cope. He succeeded to the earldom in 1710. From 1710 to 1716 he was Joint Vice-Treasurer and Treasurer at War in Ireland. Shortly before the death of Queen Anne his appointment as Lord Lieutenant was expected. On the death of the Queen, until the arrival of George I, he was one of the Lords Justices. He died in 1737. See also p. 978 n.

14. *L—ll.* Loughall, Cope's country seat.

Still pleas'd with the *good-natur'd Noise*,
And *harmless Frolicks* of her *Boys*;
Equal to all in *Care* and *Love*,
Which all *deserve* and all *improve*.
To *Kitchin*, *Parlour*, *Nurs'ry* flies,
And seems all *Feet*, and *Hands*, and *Eyes*.
No Thought of her's does ever *roam*,
But for her 'Squire when he's *from home*;   40
And scarce a *Day*, can spare a *Minute*
From *Husband*, *Children*, *Wheel*, or *Spinnet*.
The Muses when they saw *her* care,
Wonder'd the God had sent them there.
And said, "His Worship might ha' told us,
"This House don't *want*, nor will it *hold* us.
"We govern here! where she presides
"With *Virtue*, *Prudence*, *Wit* besides;
"A Wife as good as Heart cou'd wish one,
"What need we open our Commission,   50
"There's no occasion here for us,
"Can *we* do more than what *she* does.

Thalia now began to smoke,
That all this Bus'ness was a Joke.

"Sisters, said she, my Life I'll lay,
"Ye have forgot this *Month* and *Day*.—
"'Tis a *fair Trick*, by *ancient* Rules—
"The God has made us *April-Fools*.

53. *Thalia now began to smoke.* The use of 'to smoke' in the sense of 'suspect', though common for over two hundred years, died out in the middle of the nineteenth century. Swift often uses it.

P E T H O X
the Great.

Miscellanies. The Last Volume, 1727, p. 254 (1731 and 1733, p. 297;
1736, p. 277; 1742, iv. 192).
Faulkner, 1735, ii. 167 (1737, ii. 148). [Ref. F.]
The Works of Jonathan Swift, ed. Hawkesworth, 1755, 4to, iii (2), 167.

No date was assigned to this piece when first printed in the *Miscellanies.*
Faulkner attributed it to 1723, which is not improbable, for it was about
this time that Swift, Delany, and Sheridan fell into the habit of exchanging
riddles in verse. Although satirical rather than a riddle—the anagram in the
title is obvious—it bears a family likeness. Scott (1814) was the first editor
to include it, unnecessarily, with the riddles.

'SWIFT hath made his *Pethox* the Great, a piece truly historical and
learned; with as many fine strokes of satire as any in HOGARTH's. I only
wish, the subject had been less disagreeable, and the colouring in some
places, less strong' (Delany, *Observations,* 1754, p. 222).

The text is reprinted from the *Miscellanies* of 1727. Swift made one
correction, l. 83 [Ref. S.], in his copy of the *Miscellanies,* an alteration
followed by Faulkner. Hawkesworth, in 1755, deserting the London
editions, adopted Faulkner's readings in four instances.

FROM *Venus* born, thy Beauty shows,
But who thy Father, no Man knows,
Nor can the skilful Herald trace
The Founder of thy antient Race.
Whether thy Temper, full of Fire,
Discovers *Vulcan* for thy Sire,
The God who made *Scamander* boil,
And round the Margin sindg'd his Soil,
(From whence Philosophers agree,
An equal Pow'r descends to thee.)   10
Whether from War's stern God you claim
The high Descent from whence you came,

8 the Margin sindg'd his Soil,] 1733, 1736, 1742   his Margin sing'd the Soil;
F., 1755   11 War's stern God] 1733, 1736, 1742   dreadful *Mars* F., 1755

And, as a Proof, shew num'rous Scars
By fierce Encounters made in Wars;
(Those honourable Wound[s] you bore
From Head to Foot, and all before;)
And still the bloody Field frequent,
Familiar in each Leader's Tent.
Or whether, as the Learn'd contend,
You from the Neighb'ring *Gaul* descend;   20
Or from *Parthenope* the proud,
Where numberless thy Vot'ries crowd:
Whether thy Great Forefathers came
From Realms that bear *Vesputio's* Name:
For so Conjectors would obtrude,
And from thy painted Skin conclude.
Whether, as *Epicurus* shows
The World from justling Seeds arose,
Which mingling with prolifick Strife
In Chaos, kindled into Life;   30
So your Production was the same,
And from contending Atoms came.

Thy fair indulgent Mother crown'd
Thy Head with sparkling Rubies round;
Beneath thy decent Steps, the Road
Is all with precious Jewels strow'd.
The Bird of *Pallas* knows his Post,
Thee to attend where-e'er thou go'st.

Byzantians boast, that on the Clod
Where once their *Sultan's* Horse hath trod,   40
Grows neither Grass, nor Shrub, nor Tree;
The same thy Subjects boast of Thee.

16 all before;] *all before*; F., *1755*

21. *Parthenope.* The ancient name of Naples, so called from one of the sirens whose body was cast up there on the sea-shore.

24. *Realms that bear Vesputio's Name.* The New World was named America from Amerigo Vespucci, 1451–1512, who has been mistakenly credited with having reached the mainland in 1497, before Columbus.

37. *The Bird of Pallas.* 'Bubo, the Owl.'—*Miscellanies*, 1727.

The greatest Lord, when you appear,
Will deign your Livery to wear,
In all the various Colours seen,
Of Red, and Yellow, Blue, and Green.

With half a Word, when you require,
The Man of Bus'ness must retire.

The haughty Minister of State
With Trembling must thy Leisure wait;   50
And while his Fate is in thy Hands,
The Bus'ness of the Nation stands.

Thou dar'st the greatest Prince attack,
Can'st hourly set him on the Rack,
And, as an Instance of thy Pow'r,
Inclose him in a wooden Tow'r,
With pungent Pains on ev'ry Side:
So *Regulus* in Torments dy'd.

From thee our Youth all Virtues learn,
Dangers with Prudence to discern;   60
And well thy Scholars are endu'd
With Temp'rance, and with Fortitude;
With Patience, which all Ills supports,
And Secrecy, the Art of Courts.

The glitt'ring Beau could hardly tell,
Without your Aid, to read or spell;
But, having long convers'd with you,
Knows how to write a Billet-doux.

With what Delight, methinks, I trace
Your Blood in ev'ry Noble Race!   70
In whom thy Features, Shape, and Mien,
Are to the Life distinctly seen.

45 the] 1733, 1736, 1742, 1755   thy F.   68 write] 1733, 1736, 1742, 1755
scrawl F.   70 Your] 1733, 1736, 1742, 1755   Thy F.

58. *Regulus.* Marcus Attilius Regu- ing to tradition, tortured to death a
lus, defeated and taken prisoner by the   few years later. Horace, *Carm.* iii. 5.
Carthaginians, 255 B.C., and, accord-

The *Britons*, once a savage Kind,
By you were brighten'd and refin'd,
Descendents of the barbarous *Huns*,
With Limbs robust, and Voice that stuns;
But you have molded them afresh,
Remov'd the tough superfluous Flesh,
Taught them to modulate their Tongues,
And speak without the Help of Lungs.   80

Proteus on you bestow'd the Boon
To change your Visage like the Moon,
So sometimes half a Face produce,
Keep t'other Half for private Use.

How fam'd thy Conduct in the Fight,
With *Hermes*, Son of *Pleias* bright.
Out-number'd, half encompass'd round,
You strove for ev'ry Inch of Ground;
Then, by a Soldierly Retreat,
Retir'd to your Imperial Seat.   90
The Victor, when your Steps he trac'd,
Found all the Realms before him waste;
You, o'er the high Triumphal Arch
Pontifick, made your glorious March;
The wond'rous Arch behind you fell,
And left a Chasm profound as Hell:
You, in your Capitol secur'd,
A Siege as long as *Troy* endur'd.

83 So] 1733, 1736, 1742   You S., F., 1755

85–98. *How fam'd thy Conduct . . .*
Barrett, *Essay on the Earlier Part of
the Life of Swift*, p. 31, draws attention to the similarity between this
passage and that in the *Mechanical
Operation of the Spirit* relating to the
Banbury saint (*A Tale of a Tub*, ed.
Guthkelch and Nichol Smith, p. 283;
Prose Works, ed. Temple Scott, i. 204).
   86. *Hermes.* 'Mercury.' *Miscellanies*,
1727.

E P I G R A M S

Transcript by Stella; Manuscript volume in the possession of the Duke of Bedford, Woburn Abbey.
Miscellanies. The Last Volume, 1727, p. 178 (1731, p. 249; 1733, p. 249; 1736, p. 236).
Faulkner, 1735, ii. 50 (1737, ii. 39).
Miscellanies, 1742, iv. 149.

Three epigrams, linked together in subject-matter, were transcribed by Stella, without titles or indication of date, on one page of the manuscript volume now at Woburn Abbey. The first, beginning 'As Thomas was cudgelld one day by his Wife', appeared in the Pope and Swift *Miscellanies* of 1727. It was reprinted by Faulkner in 1735, and then assigned to the year 1712. The second, beginning 'When Margery chastises Ned', was first printed with Swift's poems in 1910 by W. E. Browning, i. 298, who took it from a transcript among the Forster remains at South Kensington. The third, beginning 'Joan cudgell's Ned, yet Ned's a Bully', was printed by Faulkner in 1735, and assigned to the year 1723.

Stella's transcripts appear to have been made about 1720, and later, and the accuracy of the date 1712, assigned to the first epigram by Faulkner, may be questioned. In any event the three epigrams are most naturally printed together.

The text of the epigrams is, in each case, printed from Stella's transcript.

As Thomas was cudgelld one day by his Wife,
He took to the Street, and fled for his Life,
Tom's three dearest Friends came by in the Squabble,
And sav'd him at once from the Shrew and the Rabble;
Then ventur'd to give him some sober Advice,
But Tom is a Person of Honor so nice,
Too wise to take Council, too proud to take Warning,
That he sent to all three a Challenge next morning.
Three Duels he fought, thrice ventur'd his Life
Went home, and was cudgell'd again by his Wife.   10

9 Life] Life; *printed editions*
The only differences in the editions are in printer's punctuation. There are no verbal variants.

Transcript by Stella.
*The Poems of Jonathan Swift, D.D. Edited by William Ernst Browning.
London: G. Bell and Sons Ltd.*, 1910, i. 298.

> When Margery chastises Ned
> She calls it combing of his Head,
> A Kinder Wife was never born,
> She combs his Head, and finds him Horn.

Transcript by Stella.
Faulkner, 1735, ii. 207 (1737, ii. 152).
*A Collection of Poems, &c. Omitted in the Fifth Volume of Miscellanies in
Prose and Verse. London: Printed for Charles Davis, in Pater-noster-
Row. MDCCXXXV.* p. 436.
Miscellanies, 1736, v. 208 (1745, v. 47).

> Joan cudgell's Ned, yet Ned's a Bully
> Will cudgell's Bess, yet Will's a Cully
> Dye Ned and Bess; give Will to Joan,
> She dares not say her Life's her own.
> Dye Joan and Will; give Bess to Ned,
> And ev'ry day she combs his Head.

The only differences in the editions are in spelling or punctuation. There are
no verbal variants.

1. *Margery.* The first 'r' was omitted by Stella, and is written by her above the line.
2. *She calls it combing of his Head.* *I.e.* giving him a thrashing. For examples of the use of this colloquial phrase see *O.E.D.*

2. *Cully.* A slang word of obscure origin. It was of frequent use during the seventeenth and eighteenth centuries. Two senses attached to it: (1) gull, simpleton; (2) friend, companion, mate.

POLITICAL POEMS

RELATING TO

WOOD'S HALFPENCE

POLITICAL POEMS

RELATING TO

WOOD'S HALFPENCE

About 1720 a shortage of copper money was felt, or said to be felt, in Ireland. The English government, without consulting Ireland, issued letters patent, 12 July, 1722, to William Wood, a mine-owner and iron merchant, authorizing him to mint copper coinage for Ireland to the value of £100,800, a disproportionately large sum. The Commissioners of the Revenue in Dublin took exception to the patent, and general opposition was excited. After a prorogation lasting nearly eight years the Irish Parliament met again, 9 September, 1723, and the Commons resolved themselves into a Committee to consider the new coinage. On 23 September the report of the Committee was presented and adopted by the House in the form of an address to the King objecting to the patent. On 25 September the schedule of papers relating to Wood's patent was laid before the Irish House of Lords, and referred to a Committee of the whole House. On the 28th an address to the King was agreed to the effect that the patent had been obtained in 'a Clandestine and Unpresedented Manner, and by a Grose Misrepresentation of the State of this Kingdom', that it would tend to a diminution of the revenue, and the ruin of trade. Two pointed amendments were negatived; but the address remained very frank and direct. The King's reply was laid before Parliament on 12 December, 1723. It expressed concern at the uneasiness caused, and promised an inquiry, which opened in London on 9 April, 1724. Shortly before this, in March, Swift had published his first *Letter ... By M. B. Drapier*. The fourth and much the most outspoken letter appeared on 22 October, the day of Carteret's arrival in Ireland as Lord-Lieutenant.

Swift's pamphlets fanned the flame of popular indignation. The *Dublin Gazette*, 18–22 August, 1724, contained a declaration, signed by a large number of Dublin merchants, refusing to 'import, receive or utter any of the Half-pence or Farthings coined by William Wood Esq;'. A similar declaration by merchants of Cork and Waterford appeared in the issue of 29 August–1 September. Other places followed. The *Dublin Gazette* of 15–19 September printed a petition, addressed to the King, from the Lord Mayor, Sheriffs, Commons, and Citizens of Dublin. Before this a vigorous declaration in opposition to the patent had been made at the General Sessions of the Peace held 3 September, and subscribed by the High-Sheriff, Justices, Grand Jury, Nobility, Clergy, Gentlemen, and Freeholders of Dublin.

The government took alarm, issued a proclamation, and Harding, the printer of the *Drapier's Letters,* was arrested. Swift countered by publishing a bold and provocative paper entitled *Seasonable Advice,* primarily addressed to the gentlemen of the grand jury summoned to consider Harding's case. The grand jury refused to present this paper as seditious despite Chief Justice Whitshed's attempt to browbeat them as he had done in the case of Waters (see p. 236). A letter from Marmaduke Coghill, Judge of the Prerogative Court, to Edward Southwell, Chief Secretary for Ireland, 24 Nov., 1724 (B.M., Add. MS. 21122. ff. 22-3), gives an interesting contemporary account of the discharge of the grand jury. See also *Letters of Swift to Ford,* ed. Nichol Smith, pp. 113-14.

Swift followed up the rising excitement and success with lampoons and satirical verses upon Wood. Carteret had replaced the Duke of Grafton as Lord-Lieutenant, and, on his advice, the government saw the wisdom of yielding. On 21 September, 1725, the exemplification of the deed of surrender of Wood's patent was laid before the Irish House of Lords, and on the following day before the House of Commons. The victory, for all practical purposes won nearly a year before the final surrender, was largely due to Swift's pamphleteering, and the Drapier, perfectly well known to all, became a national hero.

Apart from any question of the necessity for the new coinage, or its baseness, it was felt in Ireland that the form in which the patent was issued was an insult to the rights of the country, that it was a job for the benefit of individuals, including the Duchess of Kendal, who, it was rumoured, was to receive a commission from Wood, and that the commercial interests of the country had in no way been considered.

The ephemeral literature of the controversy is large. The exact limits of Swift's share must remain in doubt. His verses relating to Wood's coinage should be read in conjunction with the *Drapier's Letters,* ed. Herbert Davis, 1935, *Prose Works,* ed. Davis, vol. x, and *Prose Works,* ed. Temple Scott, vol. vi.

See also *Journals of the House of Lords of Ireland,* ii. 745-50, 764-5, 809-12; *Journals of the House of Commons,* iii, Part I, 319-401; Boyer's *Political State of Great Britain,* vols. xxvi, xxviii, xxx; and, for accounts of the controversy, Coxe's *Memoirs of Walpole,* i. 216-30; Scott, *Memoirs of Swift,* pp. 283-306; Monck Mason, *History of St. Patrick's Cathedral,* pp. 326-47; Froude's *English in Ireland,* i. 582-608; Craik's *Life of Swift,* pp. 346-62, 2nd edn. ii. 63-84; *Political History of England,* ix. 314-19 (I. S. Leadam). And for the coins consult Philip Nelson's *Coinage of William Wood,* and *Coinage of Ireland.*

A
SERIOUS POEM
UPON
WILLIAM WOOD,
Brasier, Tinker, Hard-Ware-Man, Coiner,
Counterfeiter, Founder and *Esquire.*

A Serious Poem upon William Wood, ... Dublin: Printed by John Harding in Molesworth's-Court. Half-sheet.
Political State of Great Britain, September, 1724, vol. xxviii. 297–9. [Ref. *P.S.*]
The British Journal, 3 October, 24 October, 1724. [Ref. *B.J.*]
Faulkner, 1762, iv. 351; 1763, xi. 337. [Refs. 1762, 1763.]
Supplement to Dr. Swift's Works, 1779 4to, p. 627.
Works, ed. Sheridan, 1784, vii. 330.
Works, ed. Nichols, 1801, vii. 322.
Works, ed. Scott, 1814, x. 482.

This ballad (advertised in Harding's *News Letter* for 15 Sept., 1724, as due for publication on 17 Sept.), after its first appearance in Dublin as an anonymous half-sheet, was soon reprinted in London periodicals. Abel Boyer, omitting 52 lines, printed it in the September number, 1724, of his *Political State of Great Britain* (xxviii. 297) as an illustration of the ferment of mind in Ireland. It appeared, also abbreviated, in *The British Journal* for the 3rd of October, 1724, and again in the issue of the 24th of October, the editor stating that the demand for copies dated 3rd of October had exhausted the supply. In neither instance was it attributed to Swift.

The poem was first collected with Swift's writings in 1762 by Faulkner, who was evidently printing from the half-sheet, for he gives the ballad in full. Nichols and Sheridan, in their editions, give the poem in its abbreviated form. In 1814 Scott restored the missing lines, printing from the original half-sheet. He failed, however, to restore the word 'Counterfeiter' to the title, which had been omitted before him by the *Political State,* the *British Journal,* Nichols, and Sheridan.

The text is here printed from the original half-sheet. Typographical usage and revised pointing have been ignored in noting variants.

WHEN Foes are o'ercome, we preserve them
          from Slaughter,
          To be *Hewers* of WOOD and *Drawers* of
          Water,
Now, although to *Draw Water* is not very good,
Yet we all should Rejoyce to be *Hewers* of WOOD.
I own it hath often provok'd me to Mutter,
That, a Rogue so *Obscure* should make such a Clutter,
But antient *Philosophers* wisely Remark,
That old rotten WOOD will *Shine* in the *Dark*.
The *Heathens*, we Read, had *Gods* made of WOOD,
Who could do them no Harm, if they did them no Good: 10
But this Idol WOOD may do us great Evil,
Their Gods were of WOOD, but our WOOD is the DEVIL:
To cut down fine WOOD is a very bad Thing,
And yet we all know much *Gold* it will bring,
Then if cutting down WOOD brings Money good Store,
Our Money to keep, let us *Cut down ONE more.*

Now hear an old Tale. There antiently stood
(I forget in what Church) an Image of *Wood*;
Concerning this Image there went a Prediction,
It would Burn a whole *Forest*; nor was it a Fiction;   20
'Twas cut into Faggots, and put to the Flame,
To burn an old Fryer, one *Forrest* by Name.
My Tale is a wise one if well understood,
Find you but the *Fryer*, and I'll find the WOOD.

I hear among Scholars there is a great Doubt
From what Kind of Tree this WOOD was Hewn out.
Teague made a good PUN by a *Brogue* in his Speech,
And said: *By my Shoul he's the Son of a* BEECH:
Some call him a *Thorn*, the Curse of a Nation,
As *Thorns* were design'd to be from the Creation.   30
Some think him cut out from the Poisonous *Yew*,
Beneath whose ill Shade no Plant ever grew.

5 hath] *P.S., B.J.*, 1762, 1763, 1779 has 1784, 1801, 1814   29 a Nation,]
P.S., B.J., 1762, 1763 the nation, 1779, 1784, 1801, 1814

Some say he's a *Birch*, a Thought very odd,
For none but a *Dunce* would come under his *Rod*.
But I'll tell you the Secret, and pray do not Blab,
He is an old *Stump* cut out of a *Crab*,
And *England* has put this *Crab* to hard Use,
To Cudgel our Bones, and for Drink give us *Verjuice*;
And therefore his *Witnesses* justly may boast
That none are more properly Knights of the POST.   40

But here Mr. *Wood* complains that we Mock,
Though he may be a *Block*-head, he is no real *Block*.
He can Eat, Drink and Sleep; now and then for a Friend
He'll not be too proud an old Kettle to mend;
He can *Lye* like a *Courtier*, and think it no Scorn,
When *Gold*'s to be got, to FORSWEAR and SUBORN.
He can RAP his own RAPS, and has the true Sapience
To turn a *Good* Penny to Twenty *Bad* Ha'pence.
Then in Spight of your Sophistry, Honest WILL. WOOD
Is a Man of this World all true Flesh and Blood;   50
So you are but in Jest, and you will not I hope
Un-man the poor Knave for sake of a *Trope*.
'Tis a *Metaphor* known to ev'ry plain Thinker.
Just as when we say, *the Devil*'s *a Tinker*
Which cannot in Literal Sense be made Good,
Unless by the *Devil* we mean Mr. WOOD.

But some will object, that the *Devil* oft spoke
In *Heathenish* Times from the *Trunk* of an *Oak*:
And, since we must grant, there never were known
More *Heathenish* Times than those of our own;   60
Perhaps you will say, 'tis the *Devil* that puts
The Words in WOOD's Mouth, or speaks from his Guts:

41–68] *Om. P.S., B.J.*, 1779, 1784, 1801   52 sake] the Sake 1762, 1763

47. *RAPS*. Counterfeit coins which passed in Ireland at this time for small change, owing to the scarcity of genuine money. See *The Drapier's Letters*, ed. Herbert Davis, p. 4: 'It having been many years since COPPER HALF-PENCE or FARTHINGS were last Coined in this *Kingdom*, they have been for some time very scarce, and many *Counterfeits* passed about under the name of RAPS.' See also Davis, *op. cit.*, pp. 188–9.

And then your old Argument still will return:
Howe'er let us try him and see how he'll burn.
You'll pardon me Sir, your Cunning I smoak,
But wood I assure you is no *Heart of* oak;
And instead of the *Devil*, this Son of Perdition
Hath joyn'd with himself two hags in Commission:

I ne'er could endure my Talent to smother,
I told you one Tale, I will tell you another.　　　　70
A *Joyner* to fasten a *Saint* in a *Nitch*,
Bor'd a large *Augre-hole* in the Image's Breech;
But finding the *Statue* to make no Complaint,
He would ne'er be convinc'd it was a *True Saint*:
When the *True* wood arrives, as he soon will no doubt,
(For that's but a Sham wood they carry about)
What *Stuff* he is made on you quickly may find,
If you make the same Tryal, and *Bore* him *Behind*;
I'll hold you a Groat, when you *wimble* his Bumm,
He'll Bellow as loud as the *Dee'l in a Drum*:　　　　80
From me I declare you shall have no Denial,
And there can be no Harm in making a Tryal;
And when to the Joy of your Hearts he has Roar'd,
You may shew him about for a new *Groaning Board*.

Now ask me a Question. How came it to pass
Wood got so much Copper? He got it by brass;

63 Argument] 1762　Arguments 1763, 1814　　70 I will] 1762, 1763　I'll
P.S., B.J., 1779　and I'll 1784, 1801, 1814　　77 on] 1762, 1763　on, *P.S.,
B.J.* of 1779, 1784, 1801, 1814　　85–108] *Om. P.S., B.J.*, 1779, 1784, 1801
85] *No Break* 1763

68 . . . *two* HAGS *in Commission.* A
reference to the fact that the patent
for the new Irish copper coinage was
granted to the King's mistress, the
Duchess of Kendal, who sold it to
Wood for £10,000, and, it was
rumoured, a share in the profits of the
coining. *Cf.* Swift's reference to 'a
Feminine Magician' in 'A Simile on
our Want of Silver', p. 354 n. His
mention, further, in that poem of
Walpole as a '*brazen* Politician' is
paralleled by his reference here, l. 86,
to 'brass'.

76. (*For that's but a Sham WOOD* . . .
Effigies of Wood were carried about
and burnt by the Dublin mob. *Cf.*
'A Full and True Account of the . . .
Execution of William Wood', *Works*,
ed. Scott, 1814, vii. 295; Davis,
Drapier's Letters, p. 173. A large
procession carrying an image of Wood
marched through Dublin on 7 September, 1724. See Davis, *op. cit.*, p. xxxvi.

This BRASS was a Dragon (observe what I tell ye)
This *Dragon* had gotten two *Sows* in it's Belly;
I know you will say, this is all *Heathen Greek*;
I own it, and therefore I leave you to seek.   90

I often have seen two Plays very Good,
Call'd, LOVE IN A TUB, and LOVE IN A WOOD.
These Comedies twain Friend *Wood* will contrive
On the *Scene* of this *Land* very soon to *revive*.
First, LOVE IN A TUB: 'Squire *Wood* has in Store
Strong *Tubs* for his *Raps*, Two thousand and more;
These *Raps* he will honestly dig out with Shovels,
And sell them for Gold, or he can't shew his Love else,
WOOD swears he will do it for *Ireland*'s Good,
Then can you deny it is *Love in a* WOOD?   100
However, if Criticks find Fault with the Phrase,
I hope you will own it is *Love in a Maze*;
For when you express a Friend's Love we are willing,
We never say more than, your *Love is a Million*;
But with honest WOOD's *Love* there is no contending,
'Tis Fifty round *Millions* of *Love*, and a *Mending*.
Then in his First *Love* why should he be crost?
I hope he will find that *no Love is lost*.

Hear one Story more and then I will stop.
I dream't WOOD was told he should Dye by a *Drop*   110
So methought, he resolv'd no Liquor to taste,
For fear the *First Drop* might as well be his *Last*:
But *Dreams* are like *Oracles*, hard to explain 'em,
For it prov'd that he dy'd of a DROP at *Killmainham*:

113 *Oracles*, hard] 1762, 1763   *Oracles*, 'tis hard *P.S.*, *B.J.*   oracles; 'tis
hard 1779, 1784, 1801, 1814   114 *Killmainham*:] *B.J.*   *Killmanham*: *P.S.*
Kilmainham: 1762, 1763   Kilmainham. 1779, 1784, 1801, 1814

92. *LOVE IN A TUB, and LOVE IN A WOOD. Love in a Tub* was the second title of Etherege's play, *The Comical Revenge*, first acted in 1664. Wycherley's *Love in a Wood* was first acted in 1671.

102. *Love in a Maze.* Shirley's *Changes; or, Love in a Maze* was first acted in 1632.

114. *Killmainham.* Kilmainham is a village on the outskirts of Dublin, where stood a jail, and the place of execution.

I wak'd with Delight, and not without Hope,
Very soon to see wood *Drop* down from *a Rope.*
How he and how we at each other should grin!
'Tis Kindness to hold a Friend up by the Chin;
But soft says the Herald, I cannot agree;
For *Metal on Metal is false Heraldry*:   120
Why that may be true, yet wood upon wood,
I'll maintain with my Life, is *Heraldry* Good.

An EPIGRAM

ON

WOODS's BRASS-MONEY.

Faulkner, 1746, viii. 317.
The Story of the Injured Lady. . . . London, Printed for M. Cooper, . . .
MDCCXLVI. p. 62.
Miscellanies, 1746, xi. 246 (1751, xiv. 219).
Works, ed. Hawkesworth, 1755, 4to, iv (1), 286; 8vo, vii. 388.

Lord Carteret, who had been appointed Lord Lieutenant, landed in Ireland on the 22nd of October, 1724, a year earlier than was expected. It was the hope of the Ministry in England that his presence and authority would moderate the violence of the agitation against Wood's coinage. This epigram was first printed by Faulkner in 1746. It was, presumably, composed at the time of Carteret's landing in 1724.

For an account of Carteret see p. 382.

*C*ART'RET was welcom'd to the Shore
First with the brazen Cannons Roar.
To meet him next, the Soldier comes,
With brazen Trumps and brazen Drums.
Approaching near the Town, he hears
The brazen Bells salute his Ears:
But when *Wood*'s Brass began to sound,
Guns, Trumpets, Drums, and Bells were drown'd.

To his Grace the
Arch-Bishop of DUBLIN,

A P O E M.

Serus in cœlum redeas diuq;
Lætus intersis Populo——Hor.

To his Grace The Arch-Bishop of Dublin, A Poem.... Dublin: Printed by John Harding in Molesworth's-Court in Fishamble-Street. Broadside. *Works*, Scott, 1814, x. 586.

This poem was first collected as Swift's by Scott, in 1814, with the curt remark, 'From a broadside printed by Harding'. It is very probable, both from the style and the person to whom the poem is addressed, that it should be attributed to Swift. Archbishop King opposed the project for a National Bank in Ireland a few years earlier, and Swift then addressed verses to him (see pp. 241–3). He also won the Dean's esteem by his strong opposition to Wood's coinage, and, at a later stage in the controversy, Swift paid him a further tribute in verse (see next poem). The present poem was probably written at the end of October, 1724, as soon as it was known that King had refused to sign Carteret's proclamation against the Drapier.

The text is printed from the broadside.

G REAT, GOOD and JUST was once apply'd
   To *One* who for his Country died,
To *One* who lives in its Defence,
We speak it in a Happier Sense.
O may the *Fates* thy Life prolong!
Our Country then can dread no Wrong:
In thy great Care we place our Trust,
Because thour't GREAT, and GOOD, and JUST.
Thy *Breast unshaken* can oppose
Our Private and our *Publick Foes*,   10

1. *GREAT, GOOD and JUST.* The opening words of an epitaph on Charles I by James Graham, first Marquis of Montrose. See Mark Napier's *Montrose and the Covenanters*, 1838, ii. 573.

The Latent Wiles, and *Tricks of State*,
Your *Wisdom* can with Ease Defeat.
When Pow'r in all its Pomp appears,
It falls before thy Rev'rend Years,
And willingly resigns its Place
To Something Nobler in thy Face.
When once the fierce pursuing *Gaul*
Had drawn his Sword for *Marius'* Fall,
The Godlike Hero with one frown
Struck all his Rage and Malice down;   20
Then how can we dread *William Wood*,
If by *thy Presence* he's withstood?
Where Wisdom stands to keep the Field,
In Vain he brings his *Brazen Shield*.
Tho' like the *Cybel*'s Priest he comes,
With furious Din of *Brazen Drums*,
The Force of thy superior Voice
Shall strike him dumb, and quell their Noise.

An Excellent

N E W   S O N G

Upon His GRACE

Our good Lord Archbishop of

D U B L I N.

By honest JO. one of His GRACE's Farmers in FINGAL.

To the Tune of

*An Excellent New Song Upon His Grace . . . Dublin: Printed by John
Harding in Molesworth's-Court, 1724.* Broadside.
*Whartoniana: Or, Miscellanies, in Verse and Prose. By the Wharton
Family, . . . 1727.* i. 127. [Ref. *Whartoniana.*]

19 one] a 1814   25 *Cybel*'s] sybil's 1814

The Poetical Works of Philip Late Duke of Wharton; . . . London: Printed for William Warner. n.d. i. 127. [A re-issue of *Whartoniana*.]
Works. Scott, 1814, x. 583. [Ref. 1814.]

Appearing first as an anonymous broadside, this poem was reprinted in *Whartoniana*, 1727 (published September, 1726), and there ascribed to Swift. It was first collected with Swift's poems by Scott in 1814. In *Whartoniana* and *The Poetical Works of the Duke of Wharton* the poem is remodelled into twenty-four quatrains.

The text is printed from the original broadside.

I Sing not of the *Draper*'s Praise, nor yet of *William Wood*;
But I sing of a *Famous Lord*, who seeks his *Country*'s Good.
Lord WILLIAM's Grace of *Dublin* Town, 'tis he that first appears,
Whose Wisdom and whose Piety, do far exceed his Years.
In ev'ry *Council* and *Debate* he stands for what is *Right*;
And still the *Truth* he will *Maintain*, whate'er he loses by't.
And though some think him in the Wrong, yet still there comes a Season
When ev'ry one turns round about, and owns His Grace had Reason.
His *Firmness* to the *publick Good*, as one that knows it Swore,
Has lost His Grace for Ten Years past Ten thousand Pounds and more: 10
Then come the Poor and strip him so, they leave him not a Cross,
For he regards Ten thousand Pounds no more than *Woods*'s Dross.
To beg his Favour is the Way new Favours still to win,
He makes no more to give ten Pounds than I to give a Pin.

1 *Draper*'s] *Whartoniana* Drapier's 1814   9 to] 1814   for *Whartoniana*
9 one] 1814   He *Whartoniana*   10 lost] 1814   cost *Whartoniana*   11 so]
Om. Whartoniana   12 For he regards . . .] 1814   For he values not five hundred Pounds Any more than *Woods*'s Dross   *Whartoniana*

11. *Cross.* See *O.E.D.* for the use of 'Cross' in the sense of a coin generally.

Why, there's my Landlord now the *'Squire*, who all in
    Money wallows,
He would not give a Groat to save his Father from the
    Gallows.
A *Bishop* says the noble *'Squire*, I hate the very Name,
To have two thousand Pounds a Year, O 'tis a burning
    Shame!
Two thousand Pounds a Year, Good Lord! and I to have
    but Five.
And under him no Tenant yet was ever known to thrive. 20
Now from his Lordship's Grace I hold a little Piece of
    Ground,
And all the Rent I pay is scarce five Shillings in the Pound.
Then Master *Steward* takes my Rent, and tells me,
    honest *Jo.*
Come, you must take a Cup of Sack or two before you go.
He bids me then to hold my Tongue, and up the Money
    locks,
For fear my Lord should send it all into the poor Man's
    Box.
And once I was so bold to beg that I might see His Grace,
Good Lord! I wondred how I dar'd to look him in the
    Face.
Then down I went upon my Knees, his Blessing to
    obtain,
He gave it me, and ever since I find I thrive amain.   30
Then said my Lord, I'm very glad to see thee honest
    Friend,
I know the Times are something hard, but hope they soon
    will mend,
Pray never press your self for Rent, but pay me when you
    can,
I find you bear a good Report, and are an honest Man.
Then said his Lordship with a Smile, I must have LAWFUL
    Cash,
I hope you will not pay my Rent in that same *Woods*'s
    Trash.

28 wondred] wonder'd *Whartoniana*   wonder 1814

God Bless your Grace I then reply'd, I'd see him hanging
high'r,
Before I'd touch his filthy Dross, than is *Clandalkin* Spire.
To every Farmer twice a Week all round about the *Yoke*,
Our *Parsons* Read the *Draper*'s Books, and make us
honest *Foke*.   40
And then I went to pay the *'Squire* and in the Way I
found,
His *Baily* Driving all my Cows into the Parish Pound.
Why Sirrah said the Noble *'Squire*, how dare you see my
Face,
Your Rent is due almost a Week beside the Days of Grace.
And Yet the Land I from him hold is set so on the Rack,
That only for the *Bishop*'s Lease 'twould quickly break
my Back.
    Then God Preserve his Lordship's Grace, and make
    him live as long
    As did *Methusalem* of old, and so I end my SONG.

PROMETHEUS,

A POEM

Prometheus, A Poem . . . Dublin: Printed in the Year, 1724. Broadside.
The Weekly Journal, or Saturday's Post, 16 Jany., 1724–5. [Ref. *W.J.*]
Fraud Detected: Or, The Hibernian Patriot. . . . Dublin: . . . 1725.
p. 214. [Ref. 1725.]
Miscellanies. The Last Volume, 1727, p. 219.

40 *Draper*'s] Drapier's *Whartoniana,* 1814   40 Our *Parsons* Read . . .] 1814
Our Parson reads the Drapier's Books And makes us honest Folk *Whartoniana*
42 *Baily*] *Bailiff Whartoniana*   bailie 1814   44 beside] 1814   besides
Whartoniana

38. *Clandalkin.* The village of Clondalkin lies to the south-west of Dublin. The older church, once one of the finest in the County of Dublin, was replaced towards the close of the eighteenth century by a new erection.
    39. *Yoke.* The word was sometimes used vaguely to denote a small manor. See *O.E.D.*

Miscellanies, 1728 (Sam. Fairbrother; Dublin reprint), ii. 125.
The Hibernian Patriot: . . . London: . . . MDCCXXX. p. 248.
Faulkner, 1735, iv. 385 (1737, ii. 197). [Ref. F.]
Miscellanies, 1742, iv. 174.

'Prometheus' was published as a broadside, probably in November 1724. On 12 December Dr. William Stratford, Canon of Christ Church, Oxford, writing to the second Lord Oxford, refers to a poem, 'the Fable of Prometheus', as having reached town, and adds, 'You will not be at a loss for the author of it'. Again writing to Oxford, 17 December, he says: 'I have seen all the Irish pamphlets. All here are of opinion that Jonathan wrote the whole fable, I must own I think so too' (*Portland MSS.*, vii. 393–4).

There are two transcripts of the poem among the Harley Papers at Welbeck Abbey, one on both sides of a folio half-sheet [Ref. W.¹], the other on pp. 1 and 3 of a folio sheet folded to make two leaves [Ref. W.²]. The latter is endorsed 'Prometheus' by Lord Oxford. There is also a transcript in the British Museum, Lansdowne 852. f. 225 [Ref. L.]. L. and W.² agree in four variants from the broadside text. A transcript in a clerical hand is also to be found among the manuscripts of the Marquis of Bath at Longleat (*Portland Papers*, xvii. ff. 117–18). Lord Rothschild has a contemporary transcript of the broadside, Catalogue No. 2269.

In 1725 'Prometheus' was included in the volume of collected 'Drapier's Letters' published as *Fraud Detected*; and in 1727 in the Pope and Swift *Miscellanies*. In the latter the title became 'Prometheus. On *Wood* the Patentee's *Irish Half-Pence*'; and this title was followed in Faulkner's edition of the *Works*, and in later collections. In the 1727 *Miscellanies* the poem was divided into three parts, marked by roman numerals, at ll. 1, 31, and 53. Faulkner divided it into four parts at ll. 1, 31, 53, and 57. In the *Weekly Journal* the name *Wood*, in ll. 1 and 60, discreetly appears as '*W*—'.

The text is reprinted from the broadside.

WHEN first the '*Squire*, and *Tinker Wood*
 Gravely consulting *Ireland*'s Good,
Together mingl'd in a Mass
Smith's *Dust*, and *Copper*, *Lead* and *Brass*,
The Mixture thus by Chymick Art,
United close in ev'ry Part.
In Fillets roll'd, or cut in Pieces,
Appear'd like one continu'd Spec'es,
And by the forming Engine struck,
On all the same IMPRESSION stuck.   10

1 WHEN first] 1725, 1727, 1728, 1730, 1742 As, when F.   4 and *Copper*,]
with Copper, *W.J.*   10 stuck.] took: *W.J.*

So to confound, this *hated Coin*
All *Parties* and *Religions* joyn;
Whigs, *Tories*, *Trimmers*, *Hannoverians*,
Quakers, *Conformists*, *Presbyterians*,
Scotch, *Irish*, *English*, *French* unite
With *equal Int'rest, equal Spight*,
Together mingled in a Lump,
Do all in *One Opinion* jump;
And ev'ry one begins to find,
The same IMPRESSION on his Mind;   20
A strange Event! whom *Gold* incites,
To Blood and Quarrels, *Brass* unites:
So Goldsmiths say, the coursest Stuff,
Will serve for *Sodder* well enuff.
So, by the *Kettles* loud Allarm,
The *Bees* are gather'd to a *Swarm*:
So by the *Brazen* Trumpets Bluster,
Troops of all Tongues and Nations Muster:
And so the *Harp* of *Ireland* brings,
Whole Crouds about its *Brazen* Strings.   30

There is a *Chain* let down from *Jove*,
But fasten'd to his Throne above;
So strong, that from the lower End,
They say, all human Things depend:
This *Chain*, as Antient Poets hold,
When *Jove* was Young, was made of *Gold*.
Prometheus once this *Chain* purloin'd,
Dissolv'd, and into *Money* Coin'd;
Then whips me on a *Chain* of *Brass*,
(*Venus* was Brib'd to let it pass.)   40

Now while this *Brazen Chain* prevail'd,
Jove saw that all *Devotion* fail'd;

12 *Religions*] Religion L.   20 on] in L.   21] *N.P.* 1727, 1728, F., 1742
21 incites,] invites *W.J.*   24 *Sodder*] 1727, 1728, 1742 *Solder* 1725, 1730, F.
26 *Swarm*:] Storm; *W.J.*   39 whips] whipt W.², L.

40. *Venus*. A reference to the Duchess of Kendal. See note p. 336.

No *Temple*, to his *Godship* rais'd,
No *Sacrifice* on *Altars* blaz'd;
In short such *dire Confusions* follow'd,
Earth must have been in *Chaos* swallow'd.
Jove stood amaz'd, but looking round,
With much ado, the *Cheat* he found;
'Twas plain he cou'd no longer hold
The *World* in any *Chain* but *Gold*;　　　　　　50
And to the *God of Wealth* his *Brother*,
Sent *Mercury* to get another.

Prometheus on a Rock is laid,

Ty'd with the *Chain* himself had made;

On Icy *Caucasus* to shiver,

While *Vultures* eat his growing Liver:

Ye Pow'rs of *Grub-street* make me able,
Discreetly to apply this *Fable*.
Say, who is to be understood,
By that old Thief *Prometheus*? WOOD　　　　60
For *Jove*, it is not hard to guess him,
I mean *His M—*, God bless him.
This *Thief* and *Black-Smith* was so bold,
He strove to steal that *Chain* of *Gold*,
Which links the *Subject* to the *King*:
And change it for a *Brazen String*.
But sure if nothing else must pass,
Between the *K—* and US but *Brass*,
Altho' the *Chain* will never crack,
Yet *Our Devotion* may *Grow Slack*.　　　　70

45 *Confusions*] 1725, 1730　Confusion W.¹, L., *W.J.*, 1727, 1728, F., 1742
47 but] 1727, 1728, F., 1742　and *W.J.*, 1725, 1730　　　53 Rock] Rack
W.J.　　53 is] was W.², L.　　56 While] 1727, 1728, F., 1742　Where 1725,
1730 Whilst *W.J.*　　58 Discreetly] Directly W.², L.　　60 WOOD] WOOD:
1725　WOOD. 1727, 1728, 1730, F., 1742　　63 This *Thief* and] This
Thief, the *W.J.*　　65] *In round brackets* 1742　68 K—] 1725, 1730
King 1727, 1728, F., 1742　70 *Devotion*] Devotions W.², L.

But *Jove* will soon convert I hope,
This *Brazen Chain* into a *Rope*;
With which *Prometheus* shall be ty'd,
And high in Air for ever ride;
Where, if we find his *Liver* grows,
For want of *Vultures*, we have *Crows*.

WHITSHED's MOTTO
ON HIS COACH.

Libertas & natale Solum.
Liberty and my native Country.

Written in the Year 1724.

Faulkner, 1735, ii. 279 (1737, ii. 172).
Miscellanies, . . . Volume the Fifth, 1735, p. 13 (1736, v. 13; 1745, v. 57).

William Whitshed presided as judge at the abortive trial of Harding, printer of the *Drapier's Letters*, and earned this lampoon, as previously he had been attacked by Swift for his behaviour at the trial of Waters, printer of the *Proposal for the Universal Use of Irish Manufacture*. See notes, pp. 236, 332.

This poem was first printed by Faulkner in 1735, and rightly assigned to the year 1724. In his 1737 edition of the *Poetical Works*, however, the date is given, in error, as 1720. This was later corrected back to 1724.

In *Miscellanies, . . . Volume the Fifth,* 1735, printed from Faulkner, the name in the title is given as '*W—D*'s', and so in 1736, but in later editions of the *Miscellanies* the name was restored in full.

In his 'Letter to the Lord Chancellor Middleton', following upon a reference to Whitshed, Swift writes: 'I observed, and I shall never forget upon what Occasion, the Device upon his Coach to be *Libertas & natale Solum*; at the very Point of Time when he was sitting in his Court, and perjuring himself to betray both.' (*Drapier's Letters*, ed. H. Davis, p. 125; *Prose Works*, ed. Temple Scott, vi. 137.)

The text follows Faulkner's 1735 edition of the *Works*.

76 For want] Instead *W.J.*

*L*IBERTAS & *natale Solum*;
　　Fine Words; I wonder where you stole 'um.
Could nothing but thy chief Reproach,
Serve for a Motto on thy Coach?
But, let me now the Words translate:
Natale Solum: My Estate:
My dear Estate, how well I love it;
My Tenants, if you doubt, will prove it:
They swear I am so kind and good,
I hug them till I squeeze their Blood.　　　　10

LIBERTAS bears a large Import;
First; how to swagger in a Court;
And, secondly, to shew my Fury
Against an uncomplying Jury:
And, Thirdly; 'tis a new Invention
To favour *Wood* and keep my Pension:
And, Fourthly; 'tis to play an odd Trick,
Get the Great Seal, and turn out *Brod'rick.*
And, Fifthly; you know whom I mean,
To humble that vexatious Dean.　　　　20

7 it;] 1735, 1736, 1737　it! 1745　　9 swear] 1735, 1736, 1745　swear, 1737
10 them] 1735, 1736, 1745　them, 1737　　18 Brod'rick.] 1735, 1736, 1745
Brod'rick: 1737

18. *Brod'rick.* Alan Brodrick, born
1656, came of a Surrey family which
had crossed to Ireland before the Com-
monwealth, and benefited by the
forfeitures. He entered the legal profession, and in 1695 became Solicitor-
General for Ireland. In 1703 he became Speaker of the Irish House of
Commons. His opposition to the Test
Act led to his removal from the office
of Solicitor-General. In 1707, however, he returned to office, as Attorney-
General. In 1714 he became Lord
Chancellor of Ireland; in 1715 Baron
Brodrick of Midleton; in 1717
Viscount Midleton. He resigned the
Chancellorship in 1725. He was re-
garded with jealousy by Whitshed,
who hoped to step into his shoes. See

Prose Works, ed. Temple Scott, vi.
135 n.; *Corresp.* i. 83 n.[4]; iii. 65 n.[2],
et passim; Drapier's Letters, ed. Davis,
pp. 304–5.
　　Brodrick inherited Whig principles,
and, as an advocate for the repeal
of the Test Act, met with Swift's
hostility. He was, however, a strong
opponent of Wood's patent, although,
in consequence of his position, he
could not avoid signing the proclamation against the Drapier. The
6th (5th) *Drapier's Letter* was addressed to him by Swift, 26 October,
1724, although this piece was not
published till the appearance of vol. iv
of Faulkner's 1735 edition of the
Works (see Davis, *op. cit.,* p. 123; *Prose
Works,* vi. 131).

And, Sixthly; for my Soul, to barter it
For Fifty Times its Worth, to *Carteret*.

Now, since your Motto thus you construe,
I must confess you've spoken once true.
Libertas & natale Solum;
You had good Reason when you stole 'um.

Verses on the upright Judge, who condemned the Drapier's Printer.

Written in the Year 1724.

Faulkner, 1735, ii. 468 (1737, ii. 200).
Miscellanies, . . . Volume the Fifth, 1735, p. 147 (1736, v. 147; 1745, v. 81).

These three squibs, directed at Whitshed, were, as stated by Faulkner, probably written at the same time as the preceding lampoon. Alderman Mark Quin, Whitshed's maternal grandfather, cut his throat in 1674. His son, James, married a lady whose husband, presumed dead, reappeared. The son of James was thus illegitimate, and the estate devolved on the Whitsheds, heirs-at-law. See Gilbert's *Hist. of the City of Dublin*, i. 221–2. Faulkner's text is reprinted.

THE Church I hate, and have good Reason:
 For, there my Grandsire cut his Weazon:
He cut his Weazon at the Altar;
I keep my Gullet for the Halter.

On the same.

IN Church your Grandsire cut his Throat;
To do the Jobb too long he tarry'd,
He should have had my hearty Vote,
 To cut his Throat before he marry'd.

22 *Carteret*.] 1737   *C—t.* 1735, 1736, 1745

On the same.
The Judge speaks.

I'M not the Grandson of that Ass *Quin*;
Nor can you prove it, Mr. *Pasquin*.
My Grand-dame had Gallants by Twenties,
And bore my Mother by a Prentice.
This, when my Grandsire knew; they tell us he,
In *Christ-Church* cut his Throat for Jealousy.
And, since the Alderman was mad you say,
Then, I must be so too, *ex traduce*.

W O O D, an Insect.

Written in the Year 1725.

Faulkner, 1735, ii. 365 (1737, ii. 212).
Miscellanies, . . . Volume the Fifth, 1735, p. 73 (1736, v. 73; 1745, v. 86).

This and the next poem, written when the heat of the conflict was over,
were first published by Faulkner in 1735, from whose text they are both
reprinted.

BY long Observation I have understood,
That three little Vermin are kin to *Will. Wood*:
The first is an Insect they call a *Wood*-Louse,
That folds up itself in itself for a House:
As round as a Ball, without Head without Tail,
Inclos'd *Cap-a-pee* in a strong Coat of Mail.
And thus *William Wood* to my Fancy appears
In Fillets of Brass roll'd up to his Ears:

5 Head] 1735, 1736   Head, 1737, 1745   6 *Cap-a-pee*] 1735, 1736   *Cap-apee*
1737   *Cap-a-pe* 1745

And, over these Fillets he wisely has thrown,
To keep out of Danger, a Doublet of Stone.   10

THE Louse of the *Wood* for a Med'cine is us'd,
Or swallow'd alive, or skilfully bruis'd.
And, let but our Mother *Hibernia* contrive
To swallow *Will. Wood* either bruis'd or alive.
She need be no more with the *Jaundice* possess't;
Or sick of *Obstructions*, and *Pains in her Chest*.

THE Third is an Insect we call a *Wood*-Worm,
That lies in old *Wood* like a Hare in her Form;
With Teeth or with Claws it will bite or will scratch,
And Chambermaids christen this Worm a Death-
    Watch: 20
Because like a Watch it always cries *Click:*
Then Woe be to those in the House who are sick:
For, as sure as a Gun they will give up the Ghost
If the Maggot cries *Click* when it scratches the Post.
But a Kettle of scalding hot Water injected,
Infallibly cures the Timber affected;
The Omen is broke, the Danger is over;
The Maggot will dye, and the Sick will recover.
Such a Worm was *Will. Wood* when he scratcht at the
    Door
Of a governing Statesman, or favorite Whore: 30
The Death of our Nation it seem'd to foretell,
And the Sound of his Brass we took for our Knell.
But now, since the *Drapier* hath heartilly maul'd him,
I think the best Thing we can do is to scald him.
For which Operation there's nothing more proper
Than the Liquor he deals in, his own melted Copper;

14 alive.] 1737   alive, 1735, 1736, 1745   17 Third] 1735, 1736, 1737
next 1745   23 Ghost] Ghost, 1735, 1736, 1737, 1745   31 it] 1735, 1736,
1737   he 1745

10. *a Doublet of Stone.* 'He was in   *favorite Whore.* Sir Robert Walpole
Jayl for Debt.'—Faulkner.   and the Duchess of Kendal. See note,
30. *Of a governing Statesman, or*   p. 336.

Unless, like the *Dutch*, you rather would boyl
This Coyner of *Raps* in a Cauldron of Oyl.
Then chuse which you please, and let each bring a Faggot,
For our Fear's at an End with the Death of the Maggot. 40

O N

W O O D the Iron-monger.

Written in the Year 1725.

Faulkner, 1735, ii. 363 (1737, ii. 210).
Miscellanies, ... Volume the Fifth, 1735, p. 71 (1736, v. 71; 1745, v. 84).
Reprinted from Faulkner 1735.

*S*ALMONEUS, as the *Grecian* Tale is,
Was a mad Copper-Smith of *Elis:*
Up at his Forge by Morning-peep,
No Creature in the Lane could sleep.
Among a Crew of royst'ring Fellows
Would sit whole Ev'nings at the Ale-house:
His Wife and Children wanted Bread,
While he went always drunk to Bed.
This vap'ring Scab must needs devise
To ape the Thunder of the Skies;   10
With *Brass* two fiery Steeds he shod,
To make a Clatt'ring as they trod.
Of polish't *Brass*, his flaming Car,
Like Light'ning dazzled from a-far:
And up he mounts into the Box,
And HE must thunder, with a Pox.

37. *Dutch*. The Dutch had counter-
feited debased Irish coinage. In his
first *Drapier's Letter* Swift writes:
'These halfpence . . . will soon be
counterfeit,... The Dutch likewise will
probably do the same thing, and send
them over to us to pay for our goods.'
(*Drapier's Letters*, ed. H. Davis, p. 9;
Prose Works, ed. Temple Scott, vi. 19.)

38. *Raps*. See p. 335 n.
1. *Salmoneus*. A king of Elis, who
incurred the wrath of Jove by usurping the sacrifices of Zeus, and by
driving a brazen chariot and flinging
torches in the air in imitation of
thunder and lightning. See Hygin.
Fab. 60, Homer, *Od.* xi. 235, Virg.
Aen. vi. 585.

Then, furious he begins his March;
Drives rattling o'er a brazen Arch:
With Squibs and Crackers arm'd, to throw
Among the trembling Croud below.   20
All ran to Pray'rs, both Priests and Laity,
To pacify this angry Deity;
When *Jove*, in pity to the Town,
With real Thunder knock't him down.
Then what a huge Delight were all in,
To see the wicked Varlet sprawling;
They search't his Pockets on the Place,
And found his Copper all was base;
They laught at such an *Irish* Blunder,
To take the Noise of Brass for Thunder!   30

    THE Moral of this Tale is proper,
Apply'd to *Wood*'s adult'rate Copper;
Which, as he scatter'd, we like Dolts,
Mistook at first for Thunder-Bolts;
Before the *Drapier* shot a Letter,
(Nor *Jove* himself could do it better)
Which lighting on th' Impostor's Crown,
Like real Thunder knock't him down.

A S I M I L E,

ON

Our Want of Silver, and the only Way to remedy it.

Written in the Year 1725.

Faulkner, 1735, ii. 361 (1737, ii. 209).
Miscellanies, . . . Volume the Fifth, 1735, p. 70 (1736, v. 70; 1745, v. 83).

  On the scarcity of silver in Ireland see notes, pp. 841–2.
  Reprinted from Faulkner 1735.

      33 we] 1735, 1736, 1745   were 1737

AS when of old, some Sorc'ress threw
  O'er the Moon's Face a sable Hue,
To drive unseen her magick Chair,
At Midnight, through the dark'ned Air;
Wise People, who believ'd with Reason
That this Eclipse was out of Season,
Affirm'd the Moon was sick, and fell
To cure her by a Counter-spell:
Ten Thousand Cymbals now begin
To rend the Skies with brazen Din;   10
The Cymbals rattling Sounds dispell
The Cloud, and drive the Hag to Hell:
The Moon, deliver'd from her Pain,
Displays her *Silver* Face again.
(Note here, that in the Chymick Style,
The Moon is *Silver* all this while.)

    So, (if my Simile you minded,
Which, I confess, is too long winded)
When late a Feminine Magician,
Join'd with a *brazen* Politician,   20
Expos'd, to blind the Nation's Eyes,
A Parchment of prodigious Size;
Conceal'd behind that ample Screen,
There was no Silver to be seen.
But, to this Parchment let the *Draper*
Oppose his Counter-Charm of Paper,
And ring *Wood*'s Copper in our Ears
So loud, till all the Nation hears;
That Sound will make the Parchment shrivel,
And drive the Conj'rers to the Devil: 30
And when the Sky is grown serene,
Our Silver will appear again.

3 her] 1735, 1736, 1745   the 1737   25 *Draper*] 1735, 1736, 1745   *Drapier* 1737

19, 20. *Feminine Magician,...brazen Politician.* The Duchess of Kendal and Sir Robert Walpole. The latter went by the nickname of Sir Robert Brass. In his epistle 'To Mr. Gay',

l. 143, Swift refers to Walpole as 'a *brazen* Minister of State' (see p. 536).
   22. *A Parchment . . . 'A Patent to* W. Wood, *for coining Half-pence.*'— Faulkner.

NOTE TO *APOLLO'S EDICT* (p. 269)

THE text of this poem is printed from the quarto pamphlet. See pp. 269–72. It has been questioned whether 'Apollo's Edict' was written by Swift, for, in an altered version, it appeared in Mary Barber's *Poems on Several Occasions*, 1734, pp. 105–10.

Although the poem may have been written at a later date than the four preceding pieces the relationship to Delany's verses, which begin by announcing Apollo's intention of appointing 'a Vicegerent in his Empire below' can hardly be questioned. 'Apollo's Edict' opens by proclaiming that his Viceroy has been 'lately fix'd' in Ireland. Smedley, reprinting the poem in *Gulliveriana*, evidently regarded it as by Swift, particularly calling attention in a footnote to this link with Delany's verses. As printed in *Gulliveriana* and in the fourth volume of Fairbrother's *Miscellanies*, 1735, the text, save for insignificant variants, is that of the pamphlet. Despite the disapprobation of Fairbrother, expressed by both Sheridan and Swift, it is worth noting that he seems to have had some relationship or connexion with the Rev. John Worrall, Dean's vicar at St. Patrick's and Swift's friend of many years' standing. This may be reasonably taken to lend some support to Fairbrother's claim to have included several pieces in his miscellany 'taken from the D[ea]ns own Original Manuscripts'.

Faulkner, it is true, did not in his edition of the *Works* print 'Apollo's Edict'. On the assumption that Swift allowed Mrs. Barber to include it in her *Poems*, as if composed by her, its omission by Faulkner becomes intelligible, for it was probably due to Swift's intervention. The disappearance of three triplets, lines 8–10, 20–2, 33–5, may reflect Swift's dislike of this poetic form. The allusion to three of Swift's friends in the altered version of the poem is of particular significance. These are Mrs. Frances Arabella Kelly; 'Rochford', that is Deborah Staunton, who became John Rochfort's wife in January 1723; and Boyle, by whom is meant the Earl of Orrery. Not one of these is named in the earlier version of the poem. Admittedly, as Mrs. Barber's volume was dedicated to Orrery, she might well have mentioned him. In addition the 'Eliza' of the new version is noted as a reference to 'Mrs. Elizabeth Penifeather'. She belonged to the family of Pennifather of co. Antrim known to Swift. These allusions should be accepted as evident proofs that Swift was active in modifications of the poem as printed in Mary Barber's volume.

Save for two poems, '*Apollo's Edict*' and '*Stella and Flavia*', p. 126, which was suspected from the first not to be hers, Mrs. Barber's volume is almost unreadable. Mrs. Pilkington in the third volume of her *Memoirs*, 1754, p. 65, tells us that when Mrs. Barber's poems were in preparation for the press 'dull as they were, they would certainly have been much worse' save for revision by a committee consisting of Swift, Delany, Mrs. Grierson, and herself. If, as may at least be assumed, Swift, out of kindness of heart, allowed Mrs. Barber to make use of 'Apollo's Edict' its marked superiority to her own poems is apparent at once. The contrast between this poem and her dull, laboured versification makes it difficult to accept her authorship. Dr. Oliver Ferguson, however, in an exact and scholarly contribution to *PMLA*, lxx. 433–40, June 1955, argues the case for Mrs. Barber's authorship, at the same time admitting that a doubt remains.